Writers for
Young Adults

Writers for Young Adults

Ted Hipple

Editor

VOLUME 1

CHARLES SCRIBNER'S SONS
Macmillan Reference USA
Simon & Schuster Macmillan
New York

Simon & Schuster and Prentice Hall International
London   Mexico City   New Delhi   Singapore
Sydney   Toronto

Scribners would like to acknowledge the following sources used in preparing marginal definitions:

The American Heritage Dictionary of the English Language. 3d ed. Boston: Houghton Mifflin, 1992.

The American Heritage Student's Dictionary. Boston: Houghton Mifflin, 1986.

Funk and Wagnall's Standard Dictionary. 2d ed. New York: Harper Paperbacks, 1993.

Merriam-Webster's Collegiate Dictionary. 10th ed. Springfield, Mass.: Merriam-Webster, 1994.

The New Shorter Oxford English Dictionary. 4th ed. 2 vols. New York: Oxford University Press, 1993.

The Random House College Dictionary—Revised Edition. New York: Random House, 1984.

Charles Scribner's Sons
An Imprint of Simon & Schuster Macmillan
1633 Broadway
New York, NY 10019

Library of Congress Cataloging-in-Publication Data
Writers for young adults / Ted Hipple, editor.
     p.   cm.
    Summary: Contains articles on writers whose works are popular with young adults, including contemporary authors, such as Francesca Lia Block and Maya Angelou, and classic authors, such as Sir Arthur Conan Doyle and Louisa May Alcott.
    ISBN 0-684-80475-1 (v. 1 : hardcover). — ISBN 0-684-80476-X (v. 2 : hardcover). — ISBN 0-684-80477-8 (v. 3 : hardcover). — ISBN 0-684-80474-3 (set : hardcover)
    1. Young adult literature, American—Bio-bibliography—Dictionaries.   2. Young adult literature, English—Bio-bibliography—Dictionaries.   3. Authors, American—Biography—Dictionaries.   4. Authors, English—Biography—Dictionaries.
[1. Authors, American.   2. Authors, English.   3. Young adult literature.]   I. Hipple, Theodore W.
PS490.W75   1997
810.9'9283'03   97-6890
[B]—DC21   CIP
                                             AC

5 7 9 11 13 15 17 19 20 18 16 14 12 10 8 4

Printed in the United States of America. The paper used in this publication meets the minimum requirements of the American National Standard for Information Sciences—Permanence of Paper for Printed Library Materials, ANSI Z39.48–1984.

REFERENCE

Editorial Staff

Project Editor
LEROY GONZALEZ

Assistant Editor
BRIGIT DERMOTT

Copy Editors
JONATHAN G. ARETAKIS   BOOK BUILDERS, INC.
EVANGELINE LEGONES

Proofreaders
RACHEL BENZAQUEN   ADRIENNE SAICH

Picture Research
BOOK BUILDERS, INC.
SANDY JONES   LAURA SMID

Index
KATHARYN DUNHAM

Manufacturing
ROSE CAPOZZELLI, *Production Manager*
BOOK BUILDERS, INC., *Interior Design*
IRINA LUBENSKAYA, *Cover Design*

Senior Editor
STEPHEN WAGLEY

Executive Editor
SYLVIA K. MILLER

Publisher
KAREN DAY

President, Macmillan Reference USA
GORDON MACOMBER

Contents

VOLUME 2

Illustration Acknowledgments

Joan Aiken: By permission of Joan Aiken. © Rod Delroy.

Lousia May Alcott: By permission of UPI/Bettmann.

Lloyd Alexander: By permission of Lloyd Alexander. Photo by Alexander Limont.

Judie Angell: Photo courtesy of Simon & Schuster Children's Publishing Division

Maya Angelou: By permission of UPI/Bettmann.

Sandy Asher: Photo courtesy of Sandy Asher.

Avi: By permission of Orchard Books. Gabriel Kahn photographer.

Joan Bauer: Photo courtesy of Joan Bauer.

Marion Dane Bauer: Photo credit: Ann Goddard.

Jay Bennett: Photo courtesy of Jay Bennett.

T. Ernesto Bethancourt: Photo by Bob Campbell.

Francesca Lia Block: Photo courtesy of Francesca Lia Block.

Judy Blume: By permission of Judy Blume. Peter Simon, photographer.

Larry Bograd: Photo by S. Stephen Hicks.

Robin F. Brancato: Photo credit: Carol Kitman.

Sue Ellen Bridgers: Photo courtesy of Sue Ellen Bridgers.

Bruce Brooks: By permission of Farrar, Straus & Giroux.

Eve Bunting: Photo credit: Hans Gutknecht.

Olive Ann Burns: Photo credit: John Sparks.

Betsy Byars: Photo courtesy of Bantam Doubleday books for Young Readers.

Alden R. Carter: Photo courtesy of Alden R. Carter.

Aidan Chambers: By permission of Aidan Chambers. Photgraph by Andy Green.

Alice Childress: Photo courtesy of Flora Roberts, Inc.

Vera and Bill Cleaver: Photo courtesy of Hugh Agee.

Brock Cole: Photo courtesy of Farrar, Straus & Giroux, Inc.
Christopher and James Lincoln Collier: Photos courtesy of Christopher and James Lincoln Collier.
Hila Colman: Photo courtesy of Hila Colman.
Caroline B. Cooney: Photo courtesy of Donald R. Gallo.
Robert Cormier: Photo courtesy of Robert Cormier.
Stephen Crane: By permission of the New York Public Library.
Chris Crutcher: By permission of Chris Crutcher.
Maureen Daly: Photo courtesy of Nancy Vogel.
Paula Danziger: Putnam's Sons.
Terry Davis: Photo courtesy of Terry Davis.
Charles Dickens: By permission of the New York Public Library.
Emily Dickinson: By permission of Pictorial History Research.
Peter Dickinson: Photo courtesy of Betty Carter.
Sir Arthur Conan Doyle: Photo by permission of UPI/Bettmann.
Lois Duncan: Photo courtesy of Lois Duncan.
Jeannette Eyerly: Photo courtesy of Jeannette Eyerly.
Paula Fox: Permission of Orchard Books.
Anne Frank: Photo by permission of Woodfin Camp.
Russell Freedman: Photo by Charles Osgood.
© 1988, Chicago Tribune Co., All rights reserved.
Michael French: Photo courtesy of Michael French.
Robert Frost: By permission of the New York Public Library.
Leon Garfield: Photo courtesy of Viking/Penguin Books.
Jean Craighead George: By permission of the writer. Allan Young, photgrapher.
Bette Greene:
Lynn Hall: Photo credit: Jan Hall.
Virginia Hamilton: Photo courtesy of Harcourt Brace and Company.
Ernest Hemingway: Photo credit: © Karsh.
Nat Hentoff: Photo by permission of National Council of Teachers of English (NCTE).

S. E. Hinton: Photo courtesy of Bantam Doubleday Dell.
Will Hobbs: Photo by Jean Hobbs.
Isabelle Holland: Photo credit: George Janoff.
Monica Hughes: Photo courtesy of HarperCollins
Publishers, Ltd., Toronto, Ontario, Canada.
Mollie Hunter: Photo courtesy of HarperCollins Publishers.
Hadley Irwin: Photo courtesy of Macmillan Books for
Young Readers.
Norma Johnston: Photo courtesy of McIntosh & Otis, Inc.
Kathleen Duxbury Yeaw, photographer.
M. E. Kerr: By permission of HarperCollins. Zo. Kamitser,
photgrapher.
Norma Klein: Photo courtesy of Penguin Books.
Gordon Korman: By permission of Scholastic, Inc.
Madeleine L'Engle: © James Phillips, 1989.
Kathryn Lasky: Photo credit: Chrisopher Knight.
Ursula K. Le Guin: Photo credit: Marion Kolisch.
Harper Lee: Photo courtesy of Twayne Publishers.
C. S. Lewis: By permission of the New York Public Library.
Robert Lipsyte: By permission of Robert Lipsyte.
Jack London: Reproduced by permission of the
Huntington Library, San Marino, California.
Lois Lowry: By permission of Lois Lowry.
Chris Lynch: By permission of Chris Lynch. Photo credit:
Kim Kenney.
Margaret (May) Mahy: Photo by permission of Margaret
Mahy.
Kevin Major: Photo credit: John Sullivan.
Harry Mazer: Photo courtesy of Harry Mazer.
Norma Fox Mazer: Photo courtesy of Norma Fox
Mazer.
Anne McCaffrey: Photo courtesy of Anne McCaffrey.
Edmund Ross, Dublin, photographer.
Milton Meltzer: By permission of Milton Meltzer.
Gloria D. Miklowitz: Photo courtesy of Gloria D.
Miklowitz.
Nicholasa Mohr: Photo by Cindy Grossman, used with
permission from Arte Publico Press.

L. M. Montgomery: Credit: L. M. Montgomery Collection, Special Collections, University of Guelph Library.

Walter Dean Myers: By permission of Scholastic, Inc. John Craig, photographer.

Phyllis Reynolds Naylor: Photo credit: Katherine Lambert.

Joan Lowery Nixon: Photo courtesy of Joan Lowery Nixon.

Scott O'Dell: Photo by permission of Houghton Mifflin Company.

Zibby Oneal: Photo courtesy of Zibby Oneal.

Katherine Paterson: Photo credit: Jill Paton Walsh.

Gary Paulsen: © Ruth Wright Paulsen.

Richard Peck: Photo by Don Lewis.

Robert Newton Peck: Photo courtesy of Bantam Doubleday Dell.

Stella Pevsner: Photo courtesy of Clarion Books.

K. M. Peyton: Photo courtesy of K. M. Peyton. Photograph by the Evening Echo, Basildon, U.K.

Susan Beth Pfeffer: Photo courtesy of Susan Beth Pfeffer. Photograph by Donol Holway.

Kin Platt: Sketch by Kin Platt. Reprinted by permission of Curtis Brown, Ltd.

Edgar Allan Poe: Credit: The Bettmann Archive.

Ann Rinaldi: Photo courtesy of Scholastic, Inc.

Colby Rodowsky: Photo credit: Sally Foster.

Marilyn Sachs: Photo courtesy of Marilyn Sachs.

J. D. Salinger: By permission of the New York Public Library.

Graham Salisbury: By permission of Bantam Doubleday Dell. Gary Nolton, photographer.

Carl Sandburg: By permission of the New York Public Library.

Sandra Scoppettone: Photo credit: Jerry Bauer.

Ouida Sebestyen: Photo courtesy of Ouida Sebestyen.

William Shakespeare: By permission of the New York Public Library.

William Sleator: By permission of the National Council of Teachers of English (NCTE).

Gary Soto: Photo courtesy of Harcourt Brace & Co. Photographer: Carolyn Soto.

Jerry Spinelli: Photo courtesy of Little, Brown and Company.

John Steinbeck: Photo courtesy of Warren French.

Robert Louis Stevenson: By permission of the New York Public Library.

Todd Strasser: Photo courtesy of Todd Strasser.

Edward Stratemeyer: Photo courtesy of Archway Paperbacks and Minstrel Books.

Marc Talbert: Photo credit: Jane Hill.

Mildred Delois Taylor: Jack Ackerman, photographer.

Theodore Taylor: Photo credit: John Graves.

Joyce Carol Thomas: Photo courtesy of Scholastic, Inc.

Julian F. Thompson: Photo courtesy of Julian F. Thompson.

J. R. R. Tolkien: Photo courtesy of the Bettmann Archive.

Mark Twain: Photo credit: Pictorial History Research.

Cynthia Voigt: By permission of Scholastic, Inc.

Jill Paton Walsh: Photo courtesy of Farrar, Straus & Giroux

Barbara Wersba: Photo courtesy of Henry Holt.

Robert Atkinson Westall: © 1993 Katie Vandyck.

Laura Ingalls Wilder: By permission of Laura Ingalls Wilder Memorial Society.

Brenda Wilkinson: Photo credit: Archie Hamilton.

Virginia Euwer Wolff: Permission by Henry Holt, Inc.

Laurence Yep: By permission of Scholastic, Inc.

Jane Yolen: Photo by Shulamith Oppenheim.

Paul Zindel: Photo courtesy of Jack Forman.

by Robert Cormier

When someone asked recently if I had noticed any change in teenagers since the publication of *The Chocolate War* more than twenty years ago, my thoughts went immediately to all the letters I receive and in particular to a girl I shall call Amanda. (All names in this article are fictitious, but the lives are real.)

I met her four years ago in upstate New York, where I was a guest at a conference of English teachers. A few students had been invited to participate in whatever manner that suited them. Amanda decided to do an impersonation. She stood bravely before three hundred teachers and declared: "My name is Robert Cormier." She embarked on an autobiographical odyssey that climaxed with rounds of applause.

Onstage, she had a wonderful presence. Offstage, she was shy and nervous. She followed me around the rest of the day, always at my elbow. She was my guest at lunch. She blushed a lot.

Later, we began an exchange of letters. Ordinarily, I discouraged long-term correspondence with students because my mail, like that of many writers whose books are studied in schools, is heavy most of the time. Amanda's letters, however, were so full of the anguish and longings of youth that I was often moved by them and allowed the correspondence to continue. She was thirteen, vulnerable, sensitive. ("I worry a lot that the kids at school don't like me.")

Abruptly, the letters stopped.

Then, a year ago, she sent a letter in which she apologized for not having written for a while. She filled me in on details of her home and school life. Now in high school, she had a steady boyfriend. And then: "I remember those days when my biggest worry was whether people at school liked me and now I worry every month about whether I'm pregnant or not."

I also think of Amy, a high school senior who heard me speak at a seminar at a prestigious women's college in New England. A straight-A student, she was given a day off from school to attend the program.

Amy was bright, articulate, passionate about reading and writing. She was dressed casually but elegantly. She was off to New York University in the fall and was excited about all that lay ahead of her. "Do you mind if I write to you once in a while?" she asked.

In October, she sent me a letter with a New York postmark. She wrote that she was taking time out from a hectic schedule to put her thoughts on paper.

She wrote: "I've been here less than a month and already a girl in my dorm tried to commit suicide, I've been approached by a drug dealer, and a girl in one of my classes has been raped."

Have teenagers changed?

Maybe a better question is: Has the world changed?

Violence stalks the streets, a plague in the form of AIDS shadows the decade, drugs are an everyday specter, and morality seems to have taken an extended vacation.

Yet, every age has its torments and terrors. My own adolescent years encompassed a nationwide depression and a terrible war that covered the globe. Later, adolescents lived under the threat of the Atomic Age and the Cold War. Still later came the social upheavals of the 1960s and the rampaging 1970s and 1980s.

When my children entered their teenage years, I learned that no single generation has a monopoly on the emotions. My children echoed my own teenage agonies and joys (the agonies far outweigh the joys) as my own adolescence probably echoed my father's. I came to see that while fashions change along with songs and slang, the emotions watch no clock or calendar. Somehow, most young people emerge intact from the catastrophes of their particular era, and I'm sure this will be true of Amanda and Amy. It's a testimony to the strength and the endurance of the human spirit across the generations.

The generation that keeps in touch with me through letter and telephone calls (it's an open secret that my telephone number appears in *I Am the Cheese*) provides insights into to-day's adolescent world. But it's important to point out that the great majority of my letters are not traumatic or weighed down with the great issues of the day. Most students are looking for background information for theme papers or book reports. Some want to touch base through a brief note with the person who wrote the book they've just finished reading. Others wish to become writers and ask for advice or tips. Some tell me about their families, their pets, their hobbies—and these students will probably become writers.

But occasionally there is the letter or call that stops the heart, that lingers in the memory, whether it was a month ago, a year ago, or ten years ago.

I remember a certain call a while back—I didn't mark the date—on a summer Saturday afternoon from a girl telephoning from a psychiatric clinic in Connecticut. She had just completed *I Am the Cheese* and told me that she had, at last, in Adam Farmer found someone she could connect with, realizing that "I'm not alone in the world." A victim of sexual abuse in a family of alcoholics, she felt lost, friendless, abandoned. Somehow, the novel awakened her spirit. She was now determined "to get out of here, to start living again." I got in touch with her former English teacher who had been kind and sympathetic to her. Together, they began a slow healing.

Thus, the shadow of your work can fall benevolently on places you can't imagine when you are simply putting words down on paper.

Conversely, the shadows of my young letter writers often fall kindly upon me.

For instance, censorship has been an enduring problem since the publication of *The Chocolate War,* accelerating in recent years. Young readers, however, have supported the books under fire with letters and petitions, even when that support causes fractures in their lives.

A young man from the Midwest recently sent me a letter that said: "I am an extremely conservative Republican Baptist. If life turns out as I plan it to, I could be a minister someday. I feel that most others in my 'situation' would not have the same opinion of you that I have."

He wrote to me because he was upset that my books have been the object of censorship (and with the knowledge that many censorship attempts come from extremely conservative Republican fundamentalists). He cited what he called the honesty he found in my novels and thanked me for allowing him "to see things through different eyes" and for preparing him for the real world.

Although such support is gratifying, I would not presume to embark on a novel to prepare young people to meet life. I am, first of all, a storyteller, an entertainer, not with jokes to divert and disarm but with suspense and conflict involving characters a reader can wither love or hate or, at least, identify with. I use all the craft at my command to keep the reader turning the pages. On another level, I try to capture the reality of life as a troubled century dies and another waits to be born, exploring themes that encompass love and hate, and the constant battle between good and evil in a world that does not guarantee happy endings. However, the novel must first succeed as a *story*—otherwise, the underlying themes would never emerge.

Young readers, somehow, glimpse not only in my novels but in those of other YA writers from Robert Lipsyte to M. E. Kerr, from Walter Dean Myers to Richard Peck, and many, many others, things that echo in their own lives. It's never easy being an adolescent and it's not always easy being a writer. YA writers and their young readers are collaborators in a sense, joined in a partnership that sustains them both. A set like *Writers for Young Adults* is a part of that alliance between writer and reader, and further extends the relationship. Readers will probably find in these pages the answers to questions they have not yet asked in letters yet to be written.

Whatever the relationship, I read each letter from young readers with pleasure whether the letter deals with a serious issue or merely asks for information. The letter that arrived as I was starting to write this foreword said: "I cried when Kate died and then got very angry," in reference to *After the First Death*. All the letters and telephone calls send me to the typewriter each day with renewed hope and energy.

A friend of mine who writes adult mysteries and seldom, if ever, receives a letter from a reader told me wistfully: "I wish somebody would write to me the way young readers write to you. It'd be wonderful."

Yes, I agreed.

It is wonderful.

by Ted Hipple

Publishing a new reference set like *Writers for Young Adults* is a large undertaking, requiring large decisions. First among these is the answer to the question: Is another reference set about writers whose works are read by young adults needed? Those of us involved in this project feel that it is, for several reasons.

Literature is important in the lives of young people. By introducing them to books, we peovide what the French author Daniel Pennac calls "the gift of reading." In his *Better Than Life* (Toronto: Coach House, 1994), Pennac examines reading as it is taught in the schools and finds the teaching generally defeating its very purpose: to help children come to cherish reading. He begins by recalling that magical threesome of early childhood—the parent (or grandparent), the child on his or her knee, and Dr. Seuss, all taking great pleasure in those green eggs and ham. It is a joyful time. But school looms ahead and with it demands that are distinctly non-Seussian: the young person *must read* and worse, *must understand*.

To these unappealing demands are often added restrictions on what counts as real reading. As defined by teachers in the past, "high quality" ofte meant too difficult. Now more teachers are wisely letting students find their own way in the literature they read, a way that includes reading contemporary works written for young people and accessible to them. No longer should the Hardy Boys be disparaged by teachers who sometimes seem to forget that they, as youngsters themselves, read about Frank and Joe and, later, replacd them with the adventure stories of Robert Louis Stevenson, Jack London, and Arthur Conan Doyle. So will today's students if allowed to choose writing intended for them, at least some of the time. My own credo about student reading is simply stated: The *that* of student reading is more important than the *what*. Schools must, I think, use young adult literature if they hope to foster the enjoyment of reading and make it the real gift Pennac so eloquently urges us to offer young people.

Happily, two things—a powerful idea and lots of books—are converging. Many teachers are aware of young adult literature and value its use in the classroom. They regularly read novels, plays, poems, short stories, and nonfiction intended for young readers. Many teachers subscribe to such journals as the *ALAN Review*, published by ALAN, the Assembly on Literature for Adolescents of the National Council of Teachers of English, and *Signal*, produced by the special interest group on adolescent literature of the International Reading Association. Reviews of works intended for adolescents appear in publications of the American Library Association and in general interest publications such as the *New York Times Book Review*. At the same time that teachers and librarians are finding classroom strategies and library space for young adult literature, both the quality and the quantity of that literature are increasing.

Thus, schools now have an alternative for the student for whom *The Scarlet Letter* is simply too tough; let him explore moral issues in *The Giver*. Teachers have come to accept the rightful place of young adult literature as readings-in-common for all students or as individual assignments. They are more willing to group novels thematically, so that Walter Dean Myers' *Fallen Angels* can be studied side by side with Stephen Crane's *Red Badge of Courage*. This increased importance of young adult literature and its greater availability and repsectability provide, then, the chief reason for this new reference set: the subject merits continuing scholarship.

It is customary to suggest that the modern era of young adult literature as a distinct genre began in the late 1960s with the publication of such works as *The Outsiders,* by S. E. Hinton, *The Pigman,* by Paul Zindel, and *The Contenders,* by Robert Lipsyte. And, shortly after the appearance of these works in the 1970s, the field grew exponentially. During these years, enormously popular and critically acclaimed authors such as Robert Cormier, Judy Blume, Sue Ellen Bridgers, and Katherine Paterson published their first books

for teenagers. In 1996, not even quite thirty years since Pony-
boy left that movie theater in the opening sentence of *The
Outsiders*, publishing companies produce each year dozens
of new works intended for an audience of young readers
and their teachers and librarians. To keep abreast of the filed,
they need new reference books.

In another decision about this work, we judged that it
was important to try to bridge the gap, ne perhaps more
imagined than real, between those authors who, like Chris
Crutcher or Francesca Lia Block, clearly write *for* young
adults, and those writers who, like Jack London or Ernest
Hemingway, had older readers in mind when they wrote but
have remained popular with teenagers. We decided, therefore, to include a dozen or so writers who can be called classic, at least in the sense of their works having stood the test
of time. Putting an essay about Mark Twain in the same collection with one about Harry Mazer underscores our judgment that the best literature for young adults will also stand
the test of time.

Another significant decision had to do with our own intended audience. Most of the contributors to these volumes
are academics—professors of young adult literature, of library science, of English, of teacher education; teachers; and
librarians. Many of them have impressive lists of published
works, written for people like themselves, other adults. What
would we get if we suggested that they prepare their essays
as if they were writing for young people? We asked them to
imagine a rather bright seventh, eighth, or ninth grader who
has read *Jacob Have I Loved* by Katherine Paterson and wants
to know more about the author. She goes to the library for
Writers for Young Adults, where she can find an essay that is
written *for her*. That idea—father essays written for an audience of young people—struck us as appealing, and we
stayed with it because the contributors responded so imag-
initively and engagingly. In short, *Writers for Young Adults* is
itself written for young adults.

Of course, we also wanted our essays to appeal to teachers and librarians, too, and that proved not to be difficult for
our contributors. After all, ninth graders who read novels can
probably handle much of what may be written for their
teachers and librarians.

We had to decide matters that are, at bottom, logistical
decisions about size that all publishing companies must

xxvi • *Writers for Young Adults*

confront—for example, are many shorter essays better than fewer longer ones? We opted for a consistent length of about 2,500 words, believing that this length would be short enough to hold the attention of today's young people and long enough to provide our readers adequate and useful information. This length, approved by some forty educators in a survey we conducted, still allowed us to cover a large number of writers, 129 in all.

Another decision is to what extent, if any, ought the essays to be formulaic, following a pattern set down by me or by the Scribner editors? We elected to let contributors have their head, go their own way, knowing as we did so that we would get a variety of formats but never daring to anticipate that this variety would prove as exciting as, in fact, it did. The results of this decision are before you; we think you will like them.

We know that users of reference books seldom sit down and read throught them essay by essay; rather, they look for the item about whom or which they want informaion, get that information, and return to their other activities. We hope, however, that users will find in these pages many essays they will want to read, even about authors whose works they may not know, just for the pleasure of reading more about them. The essays often include interviews with the authors, comments from teenage readers about the authors, and little-known historical or literary facts about their achievements.

Worries about possible sins of omission and commissions dog the selection process in any reference work: Why did you include this author, exclude that one? To such questions we can make but one answer. We did the best we could, exercised our best judgment—one buttressed by responses from a number of people about authors they believed should be included. Many writers were givens, their inclusion assured by the important critical and student acceptance of their work. A few years ago I conducted a couple of surveys of scholars in young adult literature, secondary school teachers, librarians, and publishers, and asked them to identify, in the first survey (*English Journal*, December 1989), the best young adult novels of all time and, in the second (*English Journal*, November 1992), the best written during the 1980s. It was interesting and encouraging to see that so many scholars and professionals involved in the education of young people were familiar enough with the best literature for young adults to know exactly which books were their favorites. These novels and their authors headed my returns:

The All-Time Best

The Chocolate War, by Robert Cormier
The Pigman, by Paul Zindel
The Outsiders, by S. E. Hinton
Home Before Dark, by Sue Ellen Bridgers
A Day No Pigs Would Die, by Robert Newton Peck
All Together Now, by Sue Ellen Bridgers
The Moves Make the Man, by Bruce Brooks
Jacob Have I Loved, by Katherine Paterson
Words by Heart, by Ouida Sebestyen
Dicey's Song, by Cynthia Voigt
Summer of My German Soldier, by Bette Greene
The Contender, by Robert Lipsyte
Bridge to Terabithia, by Katherine Paterson
After the First Death, by Robert Cormier
I Am the Cheese, by Robert Cormier
Fallen Angels, by Waltcr Dcan Mycrs
Roll of Thunder, Hear My Cry, by Mildred D. Taylor

The Best of the 1980s

Hatchet, by Gary Paulsen
Fallen Angels, by Walter Dean Myers
Permanent Connections, by Sue Ellen Bridgers
Jacob Have I Loved, by Katherine Paterson
The Goats, by Brock Cole
The Moves Make the Man, by Bruce Brooks
Dicey's Song, by Cynthia Voigt
Fade, by Robert Cormier
Remembering the Good Times, by Richard Peck
Running Loose, by Chris Crutcher
Stotan! by Chris Crutcher
Notes for Another Life, by Sue Ellen Bridgers
Dogsong, by Gary Paulsen
Eva, by Peter Dickinson

Izzy, Willy-Nilly, by Cynthia Voigt
Midnight Hour Encores, by Bruce Brooks
Chinese Handcuffs, by Chris Crutcher

Although many fine books for young adults have been written since this survey was conducted, this list was a good starting point for our table of contents and still makes and excellent reading list.

We were guided, too, by our knowledge about authors whose works are commonly studied in schools, particularly grades 6–10, and, thus, writers like Charles Dickens, John Steinbeck, J. D. Salinger, Louisa May Alcott, L. M. Montgomery, and Stephen Crane made the list. Though Harper Lee published but one novel, *To Kill a Mockingbird,* that novel came to be taught in virtually every school in the country; she had to be included. As, for that matter, did William Shakespeare and such poets as Emily Dickinson, Carl Sandburg, and Robert Frost.

Finally, there was one decision about which there was really no debate, provided he would agree, and he did. We wanted a writer for young adults to compose an opening statement for *Writers for Young Adults,* and our first—our only—choice was Robert Cormier. Regarded by many as *the* premier writer and storyteller among authors who write for adolescents, Cormier is thoughtful about his craft amd about youth generally. His provocative foreword follows this preface and sets the tone for what I believe is a valuable contribution to American letters.

Acknowledging the help I received in my role as Editor in Chief would, I fear, result in still more sins of omission, my forgetting to cite deserving people, some of whose assistance occurred early on, about two years ago when this project got under way. Thus, I shall limit my thanks to a few: My colleague at Scribners from beginning to end on this work was Sylvia Miller, and rarely has an editor had better support than I had from Sylvia. Thoughtful, energetic, creative, she guided this effort every step of its way, participating in the decisions I have outline here, cleaning up rhetorical infelicities, extending deadlines when needed. In her work she had two associates whom I want to thank: Brigit Dermott and Leroy Gonzalez handled the many details well, logging in manuscripts, returning copyedited manuscripts, keeping everyone on track.

I want also to applaud the contributors. All of them, from graduate students to college deans, classroom teachers to editors and novelists, have full-time jobs. Yet they took the time to write good essays and to do the preliminaries that task required: studying their authors' literary achievements, digesting reviews, conducting in-person or telephone interviews. They did do, I think, because they, too, believe in young adults and their reading and want to be instrumental in bringing them together.

To my wife, Marjorie, herself a contributor, goes my deepest appreciation, not least for her forbearance in listening to me about this effort, in what I know was occasional whining, in what I hope was more often the voice of excitement when I received the just-right essay. English teachers are fond of the story of the seventh grader whose report on a book about kangaroos begins: "This book taught me more about kangaroos than I really wanted to know." Marge may have heard more about *Writers for Young Adults* than she wanted to know, but I thank her much for never letting on and for consistently sharing my enthusiasm for this significant project.

Publisher's Note

Scribners would like to thank Patty Cambpell, Donald Gallo, and Roger Sutton for their expert advice during the early development of this project.

Did you know that when Mark Twain, the famous author of *The Adventures of Tom Sawyer* and *The Adventures of Huckleberry Finn,* was a young man his greatest ambition was to be a riverboat pilot on the Mississippi? Or that Gary Paulsen, the author of *Hatchet* and *Dogsong,* ran the Iditarod—the endurance-testing trans-Alaska dogsled race—not once but *twice?* Or that Louisa May Alcott, the author of *Little Women,* was a nurse during the Civil War? It takes an interesting person to write a good book, because in one way or another writers write about themselves even when they are making up stories.

The more you know about interesting writers, the better you can understand their books and the more of their books you will want to read. Reading is a habit that grows on you, and since it is only a little bit dangerous—when it makes you very curious or gives you new, big ideas about life, for example—you probably will not find anyone giving you a hard time for it. In fact, supporting your reading habit (or encouraging you to start one) is what this set of reference books, *Writers for Young Adults,* is all about.

Maybe you are doing research for a book report, or you are trying to find a new book to read, or you would like to know more about an author whose books you like, or you would like to know what in the world that strange book you just read is supposed to mean. *Writers for Young Adults* will help you with all those things. Although each article is different, organized in the way that suits its subject author best, every article will tell you about the author's life and about what is so important and meaningful (or not) about his or her most popular and enduring books.

Many of the articles will tell you about the origin of the author's ideas and about his or her writing habits; that is because many of our contributing writers actually talked to their subjects to find these things out. They could not talk to Twain, of course, but luckily he wrote a slew of letters that tell us about his life, ideas, and writing. Shakespeare was a more difficult case, but you will probably find that the article about him does a pretty lively job of describing him anyway.

Although your teachers and librarians and parents will find this reference set useful because it is full of accurate information and understandable literary analysis, it was not written for them. It was written for you. We—the writers and editors of the articles—think that you might enjoy browsing in these books just to see what interests you or catches your fancy. Good luck on your book report, if you have one, but when it is done, read on. And on and on!

Joan Aiken

(1924-   )

by Esther W. Glass

There are usually two questions we ask when we meet an author, especially a favorite one, face to face: (1) What made you decide to be a writer? and (2) How did you become an author? When asked these questions, Joan Aiken, the author of more than eighty books, many of them for young adults, has answered the first question by saying, "I have always wanted to write even from the time I was five years old . . ." Perhaps she did so because her father and stepfather (her mother was married twice) were both writers. In fact, Aiken's father was the well-known poet Conrad Aiken.

Although writing was very much Aiken's intended career, she admits that as she grew up, her idea of the future was to marry a man who would offer her the kind of life in which she could write "in comfort" (*Something About the Author,* p. 27). That was her wish and her plan. It worked, but only for a short time. She soon found herself a widow with two young children, in need of finding a way to keep

Quotations from Joan Aiken that are not attributed to a published source are from personal correspondence with the author on 1 April, 10 May, and 16 June 1995, and are published here by the permission of Joan Aiken.

her family going by means of her own skills and work efforts.

The answer to the second question, how she became the writer she is, will unfold as we look into the life and background of Joan Aiken as a daughter, student, wife, and mother.

Childhood Days

Joan Aiken's mother, Jessie McDonald, was a Canadian from Montreal. She was working on her master's degree at Radcliffe College in Cambridge, Massachusetts, when she met Conrad Aiken, then a student at nearby Harvard College. They were married a year after they met, and for a short time they lived in Massachusetts, where they had two children (Joan's older brother and sister, John and Jane). The family moved to England and settled in Rye, Sussex, where on 4 September 1924 Joan was born. She remembers that as a child she often observed her father at his typewriter, engaged in his writing.

When Joan was four years old, her parents were divorced. Her mother and the three children remained in England, and her father returned to the United States.

Joan Aiken describes her childhood as happy and remembers quite clearly the small English village in which she lived: the houses were built close together on a small hill, and the town was set among marshes and plains. The house on Mermaid Street in which she was born stands only two miles away from the English Channel. Aiken liberally uses these details as settings in many of her books.

After Aiken's parents divorced, times were difficult for her mother and the three young children. Nevertheless, Aiken's memories are of the good times, when her mother, sister, and brother participated in many domestic activities that kept them together.

Her mother's second marriage was to the writer Martin Armstrong, a friend of her father's. The family moved from the house on Mermaid Street, but the warm recollections of life in that house remained clearly embedded in Aiken's memory, and both father figures made a strong impression on her.

As an adult she continues to carry a notebook wherever she goes, just as she did when she was five. She jots down

Conrad Aiken won the Pulitzer Prize for Poetry in 1929 for his *Selected Poems*.

Rye is a town and **Sussex** is a county.

interesting things she sees or perhaps a title she thinks of. Ideas for her books may come from dreams, newspapers, or even overheard conversations. For most of her life she has been an avid reader. When she was a child, some of her favorite books were Rudyard Kipling's *Jungle Books,* Walter de la Mare's *Peacock Pie,* E. Nesbit's stories, and Hodgson Burnett's *A Little Princess.*

Until the age of twelve, Aiken received her entire education at home, where she was taught by her mother. While her older brother and sister were away at school, she learned French, Latin, English, history, arithmetic, geography, and some Spanish and German. The family had no radio, car, running water, or refrigerator. In fact, they had no electricity at all. At night, they lit oil lamps and candles. Aiken remembers that they had wonderful fruits and vegetables, which were grown in their own garden by her stepfather. They also had fresh eggs, cream, and milk, all from the village farms.

About five miles from the village in which Aiken lived was a movie house. Although she never went to this cinema (she was only a young child), a fourteen-year-old village girl named Lily, who worked for the Aiken family, would bicycle to the movies each week. She would carefully describe to Aiken what the movies were like. As Aiken listened intently to the exciting plots of films about Tarzan, Charlie Chaplin, and other stars, her imagination became charged. She and Lily would take long walks, discuss the films, and enjoy the natural beauty surrounding them. These clear descriptions and love of nature come through in all of Aiken's writings.

School Life

When she was twelve, Aiken was sent to boarding school near Oxford, England. Now, instead of being comfortable in a small quiet house, she found herself in what she describes as a "noisy, bare, crowded, ugly barrack . . . filled with girls in uniform" (*Something About the Author,* p. 4). Unhappy though she was, she devoted her energies to getting good grades and participating in school plays, and many of her poems were published in the school magazine. With the advent of World War II, school life changed. Aiken became ill with a swollen gland in her neck, had two operations, and spent an entire term in bed. Her schoolwork "went to pieces," she says (*Something About the Author,* p. 4). She did not attend classes and subsequently failed the entrance exams for Oxford University.

Work and Marriage

Once out of school, she found a clerical job with the British Broadcasting Corporation (BBC). She recalls that she hoped "to marry a rich man who would support me in the country while I wrote books." She was working at the United Nations Information Centre in London when she met Ronald Brown, whom she married in 1945. During this time, she continued her writing. Three of her stories for children were purchased by the BBC, some of her poems were printed in a magazine, and she completed a children's novel, which she entered in a contest. She did not win the contest but was not discouraged.

Even while she was raising her two children, John and Elizabeth, Aiken continued writing, and some of her short stories were published in magazines. In 1953 her first book of short stories for children, *All You've Ever Wanted and Other Stories,* was published, followed in 1955 by *More Than You Bargained For and Other Stories.*

When Aiken's husband died in 1955 of cancer, she became the sole support of her two small children and was left also with the responsibility of paying his debts. She took a job as story editor of *Argosy* magazine and continued to write short stories for publication. In 1960, she published her first novel, *The Kingdom and the Cave.* Three years later, she wrote one of her most popular and substantial novels for young readers, *The Wolves of Willoughby Chase.* This book brought her broad popularity and recognition from readers and critics alike. It was also her first real financial success. Afterward, her books flowed steadily, some for children, some for young adults, and others for adult readers.

Joan Aiken, Author

Joan Aiken's writings are so varied and wide-ranging that it is difficult to categorize her work. Above all, she is a very fine storyteller. She is recognized as well for her poetry, plays, and retellings of old tales. Her short stories, ghost tales, and how-to books on writing are well known and popular. Even

In *The Wolves of Willoughby Chase,* a little girl, Bonnie, and her cousin Sylvia are left in the care of a horrible governess. The two girls face many chilly misadventures in the English countryside.

a cursory examination of a list of her writings reveals that they cover a broad spectrum.

In order to create her detailed descriptions of places and of how people lived and worked in the eighteenth and nineteenth centuries, Aiken not only has done thorough research from available writings of the times but has gone, whenever possible, to see the places in which these activities or events occurred. For example, she visited a coal mine in researching her book *Is Underground* (1993), and she went to Spain to research the settings for *Go Saddle the Sea* (1977). She read as much as she could about rug-making in factories and even how people long ago lived in sewers in England, both of these for the details in *Midnight Is a Place* (1974).

When asked to share her ideas on writing, Aiken explains that early in her career, she was strongly influenced by and modeled her work after authors she admired. It is natural for young writers to follow this pattern, she believes. Her plots and characters seem to arrive together in her mind. For example, she was once inspired by a television program that included a young boy who set fires and was to be imprisoned for his actions. Aiken was so taken with the young boy as presented in this television story that she created Felix Brooke, a boy who tries to escape from a family that does not understand him. She became so fond of Felix that he developed into a major character in three of her books: *Go Saddle the Sea, Bridle the Wind* (1983), and *The Teeth of the Gale* (1988).

Writing for young readers is much more difficult than writing for adults, according to Aiken. Her advice to an aspiring author is to keep notebooks and write down any ideas that occur. "Don't be deterred by rejections," she says. Keep sending things out. Take a job so you can have many varied experiences, which will serve well in future writings. And "write in your spare time."

Some of Aiken's books can generate out-loud laughs. The series of books about a young girl named Arabel and her pet raven Mortimer include some hilarious scenes, which result from the adventures of the arrogant raven and the family members who love him. In *Arabel's Raven* (1974), the first in the series, Mortimer is described as a lover of diamonds, slot machines, and potato crisps. His entire vocabulary consists of "Nevermore." *Mortimer's Cross* (1984) continues the adventures of the raven and his adopted family. It is wildly

Her advice to an aspiring author is to keep notebooks and write down any ideas that occur.

To find out why Mortimer says "**Nevermore**," read the famous poem "The Raven," which is discussed in the article on Edgar Allan Poe in volume 3.

In *Mortimer Says Nothing,* a mouse reports, "The single thing approaching a hazard that I observed was a raven. But at the time . . . he was eating the beaters of an electric mixer. It is my belief that ravens who eat eggbeaters do not eat mice."

Jane Austen
(1775–1817) wrote *Emma,* which was made into a popular movie in 1996. The movie *Clueless* (1995) is a modern version of this story.

funny, especially the scenes in which Mortimer and Arabel save their community from all types of unholy characters who are out to do harm. Arabel and Mortimer's involvement in these events is consistently fortuitous, ending in some hilarious convolutions. Joan Aiken knows how to create situations and characters that will tickle the reader's funny bone.

She also has created several books about a period in English history in which she develops conflicting political agendas between the Hanover dynasty (of which the first king was George I in 1714) and the Stuart claimants to the British throne. The time period spans the 1700s and early 1800s, with many of the books' settings in the geographical area of her own English home in Petworth, West Sussex. These books include *Black Hearts in Battersea* (1964), *Nightbirds on Nantucket* (1966), and *The Wolves of Willoughby Chase* (1963). The stories are exciting and filled with action, and they create a picture of political behavior that we would be able to identify in people even today.

Because of her love of the work of Jane Austen, Aiken wrote *Mansfield Revisited* (1985), a sequel to Austen's *Mansfield Park,* carefully using only those words available in Jane Austen's time and rereading Austen at least once a year to capture her style. Aiken also has completed a sequel to Jane Austen's unfinished novel, *The Watsons,* titled *Emma Watson* (1996).

Many of Aiken's characters appear and reappear in subsequent books. The young urchin Dido Twite, for instance, shows up in several of the books. The reader meets her in *Black Hearts in Battersea.* Dido is described clearly as a street-smart girl who is a "shrewish-looking little creature of perhaps eight or nine, with sharp eyes . . . and no eyebrows or eyelashes . . . Her straw-colored hair was stringy and sticky with jam and she wore a dirty satin dress two sizes too small for her" (p. 16). To the character Simon "she looked so like an ugly, scrawny little bird, ready to hop out of the way if danger threatened" (p. 20). The reader gets to know this tough, ill-kempt, clever girl with a good heart as she becomes a central character in several of Aiken's adventure stories. Dido eventually shows up as a heroine when she saves the Stuart throne from the sinister Hanoverians, who are trying to replace the rightful king, James III. Dido is also central in *Nightbirds on Nantucket,* an adventure that brings her to the United States, where she lands in New Bedford, Massachusetts.

Many of the books set in the eighteenth and nineteenth centuries describe the extreme differences in the lives of the rich and the poor. Much as in the books of Charles Dickens, Aiken's characters live either in squalor or in opulence, and the author clearly depicts the unfairness of life that prevailed in England in those days. Yet we can also find romance in the novels of Aiken. For example, in *If I Were You* (1987), two young women who look very much alike exchange places with each other, with interesting results on both sides. One finds true romance and well-deserved good fortune, while the other finds unhappiness and sadness befitting her arrogance and selfishness. In *Night Fall* (1969), there is mystery as well as romance as a young woman's frightening dreams take on reality when she pursues the reasons for her nightmares. With the help of a stranger, she uncovers the mystery of her past and finds romance and love.

If you like Aiken's historical books, you might also like *Oliver Twist* or *David Copperfield* by Charles Dickens.

Joan Aiken Today

Joan Aiken continues to live a full life. She has been married since 1976 to Julius Goldstein, an American painter and teacher. She divides her time between her home in West Sussex and her husband's home in Manhattan. Although she never lived in the United States as a child, she imagined much of it from her father's stories, related to her when she was a child. Her favorite places in the United States include Cape Cod, Savannah, Boston, and New York. However, she becomes a bit frustrated by Americans because she thinks they are somewhat isolated from, and disinterested in, the woes of the rest of the world.

Joan Aiken is always at work on a new book, answers her own fan mail and business mail, does her own housework and gardening, and loves to cook and travel. Her favorite activities are listening to classical music by composers such as Bach, Monteverdi, and Purcell; walking (although somewhat hampered by an arthritic knee); working in her garden; looking at paintings, and watching television and films. Among her favorite foods are crab salad and orange cheesecake. Her favorite places include the Greek Islands, Spain, and France.

Aiken's son, John, lives in London, where he enjoys building, carpentry, and writing, including a book on the future of telepathy. Her daughter, Elizabeth, has two children, lives in

Johann Sebastian **Bach,** Claudio **Monteverdi,** and Henry **Purcell** all lived in the 1600s. Today, their beautiful, intricate music is regarded as some of the greatest music ever composed.

London, and has collaborated with her mother in creating a television program about the popular characters Arabel and Mortimer.

If you like reading books by Joan Aiken, you may also enjoy those written by Ursula K. Le Guin and Jane Yolen.

Selected Bibliography

WORKS BY JOAN AIKEN

Joan Aiken and I have selected the following titles as being the most appropriate for young adult readers.

—Esther W. Glass

All You've Ever Wanted and Other Stories (1953)
More Than You Bargained For and Other Stories (1955)
The Kingdom and the Cave (1960)
The Wolves of Willoughby Chase (1963)
Black Hearts in Battersea (1964)
Nightbirds on Nantucket (1966)
The Whispering Mountain (1969)
Night Fall (1969)
The Cuckoo Tree (1971)
Arabel's Raven (1974)
Midnight Is a Place (1974)
A Bundle of Nerves, horror stories (1976)
A Touch of Chill, horror stories (1976)
The Five-Minute Marriage (1978)
Go Saddle the Sea (1978)
Mortimer and Arabel (1981)
The Girl from Paris (1982)
Bridle the Wind (1983)
A Whisper in the Night, horror stories (1984)
Mortimer's Cross (1984)
Mansfield Revisited, sequel to Jane Austen's *Mansfield Park* (1985)
A Goose on Your Grave, horror stories (1987)
If I Were You (1987)
The Moon's Revenge (1987)
Return to Harden House (1988)
The Shadow Guests (1988)
The Teeth of the Gale (1988)

Give Yourself a Fright, stories of the supernatural (1989)

A Fit of Shivers, horror stories (1990)

Is Underground (1993)

Eliza's Daughter, sequel to Jane Austen's *Sense and Sensibility* (1994)

Emma Watson (1996)

Autobiography

"Joan Aiken." In *Something About the Author Autobiography Series.* Edited by Adele Sarkissian Detroit: Gale Research, 1986, vol. 1, pp. 17–35.

WORKS ABOUT JOAN AIKEN

Aiken, Joan. "Joan Aiken: A Writing Life." *Writers Monthly,* July 1989, pp. 34–35.

Senick, Gerard, ed. *Children's Literature Review.* Detroit: Gale Research, 1990, vol. 19, pp. 1–4.

Telgen, Diane, ed. "Joan Aiken." In *Something About the Author.* Detroit: Gale Research, 1992, vol. 73, pp. 1–7.

How to Write to the Author
Joan Aiken
c/o St. Martin's Press, Inc.
175 Fifth Avenue
New York, NY 10010

Louisa May Alcott

(1832–1888)

by Rosemary Oliphant Ingham

As I read the books, essays, and letters Louisa May Alcott wrote during her lifetime and the books written about her after her death, I kept wondering how it would feel to interview this grand lady. It might have gone something like this:

Because I had come to interview her, I was startled that she was asking me a question!

"Do you keep a diary?"

I replied, "No," wondering what that had to do with writing books. She frowned at my response and I began to be uncomfortable. I ventured, "Is keeping a diary important?"

A smile replaced the frown on the face of this tall, distinguished lady. "It worked well for me!"

Louisa May Alcott and one of her books, *Little Women,* may be the most recognizable team in American literature for young adults. The diary she kept grew into a beloved book!

Creating a Writer

Louisa was required by her parents to begin keeping a diary when she was seven years old. Her father, the educator Bronson Alcott, used this method to encourage his daughters to write their daily observations and feelings. He and their mother, Abigail "Abba" May Alcott, would often read these diaries and make comments in the margins. Ednah Dow Cheney, in her biography *Louisa May Alcott: Her Life, Letters, and Journals,* relates two example of Abba's encouragement. A tenth-birthday present with this accompanying note: "I give you the pencil-case I promised, for I have observed that you are fond of writing, and wish to encourage the habit," (p. 15) showed that Abba recognized Louisa's potential as a writer. Upon hearing Louisa's first poem, "To the First Robin," her mother's response was, "You will grow up a Shakespeare!" (p. 12).

Louisa liked to write, just as her father did. Mr. Alcott was a writer and lecturer on educational and philosophical ideas. His progressive thoughts about the education of young children had a great impact on Louisa.

Diaries and encouraging parents were not the only reasons for Louisa's interest in writing. Growing up around Concord, Massachusetts, in the mid-1800s meant that Louisa had daily contact with her father's friends Ralph Waldo Emerson, Henry David Thoreau, and Nathaniel Hawthorne. These men were frequent guests at the Alcott home, where they discussed philosophical ideas.

The Alcott sisters were read to and encouraged to read. Mr. Alcott read *Pilgrim's Progress,* an allegorical tale by John Bunyan, to the sisters as part of their moral and religious education. Books by the most respected writers for children of that day were available in the nursery: Mrs. Edgeworth and Mrs. Barbauld were read extensively.

We know from her diary entries that Louisa read a lot. The following are two examples from the Cheney biography:

Read Charlotte Bronte's life. A very interesting, but sad one. So full of talent; and after working long, just as success, love, and happiness come, she dies. Wonder if I shall ever be famous for people to care to read my story and struggles. I can't be a C. B., but I may do a little something yet." (Pp. 76–77).

Emerson (1803–1882) and **Thoreau** (1817–1862) were both American transcendentalist writers. They believed that knowledge of the physical world was secondary to the pure knowledge of a spiritual world.

Hawthorne (1804–1864) wrote imaginative, dramatic fiction about New England life and its heritage of Puritanism (the strict form of Protestant Christianity practiced by the early settlers). *The Scarlet Letter,* (1850) and *The House of Seven Gables* (1851) are two of his most famous works.

"First taste of Goethe. . . . R.W.E. gave me "Wilhelm Meister", and from that day Goethe has been my chief idol." (P. 36)

Johann Wolfgang von **Goethe** (1749–1832) is generally considered to be the most profound and influential of German writers. He wrote *Wilhelm Meister's Theatrical Mission* and *Wilhelm Meister's Apprenticeship*. Goethe is best known for his verse play *Faust*.

Louisa and her father were not the only writers in the family. Louisa's sister Anna also wrote but was not as widely published as Louisa. Anna and Louisa began their literary careers by writing, producing, and acting in plays. This was a favorite pastime of the sisters. They copied their plots and characters from the popular fiction of the day as well as from classic literature.

Diaries, family encouragement, literary friends, extensive reading, and lots of practice do create writers, but great writers need something else. Louisa had that something: she had a natural talent for telling a story.

Family Background

Louisa May was born 29 November 1832, the second daughter in the Alcott family. At the time Bronson and Abba Alcott were living in Germantown, Pennsylvania. Bronson, the schoolmaster, had been hired by a Quaker gentleman who wished his children to be schooled under Bronson's philosophy. The Alcotts, including Louisa's older sister, Anna, were very happy in Germantown, but the Quaker gentleman died suddenly and the school closed because of insufficient funds. The Alcott family's move back to Boston was the first of many relocations.

Because both of Louisa's parents had family and friends in the Boston area, they were soon able to open the Masonic Temple School. Bronson, along with Elizabeth Peabody, continued his progressive educational program for the children of some of Boston's most elite families. The Temple School, however, was closed because Bronson chose to enroll a black boy, a shocking idea at the time.

The failure of these two schools began a series of moves for the Alcotts that was to continue throughout Louisa's life. Some of the family's moves were from one house to another in the same town, while others were moves from town to town. Rather than being a step up for the Alcott family, these changes were a step down, for the family had to depend on the generosity of others. The Alcotts lived in houses provided by friends or family, lived where Bronson could be a farmhand for someone, or lived where the rent was exceedingly cheap.

During this time the family increased from the original four by two more daughters. The four Alcott sisters were Anna Bronson, Louisa May, Elizabeth Sewall, and Abba May. Judging from Louisa's diaries and the writings of biographers, it seems that the Alcott sisters had a very happy childhood. As a child Louisa was physically active; in today's language she would be called a tomboy. She had to be pulled out of the Frog Pond in Boston Common, could drive her hoop longer and up higher hills than any of the boys, and got lost while exploring the wharves of Boston harbor when she was less than six years of age.

In 1843, the Alcotts and two English gentlemen moved to Fruitlands, or the New Eden. This commune was planned as an experiment in transcendental living. Its members believed in a philosophy called transcendentalism, which emphasized feelings rather than reason. The transcendentalists also thought that people were inherently good and that Good was to be found in nature. Bronson envisioned Fruitlands as being a place in which this extended family could enjoy in-depth intellectual discussions. Besides having religious and philosophical conversations they would work together in providing for their physical needs—food, clothing, fuel for heating—in this New Eden. Charles Lane, one of the Englishmen, took over the education of the sisters at this time. He demanded a more rigorous schedule. There were extra chores for the four sisters—and less food because none of the men knew about farming. This is the only unhappy time during her childhood that Louisa mentions in any of her autobiographies.

Although they were related to the May family, one of the most respected and influential in Boston, the sisters lived a very frugal life because of their father's inability to keep a steady job. The plainness of their clothes, food, and home never seemed to bother them, but the issue of money, or the lack of it, was a constant source of worry for Louisa. In her early teens Louisa began to think about ways to help her family financially. Both she and Anna worked as governesses to supplement the meager earnings of their father. By her early twenties, Louisa was writing and getting paid for it.

Louisa's formal education was very erratic. Her father taught all the sisters at home while they were very young. Louisa and Anna also attended the Masonic Temple School. Anna went to class more than Louisa because Louisa often chose to explore her surroundings instead. Bronson, with his progressive ideas about learning, thought her wanderings were just as educational as sitting in a classroom. During the New Eden or Fruitlands experiment, Louisa and her sister were taught by Charles Lane. Yet her lack of formal education did not stop Louisa's writing.

Writings and Writing Patterns

When Louisa May Alcott's name is mentioned, the work that immediately comes to mind is *Little Women,* but her first published piece appeared in 1852. She was paid $5 for it. From the time she began her diaries until her death, Alcott wrote almost every day. She wrote partly because she needed the money but mainly because that was what she liked to do. Only in her later years, when she was in ill health and the demands of her publishers overwhelmed her did she see writing as a chore.

Like Jo, her counterpart in *Little Women,* Louisa would find a quiet place to write her stories, her poems, and the wonderful plays that she and Anna liked to perform. She wrote about what she saw in nature, as shown in her first poem; she wrote stories to entertain, as shown by the stories she wrote for Mr. Emerson's daughter; and she wrote in her diaries.

As a young adult, Louisa wrote stories for the fiction magazines that were highly popular in the mid-1850s. Because she wrote these stories strictly for the money she could make and because they were sensational in nature, Alcott did not always write under her own name. Many of these first writings were compared to stories by Charles Dickens for style. Critics readily agree that Louisa was reading Dickens at the time and modeling her works after a writer she admired.

One book of short stories that has remained of interest to the literary world is *Hospital Sketches.* Being a devoted abolitionist, Louisa wanted to help during the Civil War. Being a female, the only job available to her was that of nursing. In

Bronson, with his progressive ideas about learning, thought Louisa's wanderings were just as educational as sitting in a classroom.

Louisa's "sensational" stories are now available in a collection called *Behind a Mask.* See the bibliography at the end of this article for details. **Sensational** means shocking or gruesome.

Hospital Sketches is available to be purchased in paperback. For information, write to:
Orchard House
399 Lexington Road
Concord, MA 01742

November 1862, at the age of thirty, she decided to go to Washington and nurse at the Union Hospital in Georgetown. She left Boston on 12 December and arrived in Washington soon after. By 22 January 1863, Louisa was back home and very sick. The doctors diagnosed her illness as typhoid pneumonia, a disease she contracted while working with her patients. Of that time Louisa says, "I was never ill before this time, and never well afterward."

Even though this was a difficult time for her physically, it was a good time for her literary career. While in Washington, Louisa wrote letters home about what was happening in the hospital. Her family shared these letters with friends and publishers of the Boston newspapers. Louisa's letters became famous. After she regained her strength it was suggested that Louisa add to the letters she had sent home and *Hospital Sketches* was serialized in the *Boston Commonwealth*. The serial began in May 1863; by August the letters and stories were published in book format. Louisa was famous in the Boston area and from then on was constantly asked to write for specific journals and by specific publishers.

In September 1867, Thomas Niles, Jr., of Roberts Publishers in Boston, asked her to write a book for girls. Louisa, who had always preferred boys and boys' games, declined. The request was repeated again in May 1868. Louisa still did not want to write the book but she remembered a story she had begun years earlier, which she called "The Pathetic Family," based on the Alcotts' early life. Using "The Pathetic Family," her diaries, and her memories, she finished *Little Women* in July. Niles had some reservations about the story; he thought it read a little slow. But after asking his niece and her friends to read it, he was convinced that this book was just what young ladies wanted. Roberts Publishers accepted the book, and *Little Women* was published in October 1868.

The original *Little Women* ended when John Brooke asked Meg to marry him. But Alcott's readers were not satisfied. They wanted to know more about the March sisters, who had become not only their friends but part of their families! She finished the sequel on 1 January 1869 and published it under the title *Good Wives*. Eventually the two parts of the book were united, and today we know the result as *Little Women*.

Alcott carried the March family and its offspring into two more books: *Little Men* and *Jo's Boys*. *Little Men* was published in 1871, but *Jo's Boys* was not published until 1886, just two years before Alcott's death. Even though Fruitlands had not been a happy experience, Alcott used the idea behind it to create the school in *Little Men.*

Louisa May Alcott published seventeen other books for young readers between 1870 and her death in 1888. *An Old-Fashioned Girl* was loosely based on Louisa's and Anna's experiences as governesses. In *Eight Cousins,* Rose is surrounded by seven boisterous male cousins. She gets to do everything they do. This must have been the fulfillment of a dream for tomboyish Louisa! The sequel, *Rose in Bloom,* soon followed.

Many of Alcott's books were originally serialized in children's publications of the day such as *Merry's Museum* and *St. Nicholas.* Her other books are collections of short stories. *Aunt Jo's Scrap-Bag* turned into six different books of collected stories, and *Lulu's Library* had three volumes.

Alcott's first book consisted of the stories she wrote for Emerson's daughter and was titled *Flower Fables.* In her declining years, she wrote a collection and titled it *A Garland for Girls.* Louisa thought it appropriate to bring her works full circle.

The diaries seem to be what has made her famous, because the everyday happenings of the Alcott family are the basis for *Little Women.* The March sisters are the Alcott sisters: Meg (Anna), Jo (Louisa), Beth (Elizabeth or "Lizzie"), and Amy (May). The personalities of the March sisters reflect those of the Alcotts. Marmee is, of course, Abba Alcott.

Reading *Little Women* is much like reading Louisa's diary. The stories from real life repeat themselves in fiction. When, for example, Mr. March teaches the sisters the alphabet by shaping the letters with his body, Louisa is retelling what happened in the Alcott family. The famous plays of the March sisters are those of the Alcotts. Even the death of Beth parallels the death of the dearly loved Lizzie.

Widening the Circle

Alcott's sense of adventure took her to Europe on two occasions. The first time was as a nurse companion to an invalid lady. The second trip was to take May on the Grand Tour. May, like Amy in *Little Women,* was the artist of the family.

serialized published in short installments at regular intervals

Little Women was made into a movie three times, in 1933, 1949, and 1996.

Alcott was pleased that she could afford to give May the pleasure of visiting the great museums in Paris and Rome. In her later years, Alcott was able to make extended visits to various parts of New England. She also spent a winter in New York City to rest and indulge herself with lectures, plays, and concerts.

Her health continued to fail after the episode in Washington, and much of her later life was spent seeking treatment for the ailments brought on by her willingness to give so much of herself. Her readers were always anxious for another book, the publishers were asking when to expect the next installment, and her fans simply wanted to meet Louisa May Alcott. She gave and gave of herself.

When May died, Alcott adopted May's baby daughter and was responsible for her upbringing. Alcott also adopted Anna's son, John. This she did after he was an adult so that he could be responsible for the renewals of the copyrights on her numerous works. Until her death she was concerned about providing for her family.

Alcott was a shy person who did not understand why people were constantly trying to meet her. She considered her contributions to American literature to be less than outstanding. She grew up in a humble atmosphere and was taught to do the best she could, but not for anyone's compliments or rewards.

Louisa May Alcott would be amazed to realize that more than one hundred years after her death, young adults still read her books. Perhaps these readers often wonder, like she did with Charlotte Brontë, if they too will ever make such a lasting contribution.

If you like the works of Louisa May Alcott, then you might also like the works of Sue Ellen Bridgers, Vera Cleaver, Maureen Daly, Molly Hunter, Kathryn Lasky, Madeleine L'Engle, Katherine Paterson, Ann Rinaldi, Ouida Sebestyen, Rosemary Sutcliff, Mildred Taylor, Ted Taylor, Cynthia Voigt, and Laura Ingalls Wilder.

Selected Bibliography

FIRST EDITIONS OF BOOKS BY LOUISA MAY ALCOTT

Little Women, part 1 (1868)
Little Women, part 2, (1869; first printed as *Good Wives*)
An Old-Fashioned Girl (1870)
Little Men (1871)
Aunt Jo's Scrap-Bag: My Boys (1872)
Aunt Jo's Scrap-Bag: Shawl-Straps (1872)

Aunt Jo's Scrap-Bag: Cupid and Chow-Chow (1874)
Eight Cousins (1875)
Rose In Bloom (1876)
Silver Pitchers (1876)
Aunt Jo's Scrap-Bag: My Girls (1877)
Under The Lilacs (1878)
Aunt Jo's Scrap-Bag: Jimmy's Cruise in a Pinafore (1879)
Jack and Jill: A Village Story (1880)
Aunt Jo's Scrap-Bag: An Old-Fashioned Thanksgiving (1881)
Spinning-Wheel Stories (1884)
Lulu's Library, volume 1 (1885)
Jo's Boys (1886)
Lulu's Library, volume 2 (1887)
A Garland for Girls (1887)
Lulu's Library, volume 3 (1889)

MODERN EDITIONS OF BOOKS BY LOUISA MAY ALCOTT

Eight Cousins (1974)
Jack and Jill (1979)
Behind a Mask (1984)
Jo's Boys (1987)
Little Men (1987)
Rose in Bloom (1989)
An Old-Fashioned Girl (1991)
Under the Lilacs (1991)
The Lost Stories of Louisa May Alcott (1993)
Little Women (1994)
A Whisper in the Dark (1996)

WORKS ABOUT LOUISA MAY ALCOTT

Anthony, Katherine. *Louisa May Alcott*. Westport, Conn.: Greenwood Press, 1977.
Cheney, Ednah Dow, ed. *Louisa May Alcott: Her Life, Letters and Journals*. Boston: Little, Brown, 1928.

In Concord, Massachusetts, you can visit the Orchard House, the place Louisa May Alcott called home from 1858 to 1877. All its contents remain just as they were during her lifetime; among the items familiar to fans of *Little Women* are Lizzie's piano and the costumes the Alcott sisters wore for their play-acting.

MacDonald, Ruth K. *Louisa May Alcott*. Boston: Twayne, 1983.

———. "Louisa May Alcott." In *Writers for Children: Critical Studies of the Major Authors Since the Seventeenth Century*. New York: Charles Scribner's Sons, 1988, pp. 1–6.

Meigs, Cornelia. *Invincible Louisa*. Boston: Little, Brown, 1947.

Myerson, Joel, and Daniel Shealy. *The Selected Letters of Louisa May Alcott*. Boston: Little, Brown, 1987.

Stern, Madeleine B. *Critical Essays on Louisa May Alcott*. Boston: G. K. Hall, 1984.

———. *Louisa May Alcott*. Norman, Okla.: University of Oklahoma Press, 1950.

Lloyd Alexander

(1924-   )

by Jill P. May

Lloyd Alexander is not easily pegged as an author. His body of works does not fit neatly into one genre, and his writing style cannot be readily described. Accustomed to reading in several genres and anxious to write something that can please both himself and his audience, Alexander is continually searching for a new structure, a new setting or character type. He continually takes risks. Each time we discuss what he is writing, he tells me, "I don't know if I can do it this time. I'm afraid I've bitten off more than I can chew."

Alexander's readers have come to depend upon his ability to write in varied modes. His writings carry readers beyond one genre, into a variety of styles and tones. A twentieth-century author whose works have been published in more than a dozen languages throughout the world, Alexander has been acknowledged as a leading figure in literature for young adults. He has received the John Newbery Medal, the National Book Award, the Netherlands Silver Slate Pencil

Quotations from Lloyd Alexander that are not attributed to a published source are from personal interviews conducted by the author of this article (1986–1995) or from her correspondence with him and are published here by permission of Lloyd Alexander.

Award, the Austrian Children's Book Award, the Swedish Golden Cat, the Regina Medal, the Norwegian Children's Book Award, and the Boston Globe–Horn Book Award, among many others. He has written autobiographical books for adults as well as American biographies, fantasy stories based upon Celtic mythology, time-travel tales with cats as heroes, short picture-book fables, a time-travel novel set in the Middle East, an adventure series based upon the French Revolution, a series of mysteries based upon patterns found in the Sherlock Holmes stories, a Chinese bildungsroman (a coming-of-age tale), and a humorous adventure story for young adults, based upon Greek mythology. His eclectic writing is a reflection of his early childhood reading interests and his personal experiences.

eclectic composed of elements from various sources

Early Life

Born on 30 January 1924, five years after his sister, Florence, the young Lloyd Chudley Alexander spent most of his spare time reading and imagining how things might be. He has told me, "To the best of my knowledge, I don't remember my sister, or anyone of my immediate family, picking up a book."

His father, Alan Audley Alexander, had emigrated to the United States from Jamaica, West Indies, when he was a teenager. Alan Alexander spent his days in Philadelphia working in the stock market (until it crashed) and then as a merchant importer. Although Alan Alexander was not a reader, he filled the living room with bookshelves with "attractive volumes" as ornaments.

Once, when I asked Lloyd Alexander what made him a reader in a family of nonreaders, he replied, "I read because it gave me pleasure." Then he went on to explain, "Reading takes us where we want to go, to places where we have never been." He could choose to read Shakespeare's plays, a trashy novel, or novels by Daniel DeFoe, Edith Wharton, and Charles Dickens, Bulfinch's mythology or the romantic tales of King Arthur and his knights. He was allowed to read any book found on the family's library shelves.

Alexander was reading by the time he was three or four; he remembers his father having him read aloud for company. Although he was an avid reader, he did not enjoy entertaining adults. Still, he liked that attention better than the attention he later received from his teachers and classmates. Because he tested out of the first and second grades, Alexander was placed in the third grade when he entered Friends Central, a private Quaker school. His small size and his interest in books made him the target of bullying by his classmates. His teachers' lack of interest in what he wanted to read caused him to dislike school. At times he pretended to be ill so that he could stay at home.

War Experiences

Lloyd Alexander graduated from high school when he was sixteen. Although he wanted to become a poet, his father advised him to get a regular job. For a brief time Alexander worked in a bank as a messenger, writing at night at home. When he had saved up enough money, he entered West Chester State Teachers College. There, however, he soon discovered that he had read most of the required books in his literature classes, and after a year of college he quit. On his nineteenth birthday, he realized that he might be drafted for service in World War II and decided to join the United States Army.

Alexander likes to describe himself as a military misfit who was unable to do anything right. His interest in French kept him from having a totally miserable experience. When he discovered that his language ability would allow him to become part of a special combat intelligence team, he signed up. He has said, "It was heaven. All the misfits were in one camp together. The spit-and-polish was gone. It was a different kind of military experience." After intensive training, Alexander was shipped to Wales, where his earlier interest in Arthurian legends was rekindled. In December 1944, he was transferred to Alsace-Lorraine. His firsthand battle experiences led to his later abhorrence of war, which is reflected in his Westmark series.

While stationed in Paris, Alexander met his future wife, Janine, whom he married four months afterward. He also visited Gertrude Stein and Paul Éluard, two celebrated writers living in Paris. Although Alexander enjoyed his conversations with Stein, he was more impressed with Éluard's

abhorrence a feeling of hatred

Gertrude Stein (1874–1946) was an American author who was known for her innovative use of language. **Paul Éluard** (1895–1952) was a French Surrealist poet. Surrealist poetry reflects a world beyond reality.

record as a French resistance fighter during the war and his reputation as a contemporary poet. Alexander began to translate Éluard's poetry, an endeavor that would affect his later writing style. He thought that Éluard wrote about important aspects of life with expressiveness and feeling, that he used astonishing imagery to draw the reader into his poetry. This is something that Alexander still strives to accomplish in his own writing.

Fantasy Author

To Lloyd Alexander, a man who spent most of his life in Drexel Hill, Pennsylvania, mind traveling is a very important and pleasurable business. Long before Alexander begins to write a new book, he rereads the stories that earlier impressed him, researches other times and places, and develops a "map" for his adventures. His first fantasy book for young readers, *Time Cat: The Remarkable Journeys of Jason and Gareth* (1963), contains stories about cats in several lands. His award-winning Prydain Chronicles are set in ancient Wales. *The Cat Who Wished to Be a Man* (1973) and *The Wizard in the Tree* (1975) are set in Europe during two different eras. The hero in *The First Two Lives of Lukas-Kasha* (1978) time-travels to the Middle East, while the heroes and heroines in *The Arkadians* (1995) wander in an ancient land that resembles Greece.

Each of Alexander's portrayals of fantastic lands contains a great deal of detail that relies upon earlier myths and folkloric legend and that relies on written accounts of people and events of the past. When describing fantasy in "Identifications and Identities" (1970), Alexander wrote, "The deepest and most durable works of art . . . become explorations of the world, not only of the neighborhood; journeys not only to another country, but into the cosmos of human personality."

Alexander's youthful heroes are struggling to discover who they are. They do not reach maturity until the ends of their stories, whether they are the assistant pig-keeper Taran, the foolhardy cat who is changed into a man, or the gawky orphan Lucian. Often in their journeys an older soothsayer or storyteller accompanies them. These guides offer comic relief

> *To Lloyd Alexander, a man who spent most of his life in Drexel Hill, Pennsylvania, mind traveling is a very important and pleasurable business.*

> *In 1985, Walt Disney Productions released The Black Cauldron, an animated film based on parts of Alexander's Prydain Chronicles.*

comic relief   a relief from an emotionally tense scene through the introduction of a comic element

to the heroes' adventures, but they are also believable characters: knowledgeable and helpful, if also prone to exaggeration. In contrast to Alexander's heroes, these companions never win a damsel or seem too interested in marrying or settling in one place.

Women in Alexander's male-dominated fantasy worlds are the wiser gender; they usually marry the heroes without losing their ability to make decisions and direct their men's fate. They may appear talkative and self-centered at first, but they always know their strengths. Their marriages seem fitting endings to their interactions with men they have helped. Throughout the episodes, they have helped their heroes find themselves.

Yet Alexander's females should not be regarded as mere props for the males. They have distinctive attributes of their own. For instance, the heroine in *Wizard in the Tree* resembles Lukas-Kasha and Lionel in her early reliance on past cultural lore, but she does not have to marry in the end to complete her quest. When her wizard floats away, he tells her, "There is nothing of true value that I could give you that you don't already have." Although some feminists might find Alexander's female characters lacking in self-determination, his depiction of Mallory as a strong independent protagonist in *The Wizard in the Tree* belies such a reading.

belies contradicts

One of Alexander's most impressive fantasies, *The Remarkable Journey of Prince Jen* (1991), is set in the eighth century in China. This book has the story structure of a classic Chinese novel. The six magical objects that are central to the story come from Alexander's recollections of items that his father brought home while he was working as an importer of Chinese merchandise.

Alexander once admitted to me that he knew *The Remarkable Journey of Prince Jen* was a risky story for him to write, especially as he had read very little Chinese mythology before beginning the project. Still, he welcomed the challenge. Although the story is set in China and does contain a good deal of Eastern philosophy, it also exhibits Alexander's own belief in the human consequences of behavior within history; this we see when the elder male journeyer tells his now wiser youthful companion, "If we look backward instead of forward . . . might we not discover that one thing set in motion sets all else moving? Tug the edge of a spiderweb and the center moves."

A Mystery Series

One of Alexander's unusual accomplishments is his Vesper adventure mystery series. When I asked him if the series was influenced by the Sherlock Holmes mysteries, he wrote back:

> I was (and am) a devoted admirer of that great consulting detective. About age ten, I stumbled on a book called *The Casebook of Sherlock Holmes* and was instantly hooked. I had no idea other stories existed until a couple years later, then I gobbled up all of them. Plus seeing the movies. Trying to feel my way toward Vesper and Brinnie, Holmes and Watson were clearly, consciously, and deliberately in my thoughts; along with loving homage to Rider Haggard, E. M. Hull, and Anthony Hope.

Vesper is a strong-willed female who dares to defy society's ideas of proper female decorum without worrying about the consequences. Like Mallory, Vesper has no real need for a male counterpart. Yet at the end of the series, she is aligned with a male who is as intelligent and charming as she is. In fact, Alexander seems to have reversed his earlier gender roles within this series.

When asked why he decided to write the mystery series, Alexander explained that he created Vesper to heal his spirits after writing the Westmark series. It was, he said, "sheer fun," and he likened it to going to the Saturday matinee: "substance with zingers that sneak up on their audience." In essence, he said, the books suggested that the reader should "not be too solemn or earnest."

The History of the Westmark Trilogy

In contrast to the mysteries, Alexander's Westmark series was extremely intense and uncompromising. It was probably his greatest accomplishment. Written with great compassion and insight, the series contains the same strong elements of humanity and suffering found in the classic Russian novel *War and Peace* by Leo Tolstoy. In many ways this young adult series is an American counterpart for an audience not yet ready to read the adult war novels written in the United States during the late twentieth century. Alexander's books describe an uncertain time when political intrigue has caused men to forget themselves, allowing them to commit atrocious acts against other human beings.

Alexander wrote the Westmark Trilogy at the time of Jimmy Carter's presidency. Although the Vietnam War was over and the immediate threat of further war was absent, Alexander felt a need to revisit the horrors he had witnessed during World War II. The series broke with his earlier trend of fantasy writing and reflected his need to experiment with genres and thematic approaches that he had not used in his earlier books.

In 1987, in "Travel Notes," Alexander alluded to his newly affirmed commitment: writing young adult literature that expressed realistic concerns for humanity in the twenty-first century. Arguing that everyone must be concerned with relevancy, he said, "We can't escape from the real world. We may disguise it or turn it into metaphor, but the real world is all we have. . . . Everything in our heads comes from the same raw material, the same place." The real place that Alexander brought to life in the Westmark books was the battlefield he had seen during World War II.

The series gained international attention. *Westmark* (1981) won the American Book Award for Children's Literature and was named a Best Book by the American Library Association (ALA); *The Kestrel* (1982) was named a Parents' Choice selection; *The Beggar Queen* (1984) was named an ALA Best Book for Young Adults. At this same time, Alexander won the Netherlands Silver Slate Pencil Award for *The First Two Lives of Lukas-Kasha* and the Swedish Golden Cat Award for a body of work.

Once again, Alexander created a series with two youthful protagonists, one male and one female. The male, Theo, is an orphan struggling to find his place in society, but he is a reluctant hero at first. Forced to flee his home and take to the road, Theo encounters a group of radicals who hope to free their country from tyranny. Throughout the series, Theo struggles with his moral obligations during the war. By the

Adult novels about World War II are *The Caine Mutiny* (1951) by Herman Wouk; *The Fox in the Field* (1994) by Maynard Allington; and *Loyalties* (1994) by Thomas Fleming.

metaphor a figure of speech in which one thing is referred to as something else, for example, "My love is a rose"

second book of the series he has become a guerrilla fighter. He is the Kestrel, a famous partisan commander who kills his enemies after letting out a blood-curdling scream. Alexander writes of him:

> His desire had become very narrow and simple: to kill everyone wearing a Regian uniform; failing that, as many as possible. It seemed a modest and sensible goal.
>
> He was not sane enough to realize he had gone somewhat mad; he has only gone mad enough to believe himself completely sane.

The heroine, Mickle, is the daughter of the king, but she has been forcibly removed and is hiding with the common people. She is the strong, sympathetic personality in the Westmark series. Later, as the two youthful protagonists reach maturity, Alexander introduces a sister and brother who replace them in immaturity and insecurity. At the end of the series these younger protagonists will be left behind while the earlier pair leave Westmark.

This series illustrates Alexander's greatness as a writer. He writes with compassion and drama, and he maintains characterization, voice, tension, and adventure within the series. He carefully interweaves realism and tragedy into these mature works for young adults. The Westmark books deserve classroom attention in high schools as distinguished literary works.

Continual Themes

"One thing a cat is not is obedient. Writers aren't either, at least not the good ones."

Those who know Lloyd Alexander as a friend find him charming, witty, and a bit eccentric. He has had cats in his house most of his married life, and he shares long conversations with his cats. He keeps a regular schedule while he is writing and is rather difficult to live with during this time, according to his wife, Janine. Alexander wrote in Rojak's *The Cat on My Shoulder*, "Writers are outcasts and are thus on the defensive. Like cats, they're essentially rebels. One thing a cat is not is obedient. Writers aren't either, at least not the good ones."

There are few things more enjoyable than spending an afternoon with the Alexanders. Lloyd Alexander is attached to his house (as well as to his cats), and he takes pleasure in sharing time with his friends. He is a member of a quartet that regularly gathers at his home to practice classical music. Still, he works hard at being a writer and craves solitude for his research and writing schedule.

In the late 1990s, Alexander returned to writing fantasy, perhaps because he feels most comfortable writing metaphorically about his concerns and troubles. In every one of his books there is a dreamer/storyteller/loner who might be Lloyd Alexander. When I asked him in 1982, "Why do you write fantasy?" he wrote back, "I didn't turn to fantasy as any kind of escape whatsoever. Just the opposite. Fantasy has been, for me, the best way of expressing the real world, trying to understand or make sense of it. The books, in that aspect, are in a way messages to myself about reality."

Alexander plays the violin in this quartet. A **quartet** consists of four musicians; the instruments are usually a cello, a viola, and two violins.

Selected Bibliography

WORKS BY LLOYD ALEXANDER

The Prydain Chronicles
The Book of Three (1964)
The Black Cauldron (1965)
The Castle of Llyr (1966)
Taran Wanderer (1967)
The High King (1968)

The Westmark Trilogy
Westmark (1981)
The Kestrel (1982)
The Beggar Queen (1984)

The Vesper Holly Adventures
The Illyrian Adventure (1986)
The El Dorado Adventure (1987)
The Drackenburg Adventure (1988)
The Jedera Adventure (1989)

Other Books for Children and Young Adults
Borderhawk: August Bondi (1958)
The Flagship Hope: Aaron Lope (1960)

If you like the works of Lloyd Alexander, you might also enjoy those by Ursula K. Le Guin, Rosemary Sutcliff, and J.R.R. Tolkien.

Time Cat: The Remarkable Journeys of Jason and Gareth (1963)

The Marvelous Misadventures of Sebastian: Grand Extravaganza, Including a Performance by the Entire Cast of the Gallimaufry-Theatricus (1970)

The King's Fountain (1971)

The Four Donkeys (1972)

The Cat Who Wished to Be a Man (1973)

The Foundling and Other Tales of Prydain (1973)

The Wizard in the Tree (1975)

The Town Cats and Other Tales (1977)

The First Two Lives of Lukas-Kasha (1978)

The Remarkable Journey of Prince Jen (1991)

The Fortune-Tellers (1992)

The Arkadians (1995)

The House Gobbaleen (1995)

Adult Books

And Let the Credit Go (1954)

Janine Is French (1958)

My Five Tigers (1956)

My Love Affair with Music (1960)

Articles

"Substance and Fantasy." *Library Journal,* 14 December 1966, pp. 6157–6159.

"Truth About Fantasy." *Top of the News,* January 1968, pp. 168–174.

"Wishful Thinking—Or Hopeful Dreaming?" *Bookbird* 7, 1969, pp. 3–9. Reprinted from *Horn Book,* August 1968, pp. 383–390. Discusses the meaning of fantasy and the differences between adult and children's literature.

"A Personal Note on Charles Dickens." *Top of the News,* November 1968, pp. 10–14.

"Where the Novel Went." *Saturday Review,* 22 March 1969, p. 62.

"No Laughter in Heaven." *Horn Book,* February 1970, pp. 11–19.

"Identifications and Identities." *Wilson Library Bulletin,* October 1970, pp. 144–148. Discusses how past authors have used history in their writing and suggests that literature can help readers identify with those who are different from themselves.

"High Fantasy and Heroic Romance." *Horn Book,* December 1971, pp. 577–584.

"On Responsibility and Authority." *Horn Book,* August 1974, pp. 363–364.

"Gertrude Stein." *Cricket,* January 1977, pp. 54–59.

"Fantasy as Images: A Literary View." In *Language Arts,* April 1978, pp. 440–445.

"Notes on the Westmark Trilogy." *Advocate,* fall 1984, pp. 1–6.

"Travel Notes." In *Innocence and Experience: Essays and Conversations on Children's Literature.* Edited by Barbara Harrison and Gregory Maguire. New York: Lothrop, Lee & Shepard, 1987.

"Lloyd Alexander." In *Something About the Author Autobiography Series.* Detroit: Gale Research, 1995, vol. 19, pp. 35–52.

WORKS ABOUT LLOYD ALEXANDER

Books

Harrison, Barbara, and Gregory Macguire, eds. *Innocence & Experience: Essays and Conversations on Children's Literature.* New York: Lothrop, Lee & Shepard, 1987.

Hearne, Betsy, and Marilyn Kaye, eds. *Celebrating Children's Books.* New York: Lothrop, Lee & Shepard, 1981.

Jacobs, James S., and Michael O. Tunnell. *Lloyd Alexander: A Bio-Bibliography.* New York: Greenwood Press, 1989.

May, Jill P. *Lloyd Alexander.* Boston: G. K. Hall, 1991.

Rojek, Lisa Angowski, ed. *The Cat on My Shoulder: Writers and Their Cats.* Stamford, Conn.: Longmeadow Press, 1993.

Seales, Beth Meacham, and Michael Franklin. *A Reader's Guide to Fantasy.* New York: Facts on File, 1982.

Sullivan, C. W., III. *Welsh Celtic Myth in Modern Fantasy.* New York: Greenwood Press, 1989.

Tunnell, Michael O. *The Prydain Companion: A Reference Guide to Lloyd Alexander's Prydain Chronicles.* New York: Greenwood Press, 1989.

Tymn, Marshall B., Kenneth J. Zahorski, and Robert H. Boyer. *Fantasy Literature: A Collection and Reference Guide*. New York: R. R. Bowker, 1979.

Articles

Carr, Marion. "Classic Hero in New Mythology." *Horn Book,* October 1971, pp. 508–513.

Durell, Ann. "Who's Lloyd Alexander?" *Horn Book,* August 1969, pp. 382–384.

Greenlaw, M. Jean. "Profile: Lloyd Alexander." *Language Arts,* April 1984, pp. 406–413.

Ingram, Laura. "Lloyd Alexander." In *Dictionary of Literary Biography*. Edited by Glenn E. Estes. Detroit: Gale Research, 1986, vol. 52, pp. 3–21.

Jacobs, James S. "A Personal Look at Lloyd Alexander." In *Advocate,* fall 1984, pp. 8–18.

Kiefer, Barbara Z. "Wales as a Setting for Fantasy." *Children's Literature in Education,* summer 1982, pp. 95–101.

Kuznets, Lois. "High Fantasy in America: Alexander, LeGuin, and Cooper." *Lion and the Unicorn* 9, 1985, pp. 19–35.

May, Jill P. "Lloyd Alexander's Truthful Harp." *Children's Literature Association Quarterly,* spring 1985, pp. 37–38.

Omdal, Marsha DePrez. "For Wayfarers Still Journeying . . ." *Language Arts,* April 1978, pp. 501–502.

Scott, Jon C. "Lloyd Alexander's Chronicles of Prydain: The Nature of Beginnings." In *Touchstones: Reflections on the Best in Children's Literature*. Edited by Perry Nodelman. Children's Literature Association Publications Staff, 1985, vol. 1, pp. 21–29.

Sennick, Gerald J., ed. "Lloyd Alexander." In *Children's Literature Review,* 1983, vol. 5, pp. 13–26.

"SLJ Meets . . . Lloyd Alexander." *School Library Journal,* 15 April 1971, pp. 1421–1423.

Stuart, Dee. "An Exclusive Interview with Lloyd Alexander." *Writer's Digest,* April 1973, pp. 33–35, 57–58.

Sutherland, Zena. "Captive Author, Captivated Audience." *Saturday Review,* April 1972, vol. 22, p. 78.

Townsend, John Rowe. "Heights of Fantasy." In *Children's Literature Review,* 1983, vol. 5, pp. 7–12.

Tunnell, Michael O. "Eilonwy of the Red-Gold Hair." *Language Arts,* September 1989, pp. 558–563.

Tunnell, Michael O., and James S. Jacobs. "Alexander's Chronicles of Prydain: 20 Years Later." *School Library Journal,* April 1988, pp. 27–31.

How to Write to the Author

Lloyd Alexander
1005 Drexel Avenue
Drexel Hill, PA 19026-3306

Judie Angell

(1937–   )

by Hollis Lowery-Moore

Judie Angell and Fran Arrick are the same person. Angell also uses the pseudonym (pen name) Maggie Twohill when she publishes novels for children. Under her "real" name, Judie Angell writes and publishes books for preteens and younger teens. Angell's stories focus on coming-of-age issues and are often based loosely on people and incidents in her own life, including her experiences as a former elementary school teacher.

In *Speaking For Ourselves: Autobiographical Sketches by Notable Authors of Books for Young Adults* (Gallo, ed., 1990), Angell cites laughing as one of the terrific things in life and the breakdown of society's values as one of the not-so-terrific things in life. In Angell's books for adolescents, laughter is unavoidable, even when she is dealing with serious topics. Angell creates independent, clever characters, and the explorations of problem situations seldom interfere with the novels' entertainment value. Angell's stories fit into the broad category of not "too serious," highly readable, problem nov-

35

els for the young adolescent and are similar to many of the novels of Judy Blume, Betsy Byars, and Hila Colman. Angell's uniqueness lies in her use of many forms of humor and in the diverse supporting cast she employs in the narratives—including helpful and cooperative adults.

Memories of Growing Up

Judie Angell was born on 10 July 1937. She uses the people and events from her childhood in creating her stories, honestly recollecting the turbulent emotions of growing up. The camp antics of preteen girls make for amusing dialogue and comic events in *In Summertime It's Tuffy* (1977). Eleven-year-old Elizabeth (Tuffy to her camp mates) teams up with Iris, a new girl who's interested in witchcraft, and tries voodoo to get rid of the despised head counselor. Angell's re-creation of the familiar routines and standard personalities of camp life will delight readers who have attended their own version of Camp Ma-Sha-Na. A *School Library Journal* review (May 1977) described this novel as an obvious nostalgia trip for the author to her own camp days.

One-Way to Ansonia (1985), partially inspired by Angell's maternal grandmother, is the story of Rose Olshansky, a Russian immigrant to the United States in the late 1800s. Rose must work in a factory to pay her room and board in a crowded tenement in New York City. By the age of sixteen, Rose is married and has a baby, but she courageously sets out alone to find a better life. She has only enough money to buy a ticket to Ansonia, Connecticut, promising to send for her husband once she finds work and he recovers from pneumonia. Readers can put themselves in Rose's place and imagine how they would act in the same situations.

Music is one of the constants in the author's life, providing inspiration for characters and story lines. Angell is married to a musician who specializes in pop and jazz arrangements. In her novel *The Buffalo Nickel Blues Band* (1982), Angell's characters—Eddie, Ivy, Georgie, Shelby, and Reese—love rhythm and blues music, rather than the more usual rock and roll sounds that permeate the lives of adolescents. The five make up a band that experiences great success, but the refusal of Shelby's parents to allow him to continue playing forces the breakup of the group. Angell's focus is the funny, warm friendship of the band members, but references to great blues titles and musicians may open a whole new musical world for some readers.

Broken Families

The characters in many of Angell's stories confront the physical and emotional difficulties of broken family structures. In *Tina Gogo* (1978), Bettina Gogolavsky (the Tina of the title) battles the insecurities and pains of being a foster child—moving from family to family, always wishing for her own place in the world. Tina's brashness and duplicity make it difficult for her to find friends. Her foster family, the Harrises, and her newly found friend, Sarajane, break through the barriers and support Tina's decision to live with her mother, who is sickly and unable to provide financially for the two of them. Tina's resilience provides the reader with a sense of hope that Tina will survive the struggle that lies ahead.

Six orphans become a family headed by eighteen-year-old Arthur Beniker, who writes an advice column under the pseudonym Lola in *Dear Lola, or How to Build Your Own Family: A Tale* (1980). Slapstick humor is interspersed with the tragic stories of the children's pasts, and the reader is happy to see the youngsters escape the clutches of the Department of Social Services, which would separate them and take them away from the only family they know. They escape, however, by becoming migrant workers, a life that offers little promise of a hopeful future.

Divorce disrupts the lives of the Currie children in *What's Best For You* (1981). Despite the parents' efforts to help each child cope with the changes divorce brings, fifteen-year-old Lee, twelve-year-old Allison, and seven-year-old are frustrated and angry with their parents. Angell shows that everyone in the Currie family, young and old, must make difficult decisions and adjustments.

Variety

Reviewers praise the variety in Angell's many novels. In addition to tackling adolescent responses to society's problems, Angell parodies television soap operas in *Suds: A New Daytime Drama* (1983). Sue Sudley's parents die in a midair col-

> **On The Buffalo Nickel Blues Band:** *Angell's focus is the funny, warm friendship of the band members, but references to great blues titles and musicians may open a whole new musical world for some readers.*

duplicity deceit

slapstick humor a form of comedy that is marked by clownish and crazy chases, collisions, and exaggerated horseplay

lision and she must go to live with her mother's sister and her family in a small town somewhere in the United States. Sue solves the town mystery and exposes the respected English teacher for what she really is, the author of spicy romance novels. The heroine's romantic interest, Storm, a former football player, is paralyzed and confined to a wheelchair. In soap opera style, Storm saves the day in an important football game, is knocked out, then walks again when he regains consciousness. Those adolescents familiar with the daytime soaps will get a kick out of Angell's spoof.

Lighthearted, upbeat, inoffensive, pleasant, wholesome, and entertaining are words critics frequently use to describe Angell's novels. The middle school and junior high reader will find likable and familiar characters as well as timely topics in Angell's easy-to-read stories.

Books for Older Teens

As Fran Arrick, Judie Angell writes stories that are much more intense and that explore weighty issues such as suicide, teenage violence, prostitution, and AIDS. These novels are written for older teens and often have an obvious message. Critics disagree on the degree of didacticism and the extent to which the "preachiness" interferes with the narratives; however, most reviewers conclude that Arrick's books are loaded with honest information and realistic dialogue. Arrick frequently deals with the whole family or community in her stories, exploring issues from several points of view.

In *Steffie Can't Come Out to Play* (1978), Stephanie Rudd runs away from an unhappy home and is befriended by a slick young man, Favor, who leads Steffie into prostitution. The reader follows Steffie's story through her words and the words of a police officer who takes an interest in Steffie and is determined to get her out of the pimp's clutches.

Tunnel Vision (1980) begins with the suicide of Anthony Hamil. The reader learns about Anthony as his friends and relatives search for the reasons an academically and athletically successful fifteen year old would want to end his life. Anthony's mother, sister, girlfriend, and teacher share a sense of guilt for not recognizing the extent of Anthony's depression. Even his swim team coach questions whether he

didacticism marked by an intention to teach as well as to entertain

The books Angell writes under the pseudonym (pen name) Fran Arrick are loaded with honest information and realistic dialogue.

pushed him too hard. There are no answers in Arrick's book, but the questions raised by the characters as they seek understanding do provide opportunities for reflection on the complexities of growing up and finding personal sources of peace.

In *Chernowitz!* (1981), Emmett Sundback, the school bully, picks out Bobby Cherno to harass because Bobby is Jewish. Emmett's name-calling and pranks become increasingly vicious. Sundback and his followers burn a small cross in the Chernos' yard, paint a swastika on the Chernos' car, and ostracize Bobby. Rather than turn to others for help, Bobby plots revenge. Once the school community becomes aware of the situation, a schoolwide effort is made to raise the students' consciousness about the horrors of anti-Semitism. A chilling ending leaves the reader with unanswered questions and an unsettled feeling.

In *God's Radar* (1983), Arrick creates an ordinary, likable teenage character thrown into an extraordinary situation. Roxie Cable and her family move from Syracuse, New York, to a small Georgia town where the Stafford Hill Baptist Church becomes the center of their lives. Roxie tries to understand the sense of safety and security that the fundamentalist community provides her parents, but she resents the strict rules and the biases of the church and her new Stafford Hill friends. No one approves of Roxie's new boyfriend Jarrell Meek. Jarrell is not one of the Stafford Baptist Church members and is considered wild, but Roxie sees a different person. When the church's antenna is cracked on New Year's Eve, Jarrell is accused and Roxie is the only one who believes he's not guilty. Once again Arrick presents problems without providing answers, creating opportunity for thoughtful problem-solving and reflection.

Sixteen-year-old Billy shoots and kills his girlfriend in *Where'd You Get The Gun, Billy?* (1991). Liz and David set out to find out how Billy got a gun in the first place, providing Arrick with the opportunity to create a hypothetical story tracing the gun from its purchase, through many owners, to Billy's hands. The bottom line is that it is easy to get your hands on a gun. In his description of the gun's travels, a police officer describes all kinds of people and why each would have a gun, providing a unique look at society and at the issue of gun control. There is little opportunity to become involved with char-

swastika originally a Greek cross; was used as the symbol of Nazi Germany in World War II (1939–1945).

anti-Semitism hostility toward or discrimination against Jews

acters in this novel, but the gun's journey from person to person keeps the reader turning pages.

Another look at the way serious problems affect a community is presented in *What You Don't Know Can Kill You* (1992). Ellen is a typical suburban teenager until she contracts HIV (the AIDS virus) from her boyfriend Jack, who has been sexually active with other partners during his first year of college. Jack's feelings of hopelessness lead him to commit suicide, but Ellen survives the hostility of the community because of the support of a younger sister, Debra, friends, a support group, and, ultimately, her parents. Even though this book deals with such controversial topics as safe sex and birth control, Arrick avoids sensationalism and offensive language or descriptions, and she provides lifesaving information for readers.

sensationalism a style of writing that is shocking, intense, and disturbing (such emotional responses are often achieved by using gruesome details)

Conclusion

Honest information, respect for young people, and insight into the emotions of adolescence and young adulthood are characteristics of Angell's books. Judie Angell tackles society's problems and the impact on young adults in novels that are "quick reads" but emotionally challenging. The novels written under the pseudonym Fran Arrick beg to be discussed with peers.

One of the "terrific" times in life, according to Angell, is when a good plan comes together. The list of Angell's works for young adults attests to the fact that her book plans have often been successful.

If you like Judie Angell, you might also like the works of Judy Blume, Betsy Byars, Hila Colman, and Paula Danziger. If you like the books she writes under the pseudonym Fran Arrick, you might also like the works of Francesca Lia Block, Chris Crutcher, Lynn Hall, Norma Fox Mazer, and Ouida Sebestyen.

Selected Bibliography

WORKS BY JUDIE ANGELL

Novels for Young Adults
   In Summertime It's Tuffy (1977)
   Ronnie and Rosey (1977)
   Tina Gogo (1978)
   Secret Selves (1979)
   A Word from Our Sponsor; or, My Friend Alfred (1979)

Dear Lola, or How to Build Your Own Family: A Tale (1980)
What's Best for You (1981)
The Buffalo Nickel Blues Band (1982)
First, the Good News (1983)
Suds: A New Daytime Drama (1983)
A Home Is to Share . . . and Share . . . and Share (1984)
One-Way to Ansonia (1985)
The Weird Disappearance of Jordan Hall (1987)
Don't Rent My Room! (1990)
Leave the Cooking to Me (1990)
Yours Truly (1993)

WORKS WRITTEN UNDER THE PSEUDONYM FRAN ARRICK

Steffie Can't Come Out to Play (1978)
Tunnel Vision (1980)
Chernowitz! (1981)
God's Radar (1983)
Nice Girl from Good Home (1984)
Where'd You Get the Gun, Billy? (1991)
What You Don't Know Can Kill You (1992)

WORKS WRITTEN UNDER THE PSEUDONYM MAGGIE TWOHILL

Children's Books
Who's Got the Lucky-Duck in Class 4-B (1984)
Jetter, Mason, and the Magic Headset (1985)
Bigmouth (1986)
Valentine Frankenstein (1994)

WORKS ABOUT JUDIE ANGELL

Gallo, Donald R., ed. *Speaking For Ourselves: Autobiographical Sketches by Notable Authors of Books for Young*

Adults. Urbana, Ill.: National Council of Teachers of English, 1990, pp. 8–9.

Commire, Anna, ed. "Judie Angell." In *Something About the Author Autobiography Series*. Detroit: Gale Research, 1994, vol. 78, pp. 3–9.

School Library Journal, May 1977, vol. 23, p. 58.

Senick, Gerard S., ed. *Children's Literature Review*. Detroit: Gale Research, 1994, vol. 33, pp. 1–19

Maya Angelou

(1928-   )

by Joyce L. Graham

I first met Maya Angelou in November 1989, at a press conference at which it was announced that she had been
named a Distinguished Visiting Professor at Radford University in Radford, Virginia. She confidently strode into the
conference room, which was filled with television cameras,
flashing lights, and the expectant faces of members of the audience and reporters. Wearing an elegant red cape and smiling brightly, Angelou seemed sophisticated and worldly. Her
stature—she is six feet tall—commands attention and respect, and it was clear at that press conference that she had
received both from the audience.

Poet for President Clinton's Inauguration

When President Bill Clinton invited Angelou to write and deliver a poem at his inauguration in January 1993, her name
became a household word for people across the country and

43

> *"History, despite its wrenching pain,/Cannot be unlived, but if faced/With courage, need not be lived again." —from* **"On the Pulse of Morning"**

around the world. Clinton's invitation came to Angelou, no doubt, because she is a renowned poet and autobiographer from Stamps, Arkansas, in the president's home state. The poem Angelou wrote for the inaugural event, titled "On the Pulse of Morning," reflects Angelou's life and writing. It also illustrates many beliefs, which she shares with President Clinton, that celebrate the diversity of people living in the United States.

How is it, then, that Maya Angelou came to be such a renowned and respected scholar, poet, autobiographer, actress, civil rights activist, educator, historian, playwright, producer, and director that the president of the United States asked her to read at his inauguration? This question is an important one because in its answer we can discover much about Angelou's life and work.

Praises Sung for the *Caged Bird*

In addition to maintaining a rigorous writing and public speaking schedule, since 1982 Angelou has held a lifetime distinguished teaching position at Wake Forest University in Winston-Salem, North Carolina. She was appointed to this newly created teaching position twelve years after her first book, *I Know Why the Caged Bird Sings* (1970), was published. The book became an instant best-seller, and it received extremely positive reviews from literary critics nationwide. A review in the *New York Times* (20 March 1970) by the noted American author James Baldwin said:

> This testimony from a black sister marks the beginning of a new era in the minds and hearts and lives of all black men and women . . . *I Know Why the Caged Bird Sings* liberates the reader into life simply because Angelou confronts her own life with such a moving wonder, such a luminous dignity. I have no words for this achievement, but I know that not since the days of my childhood, when people in books were more real than the people one saw every day, have I found myself so moved. . . . Her portrait is a biblical study of life in the midst of death. (P. L45)

Such glowing reviews of the book were common and escalated Angelou's reputation as a writer. Quickly recognized as an important literary work, this first book of Angelou's autobiographical series was published at the end of a decade highlighted by the civil rights movement, and her writing continues to document the racial disparity, turmoil, and conflicts in the United States.

One of the reasons Angelou's book met with such success was that it is an excellent autobiography. Since the days of slavery in the United States and the slave narratives written by Frederick Douglass, autobiography has become a significant literary tradition for African Americans, used to capture historical and personal events and as a vehicle through which to express them creatively in written form. Angelou's writing beautifully seizes the creative opportunities offered by autobiography. Her work reads like a novel because of her ability to craft language in prose that reads easily in paragraph form yet often sounds like poetry. For example, early in *I Know Why the Caged Bird Sings,* Angelou confronts her own realization that only blond-haired, blue-eyed, white girls are regarded as beautiful and that being black brings many apparent limitations to her life. She says, "If growing up is painful for the Southern Black girl, being aware of her displacement is the rust on the razor that threatens the throat" (p. 3). Such descriptive language can be found throughout her works and enriches her frequent public presentations.

disparity inequality

Autobiographies by African Americans include *Narrative of the Life of Frederick Douglass, an American Slave, Written by Himself* (1845) by Frederick Douglass; *Black Boy* (1945) by Richard Wright; and *Dust Tracks on a Road* (1942) by Zora Neale Hurston.

Growing Up

I Know Why the Caged Bird Sings details the story of Angelou's life through the age of sixteen. The book begins with a scene in which young Marguerite Johnson (Angelou's given name) is humiliated in a church Easter pageant when she forgets the passage she is to recite. From this opening scene, in which Angelou paints a vivid picture of how difficult growing up can be, we follow her life through many equally vivid events that help readers better understand how she has become the woman she is today.

Early in the book we learn that when Maya, who is given this nickname by her only brother, is three and her brother,

Bailey, is four, they are put on a train in Long Beach, California, and travel alone to Stamps, Arkansas, to live with their grandmother after their parents' divorce. Momma, as the children call their grandmother, is a respected leader in the community; she owns a grocery store and property, and she has enough money to make loans when people need it. Regardless of these successes, Maya realizes early in life that a clear division exists between African Americans and whites in her community, and she comes quickly to understand the horrors of racial prejudice.

Establishing strict standards for her grandchildren, Momma insists that Maya and Bailey work each day in the store and at home, attend church often, and study hard in school. Maya loves books from an early age and reads with eagerness any book she is able to get.

Maya and Bailey have adjusted to their life in Stamps when, several years later, their father arrives to take them to live with their mother in Saint Louis. Soon after moving there, eight-year-old Maya is raped by her mother's boyfriend, and the day after he is released from jail with a sentence of only one year and one day to serve, several of Maya's uncles murder him. Convinced that her identification of this man has caused his death, Maya slips into a self-imposed silence; she is suddenly terrified of words and the impact that she believes they can have.

Maya and Bailey are shipped immediately back to live in Stamps, and five years after her silence has started, she is encouraged out of her muteness by an aristocratic African American woman, Mrs. Bertha Flowers. Mrs. Flowers, whom Angelou calls her "first lifeline," uses books as a vehicle through which she coaxes young Maya to speak. She encourages Maya to read aloud and to memorize and recite from books. In *Caged Bird,* Angelou recalls:

> I had read *A Tale of Two Cities* and found it up to my standards as a romantic novel. She [Bertha Flowers] opened the first page and I heard poetry for the first time in my life.

> "It was the best of times and the worst of times. . .." Her voice slid in and curved down through and over the words. She was nearly singing. I wanted to look at the pages. Were they the same that I had read? Or

A Tale of Two Cities was written by Charles Dickens. There is an article about him later in this volume.

were there notes, music, lined on the pages, as in a hymn book? . . .

I was liked, and what a difference it made. I was respected not as Mrs. Henderson's grandchild or Bailey's sister but just for being Marguerite Johnson. (Pp. 84–85)

The relationship that the young Angelou developed with Mrs. Flowers was crucial in helping her develop a clearer understanding of herself and others—and in giving her the sense of self-confidence and self-worth that she brings to her work.

Not long after her experience with Mrs. Flowers and immediately following her eighth-grade graduation, Maya is again shipped across the country with Bailey to live with their mother, this time in California. Through the remainder of the book, we find out about the difficult relationship Maya had with her father and his girlfriend and how this resulted in her running away for a month. Before her graduation from high school, Maya takes a job as the first African American streetcar conductor in San Francisco. At the book's conclusion, Maya gives birth to a baby boy and is learning how to adjust as a young single mother.

Meeting Life's Challenges

What is clear throughout *Caged Bird* is that Angelou recognized early in life that we are often faced with difficult challenges. A characteristic that distinguishes Angelou from many people in similarly harsh circumstances is that she believed, and continues to believe, that she could rise above the difficulties she encountered. This same philosophy is seen throughout the four remaining volumes of her autobiography. Angelou looks at life as being filled with opportunities, and she eagerly and confidently works to surpass these challenges.

Angelou's positive spirit and poetic talents are reflected in the intriguing titles she gives her books. Taking *I Know Why the Caged Bird Sings* from a line in a Paul Laurence Dunbar poem, Angelou leaves readers to draw their own conclusions about why caged birds do, in fact, sing. Other titles of her autobiographies are *Gather Together in My Name*

Paul Laurence Dunbar (1872–1906) was the first African American to become popular for both his poetry and his fiction. In his poems, Dunbar generally limited his racial concerns to themes praising blacks, not attacking whites.

(1974), *Singin' and Swingin' and Gettin' Merry Like Christmas* (1976), *The Heart of a Woman* (1981), and *All God's Children Need Traveling Shoes* (1986). These titles, like the works themselves, are melodious and reflect a gift at expressing language in beautiful ways.

After *Caged Bird,* the remaining books of Angelou's autobiography trace in rich detail her life from the infancy of her son, Guy, until her return to the United States after spending four eventful years in Africa with Guy, who has become a young man. Readers are able to follow Angelou's life through events such as her marriage to and divorce from Tosh Angelos, a former sailor of Greek heritage from whom she derived her name.

Beginning in the early 1950s, Angelou traveled to New York, where she frequently visited or lived for the next twenty years. It was in New York that she found a haven for her creative talents. During her early years there, she studied dance, and during the 1954–1955 season, she performed in a twenty-two-country tour of the Everyman's Opera Company production of *Porgy and Bess.* Her young son's depression during her absence, however, caused Angelou to resign from the company and return home to Guy.

For a number of years after, she supported her family by working as a singer and actress. Her growing frustration with the mistreatment of African Americans in general and with the lack of recognition, respect, and appropriate financial compensation for African American performers in particular led Angelou to leave New York with Guy in 1961 to live and work in Egypt and Ghana. During those years, Angelou worked as an editor for an English-language newspaper, as an assistant administrator at a university, and as a freelance writer and features editor for a magazine. Four years after leaving the United States, Angelou and Guy returned, and Angelou accepted a position at the University of California at Los Angeles.

Finally, in the late 1960s, at the urging of some friends, Angelou decided to write her first book (*Caged Bird*). Because of her ability as a writer and because her life is so remarkably interesting, she has been able to use autobiography as a vehicle through which she weaves language into a colorful tapestry of personal stories. The last book of the series, *All God's Children Need Traveling Shoes,* describes her years in Egypt and Ghana. We can only wait for remaining volumes to give us her account of the events that have oc-curred since the time covered in that book. What we do know is that during that time, Angelou quickly came to be recognized as a distinguished author.

A brilliant woman—she speaks French, Spanish, Italian, Arabic, and Fanti—she is also a prolific writer. In addition to the five volumes of autobiography, she has published several collections of poetry, including *Just Give Me a Cool Drink of Water 'fore I Diiie* (1971), which was nominated for the Pulitzer Prize, and "On the Pulse of Morning," her inaugural collection. As is the case with her longer, autobiographical works, in her poetry Angelou looks at issues of great impor-tance to people. Survival, freedom, love, and rising to life's challenges are themes common throughout Angelou's work.

Fanti the language of a Black tribe na-tive to Ghana, Africa

Hope is apparent in Angelou's poem "I Know Why the Caged Bird Sings," which appears in her collection *Shaker, Why Don't You Sing?* (1983) and in the 1981 *Maya Angelou: Poems.* In this poem, Angelou gives her readers her own in-terpretation of why a caged bird sings. The following is a re-peated stanza from the poem:

> **The caged bird sings**
> **with a fearful trill**
> **of things unknown**
> **but longed for still**
> **and his tune is heard**
> **on the distant hill**
> **for the caged bird**
> **sings of freedom.**

This longing for freedom suggests a belief that as long as people dream of freedom there is hope of attaining their goal. Readers see this philosophy articulated in all of An-gelou's writing.

Life Today

I first visited Angelou at her large, inviting home (it has more than sixteen rooms) in Winston-Salem, North Carolina, in the spring of 1990. The circular drive leads visitors through a tree-lined path to the front door. As she opened it and invited my companions and me into her entrance foyer, I was immedi-ately fascinated by the collection of artwork there. From vi-

If you enjoy reading Maya Angelou, you might also enjoy reading the following books: *Malcolm X: By Any Means Necessary* and *Somewhere in the Darkness* by Walter Dean Myers; *Nelson Mandela: The Fight Against Apartheid* by Steven Otfinaski; *Roll of Thunder, Hear My Cry* by Mildred D. Taylor; *Rosa Parks: My Story* by Rosa Parks with Jim Haskins; *Sorrow's Kitchen: The Life and Folklore of Zora Neale Hurston* by Mary E. Lyons; and *Words by Heart* by Ouida Sebestyen.

brant paintings to sculpture to wood carvings and ornate pieces of furniture acquired on her frequent travels throughout the world, Angelou's home reflects a keen interest in art and its preservation, particularly that of African artists. Up a half-flight of steps, she leads visitors into her enormous living room, which is both warm and bright and is furnished with huge, comfortable sofas.

Although the living room is an important hub of activity in her home, the kitchen and dining room play an even more central role in entertaining guests in Angelou's home. A gourmet cook, Angelou has a large kitchen whose long row of counters holds bright bowls, bags of flour, and a wide variety of spices and oils. It is obvious at once that Angelou is at home in her kitchen, and she welcomes her guests to enjoy the expanse of space between the kitchen, dining room, and adjoining sun room, which frames a lovely view of her tree-covered yard. Being in Angelou's home reminded me of the importance of home. Hers clearly is a sanctuary for her, a place where she can go and find peace, tranquillity, and joy after a long morning of writing. This she does in a hotel room, which she rents to secure the solitude that she needs to work. These amenities were probably dreams during many years of Angelou's life, those years when she sang freely in her cage; but long ago she discovered a door from cages that imprisoned her. We, her readers, are fortunate that she was willing to fly from the cage and share her stories and life with us.

Selected Bibliography

WORKS BY MAYA ANGELOU

Autobiography

I Know Why the Caged Bird Sings (1970)

Gather Together in My Name (1974)

Singin' and Swingin' and Gettin' Merry Like Christmas (1976)

The Heart of a Woman (1981)

All God's Children Need Traveling Shoes (1986)

Poetry

Just Give Me a Cool Drink of Water 'fore I Diiie (1971)

Oh Pray My Wings Are Gonna Fit Me Well (1975)

And Still I Rise (1978)

Maya Angelou: Poems (1981)

Shaker, Why Don't You Sing? (1983)

Now Sheba Sings the Song (1987)

I Shall Not Be Moved (1990)

The Collected Poems (1993)

On the Pulse of Morning (1993)

Phenomenal Woman: Four Poems (1994)

Poems (1994)

Memoir

Wouldn't Take Nothing for My Journey Now (1993)

Works About Maya Angelou

Bertolino, James. "Maya Angelou Is Three Writers: *I Know Why the Caged Bird Sings.*" *Censored Books: Critical Viewpoints.* Edited by Nicholas J. Karolides, Lee Burress, and John M. Kean. Metuchen, N.J.: Scarecrow Press, 1993, pp. 299–305.

Draper, James P., ed. Black Literature Criticism. Detroit: Gale Research, 1992, vol. 1, pp. 25–39.

————*Contemporary Literary Criticism.* Detroit: Gale Research, 1993, vol. 77, pp. 1–38.

Garrett, Agnes, and Heiga P. McCue, eds. Authors and Artists for Young Adults. Detroit: Gale Research, 1991, vol. 7, pp. 1–12.

Elliot, Jeffrey M., ed. *Conversations with Maya Angelou.* Jackson, Miss.: University Press of Mississippi, 1989.

Hagen, Lyman B. Review of *I Know Why the Caged Bird Sings.* In *Beacham's Guide to Literature for Young Adults.* Edited by Kirk H. Beetz and Suzanne Niemeyer. Washington, D.C.: Beacham Publishing, 1990, pp. 615–621.

Kent, George E. "Maya Angelou's *I Know Why the Caged Bird Sings* and Black Autobiographical Tradition." *Kansas Quarterly,* summer 1985, pp. 77–78.

Molotsky, Irvin. "Poet of the South for the Inauguration." *New York Times,* 5 December 1992, p. L8.

Moore, Opal. "Learning to Live: When the Bird Breaks from the Cage." In *Censored Books: Critical Viewpoints.* Edited by Nicholas J. Karolides, Lee Burress, and John M. Kean. Metuchen, N.J.: Scarecrow Press, 1993, pp. 306–316.

Tate, Claudia, ed. "Maya Angelou." In *Black Women Writers at Work.* New York: Continuum, 1983, pp. 1–11.

How to Write to the Author
Maya Angelou
P.O. Box 7314
Winston-Salem, NC 27109

Sandy Asher

(1942-   )

by John H. Bushman

"My life as a writer began in the second grade," says writer Sandy Asher. "I was fortunate," she continues. "I had good experiences most of the time throughout my years at James G. Blaine Elementary School in Philadelphia."

Early Years

The fictional role model was Jo March in Louisa May Alcott's *Little Women*. This book made a profound impact on Asher. Jo wanted to be special, and so did Asher. Jo was a writer, enjoyed every minute of it, and saw writing as a path to success. Because of Jo's example, Asher realized that she, too, could write and get paid for it—which was just what she wanted. Asher's life parallels Jo's in another way. Jo married a professor who read her writing and made constructive criticisms. Asher also married a professor who reads and makes positive, constructive criticisms of her work.

Quotations from Sandy Asher that are not attributed to a published source are from an interview conducted by the author of this article on Friday, 27 January 1995, and are published here by permission of Sandy Asher.

53

The real-life role model was Asher's second-grade teacher, Mrs. Lomozoff, who inspired Asher's writing and dramatic talents. As Asher wrote her short plays in second grade and acted them out with her classmates, Mrs. Lomozoff cheered her on. This kind of encouragement continued throughout elementary school. Asher says, "If something—a play, a folk tale—needed to be written or rewritten, teachers turned to me to get the job done. I became the school writer." Writers frequently create characters based on people who have had an effect on their lives, and Asher is no exception. "There's a little of Mrs. Lomozoff in many of my books," she says, "but she's most obvious as the flamboyant Mrs. Deveraux in *Just Like Jenny*" (1982).

School experiences strongly affected Asher, as a writer and as a person. Some experiences were positive, but others were not. Her third-grade teacher, strict and authoritarian, taught writing by drilling students in penmanship. "I don't remember being very creative in that class," Asher recalls.

The principal of the school, Mr. Meyers, had a more positive influence. His kindness and respect for individuals were the order of each day. Asher says that when he was transferred to another school, Blaine Elementary was never the same. Principal Meyers inspired the creation of Mr. Crane, the strict but lovable third-grade teacher in Asher's Ballet One series. She remembers that the replacement for Meyers did not have the same qualities. In fact, readers will find this new principal in the character of Dr. Kyle in *Summer Begins* (1980), which was reprinted as *Summer Smith Begins* in 1986.

Fifth grade brought Asher a new experience, the effect of which she did not realize until years later. The fifth-grade teacher got along with his students—perhaps too well—for he was soon gone without explanation. We meet a similar character in the form of Mr. Carraway, the well-liked drama teacher who makes sexual advances to some of his students in *Things Are Seldom What They Seem* (1983). Asher believes that she and her fifth-grade classmates should have been told more about the circumstances under which the teacher left. She and her classmates felt a sense of loss and betrayal. *Things Are Seldom What They Seem* is an attempt to help young people who may be faced with similar experiences. This book presents a good example of the compassion evident in much of Asher's writing. She portrays Mr. Carraway not as an evil monster, but as a complex human being in need of special help.

After her high school graduation, Asher attended the University of Pennsylvania and then Indiana University. She felt right at home in the University Theater at Indiana University, where she studied writing, acting, and dance. She was becoming an actress, working in theater productions on campus and on *The Majestic,* a traveling showboat that moved about the Ohio and Mississippi Rivers. All of these experiences fine-tuned the soon-to-be novelist and playwright.

Coming of Age as a Writer

When asked about her first serious writing, Asher jokingly recalls her second-grade play writing for Mrs. Lomozoff, for she does believe it all started there. It was during the 1960s and 1970s, however—when she wrote many short stories, poems, articles, and plays—that she began to be published in a more serious way. Two of her poems for adults won awards in 1970 and 1975 from *Envoi* and *Bitterroot* magazines. Her play *Afterthoughts in Eden* won honorable mention in a 1974 contest sponsored by the Unitarian Universalist Religious Arts Guild. During that period she also wrote a book of facts and fables called *The Great American Peanut Book* (1977), which coincided with the early years of Jimmy Carter's presidency. This book had more of an impact on Asher's life than you might imagine. She explains, "Completing this book, even though it was short, convinced me that I could write a book-length work—that I could fill pages with words." As the 1980s approached, Asher began her journey of filling pages with words. She turned to writing novels for young adults.

Novels for Young Adults

Summer Begins (1980) established Asher as an author for young adults. In this novel, Asher introduces a theme found in many of her works: establishing identity, specifically adolescents separating themselves from their parents to develop their own identities. Thirteen-year-old Summer Smith's father is a well-known literary critic, and her mother is a celebrated former Olympic swimmer. Summer feels that she cannot com-

> *In [Summer Begins], Asher introduces a theme found in many of her works: establishing identity, specifically adolescents separating themselves from their parents to develop their own identities.*

pete with her parents' accomplishments, and so she stays in the background. Starting with a character who voices no opinions and takes no stands, Asher draws on a conflict as a vehicle for developing Summer's identity.

After reading an editorial in a local newspaper, written by a student complaining about the food in a school cafeteria, Asher was impressed that the student writer could make such an impact on the school and the community. Inspired by this concept, but making the story her own, Asher has Summer write an editorial for the eighth-grade newspaper on what Summer believes to be an innocuous subject: consideration for non-Christians in the school Christmas program. What Summer thought would be a safe topic is anything but safe. It causes an uproar in her family, school, and community. Readers see the change, as crafted superbly by Asher, not only in Summer's actions but also in her style, syntax, and vocabulary. Early in the novel, Summer is tentative and hesitant. As the novel progresses, she sees herself in a different way, and her writing reflects this new Summer Smith. Her language becomes more emphatic, with a dramatic shift in tone, syntax, and word choice.

Asher's second novel, *Daughters of the Law* (1980), set in the 1970s, centers around two seventh graders, Denise Riley and Ruthie Morgenthau. As in the previous novel, Asher builds on the theme of identity and mother/daughter relationships. She also introduces the theme of friendship among girls. Denise tries her mother's patience, but Ruthie bears her mother's burden and protects her because her mother is a concentration camp survivor. The novel brings these two girls together through a variety of experiences, all of which help them better understand themselves and their worlds. Readers may see themselves in the characters of Denise and Ruthie.

Most importantly, this novel carries the theme of nurturing relationships that was introduced in Asher's first novel and is evident throughout her works. These strong relationships endure great hardships. Asher has found that literature for young adults often portrays the male buddy system, but it rarely shows a similar bonding between female characters. She continues, "This female relationship is so very important. In life, many women turn to their female friends when faced with uncertainty and trouble."

In *In Just Like Jenny,* Asher continues her relationship theme with Stephanie Nordland, a thirteen year old who wants to be a dancer, and Jenny Gianino, her good friend.

style a distinctive manner of expression

syntax the structure of a sentence; refers to word placement, as opposed to "diction," which refers to word choice

> *Asher has found that literature for young adults often portrays the male buddy system, but it rarely shows a similar bonding between female characters.*

Jenny seems to have everything going for her, and Stephanie would give anything to be just like Jenny. Although much of the novel centers on dancing, dancing is not of primary significance to the story. More important is the theme that Stephanie must move beyond how she sees Jennie to arrive at an understanding of how she sees herself and to come to terms with that self-image. An interesting subtheme is the motivation brought about by commitments to goals that are worthy although difficult to achieve.

Asher says that even though the novel seems to be concerned with dancing, it is really about her own writing career. "I am one of the luckiest people in the world," she says, "because I get to do something I love doing every single day of my life, and very few people have that privilege." We find many of the characters in this novel sharing their love for what they do: Mr. Oldham the dance instructor; Mrs. Deveraux the music teacher; and even Mrs. Nordland, Stephanie's mother, who strongly supports her daughter's decisions.

Things Are Seldom What They Seem, Asher's fourth book, addresses the theme that first confronted the author when she was in the fifth grade. This theme of child molestation, however, is not as important in the book as the interaction among those young people who are affected by Mr. Carraway, the drama coach. Asher introduces this sensitive topic by asking questions: What happens among friends when some of them are victimized by such abhorrent behavior? How should one react? How does one behave toward the offender and toward his victims? The struggle that Debbie undergoes when she learns that Maggie and Karen have been molested by the charismatic Carraway deeply affects her, as well as her relationship with her boyfriend, Murray. Of course, it also has a profound effect on Debbie's relationship with Maggie and Karen. Debbie must protect them while encouraging them to report Mr. Carraway to the proper authorities. The deceptions and the misperceptions are destructive. But the young people's struggles and achievements make for a complex and remarkable book.

Missing Pieces (1984), like many of Asher's other novels, focuses on the need for communication between adolescents and parents. The breaking down of barriers to communication that, perhaps unconsciously, parents and children erect is the central element of this novel. Heather, a sophomore in high school, loses her father and becomes distant from her mother while her uncle lies senile in a nursing home. Nicky,

> *Asher on writing: "I am one of the luckiest people in the world, because I get to do something I love doing every single day of my life, and very few people have that privilege."*

Heather's boyfriend, also experiences the loss of a parent. Cara Dale, Heather's best friend, has been fatherless since her parents' divorce. These three young people work to fill the void in each other's lives. The success that they ultimately achieve comes from the overwhelming support that they give each other.

The setting for *Everything Is Not Enough* (1987) is the imaginary Braden's Port on the New Jersey shore, a place known to Sandy Asher because she went to a similar place often as a child. This was the annual family vacation spot in which she, along with her brother, mother, and father, spent weeks at the ocean. This novel makes other family connections as well. During Asher's junior year in high school, she became more and more involved in theater, much to the disapproval of her rather Victorian parents. "The theater is not the life for a young girl!" Asher's parents would say. Girls could dabble in the arts, but only marriage and motherhood were regarded as the proper order in that family.

Readers find a similar situation in *Everything Is Not Enough*. Michael is the main character. His parents have his life all mapped out: winters in the suburbs, summers at the beach, then college and a career in his father's business. But one summer things seem to change. Michael meets Linda and Traci and finds himself drawn into their world, the very world of misguided youth from which his parents are trying to protect him. If he does what his parents want, he will have "everything," but for Michael, this "everything" is not enough. He is not sure just what he wants, but whatever it is, only he can determine what his future will be.

Out of Here: A Senior Class Yearbook (1993) is a collection of fascinating stories depicting the well-known nine-month snapshot known as "senior year." For one school year, readers follow the lives of Stacy Lawrence, Walt Hightower, Nicole Drake, Lee Whitaker, Jamie Bingham, and other students at Oakview High School. In one story, we are introduced to Stacy, who begins her senior year on cloud nine after spending the summer working in a drama program in the Berkshires, until she finds that none of her friends seems to feel the same excitement. In another story, we empathize with Walt, the straight-A student who has problems fitting in socially. Asher captures the essence of these two young adults and all the others, presenting them with depth as well as wit and humor. Asher comments on her writing: "Charac-

Victorian a stuffy manner that some say characterized the time of Queen Victoria of England (1837–1901)

ters and the relationship between and among them have always intrigued me as a writer. Plot is there and so is the place, but the characters—their personalities—have driven me as a writer. Perhaps this is related to my theater background. Characters are so important in drama."

The book presents excellent examples of Asher's talents, both in the story's content and in the author's craft. The stories contrast the "haves" and "have-nots" as defined by the social and value systems of high school; they also show how members of each group survive. Asher contrasts students who are accepted into popular social groups with students who don't fit in. The author's craft is evident in the way that each chapter is a short story in itself, while the book as a whole reads as if it were a novel.

The stories [in Out of Here: A Senior Class Yearbook] contrast the "haves" and "have-nots" as defined by the social and value systems of high school.

The Writing Process

In addition to these novels for young adults, Asher has written many works for children, three works of nonfiction, and many plays for children and young adults. She writes from her home in a small room "just off the kitchen." She explains her creative process:

> I write best when I write slowly, about five pages a day at first—plus a lot of thinking about the story while I'm walking the dog, doing the dishes, and so on. Each day I scribble corrections over the last five pages and type the next five, working back and forth until I complete a full draft. Rewriting tends to go faster. Once I've got something down on the page, I can play with it until I get it right.

At Present

Asher lives with her husband, Harvey, in Springfield, Missouri. They have two grown children. Harvey teaches at Drury College, where Asher is writer-in-residence. Her major responsibility in this capacity is to direct the annual Writing for Children Workshop, which she began in 1985. In addition to this project, Asher continues writing, teaching, visiting schools, and speaking at conferences.

Readers who enjoy Sandy Asher's works might also enjoy works by Louisa May Alcott. Other similar writers are Vicki Grove, Jan Greenberg, and Lois Ruby.

Selected Bibliography

WORKS BY SANDY ASHER

Fiction for Children

> *Teddy Teabury's Fabulous Fact,* illustrated by Bob Jones (1985)
>
> *Princess Bee and the Royal Good-Night Story,* illustrated by Cat Bowman Smith (1989)
>
> *Teddy Teabury's Peanutty Problems* (1989)

Ballet One Series

> *Best Friends Get Better* (1989)
>
> *Mary-in-the-Middle* (1990)
>
> *Pat's Promise* (1990)
>
> *Can David Do It?* (1991)

Fiction for Young Adults

> *Daughters of the Law* (1980), published in England as *Friends and Sisters* (1982)
>
> *Summer Begins* (1980), reprinted as *Summer Smith Begins* (1986)
>
> *Just Like Jenny* (1982)
>
> *Things Are Seldom What They Seem* (1983)
>
> *Missing Pieces* (1984)
>
> *Everything Is Not Enough* (1987)
>
> *Out of Here: A Senior Class Yearbook* (1993)

Nonfiction

> *The Great American Peanut Book,* published under the name Sandra Fenichel Asher and illustrated by Jo Anne Metsch Bonnell (1977)
>
> *Where Do You Get Your Ideas?,* illustrated by Susan Hellard (1989)
>
> *Wild Words & How To Tame Them,* illustrated by Dennis Kendrick (1989)

Published Plays (Under the Name Sandra Fenichel Asher)

> *Dover's Domain,* one act (1980)
>
> *The Insulting Princess,* one act (1988)
>
> *The Mermaid's Tale,* one act (1988)
>
> *A Song of Sixpence,* one act (1988)
>
> *Little Old Ladies in Tennis Shoes,* two act (1989)

A Woman Called Truth, one act (1989)
The Wise Men of Chelm, one act (1992)
Dancing With Strangers, three short plays (1994)
Sunday, Sunday, one act (1994)

WORKS ABOUT SANDY ASHER

Baughman, Judith S. *The Dictionary of Literary Biography Yearbook*. Detroit: Gale Research, 1983.

Gallo, Donald R., ed. *Speaking for Ourselves*. Urbana, Ill.: National Council of Teachers of English, 1990, pp. 10–12.

Nakamura, Joyce, ed. *Something About the Author Autobiography Series*. Detroit: Gale Research, 1991, vol. 13, pp. 1–16.

How to write to the Author
Sandy Asher
721 South Weller
Springfield, MO 65802

(1937-   )

by Nancy Lund

Avi grew up in a rich literary environment: two of his great-grandfathers were writers, his grandmother was a playwright, and his aunt was a journalist. Both of his parents wanted to be novelists, but his father, Joseph Wortis, became a psychiatrist, and his mother, Helen, became a social worker. Avi recalls:

> With a house full of books, being read to every night, a nearby library, the idea that writing was a splendid thing to do could hardly fail to make its mark on me. (*Something About the Author,* vol. 14, p. 270)

Biography

Born on 23 December 1937 in New York City, Avi was raised in Brooklyn. His twin sister, Emily Wortis Leider, is a poet; one of his older brothers, Henry, is an immunologist. It was his sister who gave him the nickname Avi when they were young; now it is the only one he uses. As a child, Avi was somewhat shy, not interested in sports, and not a good student. He was especially poor in spelling and writing. His parents sent him to a different school and provided him with a tutor, whose help enabled Avi to become a writer. (Years later Avi discovered that he had dysgraphia, a writing impairment.) Reading, however, was not a problem: Avi read all sorts of books all the time. He hated Friday because it was spelling-test day; yet he loved Friday because it was library day.

Avi attended the University of Wisconsin at Madison, receiving a bachelor's degree in history in 1959 and a master's degree in drama in 1962. He earned another master's, in library science, from Columbia in 1964. From 1962 to 1970 he was a librarian at the New York Public Library and from 1970 to 1986 a librarian at Trenton State College. Since 1986, he has been a full-time writer.

Avi is married to Coppelia Kahn, a professor of English at Brown University. One of his sons, Shaun Wortis, is a rock musician, while his other son, Kevin Wortis, manages rock bands. Both have written rock lyrics. Avi's stepson, Gabriel Kahn, is a journalist.

Avi believes that reading is the key to writing. Before writing a book, he forms an outline of events that will occur in it. He thinks a lot about these events, and those thoughts eventually become concepts for his book chapters. He rewrites extensively, believing that just changing a word or two can sometimes be an improvement. Avi has written a variety of stories: historical fiction, adventures, mysteries, fantasies, tales of horror, psychological thrillers, realistic novels, and humor pieces. His favorite book is always the next one.

> *Avi's favorite book is always the next one.*

Characters and Plots

I do believe that young people are special, as fascinating, as complex and compelling as any other person, no matter what age. (*Fifth Book of Junior Authors and Illustrators,* p. 16)

Avi's main characters are young people in a complex, often dangerous and violent, adult world of unsavory characters: smugglers, pirates, ruthless sea captains, treasure hunters, slave merchants, evil kings, enemy soldiers, murderers, and ghosts. The main characters are mostly in conflict with adults, not with other teens. And the conflict is usually with the father, or with school officials who are authority figures.

In *Wolf Rider* (1986), Andy receives a phone call from a man named Zeke, who claims to have killed someone. Andy takes this call seriously, although no one else does. Andy's conflict with his father intensifies as Andy pursues the truth about Zeke. The father-son relationship deteriorates: Andy tells the truth, but his father thinks he is in a "world of fantasy." In the end Andy is sent away for a rest.

In *Nothing But the Truth* (1991), the conflict is between Philip Malloy and his English teacher, Miss Narwin, who is also his homeroom teacher. Because he has made a D in her class, Philip is not allowed to try out for the track team, and he blames Miss Narwin for his missed opportunity. During the playing of the national anthem in homeroom, when everyone must be silently attentive, Philip rebelliously hums. For this he is suspended from school. Unlike Andy in *Wolf Rider*, Philip does not tell the whole truth, and in a way, he is rewarded. He wins the support of his father and mother—as well as the media, who pick up his story and embellish it. Soon Philip is a national hero, the boy who was not allowed to sing the national anthem, and he causes Miss Narwin to lose her job over the incident. But instead of taking pleasure in his revenge, Philip becomes saddened and alienated. Like Andy, he finally leaves the place of conflict to attend another school.

Avi's teen characters are generally sensitive, caring, determined, and independent. They think through difficult situations, become good detectives when necessary, and (except for Philip Malloy) communicate well with adults (ironically, the ones with whom they are in conflict). They are likable kids who face adversity with courage and survive in the adult world.

Avi's adolescent characters include several strong females: Charlotte (*The True Confessions of Charlotte Doyle,* 1990), Maggie (*Blue Heron,* 1992), Morwenna (*Bright Shadow,* 1985), Asterel (*City of Light, City of Dark: A Comic Book Novel,* 1993), Cathleen (*Captain Grey,* 1977), and Judy (*Punch with Judy,* 1993).

Charlotte Doyle is the only passenger, and the only female, aboard the *Seahawk,* a ship owned by her father's firm. A "proper lady" of social standing, she befriends the skipper,

> *Avi's main characters are young people in a complex, often dangerous and violent, adult world of unsavory characters: smugglers, pirates, ruthless sea captains, treasure hunters, slave merchants, evil kings, enemy soldiers, murderers, and ghosts.*

Captain Jaggery, and initially acts as his informer. But when Charlotte realizes his true nature, she joins the mutinous crew, passing a rigorous and dangerous test to do so. In the course of events, she is framed by Jaggery for the murder of the first mate. She stands up to the captain, whips him, and is defending herself against him when he accidentally falls overboard. With Jaggery gone, Charlotte becomes the captain, although in name only. Once she is safe at home, she makes a powerful decision: to leave home and join the crew of the *Seahawk.*

In *Blue Heron,* Maggie visits her father, his second wife, Joanna, and their new baby. What should be a pleasant month turns into an unpleasant series of revelations. Her father is moody and verbally abusive, and he refuses to take medicine for his serious health problem. Maggie copes well, even to the point of becoming the adult in the situation. It is she who comforts Joanna and confronts her father about not taking the medicine. Through the shouting and crying and general tension, Maggie finds solace in observing a blue heron. But even this causes Maggie anxiety because someone is trying to kill the bird. In the end she comes to a mature understanding when she tells the heron, "The people I love—sometimes—I don't like them" (*Blue Heron,* p. 164).

> *In the end [Maggie] comes to a mature understanding when she tells the heron, "The people I love—sometimes—I don't like them."*

Both Morwenna (*Bright Shadow*) and Asterel (*City of Light, City of Dark*) wield tremendous power. Morwenna, a lowly servant in a king's palace, is given the world's last five wishes. She is told not to waste them or use them on herself, and she uses four of them to save her friend Swen from a cruel king. Asterel is chosen by the people to keep her city from freezing. To do this, she is given special powers, including special sight and the mastery of disguises. Both Morwenna and Asterel have awesome responsibilities. Each has to make personal sacrifices for the good of others.

In *Captain Grey,* Cathleen, her younger brother Kevin, and their father set out to find peace in the New Jersey wilderness. Realizing that their father is insane, Cathleen takes charge; they survive in the wilderness because of her skills, only to be captured by land pirates. It is Cathleen who escapes and eventually rescues Kevin from a life of piracy with Captain Grey.

In *Punch with Judy,* Judy's father owns a traveling medicine show. When he dies, her mother goes mad, and Judy is left to maintain the family. She must make a number of adult decisions that include keeping the orphaned boy Punch with the show, although others think he should be let go. This decision proves to be wise because it is Punch's performances that save the show from financial ruin.

These female characters face their situations with maturity, courage, and inner strength. They may be scared; they may even cry. It would be so easy for them to crumble, but they do not.

Themes

> Fiction in children's literature is about unfairness, inconsistency, and lack of justice in the adult world. The constant struggle to adjust good with bad. ("The Child in Children's Literature," *Horn Book,* January/February 1993, p. 48)

A number of prevailing themes recur in Avi's stories: good versus evil, struggles against society, questions of freedom and truth, and the pervasiveness of death and alienation. The theme of good versus evil is most evident in his stories. The young represent what is good and innocent in the world; evil is represented by corruptible adults and wrongful situations (although well-meaning and positive adults do appear in Avi's works).

In *The Man Who Was Poe* (1989), Edmund's mother, aunt, and sister all disappear. Left alone, Edmund searches for them in a desolate and disordered world dominated by violent and greedy adults. Even the man named Poe, who helps Edmund, wavers between kindness and heartlessness.

One of Avi's most humorous stories is *S.O.R. Losers* (1984). In this book, a group of seventh-grade boys who excel in the arts and academics find that they are not interested in sports; yet school policy states that students must participate in at least one sport, so they are forced into soccer. Losing does not bother them. But society has placed such enormous importance on sports and winning that to lose and be complacent about it is unacceptable. Parents, school officials, and other students accuse the boys of having an attitude problem. The boys stick with their contention that "people have a right to be losers."

In S.O.R. Losers, the boys stick with their contention that "people have a right to be losers."

slave trade Beginning in the 1500s, Africans were bought and sold throughout Europe and the Americas. Great Britain and the United States abolished slave trade in the early 1800s although many Americans continued to hold slaves until the Civil War ended in 1865.

The bid for freedom appears in *Blue Heron*. Tucker admits that he is trying to kill the heron: "I can kill anything I want to . . . it's a free country" (pp. 103–104). In *The True Confessions of Charlotte Doyle,* Charlotte finds freedom from a structured family and society when she runs away from home and rejoins the crew on the *Seahawk.* Jonathan, in *The Fighting Ground* (1984), wants very much to fight for freedom in the Revolutionary War; he sees this as a glorious thing to do. Frankie Wattleson in *Who Was That Masked Man, Anyway?* (1992) is always imagining himself fighting for right and keeping the world free. In *Something Upstairs* (1988) Kenny witnesses the controversy over the slave trade when he travels backward through time into the past.

In *Nothing But the Truth,* freedom and truth are dominant themes. The homeroom incident involving Philip and Miss Narwin, his teacher, is blown out of proportion, and people tell "the truth" as they see it for personal gain. Philip's breaking a school rule sets off a rally for freedom and patriotism.

Avi's young characters face death in various circumstances. Some prevent it (Maggie in *Blue Heron*); some cause it (Morwenna in *Bright Shadow*); some are accused of it (Charlotte in *The True Confessions of Charlotte Doyle*); some witness it (Jonathan in *The Fighting Ground*). In ancient times or in the present, Avi shows us that death is a fact of life, that it is sometimes violent, that it strikes the young as well as the old, that it is not always easy to accept, but that life does go on. Given the dire situations in which Avi's young characters become acquainted with death, it is remarkable that they handle it so well.

Techniques

You know that there are a lot of ways to tell a story. (*Something About the Author,* vol. 71, p. 12)

Avi is a master storyteller who uses a variety of techniques. Some are evident; others are quite subtle. Avi understands his reading audience and knows that lengthy introductory material can turn away readers. He often entices them into the story by using a provocative opening scene. Before part one begins in *The True Confessions of Charlotte Doyle,* the reader is given a bold "Important Warning: If strong ideas and actions offend you, read no more." *Something Upstairs* contains Avi's explanation that he got this story from Kenny, a boy he met on one of his school visits. *The Man Who Was Poe* begins with a prologue and ends with the same piece of writing. Other narrative hooks include a riddle (*Bright Shadow*), a treasure map and a legend (*Windcatcher,* 1991), a memo with instructions for morning announcements at school (*Nothing But the Truth*), and a letter to Lord Bowden (*Encounter at Easton,* 1980).

Avi uses other techniques that provide variety to his writing. *Nothing But the Truth* is told entirely through memos, letters, telephone calls, conversations, diary entries, and newspaper reports. It has no narrator. *Who Was That Masked Man, Anyway?* is told entirely in dialogue (without a "he said" or a "she said") and is divided into episodes, both of which reflect the radio serials that dominate the story. Included are actual radio scripts of programs such as *The Lone Ranger. City of Light, City of Dark* is told in comic-book form. Charlotte Doyle's story is from the journal she kept. *Encounter at Easton* is told through testimonies. In *A Place Called Ugly* (1981), Avi uses flashbacks to recall Owen's memorable summers. *The Man Who Was Poe* is written in the atmosphere of a story by Edgar Allan Poe.

There is an article about Edgar Allan Poe in volume 3.

Other interesting devices that Avi uses include the malapropisms in *Romeo and Juliet—Together (and Alive!) at Last* (1987), the symbols before each chapter in *Bright Shadow* to indicate the number of wishes Morwenna has left, and the use of his own surname, written backwards, in *S.O.R. Losers.*

Avi's stories are packed with irony, foreshadowing, metaphor, simile, and symbolism. He sees a world full of irony. In *Nothing But the Truth* Philip, who created a furor because he wanted to be on the track team, transfers to a school that has no track team. When asked to sing the national anthem, this boy glorified in the press for not being "allowed" to sing it finally admits that he does not know the words. In *Wolf Rider,* the only person who believes Andy is Lucas, and Lucas is the one person to whom Andy has lied. In *The True Confessions of Charlotte Doyle,* Charlotte joins the mutinous crew to be free of the rigid captain's control, only to find that her father is similarly tyrannical. In *Shadrach's Crossing* (1983), Shad wants to get rid of

irony a situation in which the actual outcome is opposite or contrary to what was expected

foreshadowing the use of clues that suggest events yet to come

symbolic representative of an abstract concept

style a distinctive manner of expression

smugglers, yet it is the smugglers who support the islanders' economy.

Foreshadowing is used to make some of the story lines plausible. For example, in *Devil's Race* (1984), John Proud confronts the ghost of an ancestor with his name. In the end, we find that John's struggle is between the good and the bad forces within himself. Avi gives clues from the very beginning that this is what the struggle is about:

> **And sitting atop the stone was a boy, a teenager, fairly tall, somewhat on the thin side. He looked like anybody and nobody, a perfectly normal-looking kid. But he was oddly familiar, like someone I had met once, yet could not quite recall. (P. 44)**

Avi also uses foreshadowing effectively in *Blue Heron*. When Maggie first sees the heron, she wonders why it makes her sad. In addition, the heron becomes symbolic of the beauty of life and its fragility. The storm in *The True Confessions of Charlotte Doyle* symbolizes Charlotte's change from living a prim and proper, calm life to one radically different. And the summer cottage in *A Place Called Ugly* is symbolic of stability, home, and good memories. On a deeper level the cottage represents Owen's childhood, and when he destroys that, he has accepted adolescence.

Avi's style of description is not lengthy, but it is beautiful:

> **The old city lay dark and cold. A raw wind whipped the street lamps and made the gas flames hiss and flicker like snake tongues. Fingers of shadow leaped over sidewalks, clawing silently upon closely set wooden houses. Stray leaves, brittle and brown, rattled like dry bones along the cold stone gutters. (*The Man Who Was Poe*, p. 15)**

> **It had gotten darker, but I could make out the beach line and hear the lapping of the waves. Out to the west there was a crimson line, the last edge of day, like the crack in a doorway just before it's closed. I asked myself if I was inside or out. Even as I watched, the last edge snapped up tight and dark. (*A Place Called Ugly*, pp. 31–32)**

The endings to Avi's stories are not always neatly wrapped packages, and character motivation is not always explored, but these are not negative qualities. They make characters more complex and force the reader to probe, to put together the pieces, to make sense of Avi's clues. This is typical of good literature, and Avi's books fit that description.

Avi's works have received numerous awards and honors. Among these are the Newbery Honor Award for *The True Confessions of Charlotte Doyle* in 1991 and the Newbery Honor Award for *Nothing But the Truth* in 1992. *The Fighting Ground* received the O'Dell Award in 1984 for Best Historical Fiction.

Selected Bibliography

WORKS BY AVI

Fiction

Things That Sometimes Happen (1970)
Snail Tale: The Adventures of a Rather Small Snail (1972)
No More Magic (1975)
Captain Grey (1977)
Emily Upham's Revenge (1978)
Night Journeys (1979)
Encounter at Easton (1980)
The History of Helpless Harry (1980)
Man from the Sky (1980)
A Place Called Ugly (1981)
Who Stole the Wizard of Oz? (1981)
Sometimes I Think I Hear My Name (1982)
Shadrach's Crossing (1983)
Devil's Race (1984)
The Fighting Ground (1984)
S.O.R. Losers (1984)
Bright Shadow (1985)
Wolf Rider (1986)
Romeo and Juliet—Together (and Alive!) at Last (1987)
Something Upstairs (1988)
The Man Who Was Poe (1989)

If you like Avi's books, you might also like the books of Gary Paulsen, Katherine Paterson, William Sleator, and Cynthia Voigt.

The True Confessions of Charlotte Doyle (1990)

Nothing But the Truth (1991)

Windcatcher (1991)

Blue Heron (1992)

Who Was That Masked Man, Anyway? (1992)

Punch with Judy (1993)

City of Light, City of Dark: A Comic Book Novel (1993)

The Barn (1994)

The Bird, the Frog, and the Light (1994)

Nonfiction

"Review the Reviewers." In *School Library Journal,* March 1986, pp. 114–115.

"The True Confesions of Charlotte Doyle." In *Horn Book,* January 1992, pp. 24–27.

"The Child in Children's Literature." In *Horn Book,* January/February 1993, pp. 40–50.

"Young People, Books, and the Right to Read." In *Journal of Youth Services in Libraries,* spring 1993, pp. 245–256.

"I Can Read, I Can Read!" In *Horn Book,* March/April 1994, pp. 166–169.

WORKS ABOUT AVI

Abrahamson, Richard F. "Of Versatility and Storytelling Ability: An Interview with Avi." In *Reading Journal,* May 1987, vol. 30, pp. 738–742.

Commire, Anne, ed. *Something About the Author.* Detroit: Gale Research, 1978, vol. 14, pp. 269–270.

Holtze, Sally Holmes, ed. *Fifth Book of Junior Authors and Illustrators.* New York: H. W. Wilson, 1983.

Metzger, Linda, ed. *Contemporary Authors New Revision Series.* Detroit: Gale Research, 1984, vol. 12, pp. 517–518.

Senick, Gerard, ed. *Children's Literature Review.* Detroit: Gale Research, 1991, vol. 24, pp. 1–15.

Telgen, Diane, ed. *Something About the Author.* Detroit: Gale Research, 1993, vol. 71, pp. 7–15.

How to write to the Author
Avi
15 Sheldon Street
Providence, RI 02906

Joan Bauer

(1951-   )

by Jean E. Brown

Humor weaves the threads in the fabric of Joan Bauer's life as well as her books. She recognizes and uses humor as a way of looking at the world, a way of going beyond the difficult times, a response to painful as well as happy events in life. She recognizes that humor is also serious business that should teach profound lessons. This belief is demonstrated in her three novels. Bauer's first novel, *Squashed,* was published in 1992. It won the Delacorte Press Prize for a First Young Adult Novel, and was chosen as a *School Library Journal* Best Book of the Year, and an American Library Association (ALA) Recommended Book for the Reluctant YA Reader. It was also a selection of the Junior Library Guild and one of the New York Public Library's Books for Teenagers. Her second novel, *Thwonk,* published in 1995, made the list of the New York Public Library's Books for Teenagers and received a Kirkus starred review, thus recommending the book. Her third novel, *Sticks* (1996), is written for upper-elementary-age students.

Quotations from Joan Bauer that are not attributed to a published source are from personal correspondence and personal interviews conducted by the author of this article on November 1993 and August 1995 and appear here by permission of Joan Bauer.

Describing humor as the greatest anchor in her life, Bauer explains: "Writing, reading, and humor have always been touchstones for me. Stories and humor swirled around our house when I was growing up. My mother was an English and a film studies teacher with a great comic sense. My grandmother was a well-known storyteller. As a child, I loved to write: songs, stories, essays, letters, funny poems, and greeting cards. I was greatly influenced by the comedians of the '50s and '60s: Lucille Ball, Bob Newhart, Shelley Berman, Ernie Kovacs, Dick Van Dyke, and Bill Cosby. I was a Robert Benchley fan as a kid, but the writer who defined humorous writing at the time for me was Max Shulman (*The Many Loves of Dobie Gillis* and *Rally 'Round the Flag, Boys!*). I pored over his crisp, funny dialogue. I wanted to be a comedian or a comedy writer when I grew up. I wanted to make people laugh" (Brown and Stephens, *Teaching Young Adult Literature*, p. 238).

Max Shulman (1919–1988) was a comedy writer. **Robert Benchley** (1889–1945) was an actor and writer of humorous essays.

Becoming a Writer

Bauer was born on 12 July 1951. Before becoming a successful author, she spent ten years in marketing, promotional ventures, and advertising for the *Chicago Tribune, Parade Magazine,* and McGraw-Hill. Her career at the *Tribune* was launched when she won second prize in its Fruit and Vegetable Poetry Contest. The advertising manager identified with her poetic inspiration—a dislike of lima beans—and hired her on the spot. Even while she worked in sales, writing was a key to her success. She gained a reputation for humorous sales letters that yielded significant orders and secured major accounts. While she had a very successful and lucrative career in this field, she realized that she was not enjoying its pace and pressure. Like Gordon Mott, the publisher of the *Rock River Clarion* in *Squashed,* she had enough ulcers when she left the business world. In 1981, Bauer decided to write full-time. She credits her husband, Evan, who always recognized the writer in her, for encouraging her to pursue her lifelong dream.

In her first year as a freelance journalist, Bauer became a mother when her daughter Jean was born. A joyful addition to the Bauer family, the baby inspired Bauer to write articles

lucrative   profitable

freelance journalist journalist who does not work for an individual publication but who sells his or her writing to various publications about child-rearing and parenting for magazines. In 1987, Bauer wrote *Take It to the Streets,* a nonfiction book for adults on urban community outreach.

Building on her five years of success as a freelance writer, Bauer embarked on a new facet of her writing career in 1987 when she began writing teleplays and scripts for feature films. She had just signed a contract to write two screenplays when she was injured in a serious automobile accident, which ultimately redirected her career. She explains: "Initially, *Squashed* was going to be a screenplay. I could see the visuals of the story. Unfortunately, my screenwriting career was cut short by a crippling auto accident that made all writing for a while most difficult. When I could write again, I decided to try *Squashed* as a book" (*Teaching Young Adult Literature,* p. 238). As she was recovering from her neck injuries and neurosurgery, her writing career once again took a new direction. Because her pain was so acute that she could not sit at her computer for more than forty minutes at a time, Bauer realized that she could write only on her own schedule and not be faced with deadlines. She became a novelist as she brought to life Ellie Morgan, the dedicated and determined young woman in *Squashed,* whose dream is to grow the winning giant pumpkin at the Rock River Iowa Pumpkin Weigh-in. Humor and laughter sustained Bauer as she completed *Squashed* under such difficult and painful circumstances. Bauer believes that there is a gift that she receives in writing each of her books that more than compensates for the difficulties.

> *Humor and laughter sustained Bauer as she competed Squashed under such difficult and painful circumstances. Bauer believes that there is a gift that she receives in writing each of her books that more than compensates for the difficulties.*

Character-Driven Books

Squashed, Thwonk, and *Sticks* demonstrate the influence of Bauer's experiences writing for film as she brings the sharp visual focus of a filmmaker to the printed page. The stories are propelled by strong, interesting characters who are a bit quirky but not odd. Her books share certain features: she always creates characters with great vitality and energy; she creates vivid scenes that are easy for the reader to visualize, but she does not encumber the story with descriptive passages; she develops fast-paced stories through the crisp and witty dialogue and interaction of her characters. Bauer describes her books as primarily character-driven, meaning that character development and the interaction among characters provide the direction in them.

Bauer explains the importance of character development and relationships among characters: "The first thing that has to happen in writing fiction, not just humor, is that you have to have honest characters interacting with one another. The honesty of the characters and the fullness and the realness of the characters are the standards that help you to move beyond jokes and really move into humor. There is a difference between humor and jokes. Humor is something that stays and goes deep in the consciousness and pulls out life's truths. I find that I absolutely loathe the first draft of my books. When I'm doing a first draft, I'll do anything to procrastinate: I'll clean my closets, I'll organize my purse. It's hard for me because when I write the first draft, parts of it seem really pretty dead. Then I layer the guts on later as I get to know the characters. Humor comes from knowing the characters and ultimately knowing how they are going to respond."

Bauer describes the premises of *Thwonk* as she reflects on how a book develops.

> *Humor is something that stays and goes deep in the consciousness and pulls out life's truths.*

If anyone thinks that I just sit there and the jokes are popping, they couldn't be more wrong. I start with serious stuff, but when I get to the second draft, then I start to have some fun. My writing is a process of layering. My characterizations are created that way. Strip away the layers of *Thwonk*; it is about A. J. [Allison Jean] MacCreary, who has an abysmal love life, and it has affected her self-esteem. She is trying to find out who she is as an artist. She is alone a lot because her parents are both workaholics, and she's depressed. She's really depressed. She's struggling with very real issues. A. J. is trying to figure out if she can be an artist in this crazy world. She has to decide if she believes that she can make a go of it, if she dares take the gift that is so unique and give it a whirl by being an artist. She knows how hard and painful that will be. That's the basic story of *Thwonk,* and it's not funny at all. So through layering, I build the characters and the situations, looking for humor in all the devastation,

abysmal immeasurably low, wretched

and that comes with time as I get to know my characters better. I am very visually tuned, and I see scenes in my mind and hear the voices of my characters and their conversations in my head. I'm always tinkering, trying to think what my characters would do or think in different situations and what more can I layer on to add more power. (Personal interview, August 1995)

Believable Characters

Bauer's main characters—Ellie, A. J., and Mickey—have unique voices that make them believable for the reader, and their single-minded dedication to their dreams makes the reader root for them. Perhaps the greatest appeal of these characters is their humor. They all have a challenge, a goal that motivates them and gives direction to their lives. The protagonists of *Squashed* and *Thwonk* are both adolescent girls; the protagonist of *Sticks* is a ten-year-old boy. For Ellie Morgan in *Squashed,* the ultimate goal is growing a champion pumpkin and defeating the odious four-time champion grower Cyril Pool. Ellie describes the task:

> I grew giant pumpkins because I liked battle, and growing one was an everyday fight. You had to be in it for the long haul. Rain, frost, bugs, and fungus could strike you dead. Only certain growers are cut out to handle this pressure—tough people of steel who can stand against the odds. Richard [her cousin] says giant-pumpkin growers are the spawning salmon of agriculture, since only the strongest make it upstream each year for anything worth mentioning. (P. 6)

In *Thwonk,* "A. J. McCreary, a high school senior, has talent and a dream, but she also has a problem. Her talent is as a gifted photographer; her dream is to pursue her talent by going to a good art school where she can study photography and prepare for a career; and her problem is that she is in love with Peter, but he does not know she is alive" (*Exploring Diversity*, p. 156). A. J. believes initially that her greatest goal is to win the heart of Peter Terris, but she realizes later that the exploration and development of her art, photography, is her fundamental motivator. As she recognizes the importance of her dedication to her art, she gains perspective about her recent experiences: "I knew at that instant why artists have to suffer: It's the only way to see beneath the surface sometimes to the truth below" (p. 194).

Mickey Vernon, in *Sticks,* focuses on winning the nine-ball championship in pool and connecting with his memory of his father.

> Now it might sound impossible, me a ten year old, gunning to beat a teenager, but I can beat lots of kids my age and older in this hall. I've got pool in my blood. I'm tall for my age—five-four to be exact. This puts me dead even with Poppy [his grandmother] except when she stands on her toes to holler. I've got long arms and big hands like my dad, light brown hair like my mom. (P. 4)

The humor in *Squashed* and *Thwonk* evolves from the ability of Ellie and A. J. to look at themselves and their circumstances from a gently self-deprecating perspective. For example, both gain recognition and suddenly are no longer invisible. The irony of Ellie's sudden fame is not lost on her:

self-deprecating playing down or discrediting oneself; belittling

irony a situation in which the actual outcome is opposite or contrary to what was expectected

> Nana had me autograph each newspaper for friends and family. She said that this was going to be a whirlwind week and that true champions always keep perspective. I assured her, while applying double-strength lash-building mascara, that nothing had changed—I was the same humble Ellie. Nana said one tube of mascara per eye was probably enough. JoAnn and Grace came over and we decided the best way to handle fame was to love it. (P. 129)

While Ellie's fame came from growing Max the pumpkin and thwarting the would-be pumpkin thieves, A. J.'s fame is even more fleeting. She is a part of the Valentine's Day Court as Peter Terris' date, slumped on a spiral staircase. She feels out of place:

> Popular people know how to stand on a questionable staircase unafraid. When you're a fake, you feel every

wobble. I listed to the left and gripped the rail, figuring I could crash down the steps between Al Costanzo and Mike Griswald in case tragedy struck. Nowhere is it written that you have to go down with the ship if you are only dating the captain. (P. 181)

In *Sticks,* the humor is more situational as it evolves from the interactions of Mickey and his friends—especially Arlen, the gifted student who regularly loses his bookbag, homework, and even his Red Sox cap; and Arlen's cousin Francine, a wanna-be magician who wants two things in life: "to play Vegas" and to get a rabbit for her act.

While her main characters are truly her stars, Bauer also creates an effective supporting cast of characters in each of her books. In *Squashed,* Ellie has her omnipresent cousin Richard, who plays baseball and never fails to have an insightful observation; her grandmother, who is rooted in the soil and supports Ellie's dream; Wes, her first boyfriend, a corn grower who supports her belief in her pumpkin and admires her courage; and Max, the pumpkin, the epitome of the strong, silent type, who is the focus of her energies and hopes. A. J., in *Thwonk,* is hedged in by Peter Terris, who evolves from the insensitive, stereotypical campus star to a devoted, obsequious suitor to a "world-class chump" (p. 191); Trish Beckman, the loyal and supportive best friend; and especially Jonathan, a wise and witty cupid who came to life and helped A. J. gain perspective on her life, dreams, and values. In *Sticks,* Mickey's goal to win the nine-ball championship is aided by his father's old friend, Joseph Alvarez, who coaches Mickey, and by Arlen, who believes that math can make life better. Arlen recognizes that the path of a pool ball can be tracked as he graphs pool shots, measuring the lines and determining the angles.

In 1995, Joan and Evan Bauer were living in Connecticut with their daughter, Jean, then a teenager. Bauer was working on three books and an outline for a screenplay.

obsequious overly eager to obey; having little self-respect

chump fool

Selected Bibliography

WORKS BY JOAN BAUER

Take It to the Streets (1987)
Squashed (1992)

If you enjoy the works of Joan Bauer, you might also like the works of M. E. Kerr.

How to Write to the Author
Joan Bauer
c/o Bantam DoubleDay Dell
Books for Young Readers
1540 Broadway
New York, NY 10036

Thwonk (1995)

Sticks (1996)

WORKS ABOUT JOAN BAUER

Brown, Jean, and Elaine Stephens. *Teaching Young Adult Literature: Sharing the Connection.* Belmont, Calif.: Wadsworth, 1995, pp. 238–239.

———. *Exploring Diversity: Literature, Themes, and Activities.* Englewood, Colo.: Teachers' Idea Press, 1996.

Marion Dane Bauer

(1938-   )

by Elaine C. Stephens

Award-winning author Marion Dane Bauer grew up with stories constantly spinning in her head. "It is almost as though I was born with my head stuffed full to overflowing with stories that waited to be told," she explains in her book *A Writer's Story: From Life to Fiction* (1995, p. 5). But it was not until Bauer was in her thirties that she decided writing stories for young people would be her life's work. Since then, her novels have received numerous awards, including the Newbery Honor Book for *On My Honor* (1986), the Jane Addams Peace Award for *Rain of Fire* (1983), the American Booksellers' Association's Pick of the Lists for *Face to Face* (1991), and *School Library Journal*'s Best Books of 1994 for *A Question of Trust* (1994). In addition to novels, Bauer writes nonfiction, poetry, short stories, and picture books.

Growing Up

> *Much like herself as a child, many of her characters struggle to reconcile their fantasy worlds with real life.*

Like the early experiences of many authors, Marion Dane Bauer's experiences in childhood and adolescence profoundly influenced her writing. She was born on 20 November 1938 and reared in a small town in the Illinois River valley. Her father was a chemical engineer for the local cement mill and her mother taught kindergarten in a nearby town. There were plenty of boys for her older brother to play with, but there were no other girls in her neighborhood. Frequently alone, Bauer had a rich fantasy life and created stories in her mind that took the place of friends. Some of her earliest and happiest memories are of acting out these stories with ordinary objects, which her imagination transformed; a broom became a palomino stallion, for example, and hollyhock blossoms became beautiful ladies.

Bauer's rich imagination is still active—and readily apparent in her novels. Much like herself as a child, many of her characters struggle to reconcile their fantasy worlds with real life. When Jennifer in *Touch the Moon* (1987) angrily smashes a small figurine horse from her father, she imagines that it becomes the live horse that she really has been wanting. In *Face to Face,* Michael is devastated when he discovers that the fantasies he has created about his absent father do not match the real man.

> *"My own years in seventh and eighth grades were absolutely horrendous. I've never been able to write about who I was then, but I can take the humiliation, the powerlessness, and the rage and bring it out in my characters."*

When Bauer entered school, she found that she did not fit in with the other children. She describes her experiences in *A Writer's Story*: "It is one thing to be physically isolated. It is something else entirely to be isolated in the midst of one's peers. To be continually on the outside, ignored, sometimes even scorned, creates real loneliness. And there is no question . . . I was an extremely lonely child" (p. 9). The feelings Bauer experienced as a young person affect the stories she writes as an adult. In "Talking with Marion Dane Bauer," she states: "My own years in seventh and eighth grades were absolutely horrendous. I've never been able to write about who I was then, but I can take the humiliation, the powerlessness, and the rage and bring it out in my characters" (p. 103).

Bauer was a very truthful child, but when school assignments required that she write about her own experiences, her active imagination often transformed the truth into something much more exciting. For example, an ordinary camping trip with her family seemed too boring for an

assigned essay titled "My Summer Vacation," so she transformed it into a life-and-death adventure with a ferocious,
rabid bear—in which she herself was the hero. Although the
teachers liked her writings, Bauer was sure that her parents
would be upset by her "lying." She solved this conflict by
tearing up her papers on the way home from school and
hiding them in the city's roadside trash cans. Some of
Bauer's most powerful books explore issues of truthfulness.
Joel's series of lies in *On My Honor* leads to tragic consequences. Steve, in *Rain of Fire,* believes he must make up
"stories" to tell his friends about his older brother's war ex-
ploits in order to uphold his honor. In *A Question of Trust,*
Brad, deeply pained by his mother's decision to leave their
home, keeps an important secret from his father until something terrible happens.

When Bauer was in elementary and junior high school,
correct penmanship, which was difficult for her, was emphasized rather than creative writing. Although she loved writing
(she wrote poetry and long letters and kept a journal), Bauer
never thought of fiction writing as a career for herself until
she was in high school, where she learned to type. Even
then, the stories in her mind were so complex that she did
not know how to begin to create them on paper. In high
school, however, she found a place where she finally felt she
belonged: on the yearbook staff. She not only became the
editor of the yearbook but also wrote and directed the talent
shows, which were among the most popular events of the
school year. Bauer describes these experiences in *A Writer's
Story*: "It was like finding a world within a world, one that
was made just for me" (p. 91).

Early Career

Like many other women of her generation, Bauer married
shortly after high school, completed college while helping
her husband earn his degree, and had children. As a graduate assistant at the University of Oklahoma, she taught freshman composition. She later taught high school English in
Wisconsin while her husband attended a seminary. Bauer
never stopped writing entirely, but frequent moves and her
responsibilities as a clergyman's wife, mother of two children, and foster parent left little time for much else. She
faithfully wrote in her journal but seldom found the opportunity to write the stories that so intrigued her.

> *Even [in high school] the stories in her mind were so complex that she did not know how to begin to create them on paper.*

"I grew up in a family, as many in my generation did, where feelings were not allowed; any expression of emotion was not nice."

After her children were in school, Bauer decided to take her writing seriously and gave herself five years to learn her craft. She and her husband agreed that if she was not successful at the end of that period, she would go back to teaching and give up her dream of becoming a professional writer. Living in Hannibal, Missouri, at the time, she read voraciously from the local library, starting with picture books and then finding books for older children. When she happened upon a shelf of Newbery Medal books, she recalls, she knew she had found her life's calling:

> This . . . this was what I wanted to write! It wasn't that I was anticipating getting the Newbery. I never dreamed of such a thing. Rather, those books challenged me, excited me, sent me back to my own writing filled with fire. I discovered, for nearly the first time, books for young people that covered a wide range of topics with honesty, integrity and real literary skill. (*A Writer's Story,* p. 120)

The Writer and Her Work

Bauer's novels are not autobiographical, but her characters wrestle with many of the same issues and feelings that she did as a child and as an adolescent. In a 1995 speech given to the National Conference of Teachers of English in Minneapolis, Bauer stated that her stories reflect her belief that "feelings are the core of powerful writing." In "Talking with Marion Dane Bauer," she explains, "I grew up in a family, as many in my generation did, where feelings were not allowed; any expression of emotion was not nice" (p. 102). In *A Writer's Story,* Bauer comments, "I came to my writing with a strong need to explore feelings, to play them out, to legitimize them. The emotional self-control I learned across the kitchen table from my father, or tried valiantly to learn but too often failed at in the end, now gives power to my writing" (p. 13).

"I came to my writing with a strong need to explore feelings, to play them out, to legitimize them."

Bauer's characters struggle with strong and uncomfortable feelings, but in the end they grow in their ability to manage these feelings and in their understanding of themselves and others. Caitlin, in *A Taste of Smoke* (1993), learns to deal with her conflicting feelings about her older sister. In *A Ques-*

tion of Trust, Brad begins to accept his mother, resolving his anger to reconcile with her.

While Bauer's stories range from realistic fiction to fantasy, the universality of her themes contributes to their appeal and their ability to connect with a wide range of readers of both genders. Her novels provide an intense and compelling reading experience. Bauer's books keep readers turning the pages, not only to find out what happens next but also to experience their emotional power. It is virtually impossible to read her stories without experiencing strong reactions and then exploring what they mean for yourself and for others.

Among the themes in Bauer's works are reality versus illusion, coming of age, the search for connection, and unfulfilled longing. In *A Writer's Story* she describes what she thinks is her strongest theme:

> Another pattern that emerges again and again in my work is that of the alienated child who finally makes a connection with a parent or parent figure. *Shelter from the Wind* opens with Stacy's running away from home. On the last page of the story, she chooses to return. In *A Dream of Queens and Castles,* Diana starts out petulant and angry, resenting being forced to move to England with her mother. By the last chapter she has decided, of her own will, to stay, and she and her mother set out to explore together. *On My Honor* begins with Joel's anger and disappointment with his father. It ends not just with Joel's confession, but with a reconciliation between father and son. Joel recognizes that he can't change his father but that, still, his father is there for him. (P. 14)

petulant   irritated

Another important theme in Bauer's work is the experience of loss. Continuing in *A Writer's Story,* she explains its significance in her stories:

> However wonderful fantasy may be, the resolutions of my stories proved, it must be given up so that one may live in the real world. In *Shelter from the Wind,* Stacy pretends that she is going to find her mother,

> *"We write what we believe. [Stories] reach into an author's most private truths and give us an opportunity to explore our own."*

sidle to move sideways, especially in a shy or timid way

but accepts her real stepmother at the story's conclusion. Renny, in *Foster Child,* dreams about her nonexistent father but finally turns to the foster parents who are there for her. In *Tangled Butterfly,* Michelle creates a soothing grandmother who talks to her but gives her up in the end. (P. 28)

Bauer believes that what makes books powerful is the passion of the writers who produce them. She states, "We write what we believe. [Stories] reach into an author's most private truths and give us each an opportunity to examine our own." She has empathy for young people who struggle to express themselves through writing. She explains:

When I go into schools to talk about my books, I am drawn to the lonely kids, the outsiders, the ones in whose eyes I glimpse my own remembered isolation. I am drawn especially to the ones who sidle up to me and speak, with longing and even some pain, of the stories they "want to write." And I always wish I could say, "Just wait. I know you're hurting, but the day will come when you can transform what you're feeling now into strength and compassion . . . into stories."(Pp. 9–10)

Bauer also helps young people learn to write stories. Her popular nonfiction book *What's Your Story? A Young Person's Guide to Writing Fiction* (1992) provides beginning writers with practical information and guides them through the process of writing a short story. In 1996, she published a companion book, *Our Stories: A Workshop for Young Authors,* a collection of stories written by students in response to *What's Your Story?* with workshop commentaries.

Bauer keeps stretching and growing as an author, varying her work and exploring new dimensions. In "Talking with Marion Dane Bauer," she discusses her writing style: "When I'm writing, everything has to serve the story movement, including and particularly the language. I leave out anything that isn't contributing to the movement of my story. Compression of time also contributes to intensity; *On My Honor* takes place during only twenty-four hours. Intensity is what makes me want to write" (p. 103).

Empathy and intensity led Bauer to create and edit the highly acclaimed anthology *Am I Blue? Coming Out from the Silence* (1994). She also contributed an original short story to it. "We read stories first, to find ourselves, second, to find other people, third to be empowered," Bauer states. "We're always asking, 'But what does it mean? Why am I here? Am I the only one in the universe who feels like this, acts like this, thinks like this?'" The purpose of the anthology is to provide readers with stories that affect them both emotionally and intellectually and that help them understand themselves and others.

> *"We read stories first, to find ourselves, second to find other people, third to be empowered."*

Bauer Today

Marion Dane Bauer lives in Eden Prairie, Minnesota, where she writes full-time and also teaches writing to adults. She breeds Cornish rex and Devon rex kittens. The cat in *Ghost Eye* (1992), with some slight differences, is based on her own cat. When Bauer is asked how many more books she is going to write, she says that she always replies, "As long as my brain keeps functioning, as long as there is someone out there wanting to read my stories, I expect to go on making books. How else can I keep in touch with all those forbidden feelings? How else can I keep learning who I am?" (*A Writer's Story,* p. 20)

Selected Bibliography

WORKS BY MARION DANE BAUER

Readers who enjoy works by Marion Dane Bauer might also enjoy works by Will Hobbs.

Novels

Shelter from the Wind (1976)

Foster Child (1977)

Tangled Butterfly (1980)

Rain of Fire (1983)

Like Mother, Like Daughter (1985)

On My Honor (1986)

Touch the Moon (1987)

A Dream of Queens and Castles (1990)

Face to Face (1991)

Ghost Eye (1992)

A Taste of Smoke (1993)

A Question of Trust (1994)

Picture Books

When I Go Camping with Grandma (1995)

If You Were Born a Kitten (1997)

Easy Readers

Alison's Wings (1996)

Alison's Puppy (1997)

Nonfiction

What's Your Story? A Young Person's Guide to Writing Fiction (1992)

Our Stories: A Fiction Workshop for Young Authors (1996)

Autobiography

A Writer's Story: From Life to Fiction (1995)

Anthology

Am I Blue? Coming Out from the Silence, editor and contributor (1994)

How to Write to the Author

Marion Dane Bauer
8861 Basswood Road
Eden Prairi, MN 53445

WORKS ABOUT MARION DANE BAUER

Brown, Jean, and Elaine Stephens. "Talking with Marion Dane Bauer." *Teaching Young Adult Literature: Sharing the Connection.* Belmont, Calif.: Wadsworth, 1995.

Jay Bennett

(1912-   )

by Jeffrey S. Kaplan

He awoke in a cold sweat, pale and trembling, his eyes wildly trying to pierce the black night.

He shivered.

Then he called out, in a tight, small voice.

"Alden."

There was no answering sound.

Only silence. The dread silence of night.

He trembled again and then got out of the bed and went softly out of the dark room and down the carpeted hall, his bare feet glimmering.

He was alone in the empty house.

His parents were in Hawaii. Thousands of miles away. On vacation. And he was alone. Alone in the vast empty house.

He went slowly down the shadowy stairway and into the kitchen.

He felt nauseous.

He had drunk too much at the party with Alden.
Too much.
He went to the gas range and turned on the burner un-
der the coffeepot.
Then he sat down on a chair and waited in the silvery
darkness, his pale hands trembling.
And he said to himself what happened?
Did I dream it?
Or did something happen?
Something terrible and deadly.
"Alden."
And as he listened to his voice fade into the cold still-
ness, he felt so alone.
So desperately alone.
And terrified.

What had happened? (*Coverup,* 1991, pp. 8–9)

What has happened? What is nagging at this kid's soul?
What does this kid—Brad, another teenager with a terrific
hangover—have to fear? Does he know something no one
else does? And if so, why can't he remember it? Why?

A Realistic Mystery Writer

Welcome to the world of Jay Bennett—suspense and mystery
writer extraordinaire. Bennett writes of today's teenagers,
mixed up in a world of anger and frustration, where sometimes the only way out is violence. And the violence they see
is not cartoon violence—not scary monsters with three heads
or ghosts that go bump in the night—but everyday violence,
the kind that you see on the evening news, the kind where
people die at the hands of an unexpected killer, or perhaps
even by their own hands.

Bennett is a realistic mystery writer. And if you are looking
for a good read by an author who knows how today's kids feel
and think, then Bennett is the one you should be reading. An
award-winning author, Bennett has written countless stories
about teenagers who get themselves into life-threatening
jams and discover that their only way out is to stick up for
what they believe in, to go against their parents, to do their
own detective work, to hunt down evil people, to confront vi-

cious killers, and to fight injustice. Bennett's teenagers are people you often hear about but rarely get to see close up. They are loners and victims, out to right wrongs and defend the truth.

Take Jonathan, in the book *Skinhead* (1991), who almost singlehandedly takes on deadly, dangerous, racist "skinheads."

> The door of the barn partly opened and two figures entered silently, one after the other. A gun barrel glinted in the darkness. Jonathan shivered and tensed up. He could see the hard eyes of Carl. A panic came over him. He'll kill me now, he thought. They've decided to do it. To get rid of me. And I'm trapped. Trapped. No way out. (*Skinhead,* p. 87)

What happens next is a riveting tale of how one teenager— one lonely, brave, and clever teenager—manages to outsmart a pack of masterly evil racists.

Or take Bruce. In *The Executioner* (1982), Bruce is a teenager wracked with guilt. He feels responsible for the death of a friend.

> "Guilt," he whispered.
> The sound of his voice rustled away into the stillness.
> His hands left his face and fell to his side. Slowly, futilely. It was then the tears came. The first tears since the crackup.
> "I'm a murderer," he said, in a low bitter voice. (*The Executioner,* p. 11)

Is he a murderer? Bruce certainly thinks he is. Out joyriding in a drunken spree with his teenage friends, Bruce accidentally rattles the driver, his friend Raymond, who has also had his share of drinks, and the next thing, Bruce is attending a funeral. For Raymond.

Scared and guilt-ridden, Bruce tries desperately to forget, but first he must suffer at the hands of someone who has decided he has not suffered enough. Someone seeking revenge. The executioner.

> *Bennett's teenagers are people you often hear about but rarely get to see close up. They are loners and victims, out to right wrongs and defend the truth.*

And finally, take Ray in *The Skeleton Man* (1986). On his eighteenth birthday, Ray receives from his Uncle Ed the present of a lifetime—thirty thousand dollars in cash. There is only one catch, though. Ray cannot tell anyone how he got the money.

Ray is agreeable and content, until the next day, when Uncle Ed takes an unexpected walk off the twelfth floor of his midtown hotel. (Not exactly what Ray had in mind for his eighteenth birthday celebration.)

Sworn to secrecy, Ray tells no one—not even his mother, his girlfriend, or Ed's girlfriend—until trouble arrives in the face of Albert Dawson, a heavy hitter (in more ways than one), who kindly informs Ray that Ed owed him money. And he wants it. No matter what.

> **Albert Dawson did call.**
>
> **He seemed to know when Ray would be alone in the house. When the ring of the phone would be sudden, clear and startling.**
>
> **Ray stood there, holding the receiver with a tight grip, and listening to the man's smooth, precise voice.**
>
> **"I'd like to see you, Ray."**
>
> **"I know. I was waiting for you."**
>
> **"I thought you would be." (*The Skeleton Man,* p. 77.)**

On the run and on the loose, Ray tries to escape the clutches of a sly gangster. His fate dangles in the wind.

Bennett knows all these characters—the teenagers in trouble and in despair, in desperate straits and in lonely ways, in homes where parents fight and evil lurks, in alleyways where shady characters live and on tree-lined streets where respectable adults hold deep dark secrets. All these people and more inhabit Bennett's novels.

Jay Bennett—His Life

Jay Bennett did not start out as a writer. Born on 4 December 1912 in New York City, just after the turn of the century, Bennett attended grade school, high school, and New York University but did not graduate. So, without formal degree or training, he held many jobs until he became a successful writer. He was a farmhand, factory worker, lifeguard, mail carrier, salesman, senior editor of an encyclopedia, and, during World War II, English features writer and editor for the Office of War Information. Still, it was not until after many, many years of writing and receiving rejections that Bennett got his first big break. He sold a suspense drama to NBC-TV, and the rest, as they say, is history. Bennett's writing career was launched, and he began a lucrative career writing radio and television scripts. Then, suddenly, in the mid-1960s, he left television writing to devote himself full-time to writing for young adults.

Bennett has held many jobs, but he has always been a writer. Writing continually as a kid, his love for words and books and plays was nurtured by his parents and encouraged by his teachers.

In the early 1900s, Bennett's father, Pincus Shapiro, immigrated to the United States to escape the widespread hatred for Jewish people in tsarist Russia. Arriving in America with a mere thirteen cents in his pocket, Shapiro soon found a job in a wholesale dry goods firm. There he met and married Bennett's mother, Estelle Bennett, a bookkeeper for the same firm. Jay Bennett (as an author, he adopted his mother's maiden name) has four brothers and one sister.

Beginning in 1881 under the rule of Tsar Alexander III, Jews were massacred in Russia. To escape execution, many fled to the United States and Palestine.

Although his siblings are successful adults, Bennett is the only writer in the family. He attributes his profession to his parents' continued emphasis on the value of an education and to the many fine teachers who fostered his love for literature. As a young boy, he attended the Hebrew Institute, where he met an elementary school teacher, a writer in his own right, who introduced him to Shakespeare. For a class project, this same teacher cast Bennett in a stage production of *Julius Caesar*.

There is an article about William Shakespeare in volume 3.

At first, Bennett was frightened. He did not want his classmates making fun of him anymore than they already did, and a skinny kid with glasses wearing a toga was not his vision of "cool." Still, his teacher convinced him that even with glasses and a toga, Bennett could do Shakespeare and still keep his friends. So he did the Shakespeare play. And to this day, Bennett credits that grade school production with giving him the confidence to conquer all his fears. If he could recite Shakespeare, he figured, then anyone could, toga and all.

High School and Beyond

Next, Bennett attended James Madison High School in the Flatbush section of Brooklyn. Bennett readily admits that he was not much of a student; he passed everything, but never really studied. More interested in sports, Bennett spent his spare time participating in every sport offered there—baseball, wrestling, boxing, and weightlifting. And it was not until he attended New York University that a teacher tapped into a side that this young man had long been keeping to himself: his writing.

Since the age of sixteen, Bennett had been writing poetry, short stories, and plays, but with no luck. He had no encouraging teachers or welcoming publishers. It was only when a college professor took a liking to Bennett's work and urged him to pursue his dream that Bennett felt he had any chance to succeed as a writer.

Sadly, though, at the height of the Great Depression, Bennett, like many young people in the early 1930s, had to quit college and help his family. His father had lost his job, and along with seventeen million other Americans, Bennett was forced to look for work. Unfortunately, though, work was not to be found. Frustrated, confused, and depressed, Bennett walked the streets of New York City, looking for any kind of job, but found nothing. Finally, in desperation, he left his family and the city and went wandering aimlessly across America. He just wanted to see where life would take him.

Along the way, Bennett met the characters who would later populate his many novels—desperate, lonely people who are searching for comfort from tortured, despairing lives. On this trip across the country, he met drifters and vagrants and thieves and even murderers. He met people who felt hopeless and angry, and sometimes in their bitterness and ignorance turned to violence. Bennett now writes about these folk, warning that they often start out just like us but find themselves living very sad lives.

Returning home from his cross-country travels, Bennett attended a dance and there met Sally Stern, the woman who was soon to become his wife. Together they began a life for themselves—he as a floorboy (stockboy) at a clothing factory; she, at a beauty parlor. They lived relatively well until Bennett lost his job. His wife, though, knowing his need

The **Great Depression** was a severe recession that began when the stock market crashed in 1929 and lasted almost ten years. By the winter of 1932–1933, 14 to 16 million Americans were unemployed. Many died from a lack of food and inadequate living conditions.

During his trip across America, Bennett met the characters who would later populate his novels— desperate, lonely people who are searching for comfort from tortured, despairing lives.

to write and seeing it desperately in his eyes, told him she would go to work while he stayed home and wrote.

And write he did, all day, every day, until by chance he met a friend who knew someone working in radio who knew that a radio show called "Grand Central Station" was buying scripts. Excited and determined, Bennett ran out, bought a radio, began listening to radio shows day after day, and quickly tried his hand at turning out radio scripts. It worked. The radio show bought his scripts, asked for many more, and soon Bennett became an established writer.

Today, Bennett is a successful mystery writer. Still married to Sally, he is the proud father of two grown children, Steven and Randy.

"Grand Central Station" was a radio show broadcasted from 1937 to 1953. It consisted of conversations characters had as they left the train station in New York City.

Jay Bennett—His Writings

When asked why he writes for young adults, Bennett replies, "Well, all through my years I have been intensely interested in the young, their problems and their hopes. Their dreams and depairs" (*Speaking for Ourselves,* p. 17). Bennett's writing features a string of highly successful suspense mystery novels, all written in a taut, clipped style. Bennett frankly depicts for his readers the fast-paced and often jumbled lives that teenagers inhabit. Caught in a web of seeming indifference and loneliness, Bennett's heroes strike out at cruel teenagers and conniving adults in the hope of erasing hypocrisy from their small corner of the universe. His heroes are successful at shedding light on injustice, but only after much struggle and heartache. That is why Bennett is so popular. Reading how his teenagers struggle against impossible odds makes for highly entertaining reading.

Yet, more important, readers, especially young adults, come back to Jay Bennett's novels because they are something more than a quick read; they are strong and sustaining stories about human events of great importance: teenage suicide, gang warfare, racism, drugs, alcoholism, murder, and relationships. Bennett is a mystery writer with one eye trying to unravel a puzzle and the other trying to understand the human condition.

Bennett's suspense stories for young adults have sold millions of copies in sixteen languages, and his work for

Caught in a web of seeming indifference and loneliness, Bennett's heroes strike out at cruel teenagers and conniving adults in the hope of erasing hypocrisy from their small corner of the universe.

young readers has twice been awarded the highly coveted Edgar Award for best juvenile mysteries.

If you have already read a Jay Bennett mystery novel, then go find another, and enjoy. If not, find one now. You are in for a treat.

If you like Jay Bennett, you might also like Frank Bonham's *Durango Street* and *The Nitty Gritty*.

Selected Bibliography

WORKS BY JAY BENNETT

Mysteries for Young Adults

Deathman, Do Not Follow Me (1968)

The Deadly Gift (1969)

Masks: A Love Story (1971)

The Killing Tree (1972)

The Long Black Coat (1973)

The Dangling Witness (1974)

Say Hello to the Hitman (1976)

The Birthday Murderer (1977)

The Pigeon (1980)

The Executioner (1982)

Slowly, Slowly, I Raise the Gun (1983)

I Never Said I Loved You (1984)

To Be a Killer (1985)

The Skeleton Man (1986)

The Haunted One (1987)

The Dark Corridor (1988)

Sing Me a Death Song (1990)

Coverup (1991)

Skinhead (1991)

Death Grip (1993)

Hooded Man (1993)

Adult Novels

Catacombs (1959)

Murder Money (1969)

Death Is a Silent Room (1965)

Shadows Offstage (1974)

WORKS ABOUT JAY BENNETT

Commire, Anne, ed. "Jay Bennett." In *Something About the Author.* Detroit: Gale Research, 1985, vol. 41, pp. 35–36.

Donelson, Kenneth L., and Alleen Pace Nilsen. *Literature for Today's Young Adults.* New York: Scott Foresman, 1980, pp. 228–257.

Gallo, Donald R., ed. *Speaking for Ourselves: Autobiographical Sketches by Notable Authors of Books for Young Adults.* Urbana, Ill.: National Council of Teachers of English, 1990, pp. 16–18.

Sarkissian, Adele, ed. "Jay Bennett." In *Something About the Author Autobiography Series.* Detroit: Gale Research, 1987, vol. 4, pp. 75–91.

Marowski, Daniel G., ed. "Jay Bennett." In *Contemporary Literary Criticism.* Detroit: Gale Research, 1985, vol. 35, pp. 52–53.

Trosky, Susan M., ed. "Jay Bennett." In *Contemporary Authors New Revision Series.* Detroit: Gale Research, 1994, vol. 42, pp. 37–39.

How to write to the Author
Jay Bennett
c/o Juniper Press
1310 Shorewood Drive
La Crosse, WI 54601

T. Ernesto Bethancourt

(1932-   )

by Bruce C. Appleby

T. Ernesto Bethancourt was born Tomas Ernesto Passailaigue in Brooklyn, New York, in 1932. His father, Aubrey Ernesto Passailaigue, was born in the Dominican Republic and raised in Puerto Rico. His mother, Dorothy (Charest) Passailaigue, was born and raised in Pelham, New York.

Bethancourt was born in the midst of the Great Depression, so his father had a hard time supporting the family (which also included Bethancourt's three sisters) as a truck driver. The family moved often, so often that Bethancourt attended six different elementary schools, including one in Florida. He attended only one high school, however: Grover Cleveland High in the Ridgewood section of Brooklyn, where he graduated in 1950 with honors.

Bethancourt's family had little money, so he was not able to go straight to college. He enlisted in the navy, and the navy's support allowed him to go to college. Even then, money was still a problem, so he worked as an insurance casualty claims investigator and attended college at night.

The **Great Depression** was a severe recession that began when the stock market crashed in 1929 and that lasted almost ten years. By the winter of 1932–1933, 14 to 16 million Americans were unemployed. Many died from a lack of food and inadequate living conditions.

99

Musical Career

Bethancourt started performing publicly as a singer at the age of ten. In high school, he sang in the school chorus and with the New York City All City Chorus. When he got out of the Navy, he bought himself a guitar and taught himself how to play. In the 1950s, the guitar was thought to be for "cowboy music" and was not considered a legitimate instrument for a serious musician.

When Bethancourt was working as an insurance investigator, he followed a man who had claimed total disability to a bar where the "disabled" man danced a mean mambo. Bethancourt got his guitar out of his car and told the owner he wanted to audition. He made more in tips that night than he made in two days at the insurance company. Something had to give, so he became a full-time musician in 1957.

Bethancourt played in a number of places around New York City for a couple of years. When Harry Belafonte became a star, being a singer/guitarist became legitimate and Bethancourt played with a number of different musicians, including: Nina Simone; Peter Paul and Mary; Bob Dylan; Judy Collins; and Bill Cosby.

Bethancourt's favorite form of music—traditional jazz and blues—was then considered folk music. His work came to the attention of blues guitarist Josh White, who wanted Bethancourt to accompany his daughter, Beverly, on a tour and was also willing to teach him the approach to the guitar for which White was famous.

In addition to writing much of his own material, Bethancourt found other people picking up on his musical writing ability, asking him to write original material for them. He was also reviewing records and performances for *Stereo Review* and *High Fidelity*. RCA and Columbia Records hired him to write liner notes for records and press biographies for musical artists. He was a contract lyricist and had an Off-Broadway musical in preproduction.

In 1970, when his musical career was flourishing, Bethancourt married Nancy Yasue Soyeshima, a third-generation Japanese American whose family had been interned during World War II.

After his musical contracts were completed, Bethancourt chose to work with an ad agency. That lasted only a year because he could not stand the meetings. Because of his repu-

After the bombing of Pearl Harbor, anti-Japanese hysteria led the U.S. government to move about 110,000 Japanese Americans from the West Coast to relocation, or **internment** camps, located inland. Japanese Americans lost their homes and their jobs.

tation as a performer, he was able to get his own performing lounge at the New York Hilton Hotel.

Starting a Family and Starting as a Writer

When Bethancourt's first daughter was born in 1974, he started writing an autobiography for her so that one day she could read about her dad's background, in case something happened to him. He would take a yellow legal pad and, between sets, work on his autobiography. Bethancourt could not type, so he wrote everything in block capital letters.

One night, a customer asked Bethancourt what he was writing, assuming it was the social and political satire he was known for. When he explained what he was doing, the customer asked for copies. The customer took his manuscript to Margery Cuyler, an editor who went to Holiday House and got herself a job on the basis of his manuscript. A few suggestions and a used typewriter resulted in Bethancourt's first novel, *New York City Too Far from Tampa Blues*, in 1975. If you've read *New York City Too Far from Tampa Blues*, you know how autobiographical the novel is. Remember, he started it for his daughter to read when she became a teenager.

Tom (the hero of the novel) is a half-Hispanic singer/guitarist who is growing up in Brooklyn and Florida. The book is a series of stories told by him. He gets into a fight with Aurelio over a prime "shoeshine spot" and the two become good friends who form a group called the Griffin Brothers and work in Irish bars, are a big hit at their eighth-grade commencement, and eventually make a record of a song they wrote—the "New York City Too Far from Tampa Blues."

Most reviewers of the book found it to be realistic, irreverent, and full of joy. Jean Mercier called the book's social comments "wry, but . . . soft-pedaled" (*Publishers Weekly*, p. 45). Although some critics found the second half of the book too predictable because of the boys' musical success, others agreed with Mercier, who wrote in the same review that the author "makes it plain how hard they [the boys] had to work . . . that love, nerve and discipline are required to get where they hope to arrive" (p. 45).

satire sarcastic, ironic criticism

stereotyping creating characters that are not original or individual because they conform to preconceived categories

The critic John F. Caviston wrote that "[w]hile certain sections of this novel are insightful and entertaining, the author is as quick to categorize other groups as he is to show concern for his Hispanic central character" (*School Library Journal*, p. 117). Even though she was critical of what she saw as stereotyping, Figueroa found the story inspiring and relevant. As she stated in *Interracial Books for Children Bulletin*, "[a]lthough Tom shares the money he earns from singing with his family, his musical flight from poverty is the stuff of which dreams are made for Third World boys and girls in our urban ghettos and *barrios*" (Figueroa, p. 17).

Just before *New York City Too Far from Tampa Blues* was published, a problem arose. Bethancourt had taken the stage name of Tom Paisley because he thought his original name "would cause a fire" if featured in lights. His publisher thought that a novel about Latino life in New York City might not be well accepted by the Latino community from someone with a non-Latino sounding name like Paisley. Tom suggested another family name, Bethancourt.

Writing Career

Tampa Blues was a big hit. Bantam paid what was then a record prepublication advance for it. It was adapted for television by NBC in 1979, was nominated for an Emmy, and won the Writers' Guild of America (East) Award for 1979.

The success of his first book led Bethancourt, now known as T. Ernesto Bethancourt, to bring out his second novel for young adults, *The Dog Days of Arthur Cane* (1976), almost immediately after the first book was published. Arthur Cane, a high school student from Long Island, New York, wakes up to find he has become a dog. Arthur should not have been so insulting about witch doctors to the African exchange student.

The mongrel-that-was-Arthur is chased out of his home by his own dog and ends up wandering around the city, becomes a guide dog for a street singer, and is nearly put into a gas chamber after being caught by a dog catcher. Arthur's six weeks of adventures as a dog teach him more about human nature and life than his sixteen years as a well-to-do teenager from Long Island.

The book "is not only wise, it is very funny, and I loved it for its warmth and honesty," the critic Rosalyn Drexler said in the *New York Times Book Review.* "Bethancourt has a well tuned ear for dialogue, switching easily from the mind and speech of a sixteen-year-old boy to the miraculous conversation of a talking cat" (p. 41). *The Dog Days of Arthur Cane* was adapted for television by ABC in 1984.

Science Fiction

The success of his first two novels led Bethancourt to science fiction. *The Mortal Instruments* (1977) was highly praised. Most critics agreed with Sybil Steinberg who called it "a sophisticated, superbly crafted SF thriller (*Publishers Weekly*, p. 43).

Eddie Rodriguez is a nineteen-year-old genius—a super athlete with a super mind—from El Barrio in Spanish Harlem who gains control of the world's money markets and disappears. Even though Eddie's body is found, he isn't dead because he is living in ODIN, the secret government super-computer, from which he intends to rule the world. As in Bethancourt's earlier books, there is "wry humor" and a "fitting climax [that] ends the breakneck pace of an unusual book," as Ann Flowers says in *Horn Book* (p. 449).

The success of *The Mortal Instruments* led to a sequel, *Instruments of Darkness* (1979). Eddie—and the superhuman force that has inhabited his body—has become Ionas Iorga, who was the evil influence in the previous book. Iorga is seen as a security threat. Luis Ortiz is discovered to have psychic abilities, so he is recruited by government agencies to stop Iorga.

Once again, critics responded favorably. Karen Klockner, in *Horn Book,* said that Bethancourt "maintains suspense throughout and creates a real sense of fear of the superhuman beings" (p. 420). "The characterizations are much stronger here [than in *The Mortal Instruments*], and the author has some interesting ideas about human intelligence and mind control" Marjorie Allen said in the *New York Times Book Review* (p. 31).

Bethancourt decided to work with the idea of time travel in his next book, *Tune in Yesterday* (1978). Since *Dog Days*, Bethancourt had shown how he could make the impossible

characterization method by which a writer creates and develops the appearance and personality of a character

seem real, and in *Tune in Yesterday*, we find Matty and Richie have stumbled onto a "gate to the past." They are able to convince the gatekeeper to let them travel back to 1942, to check out the jazz scene. The story starts as a science fiction story about time travel and becomes a spy thriller when they get involved with German spies. Matty and Richie escape by going further back in time, to 1912.

As with the earlier novels, *Tune in Yesterday* was well received. The National Council of Social Studies found the book to be one of the notable children's books in the field of social studies, and the Young Adults Services Division of the American Library Association listed it as among "The Best of the Best Books" for 1970–1983.

Tune in Yesterday led to a sequel, *The Tomorrow Connection* (1984). At the end of the first book, Matty and Richie are left in 1912, so in the sequel they still need to get back to 1976. They have the key to the tomorrow gate, but must find the gate. They go back to 1906, with the help of the famous magician Harry Houdini. Richie and Matty barely survive the great San Francisco earthquake of 1906.

Many aspects of *The Tomorrow Connection* are fun. Bethancourt brings in a great deal of research on Houdini. Another interesting part is how Bethancourt portrays prejudice and bigotry. Matty is African American and we get scary insights into the treatment of minorities when Matty and Richie are stuck in 1906.

The **San Francisco earthquake of 1906** (18 April 1906) caused uncontrollable fires. Firemen were forced to dynamite entire blocks of buildings to stop the fire because of damaged water mains (the huge pipes that carry water underground). At least 3,000 people died and more than 28,000 buildings were destroyed.

Connections to Bethancourt's Life

As is apparent from the descriptions and reactions to his early books, Bethancourt uses his own life—as a musician, a Latino, and a writer—in all his books. The next books, *Nightmare Town* (1979) and *Where the Deer and the Cantaloupe Play* (1981), use the move that Bethancourt and his family (now with another daughter) made to California as part of the plot.

In *Where the Deer and the Cantaloupe Play,* we see the connections to Bethancourt's life most clearly. Teddy Machado, a Puerto Rican born in New York, is involved with his fantasies of the Wild West, fed by his great-grandfather, who has told him many stories of El Tigre, a Latino lawman. When the great-grandfather dies, he leaves his Los Angeles home to Teddy's family and leaves Teddy El Tigre's Colt .45.

Teddy and his father go through a great deal of conflict, and Teddy has to defend himself against a Los Angeles teenage gang. Eventually, Teddy wins his father's respect and Bethancourt is able to resolve the two different aspects of the story: Teddy's Wild West fantasies and the modern world of a big city.

T.H.U.M.B.B.: The Hippest Underground Marching Band in Brooklyn (1983) continues Bethancourt's use of music in his novels and is, surprisingly, a sequel to the first novel, *New York City Too Far from Tampa Blues*. Tom and Aurelio, the pair who cut the record in the earlier novel, have been doing well as musicians but decide they can form a better band than the high school marching band.

The misadventures of replacing the regular marching band with T.H.U.M.B.B. in New York City's St. Patrick's Day parade are hilarious, and the band is featured on national television. As one reviewer put it in the 1983 *Bulletin of the Center for Children's Books*, the book is "rollicking" and "funny," with an "overriding impression of a warm friendship, a sense of community, and an achievement (not probable, but possible) against odds" (p. 83).

rollicking carefree; high-spirited

The Great Computer Dating Caper (1984) and *The Me Inside of Me* (1985) are both set in California. Both also deal with problems faced by adolescent males of Latino origin in trying to find themselves. Eddie, in *Dating Caper*, and Freddie, in *The Me Inside of Me*, have to deal with money problems from the opposite ends of the spectrum, as Eddie tries to make money by starting a dating service and Freddie becomes suddenly wealthy after the death of the rest of his family in an airplane crash. Both boys have to deal with their Latino heritage and both have to come to realize how prejudice can affect all of us. In writing about *The Me Inside of Me* in *Voice of Youth Advocates*, the critic Rosie Peasley said that "as in previous works by Bethancourt, the style is sharp, almost terse. Characters are well developed, realistic and sometimes engaging" (p. 139).

spectrum range

The Doris Fein Mystery Series

Bethancourt has written a series of mystery stories that center on the character Doris Fein, a detective who is, according to the critic Mary Burns, "an intelligent, self-confident

> *"Anything that neither advances plot nor illuminates character is cut mercilessly."*

intuition the ability to know something without conscious attention or logical reasoning

narrating telling a story

teenager with remarkable intuition and a well-developed sense of humor" (*Horn Book*, 1980, p. 413). The series was given an award of "special recognition for excellence in a series" in 1983 by the Southern California Council of Literature for Children and Young People.

The series consists of eight books, all published between 1980 and 1984, starting with *Doris Fein: Superspy* (1980). The books are fast-paced, with Doris narrating the (sometimes impossible) adventures and misadventures she gets into as she solves highly complex mysteries. In her review of *Doris Fein: Superspy* in the *Bulletin of the Center for Children's Books*, the critic Zena Sutherland pointed out what makes this story stand out from other mysteries. She said: "What gives the story some substance—in addition to the pace and suspense—are the candor with which the Jewish protagonist and her Sansei (third-generation Japanese-American) colleague discuss minority groups and bias, and the cheerful honesty about her feelings expressed by Doris, who tells the story" (p. 167).

Bethancourt's Future

As is obvious, Tom Passailaigue/Paisley/Bethancourt enjoys great success as a writer for young adults. As he says in *Something About the Author*, he has used his background as a member of a minority group and his work as a musician to present characters who help readers "see that minorities are like anybody else—they have the same goals: a decent job, to live like a person, the hope that your kids grow up to live better than you did" (p. 151).

When he writes, Bethancourt says in a letter he wrote to me, he breaks down the books and stories he is working on into individual scenes. He then summarizes each scene on an index card, "along with its purpose as a component story part." For novels, he "adds another set of cards to summarize and evaluate chapters to overall structure." This technique he calls a "spinoff of the film technique of 'storyboarding.' When the story or book is all laid out, decisions are easier to make. Anything that neither advances plot nor illuminates character is cut mercilessly" (Bethancourt, correspondence with the author, February 1995).

There is more to the story of Tom Bethancourt. He has been censored. He has written "easy reader" abridgements of many classic novels. He is also a member of a large number of professional organizations for writers. His short stories have been anthologized and reprinted in a number of short story collections, most especially the well-known *Connections* from Dell, edited by Donald Gallo. In the 1990s he decided to concentrate on writing short fiction. Best known perhaps for his realistic portrayals of minorities and for his fast-paced stories that have realistic dialogue, T. Ernesto Bethancourt is a writer of books for young adults whose name will be around for a long time.

censor to suppress something that one finds objectionable

Selected Bibliography

WORKS BY T. ERNESTO BETHANCOURT

New York City Too Far from Tampa Blues (1975)
The Dog Days of Arthur Cane (1976)
The Mortal Instruments (1977)
Dr. Doom Superstar (1978)
Tune in Yesterday (1978)
Instruments of Darkness (1979)
Nightmare Town (1979)
Where the Deer and the Cantaloupe Play (1981)
T.H.U.M.B.B.: The Hippest Underground Marching Band in Brooklyn (1983)
The Great Computer Dating Caper (1984)
The Tomorrow Connection (1984)
The Me Inside of Me (1985)

The Doris Fein Mystery Series
Doris Fein: Superspy (1980)
Doris Fein: Quartz Boyar (1980)
Doris Fein: Phantom of the Casino (1981)
Doris Fein: The Mad Samurai (1981)
Doris Fein: Deadly Aphrodite (1982)
Doris Fein: Murder Is No Joke (1982)
Doris Fein: Dead Heat at Long Beach (1983)
Doris Fein: Legacy of Terror (1984)

If you like the works of T. Ernesto Bethancourt, you might also like the works of Nat Hentoff, Nicholasa Mohr, and Gary Soto.

WORKS ABOUT T. ERNESTO BETHANCOURT

Allen, Marjorie. Review of *Instruments of Darkness*. In *The New York Times Book Review,* 8 July 1979, p. 31.

Hile, Kevin S., ed. *Something About the Author* Detroit: Gale Research, 1994, vol. 78, pp. 147–153.

Bulletin of the Center for Children's Books. Review of *T.H.U.M.B.B.*, 1983, p. 83.

Burns, Mary M. Review of *Doris Fein: Superspy*. In *Horn Book,* August 1980, p. 413.

————.Review of *The Tomorrow Connection*. In *Horn Book,* March/April 1985, pp. 184–185.

————.Review of *Tune in Yesterday*. In *Horn Book,* August 1978, p. 400.

Cain, Susan. Review of *Tune in Yesterday*. In *School Library Journal,* May, 1978, p. 73.

Caviston, John F. Review of *New York City Too Far from Tampa Blues*. In *School Library Journal,* September 1975, p. 117.

Drexler, Rosalyn. Review of *The Dog Days of Arthur Cane*. In *The New York Times Book Review.* 17 October 1976, p. 41.

Figueroa, Carmen. Review of *New York City Too Far from Tampa Blues*. In *Interracial Books for Children Bulletin,* 1975, vol. 7, no. 1, p. 17.

Flanagan, Kate M. Review of *Where the Deer and the Cantaloupe Play*. In *Horn Book,* August 1981, pp. 429–430.

Flowers, Ann. Review of *The Mortal Instruments*. In *Horn Book,* August 1977, pp. 448–449.

Forman, Jack. Review of *The Tomorrow Connection*. In *School Library Journal,* December 1984, p. 88.

Forman, Jack. Review of *Instruments of Darkness*. In *School Library Journal,* September 1979, p. 152.

Grimes, Nikki. Review of *The Mortal Instruments*. In *Children's Book Review Service,* April 1977, p. 88.

Heins, Paul. Review of *The Dog Days of Arthur Cane*. In *Horn Book,* April 1977, pp. 157–158.

Heldman, Irma. Review of *Tune in Yesterday*. In *The New York Times Book Review,* April 1978, p. 44.

Klockner, Karen. Review of *Instrument of Darkness*. In *Horn Book,* August 1979, pp. 419–420.

Lipsyte, Robert. Review of *New York City Too Far from Tampa Blues.* In *The New York Times Book Review,* 4 May 1975, pp. 28–29.

McCoy, B. Review of *The Dog Days of Arthur Cane.* In *Children's Book Review Service,* September 1976, p. 6.

Mercier, Jean. Review of *New York City Too Far from Tampa Blues.* In *Publishers Weekly,* 28 April 1975, p. 45.

Nevett, Micki. Review of *Doris Fein: Murder Is No Joke.* In *Voice of Youth Advocates,* June 1983, p. 96.

Peasley, Rosie. Review of *The Me Inside of Me.* In *Voice of Youth Advocates,* April 1986–February 1987, p. 139.

Schon, Isabel. Review of *Where the Deer and the Cantaloupe Play.* In *School Library Journal,* May 1981, p. 62.

Schroeder, Melinda. Review of *The Dog Days of Arthur Cane.* In *School Library Journal,* January 1977, p. 99.

Steinberg, Sybil. Review of *The Mortal Instruments.* In *Publishers Weekly,* 4 February 1977, p. 83.

Sutherland, Zena. Review of *Doris Fein: Superspy.* In *Bulletin of the Center for Children's Books,* May 1980, p. 167

Uhnak, Dorothy. Review of *Doris Fein: Superspy.* In *The New York Times Book Review,* 5 October 1980, p. 30.

Wicher, Linda. Review of *The Great Computer Dating Caper.* In *School Library Journal,* April 1984, pp. 121–122.

How to Write to the Author
T. Ernesto Bethancourt
P.O. Box 787
Alta Loma, CA 91701

Francesca Lia Block

(1962-   )

by Patricia J. Campbell

When *Weetzie Bat* (1989) first burst over young-adult readers like a rainbow bubble showering clouds of roses, feathers, tiny shells, and a rubber chicken, some of the critics backed off in shock. They were puzzled by the freshness of Francesca Lia Block's voice and the originality of her Los Angeles–based vision and alarmed by her nonjudgmental references to sex and drugs. One librarian even condemned the book as "a glorification of pathological neurotics." But other critics were overjoyed with this unique new writer. They praised the sparkling delicacy of her style, her ability to pin down a place or a character with one striking phrase, and the strength of her underlying themes of loneliness and love.

Weetzie Bat went on to win a place on two annual American Library Association honor lists: Best Books for Young Adults and Recommended Books for Reluctant Young Adult Readers. The furor died down as timid librarians and teachers got used to Block's "strangeness" and young people dis-

> *"Weetzie knew by [her father's] eyes that he was going away forever."*
> —from **Weetzie Bat**

111

covered her with delight. Soon she had taken her place as a valued new voice in fiction for young adults. Since then Block has continued the saga of Weetzie's unconventional family with three award-winning sequels and a prequel—*Witch Baby* (1991), *Cherokee Bat and the Goat Guys* (1992), *Missing Angel Juan* (1993), and *Baby BeBop* (1996). She has also written two adult novels—*Ecstasia* (1993) and *Primavera* (1995)—and one other young-adult novel, *The Hanged Man* (1994), as well as a collection of short stories, *Girl Goddess #9* (1996).

prequel a book whose story takes place before an earlier book

Weetzie Bat

But it is Weetzie herself who first caught readers' imaginations. In an article Block wrote in the 26 July 1992 *Los Angeles Times Book Review,* she describes how the character first appeared to her:

> When I was 17 years old, my friends and I used to drive through Laurel Canyon after school in a shiny blue vintage Mustang convertible. We couldn't wait to leave the smoggy Valley we found so stifling, plunge into the canyon and come out the other side. On one of these trips, a punk princess with spiky bleached hair, a very pink '50s prom dress and cowboy boots seemed to appear out of nowhere, her thumb in the air. (P. 1)

the Valley the San Fernando Valley in California

They didn't pick her up, but her image stayed in Block's mind as the spirit of Los Angeles. Later, when they saw another blonde pixie with big pink harlequin sunglasses driving a pink Pinto on the freeway, the license plate WEETZIE gave the image a name.

When we first meet Weetzie she is sixteen, given to wearing spectacular costumes to school, and in love with the magical wonders of Shangri-L.A. Weetzie is sunny and sparkling, innocent but not empty-headed, and most of all she has a kind heart. When her best friend Dirk apprehensively tells her he is gay she says, "It doesn't matter one bit, honey-honey!" (p. 9) and gives him a hug. As the two of them seek their true loves together she grows from the experience, and when Dirk finds

Shangri-L.A. an expression for Los Angeles that refers to Shangri-La, a distant, beautiful imaginary place where life is perfect

his own Duck and Weetzie finds the older filmmaker My Secret Agent Lover Man, it is she who makes a home for the four of them full of beads and feathers and white Christmas lights and roses. Later she learns more about love from sadness, when My Secret Agent leaves her for a time when he finds she is pregnant by Duck and Dirk with the baby he has not wanted to conceive. The death of her father Charlie Bat teaches her the pain of loss, and from Secret Agent's return she learns the sweetness of forgiveness. When the witch Vixanne Wigg leaves Secret Agent's baby on the doorstep, the generosity of Weetzie's nature reaches out to accept the child into her growing family.

In the sequels it is Weetzie who holds everybody together as a loving whole: Dirk and his surfer Duck, My Secret Agent and their daughter Cherokee, Weetzie's mother Brandy-Lynn and Duck's mother Darlene, their friends Valentine Jah-Love and Ping Chong and their son Raphael, and Witch Baby and her beloved Angel Juan. As a mother Weetzie is warm and concerned but sometimes blind to troubles because she wants so badly for everyone she loves to be happy. Her greatest trial is snarly, tangly Witch Baby, who does not feel that she belongs. Weetzie reaches out persistently to her, even when Witch Baby rebuffs her with bites and kicks and runs away to seek her identity in Vixanne Wigg's coven. Weetzie's mothering style is casual, as when all the adults in the household go off to South America to make a film, leaving Cherokee and Witch Baby alone to test the precarious waters of sex and the rock nightclub scene. But even when she is far away, her spirit guides them, as they remember her counsel on birth control. In the winter gloom of New York City, where Witch Baby later goes to seek Angel Juan, it is the dead Charlie Bat's memories of his daughter's long-ago visit that warm the cold shadows. Weetzie's sparkle lights up these stories and holds back the encroaching darkness.

coven a gathering of witches

precarious uncertain and potentially dangerous

The Author's Life

Francesca Lia Block herself looks nothing like Weetzie Bat. Tall and dark, serenely beautiful, she has purple tilty eyes like Witch Baby and admits to feeling closest to that character. She lives with musician and writer Ted Quinn, a cat named Muriel, and a dog named Vincent van GoGo Boots in

"I wished I could write stories that made people react the way they do to music—sweating, dancing, crying."

decadent self-in-dulgent

the San Fernando Valley, just over the hills from the heart of Los Angeles. She has also lived for short periods in the desert at Joshua Tree. She tries to write every day. Dance is also important to her, so she takes time for classes in ballet, jazz, and Brazilian dance and has studied African dance.

As she told me in an interview for *Horn Book* magazine (January/February 1993), Block spent her early childhood in West Los Angeles and then moved to the Valley, where she went to North Hollywood High School. Her father, the renowned painter Irving Alexander Block, and her mother, a poet, nurtured her talent from the beginning. For as long as Block can remember she wrote stories, and her parents read to her and encouraged her work. At school she was in a gifted program and part of a circle of close friends who played imaginative games and made up magic lands and secret words. It was a peaceful childhood, but there were a couple of difficult years in her adolescence.

In high school Block and her friends were fascinated with the city that lay on the other side of the hills. "The short distance of the canyon separating us from Hollywood made that city a little enchanted," she writes in the *Los Angeles Times Book Review*. "There was Schwab's soda fountain where stars had been discovered and where we discovered strawberry sundaes with marshmallow topping." And there were the hip second-hand clothes stores on Melrose, a treasure trove for punk get-ups, and the Farmer's Market on Fairfax, where they gorged on a whole banana cream pie. "Our nighttime excursions were even more filled with decadent wonder." They "skulked down the aisles of Tower Records and slammed to bands like the Go-Go's, the Weirdos and the Cramps at the Whiskey and the Roxy. The music was intoxicating. . . . I wished I could write stories that made people react the way they do to music—sweating, dancing, crying."

Block went on to the University of California at Berkeley, where she majored in English literature. Workshops and classes in modern poetry helped her to find the concrete, spare images she had been seeking. She wrote a number of minimalist short stories and did her thesis on Hilda Doolittle (H. D.) and Emily Dickinson. It was a time of intense work and growth, but Block was lonesome for L.A. To comfort herself she wrote a little book about the punk princess, who had already been the subject of some stories and cartoons that Block had done in high school. She did not take the book seriously at the time, because it was so personal—and certainly not to be compared with her "real" writing for university classes. "But shortly after she graduated," I wrote in *Horn Book,* "a family friend sent a copy of the manuscript to Charlotte Zolotow of HarperCollins, who immediately recognized its quality and offered to publish it as a young-adult novel. Block was thrilled at the prospect of working with the famous editor whose books had been an important part of her childhood" (p. 59).

Sequels, Prequels, and Other Books

So *Weetzie Bat* became a reality. Under the guidance of Zolotow, and later Joanna Cotler when Zolotow retired, Block wrote two more books about the Bat family, and then interrupted herself to publish the adult novel *Ecstasia* with New American Library. This strange moody work uses poetry and fantasy to tell the story of a group of young people who live in a city of constant delight where, at the first signs of aging, they must retreat underground to a shadowy Hades. In its story of a lover retrieved from a subterranean region, it evokes the legend of Orpheus and Eurydice, as did Block's next Weetzie book, *Missing Angel Juan.*

Hades in Greek mythology, the underground home of the dead

In this story Witch Baby tells in her own voice (and in the present tense) how her clutch pig almost-mother Weetzie understands so much that she lets her go off alone to New York City to look for Angel Juan, who has left Witch Baby to find himself. Guided by the irrepressible ghost of Charlie Bat, she roller-skates through the city following a trail of unlikely clues. At last she finds Angel Juan in the basement of a fifties-style stainless-steel diner where the pale mysterious proprietor Cake has turned him into a mannequin. Charlie, in the form of a bouncing light, leads their escape. Later, the whole adventure becomes a metaphor when Witch Baby ponders whether Cake is the part of her "that wants to keep Angel Juan locked in my life" (p. 123).

A much darker, metaphor-laden adventure formed the plot of *The Hanged Man* (1994), Block's next novel for young adults. Built around the symbolic cards of the tarot deck, it is told by Laurel, who after her father's death is haunted with shame and fear. Her friend Claudia is being drawn down into a decadent world of indolent sex and easy

indolent lazy and easy

drugs. Laurel resists, but she gives in to her passionate obsession with the strange musician Jack, who appears intermittently and finally forces her to admit to herself that her father was also her lover. The identity of the enigmatic figure of Jack has been a puzzle to critics. Is he imaginary, a voice in Laurel's head? Or is he, as his tarot card indicates, a demonic apparition?

apparition ghostly figure

With some relief, Block's fans welcomed her book about the Bat family, *Baby BeBop.* In it, Dirk has a chance to tell his story—his agonized childhood struggles with homosexuality, his first love, and his ancestry. This last section gives Block a chance to try out some other milieus—such as San Francisco at the turn of the century and the dark intellectual world of the beatnik era. Block's most recent book's are a sequel to *Ecstasia* entitled *Primavera* and a collection of short stories, *Girl Goddess #9.* After that perhaps we can hope for a book about the childhood of My Secret Agent Lover Man in which we meet the eccentric parents who would burden a child with such a preposterous name. In the meantime, *Weetzie Bat* has been adapted for the stage by Ann Boyd and Julia Neary, has had a successful run at the Organic Theater Company in Chicago, and has been optioned for a film.

Pop Magic Realism

magic realism a style of fiction in which impossible or improbable events occur and are accepted as everyday occurrences

Francesca Lia Block's rich style, which she has called pop magic realism, is loaded with sensual details, allusions not only to colors and sounds, but to textures and tastes and especially smells that tell us things beyond words. In *Baby BeBop,* the beatnik Just Silver's fragrance is patchouli and incense and orange blossoms; Chinese/Jamaican Raphael Pong Jah-Love smells like powdered chocolate. Images are often drawn from food—Weetzie in her pink dress and white feathered headdress looks like a strawberry marshmallow sundae—and there is lots of wonderful multicultural eating going on. But even the celebratory menus are always vegetarian; the hamburger with which the evil Cake entices Witch Baby is the only meat in all five books. Parties in the backyard under strings of little white lights, "Love-Rice fiestas, Chinese moon dragon celebrations and Jamaican beach parties" (p. 46) show us the Bat family holding back the darkness with loving celebration of homecomings and overcomings. Dancing and making music, they are "like kids playing in the street before they have to go in for dinner" (p. 18), Weetzie tells Charlie Bat in *Missing Angel Juan*.

The City of "Devils and Angels"

Los Angeles is a pervasive presence in Block's work. Like Weetzie, she is deeply immersed in its magic, although she realizes its complexity as a place where it is "hot and cool, glam and slam, rich and trashy, devils and angels." Critics from other parts of the country have interpreted this unfamiliar setting as fantasy, not realizing that Block has rendered the lifestyle of the secret neighborhoods of L.A.—Hollywood, the canyons, Silverlake, the Melrose/Fairfax district, Venice Beach—with absolute accuracy. The streets, the buildings, and even the most fantastic-seeming details are quite real: the "fountain that turned tropical soda-pop colors" in *Weetzie Bat* (p. 4) is at Los Feliz Boulevard and Riverside Drive across from Griffith Park; there really are houses with roofs like spilled silly sand, and the bus that Witch Baby takes "up into the hills under the Hollywood sign" (*Witch Baby*, p. 89) is the Beachwood bus (I know because I rode it to school for years). The flowers, too, that blossom everywhere in the stories are the commonplace varieties in Los Angeles: poison pink oleanders, purple jacaranda, irises, and roses in a lush profusion of metaphors.

In the City of the Angels, it has been said, you are what you drive, so Block has enriched her characterizations with appropriate vehicles: Dirk's red '55 Pontiac, of course, but also Charlie Bat's pale yellow T-bird, Duck's blue VW bug, and Darlene's Volvo station wagon with a "Visualize World Peace" bumper sticker. The riotously mixed multiculturalism of Weetzie's world is also the daily reality of life in Los Angeles. The members of the Bat family are casually multiethnic, and so is their decor, their clothes, their food, even their party music and dance: reggae, surf, soul, and salsa. And the characters are drawn from California subcultures: the Santa Cruz surfer, the Sunset Strip punk, the aging Hollywood starlet, the Northern California hippie.

Their many voices, too, come from the many styles and accents in Los Angeles. Block's language has been misunderstood as "Valley Girl talk." Actually, expressions like

She describes Los Angeles as a place where it is "hot and cool, glam and slam, rich and trashy, devils and angels."

pervasive widespread

"slinkster-cool" and "lanka" were coined by her circle of friends in high school. Block is too savvy to attempt to copy current slang, and besides, nothing dates a book more quickly. But she does capture the way particular kinds of people talk and the types of things they say. Lists are a characteristic of her writing style, a kind of magical incantation of objects. So are outrageous names. "In my family names are a kind of a weird thing," says Witch Baby (*Missing Angel Juan,* p. 33). Take for instance, Duck's brothers and sisters, whose names sum up the hip interests of the sixties: Peace, Granola, Crystal, Chi, Aura, Tahini, and the twins Yin and Yang.

incantation the rhythmic uttering of words, particularly charms or spells

The Serious Side

Although Block's Weetzie books can be wonderful fun, underlying the sparkling surface is a dark sense of the world's pain, a sensibility that is even more apparent in *The Hanged Man* and her two adult novels. The comfort of love and family is her primary theme, but sexual love as a dangerous angel is a recurring motif, as is an awareness of the unnamed shadow of AIDS. Some critics have charged her with endorsing promiscuity, but a more careful reading shows that Block is celebrating faithfulness and love, even in unconventional relationships. Weetzie sums it all up when she looks happily around the table at her family and sees "all of them lit up and golden like a wreath of lights" (p. 88).

motif situation or theme

If you like the books of Francesca Lia Block, you might also like the poetry of Emily Dickinson and Carl Sandburg, or the books of Jerry Spinelli, such as *Maniac Magee.*

Selected Bibliography

WORKS BY FRANCESCA LIA BLOCK

Novels
  Weetzie Bat (1989)
  Witch Baby (1991)
  Cherokee Bat and the Goat Guys (1992)
  Ecstasia (1993)
  Missing Angel Juan (1993)
  The Hanged Man (1994)
  Primavera (1995)
  Baby BeBop (1996)

Short Stories
  Girl Goddess #9 (1996)

WORKS ABOUT FRANCESCA LIA BLOCK

Block, Francesca Lia. "Punk Pixies in the Canyon." *Los Angeles Times Book Review,* 26 July 1992, pp. 1, 11.

Campbell, Patricia J. Review of *Cherokee Bat and the Goat Guys. New York Times Book Review,* 20 September 1992, p. 18.

———. "People Are Talking About . . . Francesca Lia Block." *Horn Book,* January/February 1993, pp. 57–63.

Cart, Michael. "An Interview with Author Francesca Lia Block." *Noteworthy!,* winter 1993–1994, pp. 1–4.

———. *From Romance to Realism: Fifty Years of Growth and Change in Young Adult Literature.* New York: Harper-Collins, 1996.

Gladstone, Jim. Review of *The Hanged Man. New York Times Book Review,* 26 February 1995, p. 21.

Hearne, Betsey. Review of *Weetzie Bat. New York Times Book Review,* 21 May 1989, p. 47.

Jones, Patrick. "People Are Talking About . . . Francesca Lia Block." *Horn Book,* November/December 1992, pp. 697–701.

How to write to the Author
Francesca Lia Block c/o HarperCollins Children's Books
10 East 53rd Street
New York, NY 10022

Judy Blume

(1938-   )

by Maryann N. Weidt

Judy (Sussman) Blume always loved books. As a child growing up in Elizabeth, New Jersey, she visited the library once a week with her mother. When she was very young, her favorite book was *Madeline* by Ludwig Bemelmans. Once, when the book was due back at the library, Blume hid it. "I thought it was the only copy in the world, and I couldn't bear to part with it," she says. When her mother found the book, she told Blume she could borrow it from the library as often as she liked. Finally, her mother bought Blume her own copy. Then Blume played "library" by writing in the due date and checking out the book to imaginary patrons. Later, when Blume was a mother, she was thrilled to find her daughter, Randy, playing library, too—with the same *Madeline* book.

    Books were always a vital part of Blume's life. Often she would come home from school to find her mother curled up in a chair reading a book. Blume recalls, as an adult, forgetting to start supper because she had become so caught up in

All quotations from Judy Blume that are not attributed to a published source are from personal interviews conducted by the author of this article from 1986 to 1995.

a Joyce Carol Oates book that she had lost track of time. When Blume's daughter Randy and son Larry were young, she read to them every night before bed. Then she would go downstairs and wash dishes, all the while inventing what she calls "imitation Dr. Seuss" stories.

Blume knew she wanted to be a writer, but she was unsure how to go about it. So when she got a notice about a writing class at New York University, her alma mater, she signed up. The teacher encouraged her to continue writing realistic fiction, saying, "It's what you do best." Blume made a trip to the library and brought home stacks of books. Among them were Louise Fitzhugh's *Harriet the Spy* and books by E. L. Konigsburg and Beverly Cleary. "All of these books inspired me," Blume says, "but when I read Beverly Cleary's, I fell off the couch laughing. I knew those were the kind of books I wanted to write."

But the path to becoming a published author, Blume found, was not smooth. She collected her share of rejection letters along the way. "The first time I got a rejection," she says, "I ran to my closet and cried." With each rejection, however, she became more determined. Finally, she read about a new publisher that was interested in realistic fiction. Richard Jackson, then an editor at Bradbury Press, read *Iggie's House* (1970) and says he saw in the manuscript not just that book but "the next book and the next book and the next."

> **realistic fiction** fiction that attempts to depict life as it actually is (rather than portraying life through ideals and dreams)

> *Bloom says, "The first time I got a rejection I ran to my closet and cried."*

How She Works

Blume composed her first manuscripts on a manual typewriter she had used in college. Later she purchased a reconditioned IBM that she used until she moved to New Mexico. There she ordered her own red IBM Selectric III. In 1985, when she began putting together *Letters to Judy,* she converted to computerism. Now, due in part to her husband's interest in high-tech gadgets, Blume always uses the most current computer equipment.

No matter what she uses to write, however, Blume insists on having a special location in which to do it. "I've got to have my spot," she says firmly. In Maine one summer, it was a kitchen counter. In New Mexico, when she was finishing *Tiger Eyes* (1981), she rented a motel room because her teenage children and their friends had taken over her usual writing corner.

By the time Blume begins a book, the idea for it has been rolling around in her head for several years. Then she does what she calls "a tremendous amount of scribbling." Blume told Hilary Wilce of the *Times Educational Supplement,* "I keep a notebook, just scribbles and snatches of dialogue, before I start a book because the first draft is torture for me. Once I have that, I love the second, third, fourth drafts, and working with my editor. I tell the kids that once I've got the first draft I have the pieces of the puzzle."

Before she hands a manuscript to an editor, Blume has rewritten it at least three times. Then, after she confers with her editor, she does two more major rewrites. She says, "I'm the kind of writer who doesn't know what's going to happen until I write it. But I don't mind that. I like it."

Blume says the one person who has had the most influence on her writing is Jackson, her first editor. When Blume wrote her adult books—*Wifey* (1978) and *Smart Women* (1984)—which Jackson did not edit, she rewrote them by imagining him standing behind her asking questions. And, she says, he taught her the most important lesson in writing, one that she thinks about every day: "Show, don't tell." But, after twenty years of writing, Blume has come to trust the words will be there when she needs them. She says, "I know now that I can call forth my muse and it will come."

> *By the time Blume begins a book, the idea for it has been rolling around in her head for several years.*

muse In Greek mythology, the nine Muses are goddesses who preside over the arts, sciences, song and poetry. Today, the muse is considered a source of inspiration.

Who's Afraid?

Blume was born on 12 February 1938. As a child she was, like Sheila in *Otherwise Known as Sheila the Great* (1972), afraid of everything: attics, thunderstorms, even a stained-glass window in a church near her home. Like Sheila, she was so fearful of the water that she learned to swim with one foot on the bottom of the pool. Blume says that her mother, Esther Rosenfeld Sussman, was extremely timid and that she may have caught her mother's anxieties. Her father, Rudolph Sussman, was a dentist. Blume describes him as "an adventurous person who didn't get to live out his adventures. I wanted to be like my father, but in my early years I was certainly like my mother."

Although still afraid, Blume became more outgoing when, at the age of nine, she and her mother and brother moved to Florida for two years for her brother's health. This period in Blume's life is documented in *Starring Sally J. Freedman as*

Herself (1977), the book Blume calls her most openly autobiographical. In the book, Sally worries that her forty-two-year-old father will die because two of her uncles have died when they were forty-two. She establishes an elaborate prayer ritual, asking God to allow her father to live. When Sally talks to her father about her fears, she finds that he has had the same worries.

When Blume was a child, she, like her character Sally, agonized that her father would die young because two of her uncles had died young. On a larger scale, however, Blume worried about war generally and specifically about death at the hands of Adolf Hitler. Blume wrote in an introduction to the British edition of *Sally:* "When World War II ended I was just seven years old, but the war had so coloured my life that it was hard to think of anything else. . . . I knew that Adolf Hitler was a menace. I knew that he wanted to kill all the Jews in the world. And I was a Jew."

Blume's father did not die when Blume worried he might. Instead, he died suddenly of a heart attack at the age of fifty-four, just five weeks before Blume's wedding. The wedding went on as scheduled, because the date of a Jewish wedding, once set, may not be changed. But Blume was devastated by her father's death. However, she did not comprehend until years later the profound impact his dying had on her.

In *Tiger Eyes,* Davey's father dies suddenly when he is shot by a robber at his convenience store. Davey is overcome with grief—and fear. She says, "Newspapers are very big on facts, I think. But not on feelings. Nobody writes about how it *feels* when your father is murdered." How Davey feels is terrified. She sleeps with a bread knife under her pillow for fear that the robber will come back and kill her and the rest of her family.

Margaret Mason, in *Washington Post World Book,* praises Blume's ability in *Tiger Eyes* to get inside the head of the teenage protagonist. "She puts you inside that girl [Davey]. . . . In the proper cadence of grief—paralysis, anger, catharsis, gradual acceptance—you know how it feels, slowly, excruciatingly, over a school year's time." Davey, like Blume, struggles with fear, as she writes to a friend toward the end of *Tiger Eyes:* "I don't want to go through life afraid." She goes on to share a piece she found in a magazine. "Each of us must confront our own fears, must come face to face with them. How we handle our fears will determine where we go with the rest of our lives."

> *"When World War II ended I was just seven years old, but the war had so coloured my life that it was hard to think of anything else....I knew that Adolf Hitler was a menace. I knew that he wanted to kill all the Jews in the world. And I was a Jew."*

cadence rhythm in music and poetry; here, it means the natural progression of events

Problems? What Problems?

In *Then Again, Maybe I Won't* (1971), Tony's mother says, "What problems? A thirteen-year-old boy doesn't have any problems!" Blume told *Newsweek*, "My father wasn't a psychiatrist or counselor—he was a dentist—yet people of all ages confided in him. But not me. I was his daughter! I wasn't supposed to have problems. (At least that's what I thought.) And I didn't want to disappoint him."

Now Blume has become a confidante for the thousands of kids who write to her every year and share their problems. She says, "They write about their most immediate concerns—family, friends, love, loss, sex, school. The same concerns I had as a teenager. They wish their parents would acknowledge their feelings and take them seriously. They wish for unconditional love." Blume spent two years compiling these letters into a book: *Letters to Judy: What Your Kids Wish They Could Tell You* (1986).

Kids worry, Blume says, not only about their problems but about their parents' difficulties as well, especially drug and alcohol abuse. "They are angry, hurt, sad and fearful when their parents divorce." Some kids write and tell Blume that they want to die in order to end their pain. Blume says, "There are letters expressing such hopelessness and despair they leave me in tears." And when Blume's own two teenagers needed someone with whom to share their problems, did they turn to their mother? No. Blume remembers Randy, her daughter, telling someone, "My mother just wants to hear that everything is great!" Unfortunately, at the time her children were in their teens, Blume was going through a painful time in her life as well.

D-I-V-O-R-C-E

Three of Blume's books have divorce as the primary theme: *It's Not the End of the World* (1972), *Smart Women,* and *Just as Long as We're Together* (1987).

Blume wrote *It's Not the End of the World* at a time, she says, when, "divorce was happening all around us. I think I was trying to explain it to myself." In *Letters to Judy,* she says, "I wrote *It's Not the End of the World* at that time, to try to answer some of my children's questions about divorce, to let other kids know they were not alone and, perhaps, because I was not happy in my marriage. I kept those feelings deep

> *Kids worry, Blume says, not only about their problems but about their parents' difficulties as well, especially drug and alcohol abuse. "They are angry, hurt, sad and fearful when their parents divorce."*

inside. For years I would not, could not, admit that we had any problems."

The critic David Rees, in an article titled, "Not Even for a One Night Stand," writes that "the reactions of the central character, Karen, to the breakup of her parents' marriage seem to ring true. . . . The inability of even the most well-meaning adults to explain what is going on when a marriage collapses, in terms that a child can comprehend, is also well done."

Smart Women, a story of divorce told from a woman's point of view, is a book Blume hopes teenagers will read. She says, "It's a story about falling in love again at age forty and bringing to the relationship not only your history but your adolescent children as well." She continues, "I would like kids to be aware of what parents are feeling when they're going through a divorce." Blume's son, Larry, says he cried when he read the book because it made him think about the heartache adults suffer during a divorce.

Blume says she will never be rid of what she calls her "divorce guilt." "I was rebelling," she says, "in ways one should rebel at seventeen, not at thirty-seven. I think my divorce was all part of my rebellion."

Blume sees herself as an honest person. Yet she knows that parents are not always honest with their children. In *Just as Long as We're Together,* Stephanie's parents fail to tell her that her father's "business trip" to California is in fact a trial separation. As the reviewer Beryl Benderly writes in the *Washington Post,* "In the first of a series of damaging secrets that destroy Stephanie's peace of mind, her parents neglect to tell the children outright about their problems and plans. To the anguish caused by the split itself, this adds the anguish of betrayal; her parents' inadvertent duplicity wounds Stephanie deeply."

inadvertent unintentional

duplicity deceit

Sex Education

Blume calls *Forever* (1975) "the only book I ever wrote to order." The idea for the book came from Randy, who was fourteen when it was published. Randy, so the story goes, was reading what a librarian friend of Blume's called the "pregnant books." In looking at these books, Blume found that in most of them the boy was uncaring and the girl had sex because she was mad at her parents. In the end, the girl would be punished for her actions. So Randy begged her mother to write a book that was more realistic. Blume says, "Sex with responsibility, that's what *Forever* is supposed to be about. If you're going to do this, then you'd better know all about it and you'd better be responsible—for your body, for your actions, for your feelings."

When it came time to deal with her own children's sex education, Blume turned to books. She says her kids always knew the facts—and, to her occasional embarrassment, were all too willing to pass along reliable information to their classmates.

> *"Sex with responsibility, that's what* Forever *is supposed to be about."*

Still Censored After All These Years

When asked how she deals with the censorship of her work, Blume says, "I don't internalize it." Blume's first experience with censorship came about when *Are You There God, It's Me, Margaret* (1970) was published. She donated three copies of the book to her children's school library. The books never appeared on the shelves.

When Blume first experienced censorship of her book, she felt lonely. She says, "In the beginning, the publishers did not offer much support against censorship. Nowadays they do." And, Blume has discovered an organization that offers support as well: the National Coalition Against Censorship. She says, "The loneliness I once felt is no longer there. I now know that there are other authors whose work is being censored as well, and we're all working toward the same goal."

Almost all Blume's books have been censored at one time or another over the years. However, it is *Forever* that is targeted the most. According to a 1991–1992 report by the People for the American Way, *Forever* was one of the twelve most challenged books in the period from 1982 to 1992.

And it goes on. In the spring of 1993, Paul Peterson, a high school principal in Rib Lake, Wisconsin, confiscated *Forever* from a group of students. When he attempted to have the book removed from the school library, students hung posters on lockers reading "Censorship Sucks" and wore buttons that read "Judy Blume for Principal." Blume viewed this as a learning experience for the students. She told Hilary Wilce of the *Times Educational Supplement,* "They saw at first hand the process of book banning. They had to decide what they felt, how important it was to be an activist, they had to learn how to write letters and organise

internalize to change one's behavior or principles as a result of an experience

themselves. It was a lesson in real life. They learned about censorship and about how fearful some adults are of aspects of young people's sexuality."

On 14 March 1994, the school board in Mediapolis, Iowa, voted to remove *Forever* from district libraries. A librarian, Joanne McCabe, told *American Libraries:* "I wish there was some way that you could charge our community to deal with social and ethical problems [with which the book's detractors are concerned], but not by removing books from the shelves of our libraries."

As a way of combatting censorship, Blume established the KIDS Fund. Every year the fund grants money to nonprofit organizations working to improve parent-child communication. One year, money was awarded to a teenager who operates a hot line for kids who are home alone after school; another year to a group working with families under stress.

The Feelings Are Always the Same

> *"Velcro sneakers come and go, but that's not what really matters. The feelings are always the same."*

Blume's books have also been criticized for portraying solely white middle-class families. However, Blume maintains that young people from every level of society read her books— and they write to her and tell her their feelings.

Because Blume remembers what it felt like being a teenager, she is able to write vividly of that time in a person's life. She says, "Velcro sneakers come and go, but that's not what really matters. The feelings are always the same."

In an article Blume wrote about *Sesame Street* for *TV Guide,* she praised the program for its honesty in dealing with children's feelings: "Sesame Street characters show even the youngest children that they're not alone, that someone understands exactly how they feel."

Where Is She Now?

kayak (originally used by Eskimos) a light, narrow canvass-covered canoe with a small opening in the middle; the kayacker uses a paddle that has a blade at each end

Blume has learned, thanks in part to her husband, to enjoy many water sports including sailing, canoeing, and kayaking. "He is very adventurous," she says, "and he likes to involve me in his adventures." During the summer of 1990, the two thought they would try to kayak around every pond on Martha's Vineyard. However, by the end of the season, they had changed their goal to kayaking a different pond every summer.

During one summer Blume and her husband spent in Maine, she rode her bicycle a lot. On one of her cycling trips, she plotted out new adventures for Peter and his young brother, Fudgie. The result: *Fudge-a-mania* (1990). Bicycle Bob, the bike repairman on the island, became a character in the story.

At this point of her life, Blume was in love again—with her five-year-old grandson. She could barely stop playing with him long enough to write another book. She wrote in *TV Guide*: "We laugh together, sing together, dance together. He calls out letters and numbers and I cheer." And of course she reads to him. Perhaps someday soon, he too will be playing library with the beloved *Madeline* book.

Selected Bibliography

WORKS BY JUDY BLUME

Novels

The One in the Middle Is the Green Kangaroo (1969)

Are You There God? It's Me, Margaret (1970)

Iggie's House (1970)

Freckle Juice (1971)

Then Again, Maybe I Won't (1971)

It's Not the End of the World (1972)

Otherwise Known as Sheila the Great (1972)

Tales of a Fourth Grade Nothing (1972)

Deenie (1973)

Blubber (1974)

Forever (1975)

Starring Sally J. Freedman as Herself (1977)

Wifey (1978)

Superfudge (1980)

Tiger Eyes (1981)

The Pain and the Great One (1984)

Smart Women (1984)

Just as Long as We're Together (1987)

If you like the works of Judy Blume, you might also enjoy the works of Marion Dane Bauer, Brock Cole, Ellen Conford, M. E. Kerr, and Stella Pevsner.

Fudge-a-mania (1990)

Here's to You, Rachel Robinson (1993)

Audiovisual Materials

Deenie. Audiocassette, book, and teacher's guide. Old Greenwich, Conn.: Listening Library, no date.

Forever. Video recording. New York: CBS, distributed by EMI, 1978.

Wifey. Eight audiocassettes. Boston: G. K. Hall, 1980.

Freckle Juice. Audiocassette, book, and teacher's guide. Old Greenwich, Conn.: Listening Library, 1982.

Blubber. Audiocassette, book, and teacher's guide. Old Greenwich, Conn.: Listening Library, 1983.

The One in the Middle Is the Green Kangaroo. Audiocassette, book, and teacher's guide. Old Greenwich, Conn.: Listening Library, 1983.

Are You There God? It's Me, Margaret. Audiocassette and book. Old Greenwich, Conn.: Listening Library, 1985.

It's Not the End of the World. Audiocassette and book. Old Greenwich, Conn.: Listening Library, 1985.

Iggie's House. Two audiocassettes. Boston: G. K. Hall, 1986.

The Pain and the Great One. Audiocassette and book. Old Greenwich, Conn.: Listening Library, 1986.

Are You There God? It's Me, Margaret. Two audiocassettes. Old Greenwich, Conn.: Listening Library, 1988.

Otherwise Known as Sheila the Great. Sixteen-millimeter film and video recording. Pasadena, Calif.: Barr Films, 1988.

Fudge. Live-action television series. ABC, 1995.

Articles

"1975 Sequoyah Award Acceptance Speech." *Oklahoma Librarian,* October 1975, pp. 6–7.

"Tales of a Mother/Confessor." *Newsweek Special Issue,* June 1990, pp. 18–20.

"Hillary Clinton Toasts 25 Years of Sunny Days on *Sesame Street.*" *TV Guide,* 13 November 1993, pp. 8–14.

"Blume in Love." In *Metropolitan Home,* September/October 1994, pp. 85ff.

Nonfiction

The Judy Blume Diary: The Place to Put Your Own Feelings (1986)

Letters to Judy: What Your Kids Wish They Could Tell You (1986)

Judy Blume Memory Book (1988)

WORKS ABOUT JUDY BLUME

Benderly, Beryl. "Judy Blume: Junior High Blues." *Washington Post Book World,* 8 November 1987, p. 19.

"Board Pulls Blume's *Forever.*" *American Libraries,* May 1994, p. 390.

"*Forever* Saved (For Now)." *School Library Journal,* June 1993, p. 20.

Mason, Margaret. "Judy Blume: Growing Up with Grief," *Washington Post Book World,* 13 September 1981, pp. 9–10.

Rees, David. "Not Even for a One-Night Stand: Judy Blume." In *Marble in the Water: Essays on Contemporary Writers of Fiction for Children and Young Adults.* Boston: Horn Book, 1980, pp. 173–184.

Wilce, Hilary. "Dear Judy, You're Brilliant." *Times Educational Supplement,* 4 February 1994, supp. p. 2.

How to write to the Author
Judy Bloom
c/o Bantam DoubleDay Dell Books for Young Readers,
1540 Broadway
New York, NY 10036

Larry Bograd

(1953-   )

by James M. Brewbaker

"That guy is having my career." So observes novelist Larry Bograd of a popular young adult writer of the nineties, in some ways his rival, whose books are read widely by teens. In a 1995 interview, Bograd was philosophical—candid rather than bitter—about the derailment of his writing career, a derailment which began soon after the publication of *The Better Angel* in 1985. Having published five novels for teenage readers in six years beginning in 1981—two, *The Kolokol Papers* (1981) and *Bad Apple* (1982), before his thirtieth birthday—Bograd might well wonder what happened, might resent writers in the current limelight. Instead, he looks at his career objectively, regretting what might have been but also proud that he writes realistic, truthful fiction that high school students read and respect, even when conservatives attack its frankness and strong language.

Nearly fifteen years after *The Kolokol Papers,* a tense story of life behind the Iron Curtain, publishers—made wary

Quotations from Larry Bograd that are not attributed to a published source are from a personal interview conducted by the author of this article in April 1995, and are published here by permission of Larry Bograd.

133

by the fact that several of his books were attacked by censors—showed little interest in his work. After eight years (1987–1995) as an English professor in Denver, Colorado, Bograd, his wife, and his three daughters moved to Shaker Heights, Ohio, where he is a freelance writer and, as he puts it, "a mom." His wife, Coleen Hubbard, works with the Cleveland Theater.

Larry Bograd was born on 5 May 1953 and grew up in Denver. He was a high school freshman in 1968, the year when, in quick succession, assassins gunned down two heroes of many of that era's young Americans—Martin Luther King, Jr. and Robert F. Kennedy. Like others, he was shaken and angered by these violent events. Aware of the endless conflict with the Soviet Union, faced with the ugliness of the unpopular Vietnam War each day on the evening news, and sensitized by the civil rights movement in the South, Bograd's generation had good reason to believe that the world was a dangerous and frequently unjust place to grow up in, but it was also a place where young men and women had to contribute their energy to making things better. These beliefs led some teens of that era, Bill Clinton for one, to enter politics in later years. Larry Bograd, in contrast, became a writer who, through his fiction, attempted to help readers understand the social problems of their time. Bograd decided to be a writer at the age of nineteen; he wrote his first novel the same year.

Bograd's parents were doctors. His father emigrated to the United States from a region of Romania annexed by Russia. After completing their education in New York, the Bograds moved to Denver, where Larry was born in 1953. Though generally conservative, affluent people, they exposed their children to the issues of the day. When Bograd was nine, the family visited Washington, D.C. Inspired by Martin Luther King, Jr., poor people from all over the country had demonstrated peacefully in Washington that summer. Spotting a protest march, Dr. Bograd put young Larry on his shoulders and carried him into the middle of the demonstration. "My father wanted to make sure I didn't miss that. The father of a friend . . . well, he said that he would have headed for Baltimore when those demonstrators came along."

Bograd's European roots, along with a visit behind the Iron Curtain after his first year in college, provided an impetus for writing *The Kolokol Papers,* which portrays life in Rus-

> *Bograd's generation had good reason to believe that the world was a dangerous and frequently unjust place to grow up in, but it was also a place where young men and women had to contribute their energy to making things better.*

sia for a prominent dissident family. After several weeks in Romania and Russia, Bograd recalls, he began to feel the oppressiveness of life in the Soviet Union. He returned to his hotel room one night to find a minor official going through his luggage. The intrusion was a mistake, the man said, but Bograd realized that, as an American, he was not trusted.

In *The Kolokol Papers,* sixteen-year-old Lev faces many of the same concerns of teenage boys everywhere—in particular the need to be accepted by classmates, especially girls—but he does so at the same time his activist family is hounded by Soviet authorities. Lev's grim world is one in which a family member may be arrested and sent to a gulag, a prison for political prisoners, on trumped-up charges, or a so-called friend might report a careless remark to the KGB, the Soviet secret police.

Larry Bograd explains that he backed into writing for teenagers after he went to work for Harvey House, a small publisher of children's books, in 1977. Once Bograd had written for this age group, however, he believed he had found a niche that fit him well. Looking back today, he points out that his empathy for young people—and his talent for writing for them—is really part of a family pattern. Bograd's brother is a pediatrician and his sister is a family counselor who works with troubled teenagers.

> **dissident** one who disagrees with a particular belief, system, or organization (in this case the Soviet government that ruled Russia at that time)

Themes for a Complex World: Loss, Alienation, and Self-Discovery

Larry Bograd takes both his readers and his work seriously. In a brief autobiography he wrote for Donald Gallo's *Speaking for Ourselves* (1990), he pointed out, "I write the sort of books I wish I'd found as a teenager: no sugar coating, no mindless entertainment, but materials that would make me think." He went on, "My only rule . . . is to tell the truth, the full truth—and how people deal with it is their responsibility" (p. 26).

What sort of truths? For one, Bograd's books often portray adolescents coming to terms with the reality of loss, many times the loss of a loved one. Bograd's father died when Larry was thirteen. This event shaped his own teenage years and, in his books, is reflected in such characters as Maggie Chilton in *Los Alamos Light* (1983), whose mother

> *"I write the sort of books I wish I'd found as a teenager: no sugar coating, no mindless entertainment, but materials that would make me think."*

commits suicide, and Jack Karlstad in *Travelers* (1986), whose father died in Vietnam. Maggie and Jack are bright and resourceful; in time, they move beyond these traumatic events, building good lives for themselves despite losing a parent to a violent early death, but not without being marked by them.

A second reality in Larry Bograd's fiction is the fact that growing up hurts, maybe more today than in the past. He recalls a conversation with a high school girl following a talk to a group of students. The girl had read *Bad Apple,* Bograd's darkest, most complex novel, in which fifteen-year-old Nicky, who believes his only hope is to get away from his dysfunctional family, participates in an ill-conceived robbery of an elderly couple, a botched attempt that leads to murder. "This young girl told me that her younger brother had been driving her crazy. He was always getting in trouble," the author recalled, "But that, after reading about Nicky, she felt that she understood him better, felt greater sympathy for him."

"People don't realize sometimes that kids in trouble, kids like Nicky, are often troubled kids, seriously troubled," Bograd points out.

Like adolescents in every generation, those in Bograd's novels experience the pain of assessing who they are, how they relate to one another, and who they will become tomorrow. Jesse, Matt, and Natalie, his three narrators in *The Better Angel,* exemplify both the ambivalence and unpredictability of adolescence. Viewed as "good kids," they experiment, flirt with danger, and make choices, although not always wise ones. These choices sometimes involve drugs or sex. They behave inconsistently, displaying idealism one day, yet acting oblivious to the needs or feelings of others on the next.

In his autobiography, Bograd states that how people deal with the truth, as he writes it, is up to them. Regrettably, how many adults dealt with his novels was to restrict their circulation.

Aware of negative reactions to the gritty subjects and language of his novels, Bograd resisted temptations to tone them down. Telling the truth as he understood it and using the real speech of teenagers were each more important to him than that.

ambivalence simultaneous, contradictory feelings

Adolescents, both boys and girls, find Larry Bograd's realism appealing, a mirror of their lives told in their own language. One Iowa high school student observed that *The Better Angel* was "so close to what teenagers are like today." This novel was among the top twenty-five choices of four hundred student readers in the 1986 *Books for Young Adults Poll*. With more than three hundred eligible titles, books that made the final list were those that high school students selected on their own, read, and rated highly.

Bograd's Novels as Issues Books

Larry Bograd sees his novels as issues books, books in which a writer identifies an important contemporary issue and then builds a story and characters around that issue. In *Los Alamos Light,* the issue is the development of the first atomic bomb. In *Travelers,* it is the Vietnam War and the toll it takes on Jack Karlstad and his family a decade later; and in *The Fourth-Grade Dinosaur Club* (1989), for younger readers, it is racism directed toward young Juan Reyes and his Latino family.

The Arms Race and Nuclear War

In the seventies and eighties, many Americans, Larry Bograd among them, questioned the need to build and maintain more and more powerful nuclear weapons. Bograd's concern about this issue is central to *Los Alamos Light*. In this carefully researched novel, Bograd details from Maggie Chilton's perspective the story of the top secret development of the atomic bomb during the period 1943–1945, capturing for contemporary readers the urgency American scientists felt then to perfect, build, and test the first atomic weapon during World War II. In 1944–1945, with victory in Europe in sight, the American government and President Franklin D. Roosevelt were seeking a way to win the Pacific war without invading Japan, which they believed would involve the loss of many thousands of American lives. Atomic weapons would be the solution.

In the novel, Maggie, a Boston teenager anticipating her senior year in high school, learns abruptly that her father is to join scientists in New Mexico to work on a top secret

Pueblos members of an American Indian tribe of the southwestern United States who came from *pueblos*, or traditional American Indian villages

project. Maggie's life, already complicated by her mother's death, is all but torn apart by the move to Los Alamos. Maggie adjusts to her new home in time and writes news articles to send back to her old high school's newspaper.

Maggie is also sensitive to social issues. She questions the low status of Mexican Americans in the Southwest, and she begins to embrace values of the Pueblos she meets, one of whom teaches her how to make traditional Native American pottery.

Drugs, Crime, and Abuse

Bad Apple addresses issues of drug use, crime, and neglect. It is Bograd's most ambitious, most controversial, and—in the novelist's personal view—best book. A bleak story set in Brooklyn, it begins with what reviewer Robert Unsworth, writing for *School Library Journal,* called "a zinger of an opening. Fifteen-year-old Nicky is holding a gun to the head of his sleeping father. He calmly considers killing both his parents, but doesn't" (p. 70). Nicky is a mess and is victimized by his family. He is into drugs and petty crime and is easily led astray by others. Bograd tells Nicky's story through a series of flashbacks, each of which fills in a part of the plot. The story concludes when Nicky and a friend rob and subsequently murder an elderly couple.

flashback a section of a literary work that interrupts the order of events to relate an event from an earlier time

Bograd based *Bad Apple* on teenagers he worked with between 1976 and 1978 at Under 21 Covenant House, a shelter for runaways in Times Square, New York City. In his view, the novel is stylistically inventive while being realistic about what happens to kids like Nicky. Nicky's world, Bograd points out, is all too real. The boy, though a creation of fiction, is drawn from teenagers who are far from unique.

Books for Younger Readers

Both Larry Bograd's earliest and most recent books are for younger readers. Job hunting in 1977, he moved to New York City soon after finishing college. Before long, he found work with Harvey House. The next year he wrote the text for *Felix in the Attic* (1979), a picture book that paired him with the well-known illustrator Dirk Zimmer; the same year, *Felix in the Attic* won the Irma Simonton Black Award from Bank Street College. The next year, Bograd collaborated with Zimmer on a second book (*Egon*) and, in 1981, with the illustrator Victoria Chess (*Lost in the Store*).

Simultaneous with the negative response to his novels for teenage readers, Bograd began publishing fiction which found a readership among children in the upper elementary grades. *Poor Gertie* (1986) was the first. *Bernie Entertaining* (1987) and *The Fourth-Grade Dinosaur Club* (1989) followed.

Bograd points out that writing for and about this age group is quite different. The world of a sixteen year old, as well as his or her concerns, is bigger than that of a ten or eleven year old. "With younger characters and younger readers, a writer needs to stick pretty much to family and neighborhood, everyday life," he explains. "And you also need to have a light touch." Bograd's brother once told him that he was funny, but that his sense of humor never showed up in his books. "With these books, especially *Bernie Entertaining,* I was able to be funnier."

Despite differences between writing for adolescents and younger readers, similar themes and issues of Bograd's books for teenage readers appear in those he wrote for elementary children. In *Poor Gertie,* ten-year-old Gertie's single mother is threatened with eviction. *Bernie Entertaining* also deals with a serious issue. Bernie is led astray by an older boy who destroys a piece of jewelry with great sentimental meaning to his mother. Prejudice toward Hispanics is the subject of *The Fourth-Grade Dinosaur Club.* Billy Gelford's friendship with Juan Reyes is shaken when Billy, frozen by fear, stands by when bullies attack his Mexican-American classmate.

From the publication of *The Kolokol Papers* in 1981 onward, Larry Bograd's books for young adults have been admired by some, criticized by others. Andrea Davidson of *Voices of Youth Advocates* saw this first novel as "a fascinating, hard-to-put-down story," (p. 30), but Zena Sutherland, writing for *Bulletin of the Center for Children's Books* (p. 164) complained that "the story line is almost lost in the book's heavy emphasis on exposé and message" (p. 164). By this she means that the plot, rather than developing realistically, appears to be arranged to prove the writer's point.

exposé an exposure of an evil or a disgrace

Bad Apple was especially controversial. Some reviewers, like Robert Unsworth and Stephanie Zvirin admired *Bad Apple*'s innovations in style and theme. Zvirin wrote in *Booklist* that the novel "cannot fail to disturb and/or provoke thought among . . . mature, perceptive teenagers" (pp. 559–560). Others were put off by its dark tones, its pessimism, and its explicit sexual content. Writing for *English Journal* in 1986, teacher Sandy Miller nominated Bograd's *The Better Angel* as the one adolescent novel she admired most, because it "portrays real teens as they talk and as they behave" (p. 98). Ironically, it is this same quality which caused others, including profit-conscious publishers, to conclude that Bograd went too far in portraying the realities of the adolescent world.

Selected Bibliography

WORKS BY LARRY BOGRAD

Novels for Young Adults

The Kolokol Papers (1981)

Bad Apple (1982)

Los Alamos Light (1983)

The Better Angel (1985)

Travelers (1986)

Books for Younger Readers

Poor Gertie, illustrated by Dirk Zimmer (1986)

Bernie Entertaining, illustrated by Richard Lauter (1987)

The Fourth-Grade Dinosaur Club, illustrated by Richard Lauter (1989)

Picture Books

Felix in the Attic, illustrated by Dirk Zimmer (1979)

Egon, illustrated by Dirk Zimmer (1980)

Lost in the Store, illustrated by Victoria Chess (1981)

Short Stories

"The Reincarnation of Sweet Lips." In *Short Circuits: Thirteen Shocking Stories by Outstanding Writers for Young Adults.* Edited by Donald R. Gallo. New York: Laurel Leaf, 1993.

"Willie and the Christmas Spruce." In *Within Reach: Ten Stories.* Edited by Donald R. Gallo. New York: Harper-Collins, 1993.

WORKS ABOUT LARRY BOGRAD

Books and Parts of Books

Commire, Anne, ed. "Larry Bograd." In *Something About the Author.* Detroit: Gale Research, 1983, vol. 33, pp. 42–43.

Gallo, Donald R., ed. *Speaking for Ourselves.* Urbana, Ill.: National Council of Teachers of English, 1990, pp. 25–27.

Articles

Cline, Ruth. Review of *Poor Gertie. ALAN Review,* winter 1984, p. 23.

Conner, John W. and Kathleen Tessmer. "1986 Books for Young Adults Poll." *English Journal,* December 1986, pp. 58–62.

Gallo, Donald R. "Who Are the Most Important YA Authors?" *ALAN Review,* spring 1989, pp. 18–20.

Liggitt, Priscilla. "Growing Up in Los Alamos During WWII." *Christian Science Monitor,* 7 October 1983, p. B2.

Miller, Sandy. "Our Readers Write." *English Journal,* March 1986, p. 98.

Nelms, Ben, Beth Nelms, and Mark Vegel. "Starting Out: Personal Odysseys of the Young." *English Journal,* September 1986, pp. 80–83.

Reardon, Elizabeth. Review of *The Kokolol Papers. School Library Journal,* August 1986, p. 98.

Review of *Travelers. Kirkus Reviews,* 1 October 1986, p. 1507.

Sutherland, Zena. Review of *The Bad Apple. Bulletin of the Center for Children's Books,* May 1982, p. 164.

Unsworth, Robert. Review of *The Bad Apple. School Library Journal,* December 1982, p. 70.

Voices of Youth Advocate, December 1985, p. 318.

Wilson, Phillis. Review of *The Fourth-Grade Dinasaur Club. Booklist,* 1 May 1989, p. 1544.

Zvirin, Stephanie. Review of *The Bad Apple. Booklist,* 1 February 1982, p. 703; 15 December 1982, pp. 559–560.

How to Write to the Author
Larry Bograd
c/o Dell Publishing
1540 Broadway
New York, NY 10036

Robin F. Brancato

(1936-   )

by James E. Davis

For as long as she can remember, Robin Brancato has wanted to be a writer. The atmosphere in Wyomissing, Pennsylvania, where she grew up, provided a pleasant childhood experience. She has used this background and many of her childhood experiences in her novels, especially the first one, *Don't Sit Under the Apple Tree* (1975).

Early Life

Brancato was born in Sinking Spring, Pennsylvania, to W. Robert Fiddler and Margretta (Newroth) Fiddler on 19 March 1936. She moved with her family to Wyomissing at age four and lived there until she was fifteen, when she moved with her family to Shamokin, a coal-mining town in Pennsylvania. She spent her last year of high school in Camp Hill, Pennsylvania. To bury the sorrow resulting from the moves, she often read and wrote. Some of the books that influenced her were

John Steinbeck's *The Grapes of Wrath,* Margaret Mitchell's *Gone with the Wind,* Daphne Du Maurier's *Rebecca,* and James Thurber's *The Thirteen Clocks* (*Speaking for Ourselves,* p. 28).

Brancato graduated from the University of Pennsylvania with a degree in creative writing, a major she chose because it had fewer requirements than that of a regular English major. After college she worked as a waitress, hated the job, but saved money for a three-month trip to Europe. Following the excursion, she moved to New York City, where she served as a copy editor for technical books. Finding that boring, she enrolled at Hunter College to obtain certification to teach English. She also began writing for young adults at this time. Her first attempt at publishing was rejected; she still has this manuscript at home in a drawer.

In 1960, after a night class, she met her future husband, John Brancato. John had turned his back on a theater career, as Robin had on a textbook-publishing career, but they both loved teaching English. In the *Something About the Author Autobiography Series* she says, "Our being in the same profession always seemed an advantage. We've hardly ever gotten bored listening to each other's shoptalk" (p. 63). Their son Chris was born in 1962; Greg was born in 1964. When John was awarded a Fulbright scholarship, the family moved to Modena, Italy. He lectured at the University of Bologna, about twenty miles from Modena, and she learned Italian and taught school. Upon returning to the United States, they both resumed teaching English, but Brancato wrote in her spare time—first short stories, then novels.

John has been Brancato's first reader and editor, and her sons increasingly became her audience as they grew up. She says, "During the most turbulent years of their adolescence, they often unintentionally provided me with raw material, contributions that, in some cases, I would just as soon have done without" (p. 67).

> *Brancato on her sons: "During the most turbulent years of their adolescence, they often unintentionally provided me with raw material, contributions that, in some cases, I would just as soon have done without."*

Don't Sit Under the Apple Tree

Set at the end of World War II, *Don't Sit Under the Apple Tree* tells how that war, which began when Brancato was five, changed the world forever. Brancato has recalled that from a child's point of view the war brought excitement:

> The movies we saw made us wish we could join up and fight too. We got out of school to collect milkweed pods to be used for the war effort. Our fourth-grade teacher told us fascinating, gory stories about the capture of our enemies Mussolini and Tokyo Rose. Air-raid drills also broke up the monotony of school and created a seductive sense of danger. (*Something About the Author Autobiography Series,* P. 54)

Much of this background is worked into *Don't Sit Under the Apple Tree.* The setting, Wissining, is a thinly disguised Wyomissing, Pennsylvania. Songs of World War II, especially the song of the book's title, abound and add atmosphere.

The novel shows young Ellis Carpenter's maturation during a time of extreme turmoil—she must contend with the war's ending, a good-citizenship contest, her German grandmother's death, anti-German feeling toward her grandmother, and fund-raising for the war effort. Ellis has seen the yearbook picture of the town's missing war hero, in which he sits under an apple tree with his girlfriend, but Ellis has also seen that same girl kiss another boy. Her faith is shaken.

The movie *The Purple Heart* and other pop-culture icons are much referred to in this book, as is Emily Dickinson's poetry, particularly "I Never Saw a Moor" and "The Bustle in the House." Jules, the young brother of the soldier who is missing in action, runs away when he hears about his brother's death. Ellis knows where to find Jules. He had wanted to find the tree under which Les and Judy sat in their yearbook picture. He thought he had a message that told him to come there. There is no message, but Jules carves the lovers' initials on the tree. Ellis must also put away her love for her dead grandmother.

In *School Library Journal,* Cyrisse Jaffee calls Brancato's treatment of character here "sensitive and humorous," but she says that some of the characters, such as Ellis' father, are one-dimensional. All in all, Jaffee finds the novel satisfactory, especially in its depiction of Ellis' relationships with her grandmother, Jules, and her classmates (p. 52).

In 1942, **milkweed pods** were collected as a wartime substitute for a fiber used in life belts.

Benito Mussolini (1883–1945) was an Italian dictator from 1922 to 1943 and founder of the Fascist party. "**Tokyo Rose**" was a U.S. citizen convicted of treason for giving broadcasts from Japan to U.S. troops in order to destroy morale.

There is an article about Emily Dickinson later in this volume.

Something Left to Lose

For her second novel, *Something Left to Lose* (1976), Brancato again drew on her childhood and high school memories. This story tells of the friendship of three diverse high school freshmen. Rebbie, the rebel, is insecure, troubled by her alcoholic mother and neglected by her father. Lydia, calm and self-controlled, comes from a very stable family but is influenced by Rebbie. Jane Ann, the central character, is caught up in Rebbie's horoscope predictions, dangerous joyrides, cigarette smoking, and beer drinking. At the same time, Jane Ann is having her first romance and is bothered by her lack of life experience. Jane Ann's parents do not trust Rebbie; her family moves to another town.

Brancato juggles all of this well through dialogue and character development. Nevertheless, in the April 1976 issue of *School Library Journal*, Pamela Jajko says that Jane Ann is "a ninth grader whose thoughts and actions throughout are more appropriate for a 12 year old" (p. 84). In some ways that is the point. Jane Ann is conscious of her immaturity and wants to do something about it. It is no surprise that Rebbie idolizes rock singer Janis Joplin and that the book's title echoes a line from "Me and Bobby McGee," one of Joplin's hit songs: "Freedom's just another word for nothing left to lose." *Publishers Weekly* called the astrology portion of the plot "a deft touch, denoting the adolescent's desperate search for meaningful guidance" (p. 84).

Janis Joplin (1943–1970) was a popular blues singer in the late 1960s. She died of a drug overdose on 4 October 1970.

Winning

With *Winning* (1977), Brancato departed from her childhood memories. She took a year's leave from teaching to interview doctors and therapists in rehabilitation medicine to prepare herself for writing this novel. It is the story of a high school senior, Gary Madden, who is injured while playing football and becomes quadriplegic as a result. The story of his severe disablement is paired with that of Ann Treer, his recently widowed English teacher, whose tutoring of Gary helps her come to terms with her own loss. Gary's struggle to accept his condition is sensitively told. Brancato may gloss over some of the mental anguish, but her portrayal of the effects of Gary's condition on parents, friends, loved ones, and Ms. Treer is artfully accomplished. The book is moving without being maudlin, as it so easily could have become without Brancato's realistic plotting and use of language.

maudlin   overly emotional

Some interesting insights into Brancato's style, particularly her use of language in *Winning,* can be found in a letter published in the *Connecticut English Journal* (fall 1980). Responding to a junior high school student's objections to some of the language in *Winning,* Brancato says that she herself does not like "bad language" because it is usually unimaginative, but that an author's job is to record, not judge, speech. It is not to sell books or even to hold the reader's interest but "because sex and bodily functions and the names for them, both polite and impolite, are a part of life and I am interested in portraying life as it really is." If she fudges in language, how can a reader trust her in other things? She ends her letter with the hope that the student will come to agree that the most important thing in judging real people or characters or literary works is "not the purity of the language but the goodness of their spirits."

Brancato says that an author's job is to record, not judge, speech.

Winning is acclaimed by many as Brancato's best novel, and it probably is. *Publishers Weekly* called it "superior work" (p. 65). *Booklist* described it as "moving and involving" (p. 30). But not all criticism was so glowing. Karen Harris, in a generally positive review in *School Library Journal,* called the characters "not memorable" (p. 120). Most reviewers, however, found the characters, especially Gary and Ms. Treer, memorable indeed. The book was a Literary Guild Selection and an American Library Association (ALA) Best Book for Young Adults.

Blinded by the Light

Brancato's most daring research was in preparing to write *Blinded by the Light* (1978). She had been interested in religious cults since her college days and had done some library research on them, so it was not surprising that she would consider writing a book, especially with the notoriety that these groups were getting in the 1970s. Deciding that the best way to get firsthand knowledge was to be "inside" a cult, she attended a weekend workshop of the Unification Church, founded by Sun Myung Moon, and signed up for a three-day workshop that the group was holding in Westchester County, New York. Brancato says that playing the

notoriety   unfavorable fame

role of recruit may have been the most difficult thing she has ever done; it was not what the "Moonies" put her through, but rather that she had to pretend enjoying their attempts to make her dependent and mild.

Blinded by the Light is about Gail Brower's attempts to contact her brother Jim, who a few weeks before graduation has gone away with a Moonie-like religious group called the Light of the World. Gail is convinced that she can talk him into leaving the group, but his more realistic parents are planning a "kidnap." Gail eventually is able to talk to him after the parents' rescue attempt fails. Brancato tries to be evenhanded, but her sympathy (and the reader's) is with the bereaved family. Brancato makes interesting reference to *Antigone,* an ancient Greek play by Sophocles, through Gail's writing about it in a term paper; the reference highlights the conflict between family love and a higher loyalty.

Reviews were generally favorable, but some were mixed. A good example is Nordhielm Wooldridge's comment that the author was "heavy-handed in her manipulation of the characters' dialogue, actions, and thought processes. Despite these drawbacks, . . . the plot has the magnetism of suspense and the issue confronted is a refreshing change from the beleaguered old stand-bys."

In Greek mythology, **Antigone** defied her uncle to give her brother a proper burial. She was sentenced to be entombed alive. Rather than face an unjust punishment, she took her own life.

Come Alive at 505

Most reviewers agree that *Come Alive at 505* (1980) was not up to the quality of *Winning* or *Blinded by the Light.* The book is surely Brancato's most concerted attempt at wit. High school senior Dan Fetzer's main goal in life is to be a radio personality. He spends much of his time taping on his imaginary station 505. He enters a disk-jockey contest that he hopes will jump-start his career. The plot includes Dan's attempt to attract Mimi, a new student, and to help elect a nonexistent student president of the senior class.

It turns out that one friend, George, has supplied Mimi with amphetamines to help her lose weight, and she has become addicted. Her telling of this secret is accidentally recorded on one of Dan's tapes, which George obtains and uses as a form of blackmail. In addition to the topical subject of drugs, the book contains a teenage suicide and much profanity and vulgarity. The plot is not realistic, but Danny's disk-jockey patter is. This novel's genre is hard to pinpoint. Kathleen Leverich calls it an "old fashioned, optimistic adventure in romance" that will leave the reader "smiling and all-in from rooting and caring." That may be a little off, both on its assessment of genre and its critical estimate, but *Come Alive at 505* was selected as an ALA Best Book.

all in tired, exhausted

Sweet Bells Jangled Out of Tune

In some ways the leap from *Come Alive at 505* to *Sweet Bells Jangled Out of Tune* (1982) seems like a giant one—from winning a contest to rescuing a mentally ill grandmother. A chance sighting of her father's eccentric mother, Eva, leads Ellen to recall childhood visits with a strange woman who has become something of a bag lady. Ellen has been prohibited from seeing Eva for years because Eva is a petty thief and because her behavior is bizarre in other ways too. When she visits her grandmother, Ellen finds that Eva's only companion, a housekeeper, has died.

Believing that her grandmother's retreat from reality may soon do serious damage to herself and others, Ellen develops a compulsion to rescue her. This causes tension between Ellen and her mother, but eventually they patch things up and, with the aid of a social worker, get Eva committed to a mental hospital. As Russell Goodyear puts it, the book is about "two child-women. One, into her seventies, lives a life dominated by the ghost of her father. The other, just turned fifteen, struggles to escape the bonds of childhood." The plot is fast-paced; it has a fully developed character in Ellen, flashes of humor, a serious theme, Brancato's usual good dialogue, and sound insight into psychological cause and effect. For these strengths, the novel was selected as an ALA Notable Book.

Facing Up

Facing Up (1984) features a lot of dating, drinking, cars, and a love triangle revolving mainly around Dave Jacoby's best friend, Jepson, who is just one step ahead of the law. Dave both loves and envies Jepson, and when Jepson's girlfriend Susan hints that she is interested in Dave, he falls for her in spite of his guilt about being disloyal to his best friend. When

Dave realizes that Susan "plays the field," he stops seeing her, coincidentally just as Jepson has found out about the relationship. Drunk, Jepson confronts Dave and passes out. While Dave is driving him home, an accident occurs, resulting in Jepson's death. Dave's guilt almost destroys him.

Facing Up is filled with clichéd dialogue and stereotyped characters, which led Constance Allen to write, "It doesn't help to know that Dave rejects Susan when he finally 'faces up' to his own values. Nothing memorable here."

Uneasy Money

With *Uneasy Money* (1986) Brancato makes another attempt at a mainly humorous book. Mike Bronti wins two and a half million dollars in the New Jersey lottery with a ticket he bought to celebrate his eighteenth birthday. In addition to gifts for his family, he buys himself a car. He also starts a private charity, inviting needy people to write to him. The money and attention result in his ignoring family rules and learning that money cannot substitute for friends, family, love, or good conduct. One friend wants him to invest in townhouses, another in developing a theme park. His father wants him to follow the advice of an investment counselor. A lottery loser who bought the next ticket after Mike says he deserves half the money. Finally Mike is back at work at Beef-a-rama, a fast-food restaurant, painting a life-size Beefarama Bunny. Happiness is work! There is some humor here, but the characters are mainly stereotypical and the plot is contrived. The book does not present a pretty picture of human behavior.

Other Works

Brancato has not published a novel since 1986. Her part-time teaching of creative writing at Teaneck High School occupies her mornings, and she writes in the afternoon. Her short story "White Chocolate" appeared in *Connections,* published by Dell in 1989. Her one-act play, *War of the Words* was in *Center Stage* (1990). In an April 1995 telephone interview she reported that she had nearly finished a book, tentatively titled *A Time and Place for Us,* about an interracial teenage couple.

Brancato is still dealing with timely subjects and echoing other works from popular culture such as *West Side Story,* as the tentative title indicates. She has made frequent references to other literary works. Louise DeSalvo has said that these mentions are part of her magic—her ability to construct contemporary novels that demonstrate the intellectual principles of the works she alludes to, including *Antigone,* Arthur Miller's *Death of a Salesman,* Fyodor Dostoyevsky's *Crime and Punishment,* and Emily Dickinson's poetry. And Brancato does this "without compromising her ability to speak in a modern voice . . . a voice that young people will profit from hearing." DeSalvo is probably right.

Arthur Miller (1915–), an American playwright, won the Pulitzer Prize for drama in 1949 for ***Death of a Salesman.*** **Fyodor Dostoyevsky** (1821–1881) was a Russian novelist whose works deal with profound psychological, religious, and philosophical problems.

Selected Bibliography

WORKS BY ROBIN F. BRANCATO

Novels

Don't Sit Under the Apple Tree (1975)

Something Left to Lose (1976)

Winning (1977)

Blinded by the Light (1978)

Come Alive at 505 (1980)

Sweet Bells Jangled Out of Tune (1982)

Facing Up (1984)

Uneasy Money (1986)

Letter to Student

Connecticut English Journal, fall 1980, p. 105.

Short Story

"White Chocolate." In *Connections.* Edited by Donald R. Gallo (1989).

War of the Words. In *Center Stage.* Edited by Donald R. Gallo (1990).

Autobiography

"Robin F. Brancato." In *Something About the Author Autobiography Series.* Edited by Anne Commire. Detroit: Gale Research, 1990, vol. 9, pp. 53–68.

"Robin F. Brancato." In *Speaking for Ourselves: Autobiographical Sketches by Notable Authors of Books for Young*

If you like the works of Robin Brancato, you might also enjoy the works of Norma Fox Mazer, Kathleen Paterson, Ouida Sebestyen, Mildred Taylor, Sue Ellen Bridgers, Paula Fox, and Virginia Hamilton.

Adults. Edited by Donald R. Gallo. Urbana, Ill.: National Council of Teachers of English, 1990, pp. 28–29.

WORKS ABOUT ROBIN F. BRANCATO

Review and Articles

Allen, Constance. Review of *Facing Up. School Library Journal,* April 1984, vol. 30, p. 122.

DeSalvo, Louise A. "The Uses of Adversity." *Media and Methods,* April 1979, vol. 15, pp. 16, 18, 50–51.

Goodyear, Russell H. Review of *Sweet Bells Jangled Out of Tune.* In *Best Sellers,* June 1982, vol. 42, p. 118.

Harris, Karen. Review of *Winning. School Library Journal,* October 1977, vol. 24, p. 120.

Jaffee, Cyrisse. Review of *Don't Sit Under the Apple Tree. School Library Journal,* May 1975, vol. 21, p. 52.

Jajko, Pamela. Review of *Something Left to Lose. School Library Journal,* April 1976, vol. 22, p. 84.

Leverich, Kathleen. Review of *Come Alive at 505. New York Times Book Review,* 27 April 1980, p. 65.

Review of *Something Left to Lose. Publishers Weekly,* 10 May 1976, p. 84.

Review of *Winning. Booklist,* 1 September 1977, p. 30.

Review of *Winning. Publishers Weekly,* 2 January 1978, p. 65.

Wooldridge, C. Nordhielm. Review of *Blinded by the Light. School Library Journal,* October 1978, p. 152.

Biographical Works

Contemporary Literary Criticism. Edited by C. Riley. Detroit: Gale Research, 1985, vol. 35, pp. 65–70.

Something About the Author. Edited by Anne Commire. Detroit: Gale Research, 1981, vol. 23, pp. 14–16.

How to Write to the Author
Robin F. Brancato
c/o HarperCollins Publishers
10 East 53rd Street
New York, NY 10022

Robbie Branscum

(1937-   )

by Marjorie M. Kaiser

Welcome to Robbie Branscum's world, a realistic world in rural Arkansas, populated by real people, as the principal character in *The Girl* (1986) describes it: "Sharecroppers and little ones with no place to go . . . grannies who couldn't walk" (p. 59).

When anthropologists enter a community to record how people live and love and work and grow, they bring with them many questions, questions that can be answered only through patient and careful observation. They note the behavior, thoughts, and feelings of individuals of all ages in that community—how they interact with one another in family and community groups, how they survive the daily demands and ironies of life, what they value and believe in, and how they keep their dreams alive.

sharecroppers tenant farmers who use a part of their crops as rent for the land

The Storyteller

The **Great Depression** was a severe recession that began when the stock market crashed in 1929 and that lasted almost ten years. By the winter of 1932–1933, 14 to 16 million Americans were unemployed. Many died from a lack of food and inadequate living conditions.

> *"I think of myself as a storyteller and other people as real writers."*

And so a storyteller enters a community through memory and imagination to create for readers a picture of that world. With artistic perspective and a keen sense of narrative, Branscum retrieves a community, sometimes violent, sometimes quietly amusing, from her own past. With insight and design, she illuminates from her memory a time and place that no longer exist. Over and over, in nineteen novels, the writer invites readers into her rural farming area of Arkansas and into the daily life in tiny villages and on isolated farms during the Great Depression and the years of World War II. Readers in the 1990s approaching the work of Robbie Branscum will explore a community that is likely very different from their own.

Born to Donnie and Blanche (Balitine) Tilly in such a community, Big Flat, Arkansas, on 17 June 1937, Branscum knows what she paints for her readers. The writer's formal education began and ended in a one-room schoolhouse in Red Oak, though she was an avid and inquisitive reader from a very early age. At thirteen, after finishing the seventh grade, Branscum was sent to live in Colorado, where she resided next to a library, and she read her way through its contents. By the age of sixteen, she was writing stories, poetry, and songs. Raised by her grandparents in a family of natural storytellers, Branscum thinks of herself as a storyteller. In an interview with Hugh Agee in the *ALAN Review,* Branscum said that despite having had published twelve books between 1971 and 1983, she did not think of herself as a real writer: "I think of myself as a storyteller and other people as real writers" (p. 14).

In the same interview, Branscum openly discussed how much she relies for her stories on the family and community members she knew as she was growing up. Married three times, Branscum lived for a while in California. But by 1982, in her mid-forties, she moved to Eufala, Oklahoma, close to the Arkansas hill country she has re-created so lovingly in her books. A very private person, Branscum has one daughter, Deborah (nicknamed Debbie), to whom she has dedicated almost all her novels for young adults.

Five dimensions of the rural Arkansas community that Branscum creates in her novels will emerge for the reader who decides to know the writer's world. These dimensions provide the background for her stories of young characters in the difficult but exciting process of growing up poor.

Textures of Daily Life

Simple, weathered frame houses, many in ill repair, provide the center for all Branscum's novels. While characters come and go in their various pursuits, the home and the land around it stand as the heart of human activity in the writer's rural Arkansas. Iron bedsteads and handmade tables and chairs furnish the typically cramped dwellings. Water must be carried in, and food preparation and the sharing of meals are the focus of activity.

Chores govern daily life year-round—feeding animals, gathering eggs, milking, weeding and watering, picking vegetables and strawberries to sell and preserve, cooking, washing, mending, and so on. Making ends meet in the hard times of the Depression is the primary aim of adults and children alike, who are considered by outsiders as dirt-poor, gullible country hicks. In broad yet rich strokes, Branscum creates the hard-times, hard-work atmosphere with carefully selected images, most often from the natural world and expressed in the language of her people.

While pinto beans, greens, and cornbread are the staple fare in these farmhouses, special treats include spicy fried rabbit, baked possum, and crispy chicken. We see rivulets of melted, home-churned butter running down the sides of mountains of mashed potatoes; sweet baked yams; hot, fluffy biscuits; fried fish, fresh from the creek or river; and on the very rare and special occasion, yellow egg cake. Food is a central element in Branscum's Arkansas community. In every novel readers participate in the feasts and famines that Branscum's characters experience. The clothing worn by her families is hand-me-down or handmade, often of flour sacking. A ready-made dress is an oddity, indeed, so much so that a single store-bought party dress creates havoc. Children all make do with worn overalls and put shoes on only in winter to walk to the schoolhouse. A nail or two on the bedroom wall will hold all the extra clothing a person has use for.

This preoccupation with providing for the basic necessities of life limits the community's awareness of a world beyond rural Arkansas. Folks from "the city," though attractive to the young, are viewed with suspicion by adults. World War II is being prepared for and fought across the globe, yet readers of Branscum will get only a few glimpses of any of its impact in this isolated rural area.

> *A ready-made dress is an oddity, indeed, so much so that a single store-bought party dress creates havoc.*

The Power and Beauty of Nature

From the awesome harshness of tornadoes, storms, and droughts to the delicate sweet tastes of honeysuckle and persimmons and the soft blue glow of sweet williams discovered in a shaded hollow, nature dominates life in rural Arkansas. Ever aware of their reliance on nature, Branscum's farming families embrace its glory and live with its diverse threats.

Children learn at an early age how to give room to snakes and how to kill a rabbit or catch a fish for supper. Killing animals for food goes unquestioned among those in Branscum's community. The rare exception to this generalization is Johnny May in *The Adventures of Johnny May* (1984), whose agony over the need to shoot a beautiful deer to feed her grandparents provides a central theme of Johnny's maturing process. While every novel offers an assortment of pets, especially hound dogs like Brimstone and Sam Smith, Cheater and her menagerie of pets in *Cheater and Flitter Dick* (1983) best exemplify the friendship Branscum's farming families maintain with their animals. Sammy John in *Me and Jim Luke* (1971), for example, cannot bring himself to eat his side meat when someone refers to it as "Bessie."

In all the novels, the reader witnesses the life-death–new life cycle in the natural surroundings. Reflecting that process is the birth-death-rebirth theme in the stories of characters' lives. Grandparents die; crops are destroyed by storms; white-hooded arsonists level the barn. Coming to understand these crushing events, accepting the pain and loss but looking toward the future, ultimately brings growth for Branscum's young characters. Through her lean descriptive power, Branscum helps us see how her farming families depend on, appreciate, rejoice in, and fear nature as she exhibits her beauty and demonstrates her magnificent force.

Family Life

The makeup of families in Branscum's Arkansas farming community is remarkably consistent from novel to novel. The protagonists, from eleven to fifteen years old, are parentless. Living with grandparents, aunts and uncles, adoptive parents, a circuit preacher, or even alone, the young characters all suffer the desertion or death of parents in one way or

theme central message about life in a literary work

arsonists people who deliberately burn buildings or other property, especially with criminal intent; the white hoods refer to members of the Ku Klux Klan

protagonist the main character of a literary work

another. The most typical arrangement is developed in the three novels featuring Johnny May (*Johnny May* [1975], *The Adventures of Johnny May*, and *Johnny May Grows Up* [1987]) and the three featuring Toby (*Toby, Granny, and George* [1976]; *Toby Alone* [1979]; and *Toby and Johnny Joe* [1979]). The young protagonists, whether female or male (though most are female), must accept near-adult or adult responsibilities with little of the parental loving they yearn for. On the other hand, these characters gain strength through the wise if cool instruction of the experienced elders. All around this primary family unit, on which the novels are built, live other assorted families, but no one finds this grandparent-child family unit unusual or has the capacity to change the situation even if it should seem desirable.

In most Branscum books, the reader sees positive relationships between young protagonists and their caretakers. Nevertheless, these units resemble real families of the era, whether rural or urban, rich or poor, educated or uneducated. In all families physical abuse abounds in routine "whuppings," and even sexual abuse rears its head not infrequently (see especially *The Girl*). To balance that sadness, there are love and pride in these relationships, though both often go verbally unexpressed.

Education, Knowledge, and Wisdom

The one-room schoolhouse for children in grades one through eight is a central feature in Branscum's world. While the school setting and the idea of school are more important in some books than in others (for example, *The Three Wars of Billy Jo Treat* [1975], *To the Tune of a Hickory Stick* [1978], and *Johnny May Grows Up*), it is always there, an integral part of the landscape and the lives of the people. Used as a church meetinghouse and even, as in *To the Tune of a Hickory Stick,* a place for runaway children to live and to learn their lessons during one winter, the building figures consistently in the scene. Most folks in Branscum's community, however, value formal education less highly than they do practical knowledge and skills related to gardening, raising animals, herbing and healing, hunting, preparing and preserving food, midwifing, and, in general, getting along in the hard times of the Depression.

midwifing assisting women in childbirth

Children are kept from their book learning to work at home during picking seasons or when harsh winters make it too cold to walk to the schoolhouse. Formal exploration of history, geography, or literature interests only the schoolteacher and a few youngsters (for example, in *Johnny May Grows Up, To the Tune of a Hickory Stick,* and *The Girl*). Most adults and children much prefer active learning through authentic work and solving the problems and conflicts that they confront in their everyday lives in the community.

Despite the lack of extended formal education among those in Branscum's community, readers meet numerous bright and inventive minds of all ages. The author's young protagonists all reveal a sparkling curiosity about life, which they act upon in solving various problems and mysteries created by the silent stoicism of many members of the community. Sammy John and Jim Luke in *Me and Jim Luke* perhaps best illustrate Branscum's smart, if naive, young person growing up in an often contradictory and puzzling environment. And sprinkled throughout the novels are the wise elders who care for parentless youngsters. These individuals support the young and help them grow out of their self-centeredness while simultaneously inspiring them to hang on to their dreams. The warm, often witty and pithy guidance these elders provide comes from their life experience, their self-knowledge and understanding of others, and their religious beliefs.

naive lacking in wisdom of the world

pithy having substance; essential

Two Faces of Religion

Alongside these wise elders and a few sincere preachers, who are deeply committed to their Christian beliefs, stand others in the community who make a sham of religious commitment by their hypocrisy, pretense, and cruel manipulation of others for their own selfish ends. Thus, in both positive and negative ways, Branscum's community demonstrates the influence of religion on the fabric of life in rural Arkansas during the Depression.

Spud Tackett and the Angel of Doom (1983) introduces readers to the revivalist con man, and readers meet the dangerous cult of snake handlers in *The Ugliest Boy* (1978). Sunday meetings and revivals in the woods are satirized in nearly every novel. In *Me and Jim Luke,* the awful irony in the way members of the Ku Klux Klan justify their brutality

satirized ridiculed through sarcasm and irony

to others with their feigned Christian faith and piety escapes neither Sammy John and Jim Luke nor any reader. For counterbalance, though, readers come to know the youngsters who narrate the stories and live through their questioning about the meaning of salvation and prayer, about God in church and God in nature. While some young folks do get "saved" in Branscum's community, over and over they learn through experience and the good counsel of the elders that the real meaning of religion lies in helping one another and in kindness to all creatures on earth.

Since the mid-1860s, the **Ku Klux Klan** has opposed the social and economic advancement of minorities, particularly blacks and Jews. The Klan uses violence and fear of violence to accomplish its goals.

Growing Up in Branscum's World

Despite such detail, Branscum's books are not texts about the cultural geography of Arkansas. In each book's rich and historical backdrop, Branscum brings to life a small group of individuals and, in particular, an adolescent struggling to achieve an independent identity, groping toward mature behavior, and suffering toward self-insight. In twelve of Branscum's stories these adolescents are young women. In the other seven, the leading characters are male. But whether male or female, the adolescent characters standing out in relief on Branscum territory share certain characteristics.

Like adolescents in any culture, and in any fine literature for young adults, Branscum's leading characters struggle to know who they really are. This major task of growing up is made difficult for Branscum's young teens by the absence of real parents. Despite guidance from wise elders and others in many of the novels, these characters are often confused, rebellious, and selfish, resentful of having to do chores and being made to feel guilty about their irresponsibility. Two trilogies, the Toby series and the Johnny May series, allow readers to follow over time a character's growth away from self-centeredness and toward cooperation and the expression of self-confidence and generosity. In these trilogies, both Toby and Johnny May share with readers their sexual awakening and development. These experiences are similar to those of all teen girls, though perhaps they happen at younger ages in rural areas. These two characters suffer pain and disappointment as they grow in their abilities to relate to peers and adults and come to believe fully in themselves.

trilogy a series of three literary works that are closely related and share a single theme

Toby and Johnny May, along with Frankie in *For Love of Jody* (1978), Cameo Rose in *Cameo Rose* (1989), Cheater in *Cheater and Flitter Dick* (1983), Priscilla Sue in *The Saving of P. S.* (1977), and Nell in *To the Tune of a Hickory Stick,* are intelligent, determined, stubborn, and caring. Their brains help them solve local mysteries, as in *Me and Jim Luke* and *The Adventures of Johnny May.* These same characteristics help them survive the many emotional and physical hardships of their family situations and their environments and provide them with hope for a better future. In telling their own stories, the voices of these characters ring true. They reveal naiveté about life and consequently evoke amusement in the reader. Their speech patterns reflect both their rural upbringing and their intimate relationship with all of nature.

Similar characteristics of intelligence, determination, stubbornness, and caring can be discerned in the young male narrators telling their stories. In *The Three Wars of Billy Jo Treat, Three Buckets of Daylight* (1978), *Me and Jim Luke, The Ugliest Boy, The Murder of Hound Dog Bates* (1982), *Spud Tackett and the Angel of Doom,* and *Old Blue Tilley* (1991) male storytellers reveal in their voices the same naive local flavor as the female characters. Together, the voices of Branscum's young narrators sing a joyful anthem of celebration. In telling readers their stories of growth and hope, these Arkansas youngsters draw us in, and we cry and laugh and share their dreams for the future. Ultimately, we appreciate our own lives and are grateful.

Readers who choose one or more of Branscum's novels will engage with protagonists who find themselves in suspenseful and enlightening situations. They will also get a peek at the 1930s and 1940s in rural Arkansas, a time and place most younger readers can know only through fine, sensitive writing that draws on the memory and imagination of the writer but rises far beyond herself to speak to readers of all times.

> *In telling readers their stories of growth and hope, these Arkansas youngsters draw us in, and we cry and laugh and share their dreams for the future. Ultimately, we appreciate our own lives and are grateful.*

If you like the works of Robbie Branscum, you might also enjoy the works of Sue Ellen Bridgers, Katherine Paterson, Hadley Irwin, and Vera and Bill Cleaver.

Selected Bibliography

WORKS BY ROBBIE BRANSCUM

Me and Jim Luke (1971)

Johnny May (1975)

The Three Wars of Billy Joe Treat (1975)

Toby, Granny, and George (1976)
The Saving of P. S. (1977)
Three Buckets of Daylight (1978)
The Ugliest Boy (1978)
To the Tune of a Hickory Stick (1978)
For Love of Jody (1979)
Toby Alone (1979)
Toby and Johnny Joe (1979)
The Murder of Hound Dog Bates (1982)
Cheater and Flitter Dick (1983)
Spud Tackett and the Angel of Doom (1983)
The Adventures of Johnny May (1984)
The Girl (1986)
Johnny May Grows Up (1987)
Cameo Rose (1989)
Old Blue Tilley (1991)

WORKS ABOUT ROBBIE BRANSCUM

Agee, Hugh. "Robbie Branscum, a Natural Storyteller: An Interview." *ALAN Review,* fall 1983, pp. 11–12, 14–15, 45–46.

Evory, Ann, ed. "Robbie Branscum." In *Contemporary Authors, New Revision Series.* Detroit: Gale Research Company, 1983, vol. 8, p. 67.

Gallo, Donald R., ed. *Speaking for Ourselves: Autobiographical Sketches by Notable Authors of Books for Young Adults.* Urbana, Ill.: National Council of Teachers of English, 1990, p. 30.

How to Write to the Author
Robbie Branscum
c/o HarperCollins Publishers
10 East 53rd Street
New York, NY 10022

Sue Ellen Bridgers

(1942-   )

by Pamela S. Carroll

Her name, Sue Ellen, is sweetly Southern. When people meet Sue Ellen Bridgers in person, they think that she is a model of the grace, ease, and beauty of the American South. They are right. But if they stop there, they are wrong. Very wrong. Sue Ellen Bridgers is not merely a polite, gracious Southern lady; she is also an award-winning writer of six novels. Her books have earned a strong readership among teenagers because she deals directly with the full range of human experiences. She is concerned with the choices people make and the opportunities they miss. Her characters often find themselves in the position of trying to balance expectations their parents have for them against the goals and values they establish for themselves—much like the dilemmas many teens struggle to resolve.

Quotations from Sue Ellen Bridgers not attributed to a published source are from a personal interview conducted by the author of this article on 20 November 1988 and are published by permission of Sue Ellen Bridgers.

Love for Language: A Grandmother's Legacy

> *Her grandmothers, both of whom were talented storytellers and lived within walking distance of her childhood home, taught their granddaughter to delight in language.*

Sue Ellen Hunsucker (now Bridgers) was born to Bett Abbot and Wayland Hunsucker in 1942, in rural Winterville, North Carolina. Her grandmothers, both of whom were talented storytellers and lived within walking distance of her childhood home, taught their granddaughter to delight in language. When Bridgers was three years old, she became severely ill and had to stay indoors almost constantly for two years. During this time, her Grandmother Abbot spent many hours telling her stories and reading to her. Bridgers still remembers enjoying Winnie the Pooh stories and "The Little Engine that Could" and disliking "The Three Little Pigs" because the story has no divine hand to rescue its poor victims. Readers find that there is always someone who cares for victims in Bridgers' novels.

The love of language that she learned from her grandmothers' stories surfaced when Bridgers was in elementary school, where she composed poems for almost every American holiday. In high school, she began writing personal poems, several of which were published in the nearby Raleigh, North Carolina, newspaper.

Choosing to Be a Writer

style   a distinctive manner of expression

Her mother offered constant support for Bridgers' early writing attempts. After she saved her money and bought a typewriter, her mother would not allow friends to interrupt her daughter's typing. Bridgers describes the "double life" she led as an adolescent: at school, she was a popular cheerleader and a member of the band, chorus, and other clubs; at home, she was a serious writer. She learned early, with her mother's help, that girls have choices just as boys do, and she chose to be a solitary writer as well as a social participant in her school and community. Bridgers was also a voracious reader. She often became so involved in her reading that she temporarily adopted the author's writing style. For example, when she read Thomas Wolfe's flowing prose, she claims that she "flowed a little" herself. When she read Ernest Hemingway, her own writing became choppy and full of understated meanings (see *Something About the Author*).

Despite her early popularity at school and success as a writer, Bridgers' adolescent years were not always happy. Her home life was strained because of her father's chronic depression. At age twenty-one he had been a successful tobacco farmer and mayor of Winterville; tragically, when Bridgers was only eleven, he began suffering depression so severe that he often had to stay in the hospital. The pain that she felt for her father was powerful, but it was balanced by the incredible strength that she saw her mother, Bett, demonstrate. Bett raised the Hunsucker children in as normal a setting as possible. She became her daughter's example of a loving, strong woman, the kind of woman readers see in Jane Flanagan of *All Together Now* (1980) and in Bliss Jackson of *Notes for Another Life* (1981). Bridgers still enjoys spending family time with her mother, sister, and other relatives; her father died in 1985.

In 1960, Bridgers graduated from high school and that fall entered Eastern Carolina State College (now Eastern Carolina University). An active member of the college literary magazine staff, she met an English instructor, Ben Bridgers. The two married in 1963. The next year, with his bride's full support, Ben joined the Air Force, and the couple moved to Mississippi. Bridgers was not able to finish her college degree before she left Eastern Carolina State, but she did not choose to ignore her art in order to be a wife and then a mother; her talent for writing would reappear.

In the next few years, the Bridgers lived in Mississippi, where their daughter, Elizabeth Abbot, was born in 1963. The Air Force moved the young family far away—to South Dakota—where Elizabeth's sister, Jane Bennett, was born in 1966. In 1967, Ben left the Air Force to enroll in law school. The family moved homeward to the University of North Carolina at Chapel Hill, where their son, Sean MacKensie, was born in 1968.

With Ben's career as an attorney beginning, the family relocated to the small town of Sylva, North Carolina, which remained their home into the 1990s. Bridgers, a young mom, enrolled part-time at nearby Western Carolina University (WCU). She spent several years writing short stories that were published in small literary magazines and women's magazines, including *Redbook*. Finally, in 1976, her dedication to writing really began to bring rewards. Bridgers' first novel, *Home Before Dark,* was published, and she graduated with honors from Western Carolina University in the same year. Soon she earned a fellowship to attend the prestigious Breadloaf Writers' Conference in Vermont. As she recalls in *Something About the Author* (p.49), Bridgers shyly showed her book to another Breadloaf participant, Toni Morrison, the writer who would go on to win writing's highest prize, the Nobel Prize for Literature, in 1993.

Talking to Characters

> *A novel begins, for her, at the moment that "a person, a visual impression, a physical presence" appears in her imagination.*

Bridgers claims that her books are "character driven." A novel begins, for her, at the moment that "a person, a visual impression, a physical presence" appears in her imagination. Bridgers explains, for example: "The first sentence of *Notes for Another Life* was written on the edge of a pocket calendar because I was driving the car at the time. I heard a girl and her grandmother singing old popular songs, and I knew where they were going and why" (*Something About the Author*, p. 48). She spends a year asking the character in her mind, "'Who are you? What do you want?'" ("Notes from a Guerrilla" speech). She does not write outlines or plot summaries during that year. Instead, she jots notes about the character and drops the notes into a folder she reads through later; she imagines the character's reactions to the real-life events she experiences and the daily choices people make, such as watching sunsets and shopping for groceries. When she actually sits in front of her word processor to begin a book, it almost writes itself.

Characters and Their Choices

Following are some of the popular characters who have appeared in Bridgers' imagination and demanded that she tell their stories:

First is fourteen-year-old Stella Mae Willis, a sharecropper's daughter in *Home Before Dark* (1976), who learns the importance of feeling connected to a home. Stella understands her father's choice to return to the family's land even when it means working as a laborer for his own brother. And she finally learns that it is not a building or any other material possession, but a decision to belong, that fills her need for a home. Bridgers' loyalty to the eastern North Carolina tobacco farms she knew as a child is obvious in *Home Before Dark*.

Next there is Casey, the twelve year old in *All Together Now* who leads her friend Dwayne, who is mentally disabled, to believe that she is a boy so that he will play baseball with her. Casey is living with her loving grandparents, the Flanagans, during the summer, while her father is fighting in the Korean War and her mother is distracting herself by singing in a nightclub. When Casey becomes ill with what the Flanagans fear is polio, Dwayne discovers that Casey is really a girl, and he accepts her as she is. Dwayne and her grandparents teach Casey the value of love and honesty among family and friends, a lesson Bridgers learned from her own grandmothers.

Wren is a talented teenage pianist in *Notes for Another Life*. Wren's mother, Karen, chooses to leave her children with their grandparents so that she can pursue a career. In contrast, Wren's grandmother, Bliss, devotes her life to nurturing and caring for her family and friends. Wren struggles with the choice of following her mother's example and pursuing a career—as a concert pianist—or of following her grandmother's lead and sacrificing her talent to raise a family.

Wren and her brother, Kevin, also have a serious problem with their father, Tom. Tom is frequently hospitalized with severe depression. Bliss is tormented because she feels that Tom's illness is somehow her fault. Bridgers admits that she feels especially close to Bliss because she, like Bliss, feels the need to care for and nurture others. Also like Bliss, she has experienced the pain of believing that a family member's mental illness was related to her own weaknesses. Bliss's feelings speak eloquently for Bridgers, who suffered through her father's mental illness: "Nothing could have lessened the guilt she'd felt all these years, the agonizing soul-searching she'd spent silently replaying scene after scene between herself and [him]. Where had she gone wrong?" (*Notes for Another Life*, p. 33).

In *Sara Will* (1985), the reader first comes to know Sara Will Burney and her sister, Swanee Hope. Sara has never married, and she has grown set in her orderly, self-centered ways. Her sister is a widow who enjoys people and changes in the routines of country living. Their lives quickly change when teenage Eva, a near-relative, arrives on the scene carrying her infant daughter, Rachel. Attention to a woman's choice to protect and control her feelings (in Sara), the contrasting decision to reach out to others and enjoy life (in

The **Korean War** (1950–1953) was the first war in which the United Nations played a military role. The conflict began with Communist-ruled North Korea's invasion of South Korea. It was one of the bloodiest wars in history.

Polio (poliomyelitis) is a serious disease that affects the central nervous system, which can cause paralysis. Several severe epidemics in the U.S. led to the development of an effective vaccine in 1952. Polio has been nearly eliminated in developed countries.

Swanee), and the nonjudgmental treatment of the teenage mother (in *Eva*) reflect issues that are important to Bridgers as a woman and as a writer. This book is more appropriate for adult readers than for teens because of its focus on the lives and concerns of the adult Burney sisters.

In *Permanent Connections* (1987), readers are introduced to Rob and Ellery, teenagers who feel out of place and alone in the tiny North Carolina mountain town where they find themselves one summer. Rob is sent there to live with his father's relatives as punishment for getting involved with drugs and troublemakers in his New Jersey home. Ellery is there as a consequence of her mother's divorce and the reordering of life that her mother has begun. Rob grows extremely dependent on the free-spirited Ellery. Bridgers' concern with women's ability to resist others' demands on their time and emotions is evident when Ellery finally chooses to level with Rob. "'You expect too much'" (p. 167) and "'You wear me out. You make me hurt you and I don't want to'" (p. 169). These are words that Bridgers wishes that all young women could use when others expect too much from them.

In *Keeping Christina* (1993), readers meet a girl who seems like an ideal best friend. Once Christina, a new girl in school, enters the picture, Annie Gerhardts' seemingly perfect world begins to unravel. Annie befriends Christina, but the new girl begins to abuse the friendship. Annie does not know what to do, because her mother expects her always to be sweet to peers, even though she encourages her, in contrast, to protest an unfair school policy. Consequently, even when Christina betrays her, Annie believes she should not complain. The novel ends with unanswered questions about Christina's dangling character.

Like many mothers, Annie's mom sends the confused teenager conflicting messages: she wants sweet Annie to ignore her misgivings about Christina, yet she insists that Annie publicly voice her disagreement with the school administration. Bridgers' sincere concern with showing readers that they have choices, regardless of others' expectations, is clear in *Keeping Christina*. The character of Christina emerged in Bridgers' imagination as a fictitious response to a woman who, at one time, became overdependent on the Bridgers family. The writer's decision to extract the woman from her

> *Bridgers' sincere concern with showing readers that they have choices, regardless of others' expectations, is clear in Keeping Christina.*

family was a painful process that Bridgers refers to only in carefully selected, purposefully vague terms (see "Notes from a Guerrilla" speech).

Southern Speech and Universal Thoughts

How is it that Bridgers creates characters who speak so clearly to middle and high school readers? One answer is the characters use the natural, believable language of the South. Southern dialect is used subtly in most of her books but is obvious in the speech of older characters, like Grandpa in *Permanent Connections*: "I got baptized, didn't I? . . . Raised this family thataway. Saw to it all you young 'uns got dipped in the Little Tennessee . . ." (p. 155). An example of her characteristic reliance on natural, earthy details is in *Home Before Dark*: "Outside the sky moved slowly, still exhausted from the storm" (p. 78).

dialect a regional form of a language

A more important answer, perhaps, is that Bridgers can speak to teenagers because she understands and sympathizes with their struggles to become individuals while they maintain connections with their family and friends. In her "Writing for My Life" speech, Bridgers makes a statement that could be an adolescent's motto: "Everyday, recognizing choices challenges me to think for myself, to take responsibility for my work, to make decisions that reflect concern for other people, but for myself, too." Teenagers are drawn to her novels because she understands that "life for them is so often a series of explosions, of destroyed boundaries and tattered emotions. There is so little they can control." Bridgers' characters deal with issues concerning family, relationships, and values that are important to the writer. They trust her to tell their stories because she shows them that they have choices and that they are important.

When she is at home, Bridgers is likely to be working at her word processor or reading a book by one of her favorite writers, Katherine Paterson, Anne Tyler, Toni Morrison, or Reynolds Price. Or, she may be curled up with *The New Yorker* or *Ms.*, her favorite magazines (see *Presenting Sue Ellen Bridgers*). She recommends Reynolds Price's *A Long and Happy Life* for any reader who wants to understand where she is coming from as a

There is an article about Katherine Paterson in volume 2.

A Long and Happy Life (1962), by **Reynolds Price,** is the story of a truly good woman who learns about love as she dreams of "a long and happy life."

bombast pretentious language

patriarchal a system of society in which fathers or other male figures control most of the power.

If you like the works of Sue Ellen Bridgers, you will also want to read novels by these writers: Maya Angelou, Katherine Paterson, Ouida Sebestyen, and Cythia Voigt. Like Bridgers, they write beautifully about families, relationships, and values, and they celebrate the strengths of young women.

writer, with the claim that his novel is, "The book that showed me what I could do . . . that validates my life."

Bridgers also spends time speaking about her writing with groups of teachers and to advocates of literature for young adults. She frequently gives direct attention to women's issues when she speaks to groups such as the Assembly on Literature for Adolescents of the National Council of Teachers of English (ALAN) and is thus true to her own goal: "In my writing world, as in my real world, I want to give women priority" ("Notes from a Guerrilla" speech). Bridgers' brand of feminism is not the brash bombast that easily offends people. She does not bash men or blame them for all the problems women face in today's society. She includes men and women in her eloquent vision of a feminist stance for the late twentieth century:

> **I want a strategy for living that embraces spirituality, that frees both men and women from a patriarchal mind-set that dominates the rearing of our children even when so many children are being reared by women alone. I want a strategy that brings men in touch with their tenderness and women in touch with their choices. I want a strategy that is not power-based but that acknowledges that we are part of the whole and that this fragile earth needs our help.** ("Notes from a Guerrilla" speech)

Bridgers is committed to writing books that show young men and women that they have choices. Through her creation of small-town southern settings, lyric southern names, and turns of phrase, and with her attention to significant issues, she gently pushes readers to think about what we expect young women and men to be in our society.

Selected Bibliography

WORKS BY SUE ELLEN BRIDGERS

Novels

> *Home before Dark* (1976)
> *All Together Now* (1980)

Notes for Another Life (1981)
Sara Will (1985)
Permanent Connections (1987)
Keeping Christina (1993)

Selected Short Stories for Young Adults

"The Beginning of Something." In *Visions*. Edited by Donald R. Gallo. New York: Dell, 1987, pp. 214–228.

"Home before Dark." *Redbook,* July 1976.

"Life's a Beach." In *Connections*. Edited by Donald R. Gallo. New York: Dell, 1990, pp. 183–199.

Articles About Writing

"Acceptance Speech for the ALAN Award." *ALAN Review,* winter 1986, pp. 51–52.

"My Life in Fiction." *ALAN Review,* fall 1990, pp. 2–5.

"People, Families, and Mothers." *ALAN Review,* fall 1981, pp. 1–4.

"Responding to the Magic: Sue Ellen Bridgers Talks about Writing" [published interview with Anthony L. Manna and Sue Misheff]. *ALAN Review,* winter 1986, pp. 56–61.

"Stories My Grandmother Told Me, Part One." *ALAN Review,* fall 1985, pp. 44–47.

"Stories My Grandmother Told Me, Part Two." *ALAN Review,* winter 1986, pp. 53–55.

"Sue Ellen Bridgers." In *Something About the Author Autobiography Series*. Edited by Adele Sarkissian. Detroit: Gale Research, 1984, vol. 1, pp. 39–52.

Selected Speeches

"Finding Time." Unpublished. Given at the North Carolina Women Writers' Conference. "No More Tears." Unpublished. Given to several various audiences.

"Notes from a Guerrilla." Unpublished. Originally given at Northern Illinois University; abbreviated version given to an audience at the Annual ALAN Workshop, Orlando, Florida, November 1994.

"The Wisdom of Fiction." Unpublished. Given to several various audiences.

"Writing for My Life." Unpublished. Given to several various audiences.

How to Write to the Author
Sue Ellen Bridgers
Box 248
Sylva, NC 28779

WORKS ABOUT SUE ELLEN BRIDGERS

Carroll, Pamela S. *Sue Ellen Bridgers' Southern Literature for Young Adults*. Unpublished Ph.D. dissertation, December 1989, Auburn University, Auburn, Alabama.

Hipple, Theodore W. *Presenting Sue Ellen Bridgers*. Boston: Twayne, 1990.

Bruce Brooks

(1950-   )

by Chris Crowe

Meticulous. Fastidious. Precise. Those are the first descriptions that come to mind when you meet Bruce Brooks. His clothes, stylish and attractive, hang on him just right. His prematurely gray hair is perfectly groomed. He moves easily, talks smoothly. His eyes sparkle with intelligence, sincerity, and intensity. Smiles come frequently and readily when he speaks. He is erudite, warm, and witty. You look at him and you think, "He knows what he is doing, and he is doing it well."

You get a similar impression from reading his work. Brooks's writing is careful and precise. The protagonists in his novels—Jerome, Sib, Sam, Asa—are talented and smart, extremely smart, but also realistic. The language in his books is meticulous and calculated. When the action is fast and tense, sentences are short and tight, pulling you into the tension right along with the character. When a character is in a helpless situation, Brooks uses the passive voice to reinforce the reader's impression of the character's helplessness. The

Quotations from Bruce Brooks that are not attributed to a published source are from an unpublished personal interview conducted by the author of this article on 4 May 1995 and are published here by permission of Bruce Brooks.

passive voice a manner of writing in which the subject of a sentence is acted upon

details are always accurate, whether they are about how to dribble a basketball, the complexities of a cello performance, the life of a child with an alcoholic parent, or how predators make their kills. His fiction moves you; his nonfiction informs you—and vice versa. When you finish a book by Brooks, you think, "He knows what he is doing, and he is doing it well."

The Man

Brooks was born in Washington, D.C., on 23 September 1950 and lived his early childhood in Wilmington, North Carolina. As Brooks told Leonard Marcus in his 27 July 1990 interview in *Publishers Weekly,* his childhood was "broken-up, improvised, not the classic family setup" (p. 214). When Brooks was six years old, his parents divorced, and his life became unsettled as he endured repeated moves between homes in Wilmington, North Carolina, and Washington, D.C. His mother, who was an alcoholic, suffered a series of nervous breakdowns, one of which prompted Brooks to leave home when he was twelve years old to live with his grandmother in Washington, D.C.

The many changes in his childhood—new houses, new schools, and new friends—deeply affected Brooks. As the perpetual new kid in school, he never felt that he was among peers. "I was always somewhat different from everyone else. I was always the Yankee kid in the South, and when I went back to the North I was always the Southern kid. It led me to simply be very watchful," he is quoted as saying in *Something About the Author* (p. 23). He was both watchful and sensitive. "If you called me something horrible, I definitely felt victimized and hurt, and I worried long and angrily about what you had against me," he says in *Boys Will Be* (p. 13).

One constant in Brooks's life was his fascination with reading and writing. When he began reading stories about Dick and Jane, Tarzan, and Crusader Rabbit, he felt invited to collaborate—and did—making up stories as he read. Soon he was writing his own stories, one of the first titled "The Two Junior Detectives Catch the Bad Guys Underground"; later he wrote and illustrated his own comic books.

Brooks still enjoys reading and writing, but he also likes sports (except football), music, and nature study, and he has turned those interests into books. He explains: "I've always hopped around a lot whether it's been moving from town to town or dancing from one hobby to the next. The fact that I want to write about so many different things simply reflects a very natural part of my response to the world. I've always been terrified of being too comfortable."

When he is relatively comfortable, here are some of his other favorites. Many have found their way into his books; others have not—yet.

sports cap:	Chesapeake Chiefs Ice Hockey
professional team:	San Antonio Spurs ("Because Doc Rivers, who now plays for the Spurs, is the only professional athlete I really know.")
dessert:	brownies with vanilla ice cream
television show:	He does not watch television
musicians:	Chris Smither, Roland Hanna, Richard Goode
sport:	ice hockey
athlete:	"I tend to like players who do subtle playmaking jobs. They're usually good passers and very smart athletes who direct the play and make better players out of their teammates."

Glenn "Doc" Rivers now plays point guard for the San Antonio Spurs basketball team. Before the Spurs, he played for the New York Knicks.

Bruce Brooks apparently likes many different kinds of music. **Chris Smither** is a blues singer-songwriter, **Roland Hanna** is a jazz musician, and **Richard Goode** is a classical pianist.

Brooks attended the University of North Carolina at Chapel Hill and, after graduating, enrolled in the famous writers' workshop at the University of Iowa, where he earned a master of fine arts degree. That experience helped launch his writing career. "I went there very aggressive intellectually and came out very ambitious and increasingly confident," he says. "I used the workshop to boost my feeling that anything is possible. The only things I want to do are books that are unique and different," Christine McDonnell quotes him as saying in the March/April 1987 *Horn Book* (p. 189). His professional writing career began in earnest after he graduated from the University of Iowa in 1982. His first book, *The Moves Make the Man,* was published in 1984. He now lives and writes in Silver Spring, Maryland, with his wife, Penelope, and his two sons, Alexander and Spencer.

The Man's Books

> *About his first nonfiction book, On the Wing:, Brooks wrote, "[This book] should teach us all to be delighted that we can never find out enough."*

Few authors have written as diversely and successfully in such a short time as Brooks has. In little more than a decade, he has published five novels, four nature books, a sports biography, a collection of essays, and a picture book. In 1995, there were three other books in the works: a novel, an essay collection, and a picture book. He has earned two Newbery Honor Book awards and one Orbis Pictus Honor Book citation. All his books have been named to numerous "best books" lists.

In the introduction to his first nonfiction book, *On the Wing: The Life of Birds: From Feathers to Flight* (1989), Brooks wrote: "[This book] should teach us all to be delighted that we can never find out enough" (p. xiv). His books reflect not only his varied interests and his impressive versatility as a writer but also that he truly is delighted to find out things, things about human beings and society, about nature, and about himself.

His Diverse Interests

Brooks likes writing because it allows him to explore his many interests and to turn those interests into books. "In some ways," he says, "a book is just an another excuse for getting deeply intrigued with something else." His four nature books attest to his interest in animals and their place in our world. Music, another interest, plays a major role in *Midnight Hour Encores* (1986). But no interest manifests itself in his work more than sports does. Nearly all the essays in *Boys Will Be* (1993) are about sports or sports-related subjects, and the biography he coauthored with the NBA star Glenn "Doc" Rivers is obviously a sports book.

Sports in His Books

Though it is much more than a sports novel, *The Moves Make the Man* uses basketball as a central activity. Its narrator, Jerome, defines himself by his ability to play basketball. "The moves make the man," he says, "the moves make me" (p. 40). In addition to Jerome's basketball moves, Bix uses a one-on-one basketball game to force his stepfather to allow him to see his mother, setting up the final "move" that ends the novel. Sib's father, Taxi, in *Midnight Hour Encores,* is a decided nonsportsman, but he is athletic and soundly trounces all the other fathers in tennis, basketball, pool, and horseshoes at a weekend camp. In *Everywhere* (1990), the narrator says, "My grandfather liked the roses better than anything but the Yankees and me" (p. 7). Ollie, Sam's younger brother in *No Kidding* (1989), uses soccer practice as a cover for his secret meetings with radical religious groups. Asa, the protagonist in *What Hearts* (1992), finds that basketball and baseball are the only means (most of the time, at least) of safely interacting with his domineering stepfather.

trounces defeats decisively

Brooks's use of sports in his novels is not mere back ground; it serves to develop characters and advance plots. Jerome's technical understanding of basketball shows his intelligence and discipline while Bix's technical perfection in baseball hints at his mechanical obsessiveness. Taxi's natural and humble athleticism endears him to readers while showing him to be more than a mere hippie-intellectual. In *What Hearts,* Dave's cruel and intentional beaning of Asa with a fastball makes clear his competitive contempt for his stepson and marks the beginning of the decline of his relationship with Asa and Asa's mother. The one-on-one game between Bix and his stepfather is a pivotal scene in *The Moves Make the Man.* Phony soccer practices allow Ollie to develop his rabid religious condemnation of alcoholics in *No Kidding,* which sets up the novel's surprising conclusion. And the grandfather's passion for the fourth-place Yankees adds tension to *Everywhere* because the young narrator fears that the Yankees' losing ways may give his grandfather another heart attack.

beaning hitting a person over the head with an object

Avoidance of Labels

Replete as his writing is with sports, Brooks does not wish to be labeled, and should not be labeled, a writer of sports books. Soon after the publication of *The Moves Make the Man,* Brooks attended the annual American Library Association meeting and was shocked that so many people had immediately pegged him as a sports writer for young adult boys. He says: "That's three categories in a row nailed onto me. I thought, 'I've published one book; I'm not anything yet. And I'm certainly not fitting into three categories already for the rest of my life.'"

Brooks took some comfort in knowing his next book would be different from *Moves.* "There was a slight bit of willfulness involved in following *The Moves Make the Man* with *Midnight Hour Encores.* Avoiding that label of the boys' sports writer was a relief for me right away. I thought 'Well, if I get *Midnight Hour Encores* out there, then nobody will be able to label me for a while.'"

Brooks continued to dodge labels by writing nonfiction. He branched out into nature books, which draw on his interest in natural science and animals. He then moved into writing personal essays. In 1993, he published *Boys Will Be,* and recently completed a second collection of essays that makes use of what he calls "another part of my life that I was interested in: thinking about things that are happening between adults and kids today."

dystopia an imaginary place where people lead wretched and fearful lives

It is not surprising that his third novel, *No Kidding,* a dystopian tale of an alcoholic American society, was quite unlike his previous two novels and his nonfiction. His fourth novel, *Everywhere,* a relatively simple and short novel about a young boy dealing with his grandfather's brush with death, further makes it difficult to categorize Brooks. Then, of course, there are the sports biography of Doc Rivers and the picture book for children.

"I do continue to write about kids rather than for kids," he explains, "but that's because I'm still really intrigued with the mysteries of my own childhood."

Autobiographical Details in His Books

As a writer, Brooks follows an essential rule: write about what you know. And what does he know? He knows Washington, D.C., and Wilmington, North Carolina. He knows what it is like to live with a single parent, to be intelligent, to be a new kid in school, and to see a mother suffer. He knows that childhood and adolescence can be painful and confusing but wonderful. "I do continue to write *about* kids rather than *for* kids," he explains, "but that's because I'm still really intrigued with the mysteries of my own childhood."

Brooks admits that *What Hearts* is his most autobiographical book, the only one written consciously using his own experiences as a basis for the stories. "Asa really reflects who I was then and probably still am. The events that happen to him for the most part are pretty much things that happened to me, too." Autobiographical details "drift in and out" of his other books. In all five novels, his protagonists have a single parent, absent parents, or even a single, absent parent. The settings of his novels are either in Washington, D.C., or Wilmington, North Carolina. His characters all deal with the loss of a parent or loved one. In *The Moves Make the Man, Midnight Hour Encores, What Hearts,* and *No Kidding,* characters suffer because of their mothers' instability and depression. These autobiographical details lend a powerful honesty to the stories, giving Brooks and his readers a chance to probe the mysteries, agonies, and delights of adolescence.

Smart Characters

The protagonists in Brooks's novels are exceptionally intelligent adolescents. He writes about smart kids because he himself was a smart kid and because he chooses to write about characters who interest him. He explains: "Choosing a narrator or a character is often like choosing a friend. They don't have to be just like you but certainly you pick people who are at least stimulating and whose degree of detail will inspire your curiosity and your investigation. My characters are like that for me."

These smart kids, though, still have problems; intelligence does not guarantee that kids will avoid the "slings and arrows of outrageous fortune." Brooks says, "I like writing about kids who I hope will startle the readers by being simultaneously smarter than most people imagine children can be and also still more childish and unsure of themselves than people think most smart children are." For example, Jerome, despite his exceptional intelligence, must endure racism, the temporary loss of his mother, and the loss of his only good friend. Prodigious musical talent earns Sib offers to prestigious conservatories but does not make any easier her transformation from obnoxious teenager to sensitive human being or her decision about which parent to live with. Sam loses his younger brother despite his careful scheming to keep the family together. And Asa is unable to "cure" his

prodigious extraordinary or unusual in amount

conservatories music schools

> *Brooks wants his readers to realize that . . . everyone has problems, and that having a problem does not make a person a loser.*

mother or to establish the stable kind of life for which he longs. Instead of bailing them out of their troubles, their intelligence and insight make their losses and injuries more poignant because they are acutely aware of exactly what is happening to them.

Brooks wants his readers to realize that good grades do not guarantee an easy life, that everyone has problems, and that having a problem does not make a person a loser. "Asa has gone through some tough times, but I don't think anyone would say that he was ruined. I like that side of it too: you can be bright but still have problems; you can have problems but still be bright," Brooks explains.

The Man's Moves

Reviewers consistently praise Brooks's works for their originality, carefully developed characters, skillful use of language and dialogue, thought-provoking plots, and humor and insight into the world of adolescents. Brooks prides himself on his technical abilities as a writer, especially his careful use of language to evoke feelings and ideas in his readers. He understands and uses the power of words. As he says in *Something About the Author,* "language for me was a fascinating tool. I discovered that I could really be myself in words" (p. 23). Jerome echoes his author when he says that he had never realized "how much my way of talking was what made me who I thought and other people thought I was" (*The Moves Make the Man,* p. 56).

Brooks does not write *for* kids but for "intelligent people," he told the *Publishers Weekly* reviewer Leonard Marcus (p. 215), so his technical skills make his writing interesting, but not necessarily easy. With the exception of *Everywhere,* his novels are challenging reading. They often have ambiguous or startling endings, and the language, though precise, is at times complex. The ideas and situations are not easily resolved, the characters and their motivations not always easily understood. These difficulties, however, are not weaknesses. Good books are not easy reads that milk emotions from readers; instead they engage readers in a thought-provoking way. Brooks believes that readers value the difficulty in reading. He says in his spring 1992 article in *New Advocate,* "The Creative Process: Imagination, the Source of Reading": "It

ambiguous capable of being understood in more than one way

challenges the imagination to go beyond the immediate and familiar, to create something new. This means work. Good work, but work nonetheless" (p. 81).

Reading Bruce Brooks is good work, thoughtful work, even fun work. Careful reading of his books helps us appreciate his stories, writing skill, our world, and the people (and animals) in it. But Brooks's broad interests and his writer's moves—the technical skill he brings to writing—may ultimately be what really make his books worthwhile.

Selected Bibliography

WORKS BY BRUCE BROOKS

Novels for Young Adults

The Moves Make the Man (1984)

Midnight Hour Encores (1986)

No Kidding (1989)

Everywhere (1990)

What Hearts (1992)

Nonfiction

"In Collaboration with My Characters." *Horn Book,* January/ February 1986, pp. 38–40.

"Playing Fields of Fiction." *New York Times Book Review,* 6 April 1986, p. 20.

"The Difference between Reading and reading." *ALAN Review,* fall 1988, pp. 1–2, 6.

"Bruce Brooks." *Speaking for Ourselves.* Edited by Donald R. Gallo. Urbana, Ill.: National Council of Teachers of English, 1990, pp. 33–35.

"Pulling Proof." *Village Voice,* 21 June 1990, pp. S22–S25.

"The Creative Process: Imagination, the Source of Reading." *New Advocate,* spring 1992, pp. 79–85.

Boys Will Be (1993)

Those Who Love the Game: Glenn "Doc" Rivers on Life in the NBA and Elsewhere, with Glenn Rivers (1993)

Nature Books

On the Wing: The Life of Birds: From Feathers to Flight (1989)

Nature by Design (1991)

If you like the works of Bruce Brooks, you might also like the novels of Judy Blume and the sports books of Robert Lipsyte.

Predator! (1991)

Making Sense: Animal Perception and Communication (1993)

Picture Book

Each a Piece *(1995)*

WORKS ABOUT BRUCE BROOKS

"Bruce Brooks." Biographical Brochure from Harper-Collins Children's Books, 1993.

McDonnell, Christine. "New Voices, New Visions: Bruce Brooks." *Horn Book,* March/April 1987, pp. 188–191.

Marcus, Leonard. "Bruce Brooks." *Publishers Weekly,* 27 July 1990, pp. 214–215.

Senick, Gerard J., ed. "Bruce Brooks." In *Children's Literature Review.* Detroit: Gale Research, 1991, vol. 25, pp. 16–26.

Telsen, Diane, ed. "Bruce Brooks." In *Something About the Author.* Detroit: Gale Research, 1993, vol. 72, pp. 22–26.

How to Write to the Author
Bruce Brooks
c/o HarperCollins Publishers
10 East 53rd Street
New York, NY 10022

Eve Bunting

(1928-   )

by M. Jean Greenlaw

If you listen to Eve Bunting speak, you would know immediately that she came to the United States from Ireland. The lilt of her voice is so beautiful that you would want to listen to her speak for hours; her voice discloses that she has many stories waiting to be told. You would also see the joy of the storyteller in her snapping green eyes.

Eve Bunting was born in Maghera, County Derry, Ireland, on 19 December 1928. The daughter of the postmaster/shopkeeper, she had a lively imagination from her youngest years. She went to boarding school in Belfast when she was seven, and the experience of storytelling after the lights were turned out left a lasting impression. Ever a book lover, she shared her parents' passion for reading aloud. Bunting and her family—she and her husband have three children—decided in 1959 to emigrate to the United States, eventually settling in Pasadena, California, where she and her husband still lived in 1996.

Quotations from Eve Bunting that are not attributed to a published source are from a personal interview conducted by the author of this article on 2 March 1995 and are published here by permission of Eve Bunting.

> *"Sometimes,"*
> *says Bunting,*
> *"you possess*
> *talents you*
> *don't know you*
> *have. When*
> *you discover*
> *them, you*
> *become more*
> *than you think*
> *you can be.*

Becoming a Writer

Bunting states that writing is the driving force in her life. Until she became a writer she felt she was never any good at anything. She was not an athlete or a scholar; she dropped out of college. She felt a lack of self-worth and, when she came to the United States, she was insecure.

When Bunting learned that a local junior college was offering a writing class geared toward publication, she enrolled. Once she found writing, everything that was buried deep inside her came welling up. "Sometimes," says Bunting, "you possess talents you don't know you have. When you discover them, you become more than you think you can be. When I discovered the writing within me, I became a valuable person."

The first book that Bunting published was a picture book, *The Two Giants,* in 1972. Soon afterward, she joined her husband, Ed, the medical director of a hospital, for lunch. He took her over to the window of his office, and as they looked down on many nurses, technicians, doctors, and others streaming around, he told her, "Not one person below can write a book!" Eve Bunting can, and has gone on to write more than a hundred.

The Writing Process

Writing is so important to Bunting that she is conscious of the fact that she "must say something of worth!" She firmly believes that, as a writer, she must know what she wants to say before she writes a book. Her first goal is to be entertaining, but her books are frequently leavened by more serious matters. Bunting does not want her message to be too heavy, but the book must tell the truth.

leavened changed significantly by the addition of another element

plot the deliberate sequence of events in a literary work

theme central message about life in a literary work

In writing her books, Bunting feels that plot and theme are equally important. As she says, "Plot keeps them reading, theme keeps them thinking after reading." As a matter of fact, plot is definitely her strength. Bunting is able to hook the reader immediately and sustain the plot throughout, and her books are truly page-turners. Once you begin one of her books, you are driven to finish.

Bunting almost always keeps a pencil and notebook at hand. She writes wherever she finds herself: stuck in traffic, waiting for the doctor, on an airplane, and even sometimes at her desk. Her plots are generated by the true and the real, what she finds in the daily paper or on the news. She generally changes the location of the story because she does not want to make a mistake in describing the locale or other specifics. But before she can turn an event into a book, it must touch her. As Bunting explains it, "A book must touch the author before it touches the reader."

Books, Books, Books

An author who has written more than one hundred books over a span of more than twenty years has obviously proven herself successful. To maintain that success, Bunting writes about many subjects and is adept at portraying both the funny and the tragic. Because she is so prolific, this profile will cover only her writing for young adults, from her first book to her newest books, and a variety of genres.

Bunting wrote *The Haunting of Kildoran Abbey* in the 1970s but did not find a publisher at first. It was published by Frederick Warne, a British company, in 1978. The book is set in Ireland in 1847, the time of the great potato famine that sent many Irish people to the United States in search of a better life. This is a Robin Hood type of story in which the main characters take from the rich to feed the poor. An Englishman, Sir James Blunt, is the most hated man in Ireland because he is squeezing the life from his neighbors, and they are too sick and defeated to rebel. The story opens with twin brothers, Columb the doer and Finn the dreamer, being turned out of their home by Blunt's men. As they escape, they stumble on Witch, a girl as tough and able as they are. Taking shelter in the Abbey, which is said to be haunted, they discover other young refugees. Together with Christopher, an English boy who is staying with Sir James Blunt, they create a daring plan to steal food from Blunt to save the starving villagers. As in most of Bunting's books, there is fast-paced action blended with thoughtful interaction. She vividly portrays each character as a believable person. Each is distinctly drawn, and each has a different past and a different future. Bunting deftly intersperses vivid action with reflective moments. Even in an adventure story, there must be times of rest and thought.

Bunting got the idea for another book on a visit to the Santa Monica Pier to look at the merry-go-round, hoping

The **Santa Monica Pier** in California was a popular nightspot in the 1920s that later fell into disrepair. Santa Monica residents passed a referendum to save the pier. An addition was completed in 1990.

Joan Baez (1941–) was especially popular in the 1960s. Her music, then and now, reflects the political issues of the times and her deep belief in nonviolence.

for inspiration for a picture book. The ticket taker asked her if she knew about the abandoned apartments above the carousel, one of which had been lived in by the folk singer Joan Baez. Abandoning the idea of a picture book, she sat on the creaky stairs and wrote *If I Asked You, Would You Stay?* (1984), a story about Crow, a teenager who runs away and hides in an apartment once owned by a movie actress named Sasha. When not at his job, Crow spends his time looking at the ocean, which stretches away to nothing, and imagining what Sasha was like.

Crow meets another runaway, Valentine, who is running first from a stepfather who bothered her and then from Marty, who wants her to be a prostitute. After a prickly beginning, the two start to reach out to one another. Valentine tries to drown herself, but Crow rescues her and they realize they cannot continue their bleak existence; both then go on to other things. Valentine goes to live with a friend of her mother's, realizing she had run away to find love. People important to Crow had always left him, so he began leaving people before they became important to him. The ending is as open as life often is. Maybe Crow will return to Mrs. Simmons and Danny, in his last foster home; maybe he and Valentine will have a future someday. Life will have to play itself out.

One of Bunting's favorite books is *A Sudden Silence* (1988) because the main character is based on the personality of one of her sons. Jesse Harmon is consumed by guilt. He and his deaf brother, Bry, had been walking along the highway, coming home from a party, when a drunk driver hit and killed Bry. Jesse is tormented by the thought that he could have done something to save his brother. He is also attracted to Chloe, the girl Bry liked before his death. Because the authorities have given up on the case, Jesse and Chloe set out to find the killer. They do find the killer but their discovery shatters several families. Bunting is able to get into the mind of a teenager: the dialogue is realistic, and the fears and concerns are well expressed. She takes headlines from the newspaper and turns them into stories about the emotions and actions of real people.

For those who like mysteries and ghost stories, *The Ghost Children* (1989) will fill the bill. Matt and his sister, Abby, are orphans who go to live with a great-aunt, Gerda. She lives in a canyon in California that is becoming very popular with people who want to build a second home, thereby raising property values in the area. Gerda is not well liked by her neighbors because she has life-sized dolls in her yard that she treats as her children and that are rumored to talk. Many people try to damage the dolls; others try to run Gerda out of the canyon. The complex plot involves an art dealer, the feud in the canyon, and Matt's need to find a safe home for himself and his sister. As is usual in Bunting's work, the plot is intertwined with the needs of the characters, and as in life, people are often not what they seem.

Not Always a Happy Ending

Because Bunting writes about characters who seem real and places them in realistic situations, her endings are not always happy. *Such Nice Kids* (1990) is a cautionary tale that shows how easy it is to make a wrong decision, one that leads to other wrong decisions, which end up changing your life and those around you. Pidge is a lovable loser. Jason is his only real friend, someone who protected him when they were young children and continues to do so even now that they are teenagers. Jason has another friend, Meeker, who skates on the edge of truthfulness and morality. The tragedy that befalls these three young people starts simply: Pidge wants to borrow Jason's car, but Jason needs it himself. But Jason's parents are out of town, so—prodded by Meeker—he loans Pidge his mother's car. Like an unraveling sweater that comes completely apart, the lives of the three boys seem to be caught in an unending spiral toward catastrophe. This is an excellent example of Bunting's belief that plot keeps you reading, but theme keeps you thinking after reading. It is hard to forget this poignant story.

The In-Between Days (1994) is set on Dove Island, a tourist mecca in summer but a close-knit community in winter—especially in the "in-between days." This is the season in which the island is completely cut off from the mainland until the ice is thick enough to walk across. George lives on the island with his father and younger brother; his mother is buried in the graveyard on the island. Caroline is a tourist who rents a bike from George's dad. George likes Caroline at first and proudly shows her his island. But Caroline returns often, and

mecca a place that draws many visitors (from **Mecca,** the Islamic holy city)

George realizes that his father is falling in love with her. George does not want anyone to take his mother's place, and so he contrives to make Caroline go away. The ending is upbeat, and the book is a beautiful depiction of change and its effects. There are many kinds of love, and Bunting explores them in this book.

In *Spying on Miss Müller* (1995), Bunting returns to her roots. Using the boarding school she attended as a child as the setting, she tells of the passions that were rampant during World War II. Miss Müller was a popular teacher at Alveara School, and Jessie still likes her even though she is half German. But the students and faculty of the school turn against the teacher, and when Jessie sneaks into her room and discovers that Miss Müller's father was a Nazi, the situation gets out of hand. Along with the major plot, a subplot explores Jessie's embarrassment about her alcoholic father, a fact she has kept from all her friends. The defining moment of the book is when Jessie realizes from Miss Müller's actions that love must be strong and transcend who or what someone you love has become.

If you read a great number of Bunting's books, you will find that love in its many forms is a constant. The plot alone will keep you riveted to the books, but the humanity of the books will bring you back for more.

Eve Bunting no longer goes out on school visits. Because visiting schools is a drain on her energy, she prefers to stay home to write books. She does set aside one day a month, however, to answer letters from her readers. This prolific author says she can't stop writing. Her avid readers are happy that she is afflicted with this urgent need to write.

subplot a secondary series of events that is less important than the plot

transcend to rise above

Readers who enjoy Eve Bunting's work might enjoy books by Joan Aiken, Marion Dane Bauer, Caroline B. Cooney, Lois Duncan, Lois Lowry, Joan Lowrey Nixon, and Richard Peck.

Selected Bibliography

BOOKS BY EVE BUNTING

The Two Giants (1972; 1985)

The Haunting of Kildoran Abbey (1978)

If I Asked You, Would You Stay? (1984)

A Sudden Silence (1988)

The Ghost Children (1989)

Such Nice Kids (1990)

The In-Between Days (1994)
Once Upon a Time (1995)
Spying on Miss Müller (1995)

WORKS ABOUT EVE BUNTING

Olendorf, Donna, ed. "Eve Bunting." *Something About the Author.* Detroit: Gale Research, 1991, vol. 64, pp. 60–69.
Senick, Gerard J., ed. "Eve Bunting." *Children's Literature Review.* Detroit: Gale Research, 1992, vol. 28, pp. 41–67.

How to Write to the Author
Eve Bunting
c/o Fawcett Books
201 East 50th Street
New York, NY 10022

Olive Ann Burns

(1924-1990)

by Jane Agee

The characters and the setting for Olive Ann Burns's *Cold Sassy Tree* (1984) make readers feel that they are in the small town of Cold Sassy and know the people living there as well as they know their own family. The novel, with its teenage narrator, has been compared to Harper Lee's *To Kill a Mockingbird* and Mark Twain's *The Adventures of Tom Sawyer*. Fourteen-year-old Will Tweedy's honest and humorous appraisal of the events that follow his grandmother Blakeslee's death make the novel one that readers cannot put down.

There is an article about Harper Lee in volume 2 and an article about Mark Twain in volume 3.

Cold Sassy Tree

Cold Sassy Tree begins in the summer of 1906, when Grandpa Blakeslee, who had buried his beloved wife just three weeks before, makes a momentous decision that rocks the family and the entire town. When Grandpa summons his daughters, Mary Willis (Will's mother) and Loma, they are still dressed in mourning clothes for their mother's death. Without any warning, Grandpa announces, "I'm aimin' to marry Miss Love Simpson." As his daughters protest and cry, Grandpa says, "Well, good gosh a'mighty! She's as dead as she'll ever be, ain't she?" (p. 5). This story and Grandpa's pronouncement are actually from notes Burns made as she listened to her father tell about his grandfather, who had married soon after his first wife's death.

Yankee a native of the northern United States

In the close-knit southern community of Cold Sassy, Miss Love Simpson has two strikes against her even before the marriage proposal. She is a Yankee and a working woman, a milliner (hat maker) in Grandpa Blakeslee's store. After Grandpa Blakeslee's announcement about his intention to marry Miss Love, Will says, "Soon as Grandpa got out of sight, it was as if somebody had wound Mama and Aunt Loma up and let go the spring" (p. 6). Of course, Will has his own opinion about Miss Love: "I had always admired Miss Love, with all that wavy hair piled atop her head, and that smiley, freckedly face and those friendly gray-blue eyes. She was a merry person, like Grandpa" (p. 9). The subsequent elopement of Grandpa and Miss Love and the uproar it causes in Cold Sassy make a wonderful story.

elopement running away in secret to get married

One of the most memorable characters in the novel, other than Grandpa Blakeslee and Miss Love, is Will's Aunt Loma. Burns said she learned from watching soap operas that at least one character had to be thoroughly hateful to make a story interesting. Loma is that character. Just six years older than Will, the red-haired, gossipy Loma has illusions of grandeur that rankle Will. He traces his troubles with her back to the day she turned twelve (when he was six) and insisted that he address her as *Aunt* Loma. He refuses her demand, and to spite him she breaks his toy soldiers. When Will discovers the broken soldiers, he spits on her. No one believes his story, and he is whipped for spitting on Loma. The details of such episodes are part of Burns's craft in constructing characters that come to life.

Burns's great skill in depicting human nature with all its peculiarities produces humor that often equals the stories of Mark Twain. Some of the funniest scenes in *Cold Sassy Tree* remind the reader of scenes from *Tom Sawyer*. When Will decides to get even with his bossy Aunt Loma, he does it with nineteen big rats, one the size of a cat. Loma is directing a Christmas play for the community, and she asks Will to help her find a live mouse. When the mouse hits the stage, Will and his friend Smiley release the rats. This hilarious scene is based on a true story about Burns's grandfather.

The novel also has terrifying moments, like the time Will gets run over by the train on Blind Tillie Trestle. The moment seems so real that the reader races along with the speed of the oncoming train to find out what happens next. Just as the train appears, Will's fishing rod gets caught in the tracks at the very last second. Will falls flat onto the crossties. The train passes over leaving him unscathed except for some cinder burns.

How *Cold Sassy Tree* Started

The story of Cold Sassy actually began to take shape when Burns was diagnosed in 1975 with a serious disease. Her doctor told her she would probably develop leukemia or lymphoma, both often fatal. She decided then that she would write a novel. "I'm sure it was just trying to grab at something," she is quoted as saying in the *Atlanta-Journal Constitution* (p. 17). She discovered that writing helped her to get through the chemotherapy and the other effects of her illness.

Burns wrote from family history as well as her own experiences of growing up in North Georgia. Before beginning the novel, she spent years collecting family stories from her parents and other relatives. She carefully recorded these stories and typed them for her two children, John and Becky Sparks. Her great-grandfather, Ben Power, served as a model for Grandpa Blakeslee's character and her father for Will Tweedy's character.

As Burns points out in her introduction, the town of Cold Sassy very much resembles the North Georgia town of Commerce at the turn of the century. To write the novel, she also turned to a county history, *History of Harmony Grove-Commerce, Jackson County, Georgia, 1810–1949* by Thomas C. Hardman. But many of the stories are from her own life. She was born not far from Commerce in Banks County, Georgia, on 17 July 1924, on land that had belonged to her great-great-grandfather. Her father, William Arnold Burns, ran the family farm. Her mother, Ruby Celestia Hight Burns,

leukemia disease in which there is an abnormal increase in white blood cells

lymphoma an abnormal mass of lymph tissue in the body

was a homemaker. Burns was the youngest of four children. Her sister Margaret was the oldest, then came her sister Emma Jean, followed by Billy.

Burns's interest in writing started early. In her essay, "Olive Ann Burns—A Reminiscence," Katrina Kenison repeats a story Burns told about her ninth-grade English teacher, who was impressed with her ability with language. The teacher, trying to explain similes, wrote *violin* on the chalkboard. Burns says, as quoted in *Leaving Cold Sassy,* "I wrote 'A violin sounds like a refined sawmill.'" The teacher, impressed with her ingenious use of language, sent her to work on the school newspaper. Burns later commented that "those seven words changed my life" (p. 174).

ingenious clever

After her family moved from Banks County to Macon, Georgia, Burns enrolled at Mercer University, where she was appointed editor of the Mercer literary magazine. She later transferred to the University of North Carolina and graduated with a degree in journalism in 1946. After completing her degree, she moved to Atlanta to live with her parents.

One of Burns's first jobs was with a company that produced a trade magazine, *Coca-Cola Bottler.* In 1947, she accepted a position with the *Atlanta Journal-Constitution* as a writer for the *Atlanta Weekly,* a popular Sunday magazine. In the late 1950s, while her children were small, she wrote an advice column for the *Constitution* using the pen name Amy Larkin. This work allowed her to stay at home with her children. As a journalist, she was largely known for her stories in the *Weekly.*

While Burns was working with the *Atlanta Weekly,* she learned a lot about writing from the well-known editor Angus Perkerson. Perkerson, she says in Kenison's essay, "fired me three times in the first six months and scared me to death for five years" (p. 176). Perkerson was an extremely demanding editor who wanted stories that were not only interesting to read but also on time. His expectations were difficult for Burns to meet. She had little confidence in her writing and often labored for weeks over a story. She says that when he was tired of waiting for her to finish a story, he would yell, "Hell, Olive, if you don't finish that story by three o'clock, I'm goin' throw it in the trash can" (p. 177). Over time, though, Burns gained confidence and learned that Mr. Perkerson was a fine editor and mentor. She often said that her newspaper work taught her what she needed to know to write a novel.

mentor a wise or trusted teacher

The Beginnings of *Cold Sassy Tree*

While working with the *Weekly,* she met Andrew Sparks. They worked together for nine years before they were married on 11 August 1956. *Cold Sassy Tree* is dedicated to "Andy, my beloved" and their children, John and Becky. She left the *Weekly* in 1957, after her daughter was born.

Before writing *Cold Sassy Tree,* Burns had not written fiction. However, she had been a member of a "plot club," which included other Georgia writers like Robert Burch, Wylly St. John, and Celestine Sibley. Once she decided to write a novel, she approached the craft of writing fiction in a practical way. She read a book on how to write a novel and analyzed soap opera characters and plots on television.

Burns began her journey to publishing fame with a couple of lucky meetings. In 1980, she took the *Cold Sassy* manuscript to Ossabaw Island off the coast of Georgia, a private retreat for writers and artists. While there she met Menakhem Perry, a professor and literary critic from Tel Aviv University in Israel. He read the manuscript and strongly encouraged her to finish it. Then, in 1982, she met Anne Edwards, an author who was in Atlanta to gather information for a biography of Margaret Mitchell, the author of *Gone with the Wind.* She stayed with Burns and her family on one of her trips. While in Atlanta, she heard about Burns's novel.

A year later, Anne Edwards arranged for Burns to meet the president of Ticknor & Fields, Chester Kerr, and his wife Joan. Ticknor & Fields had published Anne Edwards' book. Joan Kerr was very interested in seeing Burns's story. At a party in Atlanta celebrating the publication of *The Road to Tara,* Edwards' book on Margaret Mitchell, Kerr invited Burns to send her the *Cold Sassy* manuscript.

Once Joan Kerr read the 825-page draft of Will Tweedy's story, she knew that with some cutting and editing, it would be a wonderful novel. She passed the manuscript on to Katrina Kenison, an editor at Ticknor & Fields. Working with Kenison, Burns cut 250 pages and made many revisions. When she sent her final manuscript to the publishers, they scheduled an initial printing of five thousand copies.

The enthusiastic response to *Cold Sassy Tree* surprised everyone, especially Burns. Ticknor & Fields quickly sold out the first printing. By the end of 1985, more than fifty-

The made-for-cable movie *Cold Sassy Tree* was released in 1989.

The **Great Depression** was a severe recession that began when the stock market crashed in 1929 and that lasted almost ten years. By the winter of 1932–1933, 14 to 16 million Americans were unemployed. Many died from a lack of food and inadequate living conditions.

thousand copies had been sold, and paperback rights were sold to Dell Publishing Company.

The novel rapidly gained national and international attention. It became a Book-of-the-Month Club alternate selection in 1984, the American Library Association included it on its list of 100 Best Books for Young Readers, and the New York Public Library listed it as one of two-hundred books recommended for teenagers. Burns's novel quickly hit the best-seller list and received numerous enthusiastic reviews. The 21 September 1984 *Publishers Weekly* concludes, "Burns . . . has written a book with such fine characterization and rich detail that it hurts to turn that last page." In 1986, the actress Faye Dunaway announced plans to make a television movie based on *Cold Sassy Tree*. She said she would play the role of Miss Love Simpson. Although Burns said she did not think Dunaway had a mouth big enough for the character of Miss Love, she was happy that the actress was anxious to preserve the story as told in the book.

The Sequel

Burns began the sequel to *Cold Sassy* in response to fans' questions about what happened to Will Tweedy. She started the sequel about 1985, after her husband Andy had also been diagnosed with lymphoma. Her own health began to deteriorate during this time. Grieving after the death of her husband in 1989 and suffering from congestive heart failure and the advanced stages of lymphoma, she worked from her bed to finish Will Tweedy's story. A neighbor, Norma Duncan, helped out by having Burns dictate the story to her. Unfortunately, only fifteen chapters were completed before Burns died on 4 July 1990. The unfinished sequel to *Cold Sassy Tree* is titled "Time, Dirt, and Money" (published in *Leaving Cold Sassy*) and is based on the story of Burns's parents' marriage during the Great Depression.

"Time, Dirt, and Money" opens in 1917, when the United States is involved in World War I and Will Tweedy is twenty-one years old. He has completed a degree in agriculture at the University of Georgia and is a county agent (an expert in agriculture and home economics) living in Athens, Georgia. When Will runs into Smiley Snodgrass, his old friend who helped him catch the rats in *Cold Sassy Tree,* Smiley persuades Will to come to a watermelon cutting in Cold Sassy, which is now named Progressive City. At the watermelon cutting, Will meets a pretty young schoolteacher, Sanna Klein, who is renting a room from Miss Love, Grandpa Blakeslee's widow. Sanna, a refined dark-haired beauty from Mitchellville, Georgia, teaches fourth grade. One of her pupils is the mischievous Sampson Blakeslee, the child of Grandpa Blakeslee and Miss Love. The sequel traces the courtship and marriage of Will and Sanna.

Some of the same characters appear in "Time, Dirt, and Money"—Miss Love, Loma, Will's parents, his sister Mary Toy, and his old friend Smiley Snodgrass—but the fifteen chapters suffer in comparison with *Cold Sassy Tree.* The sequel is clearly a work in progress. When Ticknor & Fields published the unfinished sequel in 1992, the decision caused a stir in publishing circles. It is extremely rare for an unfinished novel to be published. Some people in the publishing business thought it was a mistake to publish "Time, Dirt, and Money" because it was not a polished, finished story.

However, John Herman, editor at Ticknor & Fields, saw things differently. He wanted to honor Burns's dying wish that the sequel be published. Katrina Kenison, the editor who had worked with Burns so closely on *Cold Sassy Tree,* added a personal reminiscence to "Time, Dirt, and Money." The unfinished sequel and the reminiscence were published together as *Leaving Cold Sassy.*

reminiscence an account of memorable past experiences

Although the fifteen chapters and the collection of notes for what Burns was planning to write about in the sequel are far from a finished story, they offer valuable insights into the process that a writer goes through to create a work of fiction. More importantly, the sequel offers a tribute in two ways, one to Burns's readers, for whom she so desperately tried to complete the sequel, and a second to Burns herself. She was much loved by those who knew her. Lee Walburn, a fellow journalist, said in the October 1990 *Atlanta Magazine* that he and his wife wore their underwear inside out at Burns's funeral when she was buried beside her husband Andy in the family plot in Commerce, Georgia. He explained that Burns "thought it patently silly to wear seams next to the skin, chafing you like some cotton-and-polyester mosquito. So she didn't" (p. 152). As Walburn and many others noted, Burns wrote a remarkable book that has all the qualities of an American classic.

If you enjoyed *Cold Sassy Tree*, you might be interested in *A Solitary Blue*, by Cynthia Voigt, or *Park's Quest*, by Katherine Paterson.

Selected Bibliography

WORKS BY OLIVE ANN BURNS

Cold Sassy Tree (1984)

Leaving Cold Sassy: The Unfinished Sequel to Cold Sassy Tree (1992)

WORKS ABOUT OLIVE ANN BURNS

Kenison, Katrina. "Olive Ann Burns—A Reminiscence." In *Leaving Cold Sassy: The Unfinished Sequel to Cold Sassy Tree*. New York: Ticknor & Fields, 1992.

O'Briant, Don. "Laurels to 'Sassy Tree': Idea for Atlantan's Novel Grew Out of Family History." *The Atlanta Journal-Constitution,* 13 July 1986, p. 11J.

Betsy Byars

(1928-   )

by Colleen P. Gilrane

Do you want to be a professional writer someday? Betsy Byars did not, not when she was a young person! In *Something About the Author Autobiography Series,* she said, "Writing seemed boring. You sat in a room all day by yourself and typed. If I was going to be a writer at all, I was going to be a foreign correspondent like Claudette Colbert in *Arise My Love.* I would wear smashing hats, wisecrack with the guys, and have a byline known round the world" (p. 57).

However, Byars found herself "at loose ends" (p. 61) in 1955 when she and her husband, Ed, and their children moved to Urbana, Illinois so that Ed could get his Ph.D. at the University of Illinois. Ed and the children had school to keep them busy, and Byars was lonely. She bought an old typewriter, put it at her place at the kitchen table, and began to write! For the next two years, she would push the typewriter aside when she sat down to eat and then pull it back so she could continue writing. She wrote mostly articles

In *Arise My Love* (1940), **Claudette Colbert** plays a reporter who saves a airman from an firing squad during the Spanish Civil War.

then; her first book, *Clementine,* was published seven years later in 1962.

Discovering the Realistic Novel

Betsy's early books were not at all realistic, being about make-believe characters such as performing pigs and an orangutan who went to school. They were not well received by critics, either, and are not popular with readers. She believed then that her own life experiences were not interesting enough to write about, as she explains in *The Moon and I* (1991):

> The first (and possibly the best) piece of writing advice I ever got was in third grade. "Write about what you know," Mrs. Stroupe told us.
>
> At that time I went to school in rural North Carolina, and I thought, Well, that is the stupidest thing I ever heard in my life. I mean, it may be fine to write about what you know if you're Lindbergh, but if you're a third grade girl in rural North Carolina, you better make up some stuff.
>
> That's what I did. Through grade school, through high school, through college, even into my professional career, I made up stuff.
>
> But at some point finally—finally!—I got smart. I saw why you write about what you know. (P. 34)

niche place or position best suited to the person

When Betsy discovered the realistic novel, she found her niche as a writer, and she was to discover, in her enormous success, the truth of Mrs. Stroupe's advice.

Byars believes that "one of the best gifts a writer can give a reader is the feeling 'This writer knows what she's talking about'" (*The Moon and I,* p. 34). When she is working on a book about a topic she does not know much about, she does a lot of research. She gathers a great deal of information by reading in the library, but just as important is what she learns by having the experiences herself that her characters have in her books. In her autobiography, *The Moon and I,* you can read about how Byars carefully studied a snake, Moon, who lived on her land; how she bought another snake, Satellite, from a neighborhood boy who had caught it; and how she bought still another snake, Freckles, in the pet store—all while she was reading about snakes in books and asking her husband, Ed, and the pet shop owner questions about snakes. *And* while she was being bitten by Moon! Byars did all of this so that if she wrote about snakes, she would know what she was talking about!

Byars has a pilot's license and loves planes and flying, and one day she got the idea of writing a book about a girl and her grandfather flying across the country in an old airplane. When Byars asked Ed to map out the route, he reminded her that she needed to experience it if she was going to write about it, so they set out on a cross-country flight in Ed's 1940 J-3 Piper Cub, with Byars keeping a journal. Another well-researched book is *The Summer of the Swans* (1970). After working as a volunteer with two students who were having learning difficulties, Byars did research in the medical library and found case histories of children who had suffered brain damage as a result of high-fever illnesses. She created the character of Charlie from what she learned, and *The Summer of the Swans* won the John Newbery Medal in 1971.

Byars has a pilot's license and loves planes and flying.

Characters Are the Key

According to Byars, there are four important elements to a good story: characters, plot, setting, and "good scraps." She says the plot is the "seed" that comes first, but "the characters are the key to the story. They unlock the plot. They make it happen. So the characters, for me, are the most important element." (*The Moon and I,* pp. 38–39)

"The characters are the key to the story. They unlock the plot. They make it happen."

Most of Byars' characters are young people trying to figure out how to make it through the ups and downs of everyday life without being lonely or getting hurt. Some of the characters have the assistance and support of the adults in their lives, and others survive *despite* the adults! Few of Byars' characters cope with ordinary circumstances. Even Bingo Brown, who has a mother, a father, and a grandmother he can count on, finds himself dealing with a school-wide rebellion and with a suicidal teacher in *The Burning Questions of Bingo Brown* (1988). In *Cracker Jackson* (1985), "Cracker" Jackson Hunter and his friend, Ralph "Goat" McMillan, deal with spouse abuse when Cracker discovers that his old baby-sitter, Alma, is being beaten by her husband, Billy Ray. And Jimmy Little, who is loved by all the adults in his family, often finds himself embarrassed by their zany and foolish antics in *Good-bye, Chicken Little* (1979).

Many of Betsy's characters are dealing with extraordinary circumstances *without* help from the adults in their lives; in fact, the adults are part of the problem that the young person is left to solve! After spending some time with her mother on the rodeo circuit in *A Blossom Promise* (1987), Maggie Blossom explains to her friend, Ralphie, that her mom has never grown up and still wants the same things she wanted when she was eighteen years old, while Maggie has grown up too fast and is taking on too much family responsibility: "You know, Ralphie, the people who are lucky grow up when they're supposed to, not too fast, not too slow—on schedule. The people who aren't lucky—well, they either never grow up, like my mom, or they grow up too fast" (p. 141). Later in that conversation, Maggie decides she's had enough:

> "Only, Ralphie, this time I'm going to see that it happens. I'm going to see that we do open a riding school. I'm going to see that we settle down whether my mom likes it or not. This is a Blossom promise to myself. I'm going to take over this family if I have to."
>
> "Mutiny!" Ralphie said.
>
> "Exactly!" Maggie answered. (P. 141)

Several of Byars' characters find themselves being in charge, without "grown up" adults in their lives, just as Maggie did. Retta, in *The Night Swimmers* (1980) is raising herself and her two younger brothers while her father sleeps most of the day and is gone after supper (cooked by Retta) every night to perform as a country-and-western singer at the Downtown Hoedown. She has been in charge ever since her mother died. In *After the Goat Man* (1974), Figgy finds himself abandoned when his grandfather takes a shotgun and returns to the cabin in the woods they were forced out of for the construction of a highway. And poor Alfie is trying to find space to be himself and concentrate on his work in *The Cartoonist* (1978), only to meet resistance from his mother, who wants him to keep her company watching TV and recalling the antics of his older brother, Bubba, who stole cars and carried

Maggie Blossom explains to her friend, Ralphie, "You know, Ralphie, the people who are lucky grow up when they're supposed to, not too fast, not too slow—on schedule."

out other pranks his mother found delightfully funny when he was in high school. A crisis arises for Alfie when Bubba loses his job and their mother plans to turn Alfie's sanctuary, the attic, into an apartment for Bubba and his wife, Maureen.

The characters in *The Pinballs* (1977)—Carlie, Harvey, and Thomas J—find in their foster parents adults they can count on, in contrast to their parents. Carlie's stepfather beat her, Harvey's father ran over both of Harvey's legs with his car, and Thomas J's parents abandoned him when he was a baby, to be taken in by the Benson twins—women in their eighties. However in their foster parents, Mr. and Mrs. Mason, the three children find adults they can relate to and depend on, and they build from there. Many of Byars' characters find someone like the Masons to call on in a crisis, if their parents are unavailable. Some of the adults the young persons turn to are Mad Mary in the Blossom Family Quartet (*The Not-Just-Anybody Family* [1986], *The Blossoms Meet the Vulture Lady* [1986], *The Blossoms and the Green Phantom* [1987], and *A Blossom Promise* [1987]) and in *Wanted . . . Mud Blossom* [1991], Aunt Willie in *The Summer of the Swans*, and Ada's father in *After the Goat Man*.

These trustworthy adults share a trait with Betsy Byars: They respect young people and take them seriously. They treat young people's ideas, feelings, worries, and concerns as important, not as things to be laughed at or ignored. Byars believes that remembering her own experiences growing up, and having four children herself, are important to her as a writer. While some adults (including Cracker Jackson's mother!) believe that topics such as spouse abuse, suicide, and jailed relatives are too disturbing for young readers to deal with, Byars believes that she must write up to her readers rather than talk down to them (*Twentieth-Century Children's Writers*, p. 167). By caring about them and taking them seriously, Byars brings her characters to life and makes her readers care about them too.

> *Byars believes that she must write up to her readers rather than talk down to them.*

Plenty of Good Scraps

Plenty of good scraps are as important in making a book as in the making of a quilt.

I often think of my books as scrapbooks of my life, because I put in them all the neat things that I see and read and hear. I sometimes wonder what people who don't write do with all their good stuff. (*The Moon and I,* p. 39)

Betsy Byars' books are full of "good scraps," fascinating events and characters that she notices and stores away until she has a place for them in a story. In *The Pinballs,* one of the scraps is a story Mr. Mason tells Thomas J about a time when Mr. Mason was a child and went with his father to see an old man, Mr. Joe, who had died. When his father picked him up, the child's foot hit the coffin and jarred Mr. Joe's mouth open, which scared the child so much he ran away. This is a scrap from Byars' own childhood, when she went with her grandfather to see the real Mr. Joe.

Many of the incidents in her books are from her own life. Byars herself touched a mummy in a museum as someone else held the case open, as she has Birch do in *Coast to Coast.* And Byars' daughter once plotted—and attempted—to drill a hole in the wall of the school so that she and her best friend in the classroom next door could pass notes to each other! Byars found out when she had to go to the school to talk with the principal about it, and she gave Simon Newton and Tony Angotti this scrap in *The Cybil War* (1981). If you want to discover more of the scraps that are events from Byars' own life, you'll want to read her autobiography, *The Moon and I,* as well as the entry she wrote for *Something About the Author Autobiography Series.*

Other scraps come from being a careful observer of life around her, whether from news stories or from people she sees in the grocery store. The Benson twins, Thomas and Jefferson, in *The Pinballs* are based on a pair of twins in their eighties, dressed alike, that Betsy saw one day when she was buying sandwich ingredients in a grocery store. And a news report of a man who tried to cross a frozen river after he had been drinking too much turned into Uncle Pete in *Good-bye, Chicken Little.*

Sometimes the news items grow from scraps into whole books when Betsy gets excited about an idea and begins to do research on it, as in the case of *The House of Wings* (1972). When a "monster" in the news turned out to be a crane that had been lost and injured, most newspaper readers lost interest in the story, but Betsy began uncovering all she could about sandhill cranes and people who rescued and nursed injured birds and then set them free.

Wait Till You See . . .

In 1996, Byars was still writing in a log house in South Carolina, about five minutes away from the condominium she and Ed lived in. At the time she wrote *The Moon and I,* she had written the manuscript of the cross-country flight seventeen times, and her publisher still did not like it. Byars did not know if it would ever get published. But she did not give up, as she explained in *Something About the Author*:

> I know of writers whose creative drive begins to fade in the face of seemingly endless rejection slips. Starting a new writing project does require enormous energy, and it gets harder and harder to sustain this creative energy when you are being continuously turned down.
>
> In Illinois, out of necessity, I developed a kind of tough, I'll-show-them attitude that I have maintained to this day. Sort of—All right, you don't like that one, wait till you see this one. All right, you turned that down and you'll be sorry. I am now going to do the best book in the entire world. (P. 61)

Coast to Coast was finally published in 1992, so Byars' perseverance paid off. And her readers can look for new stories to follow *McMummy* (1993) and *The Dark Stairs* (1994) because Byars loves what she's doing!

Selected Bibliography

WORKS BY BETSY BYARS

Fiction

Clementine (1962)

The Dancing Camel (1965)

Rama, the Gypsy Cat (1966)

The Groober (1967)

Midnight Fox (1968)

Trouble River (1969)

The Summer of the Swans (1970)

If you like the works of Betsy Byars, you might also like the works of Francesca Lia Block and Judy Blume.

Go and Hush the Baby (1971)

The House of Wings (1972)

The Eighteenth Emergency (1973)

The Winged Colt of Casa Mia (1973)

After the Goat Man (1974)

The Lace Snail (1975)

The TV Kid (1976)

The Pinballs (1977)

The Cartoonist (1978)

Good-bye, Chicken Little (1979)

The Night Swimmers (1980)

The Cybil War (1981)

The Animal, the Vegetable, and John D. Jones (1982)

The Two-Thousand-Pound Goldfish (1982)

The Glory Girl (1983)

The Computer Nut (1984)

Cracker Jackson (1985)

The Blossoms Meet the Vulture Lady (1986)

The Golly Sisters Go West (1986)

The Not-Just-Anybody Family (1986)

The Blossoms and the Green Phantom (1987)

A Blossom Promise (1987)

Beans on the Roof (1988)

The Burning Questions of Bingo Brown (1988)

Bingo Brown and the Language of Love (1989)

Bingo Brown, Gypsy Lover (1990)

Hooray for the Golly Sisters! (1990)

The Seven Treasure Hunts (1991)

Wanted . . . Mud Blossom (1991)

Bingo Brown's Guide to Romance (1992)

Coast to Coast (1992)

McMummy (1993)

The Dark Stairs: A Herculeah Jones Mystery (1994)

The Golly Sisters Ride Again (1994)

Autobiography

The Moon and I (1991)

"Betsy Byars." In *Something About the Author Autobiography Series*. Edited by Adele Sarkissian. Detroit: Gale Research, 1986, vol. 1, pp. 53–68.

WORKS ABOUT BETSY BYARS

Hile, Kevin, ed. "Betsy Byars." In *Something About the Author*. Detroit: Gale Research, 1995, vol. 80, pp. 29–36.

Lesniak, James G., ed. "Betsy Byars." In *Contemporary Authors New Revision Series*. Detroit: Gale Research, 1992, vol. 36, pp. 68–70.

How to Write to the Author
Betsy Byars
c/o HarperCollins Publishers
10 East 53rd Street
New York, NY 10022

Alden R. Carter

(1947–   )

by Terry C. Ley

Alden R. Carter decided in the third grade that he wanted to become a writer. One day at school he wrote a story about Percy, a racehorse who comes out of retirement to run one final, glorious race. During the race, however, while trying to leap over a picket fence, Percy is impaled upon its sharp points. Carter read his story to his mother and his little sister while riding home from school that day. When Percy's fate moved his sister to tears, Carter knew that he had to become a writer, one who could use words to make people happy or sad. Since then, he has written many books, fiction and nonfiction.

> **impaled** pierced by a sharp point or pointed weapon

Early Influences

As he grew up in Eau Claire, Wisconsin, with his older brother, Bill, and his younger sister, Cynthia, Carter read a great deal. When he was very young, his father, John Kelley

Carter, often read to him favorite stories about dogs, pirates, and cowboys. His father also told him stories about Eau Claire when it was a rowdy lumbering town, and these stories created in Carter an early interest in history, which was sustained by the Landmark Series books that his father bought for him. Carter also remembers his mother, Hilda Small Richardson Carter, reading *The Swiss Family Robinson* aloud while the family traveled, pausing often to offer critical commentary on the author's style.

Like many young readers, Carter often read late into the night, under the covers, fascinated not only by the stories that he read but also by the ways in which authors created magical effects with their sentences and paragraphs. He thinks that reading the fiction of Ernest Hemingway and F. Scott Fitzgerald influenced his own writing style. A good student, Carter wrote for his high school newspaper, and during his senior year, his English teacher encouraged him to devote a month or more to writing a single short story. By the time he graduated from high school, he had completed drafts of two novels, both of them rejected by publishers.

style   a distinctive manner of expression

Ernest Hemingway (1899–1961) and **F. Scott Fitzgerald** (1896–1940) are two of the most popular and critically acclaimed writers of contemporary American fiction. There is an article on Hemingway in volume 2.

Becoming a Writer

After earning a bachelor's degree in English and the humanities at the University of Kansas in 1969, Carter served as a U.S. Navy officer for five years and as a high school English and journalism teacher for four years. While he was teaching, he completed drafts of two novels, both of which were rejected by publishers. In 1980, determined to succeed as a writer but having little time for sustained writing, he decided to write full-time.

During the next two years, he produced short stories, articles, a third novel, and part of a fourth novel. Unfortunately, publishers sent only rejection letters, not praise and checks, when he submitted his manuscripts. Naturally he became discouraged. Finally, one editor showed enough interest in *Growing Season,* a novel for young adults, to offer suggestions for revision. Hopeful, Carter thoroughly reworked his novel, beginning with page one. Disappointed when that editor rejected his revised draft, Carter examined the sizable stack of rejection letters he had received, searching for the editor who had been most gracious in her rejection. That editor agreed to read his revision of *Growing Season,* suggested further revisions, and offered him a contract.

Growing Season was finally published in 1984, several years after Carter had begun writing it. He was encouraged when reviewers praised his first book and the American Library Association named it a Best Book for Young Adults. His second novel, *Wart, Son of Toad,* was published in 1985, followed by *Sheila's Dying* in 1987, *Up Country* in 1989, *Robo-Dad* (later published in paperback as *Dancing on Dark Water*) in 1990, *Dogwolf* in 1994, and *Between a Rock and a Hard Place* in 1995.

Nonfiction: A Second Writing Phase

Soon after the publication of his first novel, Carter began a second phase of his writing career. Between 1985 and 1994, he wrote twenty nonfiction books for young adult readers, including books about computers, the history of radio, and the Shoshoni Indian group, and a series of four books about the American Revolution. *China Past—China Future* (1994) is the second book that he has written about that country, which he visited in 1984. Although finding out more about his subjects does not always involve travel, Carter enjoys the research that writing nonfiction requires, particularly when he is preparing to write about history. Fitting a great deal of information on a complex topic into a publisher's six-thousand-word format is not always easy, but Carter thinks it has made him a more careful writer.

The **Shoshoni** Indians once lived from Eastern Oregon to Central Wyoming. They lived modestly in small huts, gathering most of their food.

Writing for Young People

Although Carter enjoys writing nonfiction, he views himself primarily as a novelist for young adult readers who are struggling with tasks common to everyone approaching adulthood. Often, those tasks are related to establishing independence, making moral choices, testing the limits of physical or mental strength, or pursuing friendship and romance. Carter thinks that his stories about teenagers dealing courageously with such tasks can offer his readers both encouragement and hope. "Young adult novels provide no miraculous cure for the age-old problems of growing up," he said in the *Something About the Author Autobiography Series.* "Yet, such novels can offer a respite of sorts. For a few hours, the young adult reader can escape into the lives of fictional young people who are also fighting to make some sense of life: young people who are, in short, proving that the teenage years can be survived." On the other hand, if young readers get nothing more than relaxation and a few laughs from his books, he is satisfied.

Carter's Characters

In Carter's novels, imperfect teenage protagonists deal imperfectly with the challenges of adolescence that confront them. They stumble and sometimes retreat, at least temporarily, but most of them meet those challenges with admirable measures of courage, integrity, and what Carter calls grit. For example, Rick Simons in *Growing Season* resents having to move from Milwaukee to a dairy farm in rural Wisconsin during his senior year. But because owning a farm has long been his parents' dream and because his five younger brothers and sisters look forward to the pets they have been promised, Rick reluctantly exchanges city life for life on a struggling dairy farm. It comforts him to know that he will leave the farm in the fall to study architecture at the university.

The struggle to succeed that first year tests the family's enthusiasm in many ways, for money is short, everything is risky, and no one in the family knows much about farming. They all make mistakes and, at times, become discouraged and out of sorts with each other. But Rick works hard to help his parents manage, and as the big brother he helps his brothers and sisters deal with their respective physical and emotional problems. Sometimes he longs to be back with his friends in Milwaukee, but as summer progresses, Rick finds satisfaction in his accomplishments and challenges himself to learn more about how to make the farm succeed. By the end of the summer, his dream to become an architect has faded, and he decides to remain on the farm for a while. Later, perhaps, after studying agricultural design, he will design the perfect dairy farm. Rick finds his future in an experience that he initially resists.

Like Rick, Carl Staggers in *Up Country* must leave Milwaukee to make his life in rural Wisconsin. He goes there alone, however, to live with relatives he barely knows after his alcoholic mother has been arrested for a hit-and-run accident and assigned to a rehabilitation program. Carl resists going because he needs the money that he makes repairing stolen electronic equipment. He plans to use that money to study engineering, and without it, his plans for escaping his unhappy life seem doomed.

At first he resists the overtures of people whom he considers to be hicks, but as his hard shell cracks, he responds to the kindness of his aunt, uncle, and cousin—and to the friendship of Signa, whom he loves. Carl's rural friends remain loyal to him when he must return to Milwaukee to face charges related to the electronics thefts. Later, when he has an opportunity to return to the city to live with his recovering mother, he chooses instead to return to the country, where he seeks alternative means to fulfill his plan to become an engineer.

In *Between a Rock and a Hard Place,* cousins Mark and Randy Severson are also city kids who must cope with life in the country. As a rite of passage, several generations of Severson youths have traveled the Minnesota lake country in canoes, and now it is Mark and Randy's turn. They dread the thought of spending time together in the wilderness. Mark is overweight and does not like either the water or himself very much; Randy seems obsessed with his diabetes. Neither likes to fish. Just as they begin to enjoy each other's company and their surroundings, however, nature tests them both. After rapids sweep away Randy's insulin, Mark takes great risks to save his cousin's life. Having survived their initiation journey, they are eager to plan the next.

In *Wart, Son of Toad,* Steve Michaels and his father both have a tough time after the accidental death of Steve's mother and younger sister. They offer little comfort to each other. In fact, they fight more than they did before, often over Steve's hair, his clothes, his grades—and his friends. Seeing himself as a misfit and something of a rebel, Steve befriends the "dirts" in his school, who "on the average . . . drink more, smoke more, skip more classes, and study less than most kids" (p. 16). To make matters worse, Steve wants to enter the Capstone, a special two-year apprentice program that will prepare him to become an auto mechanic, not the sort of future that his father has in mind for him.

Life at school is no easier than life at home for Steve. He suffers the consequences of being a student of Mr. Michaels, a strict, cheerless biology teacher whom nearly every student

rite of passage a ceremonial act or procedure associated with a crisis or change in status of a person, such as the change from childhood to adulthood.

insulin a hormone that regulates the amount of sugar in the blood; people with insulin-dependent diabetes must have insulin daily to survive.

dislikes. Behind his back, students call Mr. Michaels "Toad." When they want to tease Steve, they call him "Wart, the son of Toad." Attaining the C grade average that he must have to enter the Capstone is quite a challenge for Steve, who is nearly failing in every subject, but it keeps him in school and gives him a goal worth achieving. He almost sacrifices his future when he defends his father by fighting the school's quarterback, but in the end his grit and determination help him to befriend his enemy, strengthen his relationship with his father, and face the future on his own terms.

Shar Zarada's father is also at the center of the challenges she faces in *RoboDad*. Shar finds it difficult to reestablish her relationship with her father after an aneurysm destroys the part of his brain that controls his emotions. His consequently erratic and reckless behavior often embarrasses and frightens Shar, and his lack of emotion makes her yearn for the loving father she has lost. She shares with her mother the responsibility for her father's care. One day, out of pity, she decides not to give him his tranquilizers. Following the crisis that ensues, Shar acknowledges the permanent loss of the father whom she misses and vows to "give this stranger what love I can in memory of that dad I once had" (p. 144).

Like Shar, Jerry Kincaid in *Sheila's Dying* also matures after he assumes responsibility for someone who is very ill. About the time Jerry decides to break off his relationship with Sheila Porter, she discovers that she is suffering from terminal cancer. Because Sheila has meant something to him and she otherwise has only her alcoholic grandmother to care for her, Jerry decides to stay with Sheila throughout her ordeal. Sheila's friend Bonnie, Jerry's abrasive adversary at school, becomes his partner in caring for Sheila. Their mutual concern for Sheila slowly turns to respect and, eventually, love. In caring for Sheila, Jerry observes the stages of her illness, her medical treatment, and her responses to pain and dying. For the most part, he deals maturely with the resentment, fear, fatigue, anger, and grief that he feels as Sheila's advocate.

A mix of Chippewa, Metis, and Swede, Pete LaSavage explores his racial identity in *Dogwolf*. Intrigued and angered by a howling half-dog, half-wolf that his neighbor seems to have abandoned, Pete prepares to end the animal's misery. When he approaches the animal to shoot it, however, he lets it escape into the forest instead, perhaps because he identi-

aneurysm an abnormal swelling of a blood vessel

Chippewa an Indian tribe that lived in Southern Canada

Metis communities in Canada of a mixed European and Indian ancestry

fies with its mixed blood. Pete worries about the consequences of that private act while sitting in a fire tower watching summer fires claim hundreds of acres of national forest,
near which he lives in Wisconsin. Tension builds until, in the
midst of a devastating fire that threatens his community, Pete
discovers that the dogwolf has killed his best friend, Jim Red-
wing. Pete paints his face with the blood of his friend and
stalks the savage that he once spared. In many ways, Pete is
Carter's most complex character.

Processes and Praise

Carter does not have trouble finding something to write
about. As he says in *Something About the Author Autobiography Series,* he believes that writers who keep their eyes
and ears open find that "life is absolutely thick with stories."
His stories often develop out of games he plays with his
imagination, placing possible characters into possible situations and shaping plots based upon the consequences. When
an idea works, he writes it in a notebook that he carries in
his back pocket. Such ideas sometimes continue to grow, often for years, before he transforms them into short stories or
novels. Although Carter claims that his stories generally are
not autobiographical, he admits that events in his short comical play *Driver's Test* do parallel his memories of failing his
own first driver's test.

Before he can begin writing, Carter usually must do some
research. Generally he consults two kinds of sources: printed
and human. For *Sheila's Dying, RoboDad,* and *Between a
Rock and a Hard Place,* he sought medical information about
cancer, aneurysms, and diabetes. Because he had been a city
boy, he sought information about farming before beginning
to write *Growing Season.* Although as a boy he had known
some Chippewas and as a young man had worked briefly for
the Native American Studies Department at Montana State
University, before beginning to write *Dogwolf* he sought expert advice from friends familiar with the history, beliefs, and
current lifestyles of the Chippewa. He also had to research
methods of fighting forest fires before writing that book.

Because his own father had been an alcoholic, Carter assumed that he would not need to research alcoholism before
portraying Carl Staggers' alcoholic mother in *Up Country.* But

while reading a nonfiction book about the adult children of alcoholics, he learned that he had not really understood very much at all about the families of alcoholic parents. Not until he had read many more books on the subject, joined a group for adult children of alcoholics, and attended related workshops was he ready to write *Up Country.* That book is not autobiographical, he says, "but many of Carl's emotions are definitely mine."

By the time he begins a novel, Carter generally knows his characters quite well and knows where he wants them to go. After he has rewritten the opening chapters several times, his characters find their voices and take over the story. He does not always approve of what they choose to do, but if their actions are in character and are important to the story, he lets them make their own choices. Two rules guide his writing: do not lie and do not preach. A deliberate writer, Carter reads and revises each chapter many times before a book is published. Over a ten-year period, *Dogwolf* went through five major drafts before its publication. Carter believes that a wastebasket is an important tool for writers.

Critics generally give Carter extremely high marks for characterization, not just for main characters but for supporting characters as well. Shar's mother in *RoboDad* and Signa in *Up Country* are especially strong supporting characters. Critics also praise his positive portrayals of family life, as in *Growing Season* and *Dogwolf,* and of rural Midwestern life, as in *Growing Season* and *Up Country.* Expert readers also admire his action scenes, including forest fires in *Dogwolf* and shooting the rapids in *Between a Rock and Hard Place.* Carter's nonfiction often wins praise for scholarship, readability, and style. Five of his novels have been selected by the American Library Association as Best Books for Young Adults. *Sheila's Dying, Up Country,* and *Wart, Son of Toad* are among "The 100 Best Books of the Last 25 Years" selected by the Young Adult Library Services Division of the American Library Association.

In 1996, Carter lived with his wife, Carol Ann Shadis, and their two children, Brian and Sisi, in Marshfield, Wisconsin, where he wrote in a small office at the local airport. When he was not writing, he enjoyed canoeing, hiking, camping, photography, traveling, and reading. And whose books did this writer enjoy? He cited books by Tony Hillerman, Stephen King, Larry McMurtry, and Paul St. Pierre, among others.

Tony Hillerman writes mystery and non-fiction novels featuring Native Americans. **Stephen King** writes horror novels. **Larry McMurtry** writes Western novels, including *Lonesome Dove.* **Paul St. Pierre** writes Westerns set in Canada, particularly in British Columbia.

Selected Bibliography

If you like books by Alden R. Carter, you might also like those by Robin Brancato, Brock Cole, Chris Crutcher, Will Hobbs, Kevin Major, and Gary Paulsen.

WORKS BY ALDEN R. CARTER

Novels

Growing Season (1984)

Wart, Son of Toad (1985)

Sheila's Dying (1987)

Up Country (1989)

RoboDad (1990), published in paperback as *Dancing on Dark Water* (1993)

Dogwolf (1994)

Between a Rock and a Hard Place (1995)

Short Stories and Plays

"Tree House." In *Connections: Short Stories by Outstanding Writers for Young Adults*. Edited by Donald R. Gallo (1989).

Driver's Test. In *Center Stage: One-Act Plays for Teenage Readers and Actors*. Edited by Donald R. Gallo (1990).

"No Win Phuong." In *Join In: Multiethnic Short Stories by Outstanding Writers for Young Adults*. Edited by Donald R. Gallo (1993).

Nonfiction

Supercomputers, with Wayne Jerome LeBlanc (1985)

Modern China (1986)

Modern Electronics, with Wayne Jerome LeBlanc (1986)

Illinois (1987)

Radio: From Marconi to the Space Age (1987)

At the Forge of Liberty (1988)

Birth of the Republic (1988)

Colonies in Revolt (1988)

The Darkest Hours (1988)

The Shoshoni (1989)

The Battle of Gettysburg (1990)

Last Stand at the Alamo (1990)

The American Revolution: War for Independence (1992)

The Civil War: American Tragedy (1992)

Clashes in the Wilderness: The Colonial Wars (1992)

The Mexican War: Manifest Destiny (1992)

The Spanish-American War: Imperial Ambitions (1992)

The War of 1812: Second Fight for Independence (1992)

Battle of the Ironclads: The Monitor and the Merrimack (1993)

China Past—China Future (1994)

WORKS ABOUT ALDEN R. CARTER

Carter, Alden R. *Something About the Author Autobiography Series.* Detroit: Gale Research, 1994, vol. 18, pp. 77–94.

———. "Alden R. Carter." In *Speaking for Ourselves Too: More Autobiographical Sketches by Notable Authors for Young Adults.* Edited by Donald R. Gallo. Urbana, Ill.: National Council of Teachers of English, 1993.

Olendorf, Donna, ed. "Alden R. Carter." *Something About the Author.* Detroit: Gale Research, 1992, vol. 67, pp. 40–43.

Poe, Elizabeth A. *Twentieth-Century Young Adult Writers.* Detroit: St. James Press, 1993, pp. 105–106.

Senick, Gerard J., ed. *Children's Literature Review.* Detroit: Gale Research, 1991, vol. 22, pp. 16–23.

How to write to the Author

Alden R. Carter
1113 West Onstad Drive
Marshfield, WI 54449

Aidan Chambers

(1934-)

by Ted Hipple

Aidan Chambers is a master wordsmith, a writer whose affection for language—its sounds and shapes and meanings, its awesome variety, and its amazing versatility—enables him to use it well in the service of his stories. Chambers engages readers in several ways, composing ingenious plots, creating memorable characters, exploring important ideas, yet always dazzling us with his skill with language. He likes to use plays on words, double-edged names for his characters, whimsical descriptions, *italics* and other **alternative** fonts (even within one sentence), quotations from authors such as Franz Kafka or Charles Dickens, letters, newspaper columns, diary entries, shifts in narrative point of view from the first to the third person, interior monologues, and on and on.

There is an article about Charles Dickens later in this volume.

interior monologue
a representation of a character's inner thoughts and feelings

The Author's Work

Reading Chambers is a bit like going on a linguistic safari: you do not know what you will find on the next page or in the upcoming chapter. Will it be the full-page drawing of a fist coming at you in *Breaktime* (1978) or the poem in three parallel columns in *N.I.K.: Now I Know* (1987), a novel whose very title is a pun on the name of its major character? Note this introductory page to another of his novels:

DANCE
ON MY GRAVE

Aidan Chambers
A Life and a Death
in Four Parts
One Hundred and Seventeen Bits
Six Running Reports
and Two Press Clippings
with a few jokes
a puzzle or three
some footnotes
and a fiasco now and then
to help the story along

fiasco a humiliating failure

True to his words, Chambers does include all these items in this novel.

Yet it would be doing Chambers a considerable injustice to classify him as merely a clever practitioner of language, although that he indeed is. He also tells good stories, dramatic and complex narratives that focus on young people who face situations that must be confronted. Moreover, he tells these tales *for* young readers, people he envisions as having problems similar to those his characters encounter, and thus his writings take on an instructional dimension as well as an entertaining one.

From the age of fifteen, the time he recalls as the first when he knew he would try to be a writer, Chambers has been interested in young adult literature: as critic, as publisher, as playwright and, most particularly, as novelist. He is an author worth reading—and reading about.

The Author's Life

Aidan Chambers was born 27 December 1934, to George Kenneth Blacklin (a funeral director) and Margaret Hancock Chambers, in the small coal-mining town called Chesterle-Street in England. He lived there until he was ten. Those years shaped Chambers' life. He had few close friends and was essentially a loner, characteristics of many of the protagonists in his novels. He loved movies and developed an interest in drama that would find an outlet in his writing. He loathed school and did poorly there; his teenage protagonists typically have little regard for school in general, although, like Chambers himself in later school days, they often are fond of individual teachers and are significantly influenced by them.

protagonist the main character of a literary work

In Chambers' case this one teacher was Jim Osborn, whom he encountered in Darlington, a larger town to which his parents moved when he was ten. Osborn insisted that Chambers become a reader and that he participate in drama and debate clubs. Chambers developed skill in speaking and writing and, more important, confidence in his abilities. (In *Dance on My Grave* (1983), both Hal and Barry revere their English teacher—named Jim Osborn.)

After his initial schooling, Chambers spent two years in the navy and then returned to college, where he studied English and produced, wrote, and acted in plays. He next became an English teacher in secondary schools and renewed his longtime interest in religion, specifically in the nature of belief and how people ought to act in response to their beliefs. After three years of teaching, Chambers helped found a monastery devoted to helping young people. He spent seven years in the order, but not exclusively at the monastery; he taught part-time and later assumed an editorship of books written for youth. He also continued with his writing.

Finally, he had to make a choice: should he be a monk? an editor? a writer? Chambers left the monastery in 1967, intent upon serving young people through his writing. In 1968 he married Nancy Lockwood, and together they have continued the work to which Chambers has devoted his considerable talents—the production of and support for writing of high quality for children and young adults. They edit *Signal,* a British magazine about literature for children and adolescents that attempts to increase the critical attention to this field. They also founded Thimble Press, which publishes books for children.

Finally, he had to make a choice: should he be a monk? an editor? a writer?

advocate one who defends or maintains a cause

In effect, Chambers became as much an advocate as an author; he urged that literature written for children receive the same attention afforded so-called adult novels and stories. He also wrote about teaching literature to young people, most notably in *Introducing Books to Children* (1983), a work intended for teachers, librarians, parents, and anyone else who participates in the interaction between a youthful reader and a book. In a chapter called "Why Bother?" he poses the question, "Why bother so much about children's reading?" Chambers offers a few answers, among which are the following.

Reading literature:

helps extend a child's experience and knowledge of life;

helps a child's personal growth—you discover yourself in literature and therefore learn to understand more about yourself; . . .

challenges and changes us; . . .

allows us to experience all kinds of human possibilities, from murder to childbirth, without suffering the consequences of undergoing the experiences in real life;

is a game-playing activity in which we "try out" various possible solutions to life-problems and see how they might be worked out before having to tackle them in reality.

In this important piece of scholarship, Chambers implicitly charged himself with writing the very kind of demanding yet rewarding, thoughtful yet entertaining literature he wanted all children to experience; he must practice what he preaches. Chambers has met this challenge with brilliance.

Chambers' Novels for Young Adults

Breaktime was not Chambers' first piece of fiction. He had written earlier novels for younger readers, collections of ghost stories, and several plays. *Breaktime,* published in 1978, was certainly the riskiest undertaking of his developing literary career, however. The novel contains a vivid description of sex, printed on a half-page with a pedantic excerpt from a sex manual on the other half. The book contains letters, drawings, imagined and real conversations, blurbs from travel brochures, and a takeoff on the burglary scene from *Oliver Twist*. Throughout, Chambers creates a suspicion among readers that maybe all of this is really happening and maybe it is not.

pedantic overemphasizing minor details

The thrust of *Breaktime* is an argument between Ditto, the seventeen-year-old protagonist, and his schoolmate Morgan about whether "literature is crap," to use Morgan's disparaging comment. Ditto proposes to take a holiday during which he will record events—some real, some he may make up—and give this record to Morgan to counter the latter's attack on fiction. One of the events Ditto hopes to report is the loss of his virginity to the willing Helen, and he arranges to rendezvous with her on his outing. When he returns, Ditto gives his story to Morgan, who reads it and notices that he himself appears in Ditto's escapades:

> **"I'm in the thing [Ditto's adventure]. Are you saying I'm just a character in a story?"**
>
> **"Aren't we all?" said Ditto and laughed.**

Chambers held out little hope for the publication of *Breaktime*. Not only would its sexual content worry potential publishers, he figured, but also the narrative techniques violated so many conventions of the generally conservative nature of works for adolescent readers (at that time) that he feared it would never see print. He was wrong. The second editor to whom he sent the work published it to generally very excited critical praise and Chambers was off and running. As it happens, he was running to what he wants to become a sextet of young adult novels that explore important developments and problems in the lives of young adult males. Four of these novels had been published by the mid-1990s—*Breaktime, Dance on My Grave, N.I.K: Now I Know*, and *The Toll Bridge* (1992)—and Chambers is at work on the fifth. Because he takes a long time to write his novels, with numerous revisions, it may be a while yet before numbers five and six in the series appear, but in the meantime we have these four. And they are outstanding.

sextet a group of six

desecrating treating
with disrespect

first-person narration
a story told from the
position or perspec-
tive of someone in-
side the story, using
the pronoun "I"

Dance on My Grave, which Chambers wrote over a
twelve-year period, describes the guilt-free sexual bonding
of two gay teenagers. The story opens with a newspaper
clipping about the arrest of Hal Robinson, a sixteen year old
charged with desecrating the grave of recently deceased
Barry Gorman, also sixteen. Readers soon learn that Hal and
Barry are lovers and that Barry has insisted upon a pact: if
one of them dies, the other has to dance on his grave. Barry
is killed in a motorcycle crash, just after he and Hal have
fought over their differing attitudes about their relationship.
Hal wants it to be forever, but to Barry it is only a passing
fancy. The distressed Hal feels that he must honor their
agreement. Interspersed in Hal's first-person narration is the
formal report of the social worker assigned to the case, who
interviews Hal's parents and his supportive teacher named
Jim Osburn.

N.I.K.: Now I Know (this is the American title; in England,
the *N.I.K.* is omitted) explores religion and teenagers' various
beliefs about its tenets and practices. Nik, seventeen, is urged
by his history teacher to help a youth group with their drama
production, a pageant about Christ's returning to earth. Although he is reluctant, Nik, an atheist, takes on the task and
ends up being assigned the role of Christ. At a rally Nik
meets Julie, who is religious yet not exactly orthodox in her
beliefs. She refers to God and Jesus with feminine pronouns.
When Julie is critically injured, both she and Nik have to examine their attitudes about religion and about each other.
Their private thinking and personal conversations cover a
wide spectrum of teenagers' beliefs and doubts, making this
novel Chambers' most philosophical.

Fourth in the series is *The Toll Bridge,* and in it Chambers
unleashes a substantial amount of overt symbolism to support his story about seventeen-year-old Piers, who simply
does not know whether he is coming or going. To find out,
Piers leaves his home and girlfriend to take a job in rural
England as the collector of tolls at a seldom-traveled bridge,
a structure that is used for coming and going. Piers lives
alone in a small cabin alongside the bridge, where he hopes
to have ample time to reflect on life and its quirks. Tess, his
boss's daughter, senses his ambivalence and quickly begins
calling him Jan, after Janus, the Roman two-faced god who,
like a bridge, faces two directions at once. Enter Adam, a
mysterious teen whose past seems to change each time he

describes it. Jan wants Adam to leave, yet he is drawn to him too. A sexual urge? A need to know about Adam? Equally annoying to Jan (or is it?) is the obvious attraction between Adam and Tess, about whom he is also undecided. An unexpected visit from Jan's old girlfriend, whom he had ignored, and a wild party add to the climax of this novel and reveal insights into all the teenage characters.

Four Special Novels

Each of these remarkable novels differs from the others in many ways, yet there are similarities worth noting. They all feature a male around seventeen years of age, usually somewhat of a loner, usually more than a bit mixed up. All four boys—Ditto, Hal, Nik, and Piers/Jan—are smart, and each of them is aware of at least some of his hang-ups and is willing to try to confront them. All four boys like language, perhaps as much as their creator, and that is saying a lot; Chambers has said that language is "the god who makes us." Love, often physical love (sometimes graphically depicted), plays a central role in the life of each protagonist. Parents are generally less consequential than are the boys' teachers, but schooling itself is seldom mentioned and then not always favorably. The settings of the novels are rarely significant, affording them a universality that they might not have if they were placed more particularly or if they were locales that shaped or limited the kinds of stories Chambers wants to tell.

> *Chambers has said that language is "the god who makes us."*

Writing about his first three novels in the *Something About the Author Autobiography Series,* Chambers says:

> *Breaktime* is largely to do with physical sensation— the life of the senses. *Dance on My Grave* is largely to do with the emotions—kinds of love and our personal obsessions. *Now I Know* is largely about what people often call spiritual experience and about thought, and how they clash and blend and complement each other.

To this it may be added that *The Toll Bridge* explores introspection and depression—or "the glums," as Jan calls the feeling. In effect, the protagonists face a kind of bewilderment about life—its physical, emotional, spiritual, or psychological aspects. The trials that Chambers puts them through

sine qua non something absolutely necessary

help them confront their uncertainties, although without total resolution and never with ultimate happiness. A summary statement about these four novels might suggest that Chambers is more interested in ideas than in events; the latter provide a vehicle for the former. In this way he differs from those writers for young adults who seem more interested in actions and less in their philosophical significance.

Perhaps more than their other compelling thematic features, these four novels focus on change, that ever-present characteristic of adolescent life, the sine qua non of existence. Although it happens to everyone, change can be frightening if it goes unrecognized, if the adolescent knows only that something about him or her is different without also understanding why. This may be the reason that Chambers writes of change—to help his teenage readers recognize and understand it. Near the conclusion of *The Toll Bridge,* Jan becomes aware of some of his own changes and notes:

phonemes speech sounds

> **There are moments that change people. No, wrong; try again. There are moments when people change. These moments are not isolated, not separate, not removed from the rest of life. They are not independent atoms of existence that suddenly break into your life— the ever-shifting phonemes of existence, which sometimes gather into concentrated patterns of such intensity, such unmistakable clarity and significance, that suddenly you know something about yourself, your own *self,* for the first time. Some hidden part of you enters your consciousness. Recognized, acknowledged, accepted, it becomes part of the you you know.**

These four novels demand and reward intelligent reading— and rereading. Chambers in an interview remarked that "you have to read the books two or three times to enjoy them." He knows that this suggestion will mean fewer readers among those who want their fiction "once and fast," but he refuses to compromise his standards in order to deliver "sensational entertainment." Yet it is sensational entertainment that he, in fact, does deliver for those readers who appreciate good stories told interestingly, stories in which the telling matches the tale. Aidan Chambers does not deliver the straightforward, beginning-to-end, action-packed thrill on every page, the cliff-hanging adventure. His characters pause to examine events, to study their significance.

Furthermore, Chambers writes not only in simple prose but also in poetry; he uses flashbacks and flashforwards; he shifts narrators and matches style to character; he sends readers to the dictionary hunting for meanings of words such as "leptonic" and "estragonist." He plays with the spacing on the page. In being philosophical and in doing these linguistic magic acts, Chambers is showing enormous respect for his readers, an awareness that they, too, can and will join in the fun. And yet all his stories, no matter how amusing or amazing, speak of real issues that confront real teenagers and require real attention—attention that Chambers always gives them.

Selected Bibliography

WORKS BY AIDAN CHAMBERS

Breaktime (1978)

Dance on My Grave (1982)

Introducing Books to Children (1983)

The Present Takers (1984)

Booktalk: Occasional Writing on Children and Literature (1985)

N.I.K.: Now I Know (1987)

The Toll Bridge (1992)

WORKS ABOUT AIDAN CHAMBERS

Chambers, Aidan. "Aidan Chambers." In *Something About the Author Autobiography Series*. Detroit: Gale Research, 1986, vol. 12, pp. 37–55.

Gowar, Mick. "Interview with Aidan Chambers." In *Living Writers: A New Approach to English Novelists*. Edited by Mick Gowar and Dennis Hanley. London: Nelson, 1992, pp. 111–115.

If you like the works of Aidan Chambers, you might also enjoy the works of Robert Cormier, Chris Crutcher, Chris Lynch, Bruce Brooks, and J. D. Salinger.

How to Write to the Author
Aidan Chambers
c/o HarperCollins Publishers
10 East 53rd Street
New York, NY 10022

Alice Childress

(1920–1994)

by Linda Miller Cleary

Alice Childress (pronounced CHILL-dress) was born in Charleston, South Carolina, on 12 October 1920. She was the great-granddaughter of a slave. Raised by her grandmother after her parents divorced, Childress was taken to New York City at the age of five, on the "journey from the South to the promised land of the North that generations of blacks had taken before her," as Trudier Harris calls it in the introduction to Childress' *Like One of the Family* (p. vii). Childress went to grade school at Public School 81 in Harlem, then to the Julia Ward Howe Junior High School; she had to leave Wadleigh High School after three years because both her mother and grandmother had died.

Before Childress' grandmother died she encouraged her granddaughter to write down ideas that seemed important to her, and this probably began Childress' life as a writer. Later, Childress immersed herself in the literature of the time to find her place as a writer.

Artistic Beginnings

Childress' first creative home was the theater. She worked with the American Negro Theater in Harlem from 1943 to 1954. The actor Sidney Poitier, who worked with Childress during that time, said: "She opened me up to positive new ways of looking at myself and others, and she encouraged me to explore the history of the black people" (*Dictionary of Literary Biography, Afro-American Writers After 1955,* p. 68). Even though Childress wanted to act and write, she worked at many other jobs—assistant machinist, domestic worker, insurance agent, photo retoucher, and saleslady—so she could support her daughter, Jean. The varied and rich characterization found in her plays, screenplays, and novels reflect that work experience.

characterization a method by which a writer creates and develops the appearance and personality of a character

Though drama critics have generally praised her work, her plays have been underproduced. Some critics and scholars think that this relative obscurity is because her presentations of African Americans are so realistic that she did not always endear herself to white audiences. Others think the cause was her politics: in the 1950s, when many writers and actors were accused of being communists, Childress had written sketches that were included in Paul Robeson's magazine, *Freedom,* and Robeson had connections with the Communist Party. Finally, another explanation some critics give is that Childress lived her life as a writer with great determination and integrity, a writer who did not take popular routes to fame but followed artistic paths that she thought were important. For instance, when her play *Trouble in Mind* (1955) was sought for a Broadway production, Childress refused to make changes to appeal to Broadway audiences and withdrew the play. She was interested in making her audiences think about the harshness and unfairness that African Americans have faced and was not willing to sacrifice that mission for the sake of making it more entertaining or profitable. As was the case with Langston Hughes, many observers thought that she might receive more attention after her death.

Paul Robeson was a singer and actor who also was a supporter of the black civil rights movement.

When Childress died in 1994, she had written novels for young adults, novels for adults, and plays, and she had collaborated on musicals with her husband, Nathan Woodward. She received many awards for her work, including the Obie Award for *Trouble in Mind,* and two *New York Times Book Review* Outstanding Books of the Year Awards in 1973 and

Nathan Woodward was a musician who wrote the music for several of Childress' plays.

1981. In 1978, her novel *A Hero Ain't Nothin' but a Sandwich* (1973) was made into a film starring Cicely Tyson and Paul Winfield.

Novels for Young Adults

The books by Childress that you are most likely to find in your school library are in *A Hero Ain't Nothin but a Sandwich*, *Rainbow Jordan* (1981), and *Those Other People* (1989). With courage and dignity, the main characters in each of these books face difficulties that trouble many young people. As Benjie, the main character in *A Hero Ain't Nothin' but a Sandwich,* is told by one of his teachers, "You can face hardship if you realize it's not all your fault" (p. 43). The main characters in these three books come to know that their troubles are not all their own doing.

Benjie has a hard time understanding that people care for him: "I feel like a accident that happen to people. My blood father cut out on Mama. Musta gone cause he didn't dig me" (p. 70). Later he says, "Nobody care, why should they if your own daddy run off?" (p. 74).

By using multiple narrators (Benjie's mother, stepfather, grandmother, teachers, principal, best friend, and even a drug pusher), Childress tells of Benjie's growing addiction to drugs. He becomes hooked because he needs to prove himself to his so-called friends. At first Benjie's family does not know what to do when they see him going down a self-destructive path. Benjie's grandmother says, "One day I almost said . . . 'Benjie, the greatest thing in the world is to love someone and they love you too.' But when I opened my mouth, I said, 'Benjie, brush the crumbs off your jacket'"(p. 54). Benjie's stepfather has to realize that he cares for Benjie; Benjie has to come to believe it; and others have to show that they care. When these things happen, it makes all the difference. "I can do it [stay off drugs] . . . long as somebody believe in me," Benjie discovers. But his stepfather says, "Dammit, Benjie . . . you gotta do it even if *nobody* believe in you, gotta be your own man, the supervisor of your veins, the night watchman and day shift foreman in charge-a your own affairs" (p. 120).

As Benjie is finding out how much people care about him, Rainbow in *Rainbow Jordan* comes to understand how

As Benjie, the main character in A Hero Ain't Nothin' but a Sandwich, is told by one of his teachers, "You can face hardship if you realize it's not all your fault."

narrator a speaker or character who tells a story

alone she is. Her mother, who wants to be called Kathie, "doesn't love me as much as I love her" (p. 123). Kathie was only fifteen years old when Rainbow was born. By the time Rainbow is fourteen, she has often been left on her own, and is sometimes sent by the family social worker to her "interim home" with her foster mother Miss Josie. Only inner strength allows Rainbow to get through her problems with her girl-friends; her boyfriend, Eljay; and her school. This excerpt shows one of her dilemmas:

> **Wish I could tell Eljay all that's in my heart . . . but can't yet trust to tell him all. Must be eight girls fol-lowin after him. Some lookin fine as movie stars. More than a few also *puttin out* . . . Nobody gets laughed at as much as those, like me, who not puttin out . . . I don't wanta . . . yet. (P. 47)**

Eljay tries one of the oldest and stupidest arguments known to woman to try to convince Rainbow to have sex with him: "Girl, you got hang-ups bout sex. Nothin wrong with sex. It's a natural thing. If a guy don't get off, once in a while, like his health'll be broke. . . . Can get a hernia" (p. 97). Rainbow almost gives in because she fears losing the one person with whom she feels close. She is saved by circumstance and her own presence of mind and she couragously continues with-out the support of Eljay. Even before she broke up with El-jay, there was no one with whom she could share the truth about her family situation, so she makes up stories.

> **Wish I could tell somebody how I/feel, bout Kathie droppin in and out like she do once in a while. . . . I lie to keep the family situation in check. I tell Eljay and my friend Beryl that Miss Josie is my aunt . . . how the reason I'm back and forth with her is cause my mother be working outta town. . . . Lotta people will mouth your business to the world if they ever peep your per-sonal secrets. Like when I went to the circus and saw a man walkin the high wire and keepin his balance . . . Ha! Ask me about it. I do it every day. (P. 48)**

It takes courage for Rainbow to keep on in the face of aban-donment. She holds herself back from people because she is afraid of being hurt again: "Would be easy to like her [Miss Josie] a lot if I wasn't wise to how people can draw you close, then turn you loose" (p. 50). Rainbow may have to hide the truth from other people, but she thinks hard about what is happening to her and ends up knowing that she can trust Josie. "It's the big ones [lies] I'm gonna stop . . . like me telling myself Kathie be gone cause-a her career or cause somebody is *makin* her do it. She gone cause that's what she wanta do . . . just like Mr. Harold [Josie's husband] and Eljay. They gone, gone, gone, while we standin round actin simple" (p. 126). Miss Josie and Rainbow are ready to face up to the truth of their being abandoned by those for whom they have cared the most.

What is remarkable about Childress' characters, whose ages range from twelve to seventeen, is that they do not hide themselves from the truth as they know it. Both Benjie and Rainbow learn to see themselves and the world around them with more clarity, and as a result they see better how they can get along in their worlds.

Jonathan, in *Those Other People* (1989), is another character with such strength. He is gay, and he has known it for years before the action of the novel begins. At seventeen, Jonathan has graduated from high school; postponed college plans; escaped to New York City, where everything went very wrong; and is working at Minitown High School as a temporary computer instructor. Jonathan's parents accept the fact that he is gay, but they want him to keep up his connection with his friend Fern so that he will look "normal," and he gives in. "Maybe that's why I keep running," he says, toward the beginning of the book. "Too chicken. . . too cowardly to stand my ground and face the future" (p. 25). Jonathan finds the courage to come out with the truth—to Fern and to others around him—even when it means losing his job.

The teens in *Those Other People* are all more willing to face the real issues of life than the adults are. Jonathan is not much older than his students, who find equal courage: Theodora is willing to bring charges of sexual assault against the physical education teacher; Tyrone and Susan, the only African American students in the suburban town, find the courage to maintain their racial pride, even though their father is trying to assimilate into the white neighborhood. Tyrone and Susan find the courage to come forth with evidence for Theodora when it would be easier not to get involved.

Rainbow says, "Would be easy to like her [Miss Josie] a lot if I wasn't wise to know how people can draw you close, then turn you loose."

Childress allows you to see different ways people think about the same situations.

monologue extended thoughts of a character, especially those spoken aloud while the character is alone

stereotype a character that is not original or individual because it conforms to a preconceived category

Benjie, Rainbow, and Jonathan all have the courage to tell the truth to themselves. They are in many ways like Childress, who found the courage to live—and write—with integrity in a world that was not always hospitable.

Style

Childress is, at heart, a dramatist. If you read her plays, it is clear how she uses dramatic techniques in her novels, building a narrative through a succession of monologues. In her novels for young adults, the multiple narrators talk to the reader about their connections with the main characters; and the main characters, Benjie, Rainbow, and Jonathan, talk directly to the reader, as well. By using more than one narrator, Childress allows you to see different ways people think about the same situations. Your job as reader is to piece together the story and to think about who and what to believe. This technique shows characters as full-blown personalities, not just stereotypes.

Because the characters speak for themselves, all their faults and strengths push through Childress' words and are revealed. In "Those Were the Days, My Friend," an article in the 3 December 1972 *Sunday News*, Childress says:

> Characters know, they won't be fooled, not even by their medium, the writer. They *allow* you to write them, pushing you along until they're satisfied that they've done their thing to the utmost of your ability . . . . The characters kept chasing me down . . . . They tap at the brain and move a pen to action to the middle of the night. They are alive, they really are, pushing and shoving interfering creators out of the way.

In *Something About the Author,* Childress says,

> "When I'm writing a character that I see as a villain, I try to take the villain's side and believe in the righteousness of the villainous act. In *A Hero* . . . we [Childress and the editor] pondered long over cutting out the drug pusher's side of the story [because of the

young readers] . . . but after a great deal of talk about it, we decided to leave the character in." (P. 54)

Childress respects the young readers and challenges them to think about events from many points of view and to decide for themselves where truth and goodness lies.

Another interesting aspect of Childress' style is her use of imagery. She weaves pictures into what her characters say instead of embedding them into description, as many other authors do. Josie in *Rainbow Jordan* describes a gossipy neighbor using this vivid image: "She also needs a lock-type zipper for her big, destructive mouth" (p. 91). Rachel in *Rainbow Jordan* says: "Our heads and hearts have to stay in training for it [thinking], like athletes preparing for the Olympics" (p. 87). As Jonathan in *Those Other People* resigns from his job, he observes, "Everyone is quiet. You could hear a flea piss on a piece of cotton" (p. 184).

imagery words or phrases that appeal to one or more of the five senses in order to create a mental picture

Language

Childress dared to write in her language, Black English. If you understand Black English, then Childress' books will be just a little easier for you to read than works that do not use Black English. Nigeria Greene, one of Benjie's teachers, who is African American, defends Black English: "Right on . . . I'm one of the underprivileged, and I dig Black talk, I smile Black, think Black, walk Black . . . You get off my kids!" (p. 46). He is talking to Bernard Cohen, another teacher who says about Greene, "Nigeria likes to say 'ain't' even though he knows better. That's *their* way of trying to invent a language because they don't have one" (p. 37). Many linguists, scientists who study language, would say that Cohen was wrong. They would say that Black English is a complete language and has rules just as standard English does; they are just different rules.

Black English a form of English spoken by some African Americans

Some people, like Josie, think that African American students should change their language so they can speak and write in a way that will empower them in the mainstream society. In these two scenes, she is trying to convince Rainbow to do so, but Rainbow resists:

mainstream the widely accepted current of thought or way of life

"Miss Josephine, today's Monday. Tomorrow is my deadline for bringin a parent to school."

"Say bring*ing*. You write compositions in good English. Speak that way."

"I like to sound like my friends. Nobody wants me bringin them strange sounds."

"Say bring*ing*." (P. 93)

"Didn't mean to bug you, Miss Josie. If nobody shows, it'll make me the onliest one who hasn't had a parent-teacher evaluation."

"Don't say 'onliest.' You will be the only one, not the 'onliest.'"

"Last night you said . . . 'I feel like the loneliest woman in town.' If you can be the loneliest, how come I can't be the onliest?" (P. 93)

If they were characters in the same novel, Nigeria and Josie would disagree. Language experts think students can know both varieties of English and use whichever one serves them better, depending on to whom they are writing or speaking. This juggling of languages makes school harder for many African American students, but as Nigeria says: "Most of the kids don't talk anything but Harlemese, but have minds as sharp as a double-edge razor" (*A Hero,* p. 43).

Beyond Childress' Novels

If you like Childress' novels for young adults, you may appreciate other African American writers, such as Rosa Guy, Langston Hughes, Zora Neale Hurston, Nella Larsen, Walter Dean Myers, and Ann Petry. You also may be ready for Childress' other works. One play that you might find particularly interesting to read or perform is *When the Rattlesnake Sounds* (1975), a one-act play that pays tribute to three women who worked for the Underground Railroad. Harriet (Tubman), Lennie, and Celia are earning money at a Cape May, New Jersey, hotel so that more Southern slaves can be brought to freedom. Celia, the youngest, finally says to Harriet, "If these people in this hotel knew who you was. Forty thousand dollars' reward out for you! . . . I'm just scared and shame cause I'm afraid." (p. 24)

Harriet responds sensitively, "Counta you some little baby is gonna be born on free soil. It won't matter to him that you was afraid . . . Won't nothin count ceptin he's free. A livin monument to Celia's work" (p. 31).

A glimpse of the novel *A Short Walk* (1979), which was written for adults, might provide an apt conclusion to Childress' work because in many ways it sums up Childress' strongest theme. In this scene, the heroine Cora is getting advice from her dying father:

> "I leave you with this piece of knowledge: don't let the slave market have every bit of you . . . understand?"

> "Slavery's over."

> "Only in a way a speakin, daughter. The law still pushes us to the back entrances and separate lines. But while you standin separate just keep tellin yourself that Jim Crow law is nothin but some bad echoes from a old slave market."

> "It doesn't make me as mad as it use ta."

> "Hang onto 'mad'. When you stop mindin, that's when they got every bit a you and have fulfill the purpose of their meanness, which is to turn us into wrung-out, tuck-tail dogs; whatcha call 'defeat.'"

> "I'll never act like a tuck-tail dog."

> "They don't wantcha to act like one—they wantcha to be one and act like you not." (P. 100)

When Childress died, there were no back entrances or separate lines, but she was still fighting the problems that persist for African Americans. The "race pride" that pervades her literature, the awareness that her young adult characters gain about the world and how the world acts upon them, and their growing ability to act on their own behalf is what Childress was fighting for. Through courage, these characters move to a higher level of emancipation. As Childress did in her own life, her characters move through their lives, and they learn just how much second-phase slavery (from drugs,

Harriet responds, "Counta you some little baby is gonna be born on free soil. It won't matter to him that you was afraid . . . Won't nothin count ceptin he's free. A livin monument to Celia's work."

Jim Crow Laws the legal enforcement, from 1890 to the 1960s, of racial segregation and social exclusion of African Americans

prejudice, and poverty) their souls can bear and what they can do about it.

If you like the works of Alice Childress, you might also enjoy the works of Walter Dean Myers and Virginia Hamilton.

Selected Bibliography

WORKS BY ALICE CHILDRESS

Novels for Young Adults

Like One of the Family . . . Conversations from a Domestic's Life (1956)

Wine in the Wilderness: A Comedy-Drama (1969)

A Hero Ain't Nothin' but a Sandwich (1973)

Wedding Band: A Love/Hate Story in Black and White (1973)

Let's Hear It for the Queen (1976)

A Short Walk, novel for adults (1979)

Rainbow Jordan (1981)

Those Other People (1989)

Plays

Florence (1949)

Just a Little Simple, based on Langston Hughes's collection *Simple Speaks His Mind* (1950)

Gold Through the Trees (1952)

Trouble in Mind (1955)

Wedding Band: A Love/Hate Story in Black and White (1966)

The World on a Hill (1968)

A Man Bearing a Pitcher (1969)

Martin Luther King at Montgomery, Alabama (1969)

String (1969)

The Freedom Drum, retitled *Young Martin Luther King* (1969–1972)

Mojo: A Black Love Story (1970)

The African Garden (1971)

Mojo and String: Two Plays (1971)

When the Rattlesnake Sounds (1975)

Sea Island Song (1977)

Gullah (1984)

Moms: A Praise Play for a Black Comedienne (1986)

Screenplays

Wine in the Wilderness (1969)

Wedding Band (1973)

A Hero Ain't Nothin' but a Sandwich (1977)

String (1979)

WORKS ABOUT ALICE CHILDRESS

Abramson, Doris E. *Negro Playwrights in the American Theatre, 1925–1959.* New York: Columbia University Press, 1969, pp. 188–204, 258–259.

Brown-Guillory, Elizabeth. "Alice Childress: A Pioneering Spirit." *SAGE,* Spring 1987, pp. 66–68.

Brown, Janet. *Feminist Drama: Definitions and Critical Analysis.* Metuchen, N.J.: Scarecrow, 1979, pp. 56–70.

Brown-Guillory, Elizabeth. "Images of Blacks in Plays by Black Women." *Phylon,* September 1986, pp. 230–237.

———. "Alice Childress." In *Black Women in America: An Historical Encyclopedia.* Edited by Darlene Clark Hine. Brooklyn, N.Y.: Carlson, 1993, pp. 233–235.

Childress, Alice. "Those Were the Days, My Friend." *Sunday News,* 3 December 1972.

Commire, Anne, ed. "Alice Childress." In *Something About the Author.* Detroit: Gale Research, 1987, pp. 50–56.

Davis, Thadious M., and Trudier Harris, eds. "Alice Childress." *Dictionary of Literary Biography, Afro-American Writers After 1955: Dramatists and Prose Writers.* Detroit: Gale Research, 1985, vol. 38, pp. 66–79.

Evans, Mari. *Black Women Writers (1950–1980): A Critical Evaluation.* Garden City, N.Y.: Doubleday/Anchor, 1984, pp. 111–134.

———."Black Women Playwrights: Exorcising Myths." *Phylon,* fall 1987, pp. 229–239.

Harris, Trudier. *From Mammies to Militants: Domestics in Black American Literature.* Philadelphia: Temple University Press, 1982.

————. Introduction to *Like One of the Family* by Alice Childress (Boston: Beacon Press, 1986, pp. xi–xxxviii).

Hughes, Langston and Milton Meltzer. *Black Magic: A Pictorial History of the Negro in American Entertainment*. Englewood Cliffs, N.J.: Prentice-Hall, 1967.

Miller, Jeanne-Marie A. "Images of Black Women in Plays by Black Playwrights." *College Language Association Journal,* June 1977, pp. 494–507.

Mitchell, Loften. *Black Drama: The Story of the American Negro in the Theatre*. New York: Hawthorn Books, 1977.

Vera and Bill Cleaver

(1919-1992; 1920-1981)

by Hugh Agee

The publication of *Ellen Grae* in 1967 launched the career of Vera and Bill Cleaver as successful novelists for young adults. Ellen Grac Derryberry's independence, imagination, quick wit, and love of language make her the first in a series of strong female characters in a variety of settings. These settings include South Dakota, the southern Appalachian Mountains, the Ozark Mountains, Florida, and Seattle. The Cleavers were intimately familiar with these locales and drew effectively upon the language and folkways of each region. The Cleavers' novels realistically address a variety of social issues, including mental retardation (*Me Too,* 1973), illegitimacy (*I Would Rather Be a Turnip,* 1971), divorce (*Ellen Grae* and *Moon Lake Angel,* 1987), and the trials of poverty (especially *The Mimosa Tree,* 1970). Their most compelling theme overall, however, is the struggle of young people coming to terms with themselves and coping with stressful family situations.

> *Vera and Bill Cleaver's most compelling theme is the struggle of young people coming to terms with themselves and coping with stressful family situations.*

241

Ellen Grae

Ellen Grae opens with tomboyish eleven-year-old Ellen Grae returning to Thicket, a small Florida town where she attends school and lives with the McGruders. Ellen Grae informs Mrs. McGruder that she has changed: she now bathes every night without having to be told to, and she no longer swears. She has not lost her talent, however, for creating interesting stories that she loves to share about people. She rooms at the Mc-Gruders' with another boarder, Rosemary, who has not changed but arrives "her same old gloomy self." The two girls are opposites in many ways, but both are children of divorced parents. Among the many people Rosemary dislikes, aside from a roommate who refers to her parents by their first names, are Ellen Grae's two local friends, Grover and Ira. Grover, a classmate, is twelve. He missed a year of school after his terminally ill mother killed herself.

Ira, a simple, gentle man, harbors a dark secret concerning the death of his mother and stepfather in the swamp years earlier, but he does share it with Ellen Grae. Because townspeople believe that Ira's parents went north, Ellen dismisses Ira's story at first. But when they go into the swamp with Grover on a treasure hunt, Ira takes her to the spot where he buried the bodies and the snake that had bitten them. Ellen Grae's moral dilemma—whether or not she should report this discovery—hinges on her belief that "dead people, even bad ones, belonged in cemeteries" (p. 49) and her wish to protect Ira: "They'll put him in jail or the crazy house. . . . And he'll die and it'll be my fault" (p. 66). Her altered behavior prompts Mrs. McGruder to summon her parents, who persuade her to tell them about Ira. Ellen Grae agrees to tell the sheriff Ira's story, but he dismisses it. His wife, he announces, is in a bridge club with Mrs. McGruder, where, it appears, Ellen Grae's unusual stories are well known. Ellen Grae's dilemma has resolved itself, and she is free to enjoy her time with Grover.

Lady Ellen Grae (1968) traces Ellen Grae's continuing development as her father decides to send her to Seattle with her aunt Eleanor and her cousin Laura, where she is to be schooled in becoming a lady. The visit, however, is brief, as her parents decide they want Ellen Grae in the same state with them, though she will still live only with her father. Although the story highlights Ellen Grae's adaptability, this sequel lacks the more substantial elements of *Ellen Grae*. In

Grover (1970), the third Thicket book, the Cleavers tell Grover's story of his mother's illness and suicide and how Grover and his father work through their grief. Ellen Grae is a part of this story, not as the narrator but as a friend. This story measures the depth of friendship when someone needs comforting.

Many of the Cleavers' protagonists are engaged in journeys of growth and self-discovery. In *The Mimosa Tree,* Marvella Proffitt's family migrates to Chicago when the last of their hogs dies and life on the farm becomes intolerable. The family discovers that being in a big city without jobs and resources presents a new set of problems, including the children's becoming involved in stealing. In the end, the family returns home to an environment that, while harsh at times, is at least familiar. In *The Kissimmee Kid* (1981), Evelyn and Buell Chestnut travel from the Gulf Coast to the Kissimmee Prairie in Florida to visit their sister, Reba, and her husband, Camfield. The journey is no great distance in geographical terms, but the impact on Evelyn is significant. She adores her brother-in-law. He works as a cowboy for Major Peacock, who nicknames Evelyn "the Kissimmee Kid." When she learns that Cam is involved in the theft of the Major's cattle, she faces a dreaded decision. Despite her nine-year-old brother's disapproval, her values override her emotions, and her sister, Reba, is understanding.

Gulf Coast the area of coastline along the Gulf of Mexico, between Texas and Florida

Kissimmee a city in Florida, south of Orlando

The Cleavers' Collaboration

In their own lives, Vera and Bill Cleaver, who were married in 1945, were involved in journeys of their own. Vera, a South Dakota native born on 6 January 1919, went to school there and in Florida. Bill, an Ohio native born on 24 March 1920, attended schools in British Columbia and Seattle. The Cleavers lived abroad for a while, first in Japan (1954–1956) and then in France (1956–1958), where Bill served in the United States Air Force and Vera worked as an accountant. When they returned to the United States, they settled in Boone, North Carolina. This mountain region is the setting for *Where the Lilies Bloom* (1969) and *Trial Valley* (1977). Before *Ellen Grae* charted their future journeys as a team, the Cleavers wrote many short stories for popular magazines. They later moved to Florida, where Vera had lived during her youth when her father's job took her family many places.

> *Questioned about the nature of their collaboration, the Cleavers spoke consistently of their work as a team effort.*

Questioned about the nature of their collaboration, the Cleavers spoke consistently of their work as a team effort. Neither had any formal training as a writer of fiction, but one of them (presumably Vera) wrote in John Townsend's *A Sounding of Storytellers*:

As a very young child I knew that I was going to be a writer. Also, in that way children know things without being told or shown, I knew that I was going to have to be my own teacher. I have been my own teacher. I am a graduate of the public libraries of the United States of America. (P. 39)

The prevailing assumption, especially in light of Vera's output after Bill's death in 1981, is that the two worked closely in plotting their stories, with Bill contributing research and editorial feedback, while Vera did more of the actual writing. The most important point is that the Cleavers have contributed a significant body of fiction for young people that is of high quality overall and generally well received by their readers.

Mary Call Luther

The Cleavers' masterpiece is *Where the Lilies Bloom,* the story of fourteen-year-old Mary Call Luther's challenge to keep her siblings together in Trial Valley after her father's death. Knowing that he was dying and aware of the potential impact on his family, Roy Luther had dug his own grave up on the mountain and charged Mary Call with burying him at night, leaving the children to keep up the pretense that their father was still alive—so that they would not be separated and sent to foster homes. They live on property owned by Kiser Pease, who wants to marry Devola, the "cloudy-headed" older sister. Mary Call must keep him and others away by pretending that her father is too ill to see anyone.

Meanwhile, Mary Call, Devola, Romey, and Ima Dean continue their wildcrafting—the collecting of plants and herbs on the mountain to sell for medicinal use. Mary Call's daring and resourcefulness pull the family through much adversity, and the book's tense moments are balanced by points of comic relief, such as when Mary Call and the children administer a hot onion treatment to a very sick Kiser Pease. In the end Devola marries Kiser, who puts the Luther

comic relief a relief from an emotionally tense scene through the introduction of a comic element

land and property in Devola's name, thus giving Mary Call and the children more freedom.

In his review of *Where the Lilies Bloom,* in the 28 September 1969 *New York Times Book Review,* William Saroyan found the book "immersed in a sense of the deep kinship between human beings . . . a story of good people, with real natures, living under conditions of hardship, in poverty, in the midst of bereavement, maintaining their independence, wit and dignity." Saroyan concludes: "Reading the book has been like eating a good meal of bread, cheese, onion and cold water. I tend to have this feeling of hunger satisfied when I read very good writing." This novel, obviously satisfying to many, was a Newbery Honor Book and earned a National Book Award nomination; it was also made into a film. It is familiar fare in many secondary school classrooms.

Trial Valley extends the story of Mary Call Luther, now sixteen, as she continues to lead her none-too-enthusiastic business partners, Romey and Ima Dean, in wildcrafting as a symbol of their financial independence. Devola's cloudy-headedness seems less obvious now. When the children find a caged child who's been abandoned in the valley, Devola and Kiser take charge of this mysterious youngster, ready to lavish upon him their affection and affluence. However, Jack Parsons is attracted to the nurturing Mary Call and insists on being with her. This emotional tug-of-war builds toward a search for a lost child that brings the story to a close. The two young men who vie for Mary Call's attention add a weak romantic element to the plot. Overall the sequel fails to match the depth and intensity of the initial story. Nonetheless, Mary Call displays the same spunk and resourcefulness she exhibited in *Where the Lilies Bloom.* The stakes simply are not as high.

Another Cleaver heroine of note is Littabelle Lee of *The Whys and Wherefores of Littabelle Lee* (1973). In it Littabelle, at age sixteen, becomes out of necessity a schoolteacher in her Ozark Mountains community. When her elderly grandparents' house is destroyed by lightning, they move into the barn. Her Aunt Sorrow, who uses folk remedies to help the sick, leaves the community. Unable to count on other family members, Littabelle demonstrates that hard work and determination pay off. Some of Littabelle's classroom scenes are gems of humor. At one point she observes: "I am certain many heroes and saints, inventors and great world investigators have been lost in classrooms because of teachers who

Ozark Mountains a mountain range in northern Arkansas

only thunder instruction every minute" (p. 64). In his praise of this novel in the 4 March 1973 *New York Times Book Review,* Jonathan Yardley found it "of the caliber of William Armstrong's 'Sounder' and Laura Ingalls Wilder's 'The Little House in the Big Woods.'"

After Bill Cleaver's death on 20 August 1981, Vera completed *Hazel Rye* (1983), their final collaboration. Hazel Rye is an eleven year old who struggles to turn an old orange grove into a productive venture that will give her money to pursue her dreams. Her father places little value on education, but Hazel learns from a young boy she hires to work for her.

Vera Alone

After completing *Hazel Rye,* Vera Cleaver continued to write alone, publishing *Sugar Blue* (1984), *Sweetly Sings the Donkey* (1985), *Moon Lake Angel,* and *Belle Pruitt* (1988). Each of these novels focuses on a young female challenged by a family situation. Amy Blue must adjust to having her four-year-old niece in her life when Ella, who calls Amy "Sugar Blue," joins the family. Amy does bond with Ella and misses her when she leaves. The plot is similar to that of *I Would Rather Be a Turnip,* in which Annie Jelks has to overcome her feelings of humiliation when eight-year-old Calvin, the illegitimate child of her older sister, comes to live with her family. Annie's friends reject her, but in time she realizes that the precocious bookworm Calvin is far more caring and supportive than any of her friends have ever been. Annie's discovery, with Calvin's assistance, of the power of reading and writing foreshadows Hazel Rye's awakening to knowledge.

In *Sweetly Sings the Donkey,* fourteen-year-old Lily Snow has to take charge after her dreamer father moves the family from South Dakota to Florida, where the land they have inherited is as bleak as their future. She enlists the help of some local men to begin building a log house on the land. When her mother deserts the family, Lily helps her father and her siblings cope with their loss. Lily even agrees with her father that a peanut farm on this land is a possibility. Therein lies a ray of hope.

In *Moon Lake Angel,* ten-year-old Kitty Dale's parents have divorced and remarried. Kitty lives with the Fords during the school year. When she leaves the Fords' place for her

There is an article about Laura Ingalls Wilder in volume 3.

precocious unusually mature for one's age

foreshadowing the use of clues that suggest events yet to come

father's, she finds that he has moved to another state. Kitty travels to her mother's home, arriving unexpectedly for the summer just as her mother is settling into a new marriage to a man who has no place in his life for a stepchild. As Kitty finds herself placed with the eccentric Aunt Petal, she plots her revenge. The plan, however, becomes a healing process for Kitty and a boon to Aunt Petal. When Kitty goes back to school, she has learned much about herself and is more accepting of life apart from her parents.

Vera Cleaver's final book, *Belle Pruitt,* is the sensitive treatment of a family racked by the death of Belle's baby brother. Her mother's emotional retreat into a world of solitude prompts Belle to devise a bold plan to help her mother emerge from her grief and become once again the vibrant center of the family. Belle makes her seemingly impossible plan work, placing her among those resourceful protagonists that characterize the Cleavers' fiction.

Vera Cleaver died on 11 August 1992. Together, the Cleavers left a unique legacy to the world of young-adult fiction. John Rowe Townsend sums it up well in *A Sounding of Storytellers*: "By and large it is a poor, rural and curiously innocent America that emerges from the novels of Vera and Bill Cleaver. Life is hard, and must be faced with determination and without illusion. Subsistence has to be worked for. Values are traditional, good people are upright and self-respecting and inclined to be stern" (p. 28). Readers may be challenged, but the results will be well worth the effort.

Selected Bibliography

NOVELS BY VERA AND BILL CLEAVER

Ellen Grae (1967)

Lady Ellen Grae (1968)

Where the Lilies Bloom (1969)

Grover (1970)

The Mimosa Tree (1970)

The Mock Revolt (1971)

I Would Rather Be a Turnip (1971)

Delpha Green and Company (1972)

Me Too (1973)

The Whys and Wherefores of Littabelle Lee (1973)

protagonist the main character of a literary work

subsistence the maintenance of the basic necessities of life

If you enjoy the works of Vera and Bill Cleaver, you might also enjoy: Robbie Branscum's *Toby, Granny, and George* and *Johnny May;* Sue Ellen Bridgers' *Home Before Dark* and *All Together Now;* Olive Ann Burns's *Cold Sassy Tree;* Laura Ingalls Wilder's *The Little House in the Big Woods;* Brenda Wilkinson's *Ludell;* and Cynthia Voigt's *Dicey's Song.*

Dust of the Earth (1975)

Trial Valley (1977)

Queen of Hearts (1978)

A Little Destiny (1979)

The Kissimmee Kid (1981)

Hazel Rye (1983)

NOVELS BY VERA CLEAVER

Sugar Blue (1984)

Sweetly Sings the Donkey (1985)

Moon Lake Angel (1987)

Belle Pruitt (1988)

WORKS ABOUT VERA AND BILL CLEAVER

Cianciolo, Patricia J. "Vera and Bill Cleaver Know Their Whys and Wherefores." In *Top of the News,* June 1976, pp. 338–350. Portions reprinted in "Vera and Bill Cleaver." In *Children's Literature Review.* Edited by Gerard J. Senick. Detroit: Gale Research, 1984, vol. 6, p. 103.

Saroyan, William. Review of *Where the Lilies Bloom.* In *New York Times Book Review,* 28 September 1969, p. 34. Portions reprinted in "Vera and Bill Cleaver." In *Children's Literature Review.* Edited by Gerard J. Senick. Detroit: Gale Research, 1984, vol. 6, p. 103.

Townsend, John Rowe. "Cleaver, Vera and Bill." In *Twentieth-Century Children's Writers,* 3d ed. Edited by Tracy Chevalier. Chicago and London: St. James, 1989, pp. 210–212.

———. "Vera and Bill Cleaver." In his *A Sounding of Storytellers: New and Revised Essays on Contemporary Writers for Children.* New York: J. B. Lippincott, 1979, pp. 30–40.

Yarbrough, Jane Harper. "Vera Cleaver (6 January 1919) and Bill Cleaver (24 March 1920–20 August 1981)." In *Dictionary of Literary Biography.* Edited by Glenn Estes. Detroit: Gale Research, 1986, vol. 52, pp. 91–97.

Yardley, Jonathan. Review of *The Whys and Wherefores of Littabelle Lee.* In *New York Times Book Review,* 4 March 1973, pp. 6–7. Portions reprinted in "Vera and Bill Cleaver." In *Children's Literature Review.* Edited by Gerard J. Senick. Detroit: Gale Research, 1984, vol. 6, p. 109.

Brock Cole

(1938-   )

by Jeannie G. Borsch

"The only thing I have to worry about is dying before it is finished," says Celine Morienval, heroine of Brock Cole's novel *Celine* (1989), about her latest painting. Her words echo Cole's own words about his work. When Cole writes, he gets completely engrossed in his characters and their stories. "What if I get killed before I get it done?" he often asked himself while writing *The Goats,* his first young adult novel. This feeling for his characters really shows in Cole's novels. Howie and Laura, in *The Goats,* and Celine Morienval, in *Celine,* are strong, interesting characters—and perhaps even more satisfying, they are real people.

Cole was born in a small town in Michigan on 29 May 1938, but spent most of his childhood moving from town to town. He changed schools frequently. Cole claims to have enjoyed getting to start over all the time, since he defines himself as "a terrible student." He also remembers that when he was a child, adults did not have to worry so much about

> *Cole's childhood left him with a belief in the power of innocence and innate goodness that most children possess.*

children and what they were doing. He recalls days of swimming and sailing, spending days from morning till evening out of the house, falling off a hay wagon. His childhood left him with a belief in the power of innocence and innate goodness that most children possess.

The Goats

This belief is evident in Cole's first young adult novel, *The Goats,* published in 1987. The book is a survival story about two teenagers searching for recognition and identity. In the middle of the night, a boy and a girl are stripped and abandoned on an island by their fellow summer campers. They are the "goats"—social outcasts who have no friends, teased and made fun of by the other campers. The boy and the girl know they are social misfits. "'I'm socially retarded for my age,'" the girl tells the boy. "'Yeah. Me too,'" he replies. Knowing that they are "socially retarded" does not make the joke hurt any less, though. The boy and girl escape the island and decide to disappear, so that the people at the camp cannot find them.

Cole deliberately does not use the names of the boy and girl in the book, except in conversations between the camp counselors and the girl's mother. To each other, they remain nameless until near the end of the book. Cole explains that this is because they have left their old identities behind on the island. They are searching for new ones, which they begin to develop as they learn how to fend for themselves. They steal money for food from a pickup truck and clothes from the concession stand at the beach. They join a group of inner city kids being bussed to a camp. These kids understand what it is like to be outcasts. They take the boy and girl in, accepting them in a way no one ever has before.

> The girl didn't know why she felt like crying. She didn't feel nervous and scared anymore. Maybe it was because they were nice to her. Nice to a goat. She'd almost forgotten that she was supposed to be a goat. No, not forgotten. She wouldn't forget, and she wouldn't forgive, either. But it didn't seem important in the same way. It was as if it had all happened to some other, littler kid. She was crying a bit for that

kid, too. It wasn't the same as feeling sorry for herself, because she wasn't quite the same person. But she still felt bad about what had happened to that kid. (Pp. 93–94)

The boy and girl have already become more confident. They are less uncertain of themselves, each other, and their ability to survive on their own.

As their friendship develops, the boy and girl begin to understand that together, they can make a stand. They have a sort of "us against the world" attitude that strengthens the bond between them. At first, the boy believes that this will last only as long as they are runaways: "They might try to stay together, but he didn't think they would be strong enough. They were really strong enough only when they were alone." (p. 101) The boy dreams of the two of them disappearing together, living alone in the woods, where no one can find them. By the end of the book, though, he is stronger.

Suddenly he was very sure that everything was going to be all right. He wasn't a fool. He knew that there would be arguments and long-distance phone calls, and parents and camp counselors and policemen talking over their heads about things he didn't understand. He would want to crawl in a hole, and she would cry. It didn't matter. They would think of something.
They could look at each other now and smile. (P. 183)

They have found their new identities, and can now take their names, Howie and Laura, back.

Cole believes in the judgment of children and their ability to define and understand their own places in the world. He seems to feel that many adults do not give children enough credit. He also criticizes the way that adults seem to apply their own standards to children. The adults in *The Goats* misjudge Laura and Howie. Besides being goats, they are called wild wicked things, sneaky, foxy. A deputy asks Howie if he has been getting a little "nudgy," the cleaning

Cole believes in the judgment of children and their ability to define and understand their own places in the world.

> *Even in Cole's children's picture books, though, the story is most important.*

lady at the motel thinks Howie is Laura's boyfriend, and even the camp director keeps assuring Laura's mother that she doesn't have to worry about Howie "harming" her daughter. None of the adults understand Laura and Howie, or their deep friendship, at all.

In the end, this idea of recognizing people for what they are is at the root of most of Cole's books, his children's picture books as well as his two young adult novels. Before turning to writing, Brock Cole taught philosophy at the University of Wisconsin, but he began working as an author and illustrator of children's books in the late 1970s. Cole's self-illustrated book *The King at the Door* (1979) won the 1980 Friends of American Writers Juvenile Award. In this book, Little Baggitt recognizes the king at the door although the king is dressed in ragged clothes, and Little Baggitt is rewarded well for his ability to see past the surface to understand who the king really is. In *No More Baths,* published in 1980, Jessica finds that she cannot be a chicken, or a cat, or a pig. She must learn to accept that because she is a girl, she has to take baths. In *Nothing But a Pig* (1981), Preston the pig escapes recognition by dressing up like a person, but soon finds that "fine clothes do not make a man."

Cole taught himself to draw by studying the works of illustrators he liked—illustrators such as Maurice Sendak, writer and illustrator of children's classics like *Where the Wild Things Are* and *Chicken Soup with Rice.* Even in Cole's children's picture books, though, the story is most important. He writes the text first, then begins to sketch out the illustrations. He tries to keep his style simple and straightforward, leaving a lot to the imagination of the reader. In 1986, Cole won a Parent's Choice Award from the Parent's Choice Foundation for *The Giant's Toe* (1986). Cole also did the illustrations for Lynn Reid Banks's wildly popular children's book *The Indian in the Cupboard* (1980).

Like her creator, Celine Morienval of *Celine* is an artist, and her artist's perspective colors her view of the world. Celine's hilarious observations on her world are bright, sharp, and usually wildly imaginative. Her moods can change from minute to minute, and she's struggling to figure out who she wants to be and how she fits in the world. Her father, a professor, has gone off for a seven week tour of Europe, leaving Celine with her new stepmother Catherine, who is only six years older than Celine. Celine and Catherine don't care much for each other, but they seem to be stuck with each other.

> Whenever I drift into view, I seem to induce in Catherine profound existential anguish. What my old friend and Godpapa Jean-Paul calls *nausea.* She watches me closely for signs of fading around the edges, indications of growing insubstantiality, the first symptoms of deconstruction. This is not, perhaps, as loony as it sounds. After all, no one told her when she was a young graduate student brushing strands of hair from her ovoid face that the French professor with whom she had fallen in love had secreted somewhere in Iowa a lumpy adolescent. I was an unlooked for absurdity, a serpent in the bosom, a cloud before the sun, a shock, a handful, as my grandmother announced upon her sudden decision to move to Sun City, where to her intense regret, teenagers are allowed only on closely supervised visits. There was a short, bitter custody battle between my mother and my father, and Catherine lost. My father hopes that we will grow to love one another . . . A man of powerful imagination and boundless hope, he has been gone six weeks now. (Pp. 13–14)

Existentialism is a philosophical movement that began in the 1800s. It concerns the nature of existence or being and the struggle for freedom. An awareness of the difficulties involved in attaining freedom causes existential anguish.

Godpapa Jean-Paul refers to Jean-Paul Sartre, a French existentialist writer.

This amusing commentary on a major problem in her life is typical of Celine.

At the beginning of the book, Celine meets Jake Barker, the boy next door. Sounds promising, until you discover that Jake is an 8-year-old who still wears Superman underwear and, like Celine, loves TV. Jake's parents are getting a divorce, and Celine soon becomes his best buddy. She offers him some control over his world when she teaches him about the television remote control, which she calls her "zapper." With a remote control, she believes, life becomes new and exciting. "Even if all the channels have boring stuff, you can zip through them, looking for that little high, or you can construct interesting dialogues by going back and forth between one program and another. . . You don't want to even consider buying three rooms of carpeting for $212 . . . ? *Zap!*" (p. 12) Television is comforting. You do not have to think when watching television. You can just sit in front of it like a limp little mummy. With the remote, you can even create your own reality. Celine and Jake, who find the world fascinating but also frightening and confusing, like the ability to create their own reality using television.

Through her art, Celine tries to define her own identity. She destroys *Test Patterns,* her masterpiece, but she does not care. In a way, it frees her to continue to explore her feelings about the world in other paintings. Soon she is beginning work on her next project, a self-portrait she calls Celine-Beast. This painting, she thinks, will "triumph over boredom, depression, falling in love, cold sores, headaches, homework, other people, all the things that conspire against getting a painting together" (p. 76). The Celine-Beast is fat, and crazy, and blurry, done in bright colors like orange and yellow. Useless wings sprout from her shoulders. Jake tells her the painting does not look like her at all. Celine thinks it does, sometimes. Like Howie and Laura, Celine wants to be recognized for who she is. The problem is, who is she?

> In Celine, Celine and Jake, who find the world fascinating but also frightening and confusing, like the ability to create their own reality using television.

Celine's Maturity

Celine is hoping to graduate from high school a year early and go to live with her best friend in Italy. The only thing she has to do, says her father, is "show a little maturity," which she figures means, "Pass all your courses, avoid detection in all crimes and misdemeanors, don't get pregnant" (p. 18). Getting pregnant is no problem; Celine "never felt the need." She usually avoids being detected. Her only problems are that she is going to fail English if she can't rewrite her essay on J. D. Salinger's *Catcher in the Rye.* She has also skipped her mandatory swimming class all term and will fail it as well, unless she gets a doctor's note. Still, Celine wonders how much more mature she needs to become. As she says, "it's hard not to be offended. If I was any more mature, I'd have Alzheimer's disease" (p. 19).

While Celine offers Jake the stable friendship he needs, she finds comfort in the friendship too. She feels responsible for him and is surprised to find that she likes the responsibility. The adults in Celine's and Jake's life do not seem very responsible. Celine's father has gone off to Europe. Jake's father has left his mother and is dating Celine's art teacher. Catherine leaves for a conference with one of her art professors. Through a series of miscommunications, Jake is left alone with Celine for a whole weekend. She takes him to his appointment with his counselor, keeps him fed, and makes sure he gets to bed at night. "Show a little maturity," her father has told her. But as in *The Goats*, it is the adults who are not very mature. Cole believes that it is often children who really see the world clearly and know how to do the right thing. As Celine says at the end of her weekend with Jake:

> My dad is out there somewhere. Probably packing his bag in a Frankfurt hotel or stepping off the curb in the rain to hail a cab. And Mrs. Barker is there, making phone calls, making memos and explanations, putting on her hat and coat. It's all very comforting really. I bet even Catherine is heading this way, little nose sticking out of the turned-up collar of her coat . . . They're all out there somewhere, rushing home to save the children. They'll be tired and hungry. I wonder if I should make some waffles. (p. 215)

Laura, Howie, and Celine all demonstrate Cole's belief in the power of young adults. Remembering the days of his childhood, when children's worlds were simpler than they are today, he has commented that miracles were more common then. In his books, he seems to urge a return to a time when kids were allowed to be kids, and when adults recognized kids' strengths. About himself, he has said, "I think I would be a very disappointing child today. I suppose I never really learned any discipline. Never really learned to apply myself. . . Here I am a writer and illustrator with no proper job experience at all." (*Speaking for Ourselves, Too*, p. 39) Fortunately for his readers, he seems pretty happy with this state.

> *Cole believes that it is often children who really see the world clearly and know how to do the right thing.*

> *In his books, he seems to urge a return to a time when kids were allowed to be kids, and when adults recognized kids' strengths.*

If you like Brock Cole, you might also like M. E. Kerr and Graham Salisbury.

Selected Bibliography

WORKS BY BROCK COLE

Books for Young Adults
The Goats (1987)
Celine (1989)

Picture Books
The King at the Door (1979)
No More Baths (1980)
Nothing But a Pig (1981)
The Winter Wren (1984)
The Giant's Toe (1986)
Alpha and the Dirty Baby (1991)

WORKS ABOUT BROCK COLE

Berger, Laura Stanley, ed. *Twentieth-Century Young Adult Writers*. Detroit: St. James, 1994, pp. 140–142.

Campbell, Patty. "The Young Adult Perplex." *Wilson Library Bulletin,* January 1988, p. 75.

Gallo, Donald, ed. *Speaking for Ourselves, Too.* Urbana, Ill.: National Council of Teachers of English, 1990, pp. 38–39.

McDonnell, Christine. "New Voices, New Visions: Brock Cole," *Horn Book,* September/October 1989, pp. 602–605.

Nilsen, Aileen Pace, and Ken Donelson. "Honor Listing Update, 1989: Some New Kids on the Block." *English Journal,* December 1990, pp. 77–78.

How to Write to the Author
Brock Cole
c/o Farrar, Straus & Giroux, Inc.
19 Union Square West
New York, NY 10003

Christopher Collier
James Lincoln Collier

(1930-   ; 1928-   )

by Patricia J. Cianciolo

Christopher and James Lincoln Collier came from a family of writers. Their father, Edmund Collier, wrote adventure stories, most of which were about cowboys, and some of these stories were for children. He also wrote biographies of people such as Kit Carson, Annie Oakley, and Buffalo Bill. An uncle, Slater Brown, was a novelist; a cousin, Gwilym Brown, was a staff writer for *Sports Illustrated* for twenty years; and an aunt, Susan Jenkins Brown, wrote a book about her friendship with the American poet Hart Crane.

Alluding to this multitude of writers in the family, James Lincoln Collier said in the *Fifth Book of Junior Authors and Illustrators* (1983), "I became a writer the way other people go into the family business. It never occurred to me that I couldn't write what people did" (p. 80). In contrast, Christo-

> *On the number of writers in his family, James Lincoln Collier said: "I became a writer the way other people go into the family business. It never occurred to me that I couldn't write what people did."*

257

pher Collier never wanted to be a writer and chose teaching instead, for as he said in his autobiographical sketch in the *Fifth Book,* "Teaching is just as much fun [as writing], and you earn a lot more money. Now I still teach, but I manage to find the time to write all sorts of things, too" (p. 78).

James Lincoln Collier, Accomplished Writer and Musician

James Lincoln Collier, who also writes under the pseudonym Charles Williams, was born on 27 June 1928 in New York City, the son of Edmund and Katharine Brown Collier. He married Carol Burrows on 2 September 1952; they since divorced. They had two sons, Geoffrey Lincoln and Andrew Kemp. Collier then married Ida Karen Potash, and they resided in Pawling, New York. He earned a B.A. degree from Hamilton College in 1950 and then served in the army infantry during the Korean War. His first job was editor of a magazine, a position he held for six years, during which he wrote in his spare time. He quit that position in 1958 and worked as a freelance writer, specializing in music (especially jazz), social science reporting, sex education, and related fields. He traveled widely in Europe and has lived in Paris and London.

Besides being a writer, James Lincoln Collier is an accomplished professional trombonist. He has worked as a jazz musician for many years and has played with groups in New York and around the world. He is thought to be the only American writer on jazz to gain official acceptance in the former Soviet Union. His work has been published in *Playboy, Esquire,* the *New York Times Magazine,* the *Village Voice,* the *Wall Street Journal,* and *Horn Book Magazine.*

James Collier also has written nine books for adolescents in collaboration with his brother, Christopher Collier, and is sole author of more than twenty books for children and young adults. He won high praise from literary critics for a number of the books he wrote alone. They show a remarkable versatility in the author, as they span a variety of literary genres.

Historical Fiction

The hero of *The Jazz Kid* (1994), twelve-year-old Paulie Hovarth, hears jazz by accident from the basement of a speakeasy, where he has gone with his father to repair

The **Korean War** (1950–1953) was the first war in which the United Nations played a military role. The conflict began with Communist-ruled North Korea's invasion of South Korea. It was one of the bloodiest wars in history.

speakeasy a place where alcohol was sold illegally during the 1920s, when alcohol was prohibited by the Constitution

frozen plumbing pipes. He quickly becomes obsessed with this kind of music and wants to make it his life, but this ambition leads him into conflict with his parents and eventually into the tough underworld of Chicago in the 1920s. Even though Paulie's father calls jazz "nigger music," Paulie lies, cheats, and skips school to get time for lessons, to practice and build a repertoire of music, and to sneak across town to cheap bars, just to hear the jazz greats play. James Collier shows Paulie struggling to find answers to questions that still concern us today: What exactly is jazz? Why do so many people respond negatively to this kind of music? What is the relationship between white and black musicians?

In the author's note at the beginning of the book, James Collier informs his readers that at the time this story took place, the use of insulting racial and ethnic slurs was standard usage in common speech. He states clearly that he does not encourage the use of such words and emphasizes that they should be avoided. He says that he included them in the dialogue spoken by some of the characters for the sake of historical accuracy and to dramatize the derogatory and racist attitude they convey.

> *What exactly is jazz? Why do so many people respond negatively to this kind of music? What is the relationship between white and black musicians?*

Modern Realistic Fiction

The Teddy Bear Habit or How I Became a Winner (1967) and its sequel *Rich and Famous: The Further Adventures of George Stable* (1975) are engrossing tales of satirical humor and mystery loaded with characters from New York City's Greenwich Village underworld, people associated with talent agencies, television studios, popular music and the record business, and drug trafficking.

> **realistic fiction** fiction that attempts to depict life as it actually is (rather than portraying life through ideals and dreams)

The Teddy Bear Habit starts as a psychological novel about George Stable, an adolescent who has a secret obsession with his teddy bear, but it quickly turns into an exciting and suspense-filled account of what happens when Wiggy, George's guitar teacher, packs the teddy bear with stolen jewels. The zany cartoon-styled illustrations by Lee Lorenz (who plays jazz trumpet in his spare time) effectively extend and enhance the high comic adventure. The story's climax is a hectic, frightening chase scene, which takes George (and the readers) through the streets of Manhattan to the rooftops and basements of city tenement buildings.

In *Rich and Famous,* the sequel to *The Teddy Bear Habit,* George again manages to have some frightening adventures.

Without his father's consent, he sets out to be groomed for pop-record stardom, but he learns the hard way that, too often, all one seems to need to reach stardom in the record business is a little talent, a smidgen of intelligence, and some clever packaging.

Biographies

James Lincoln Collier's particular talent is evident in his books about the lives of musicians, especially jazz musicians. His biographies *Duke Ellington* (1985), *Benny Goodman and the Swing Era* (1989), and *Louis Armstrong* (1985; 1991) reveal Collier's thorough research as well as his vast knowledge and intense passion for his subject. In each of these books he develops the fascinating life stories of each of these great jazz musicians. His respect for them is evident, but his praise for their accomplishments is never excessive or unwarranted. He reveals their personality and character, their childhood experiences, and their family circumstances with sympathy. He gives his readers a great deal of information and insight about the times in which these musicians lived, and he does all this in a manner that makes their accomplishments very significant to the reader. The bibliographies and indexes in each biography list excellent books and articles about these famous persons, as well as some of their most famous recordings.

A first-class collection of biographical sketches of some of the greatest and most influential jazz musicians can be found in James Collier's book *The Great Jazz Artists* (1977). Robert Andrew Parker's stunning full-page, black-and-white prints of Scott Joplin, Leadbelly (Huddie Ledbetter), Blind Lemon Jefferson, Bessie Smith, Bix Beiderbecke, Fats Waller, Lester Young, Charlie Parker, and John Coltrane help to bring them alive for readers.

Science Fiction

Planet Out of the Past (1983) depicts the dangerous adventures that three young people experience during their search for prehistoric people (humanoids) on Pleisto, a planet similar to Earth. James Lincoln Collier creates a rudimentary spoken language for the early humanoids that populated Pleisto. This language consists of a series of cries, or "words," for im-

rudimentary primitive

portant things they have to communicate, such as "Watch out" and "friend." Collier also gives them a simple system through which they can express an understanding of opposing concepts such as good and bad.

In the afterword, the author explains that on the basis of what we know about chimpanzees, we can be fairly certain that the early humanoids possessed a simple set of symbols for things and acts that were important to them. He also says that we cannot be certain, however, that they were capable of understanding concepts like "negative" and "positive."

Nonfiction Books

We should not be surprised that James Lincoln Collier's fascination with, and vast knowledge of, jazz and music in general has led him to write nonfiction books about numerous aspects of this subject, ranging from making music for money to music theory and the history of jazz. In one of his nonfiction books, *Inside Jazz* (1973), James Collier tells his readers early in the first chapter that it is very difficult to translate musical sounds into words, but they will appreciate his fine explanations of jazz and its distinguishing features, as well as its brief history. Through the words of some of the jazz greats who were addicts, the author also informs his readers (without moralizing) about the bad effects of alcohol and drugs, which are all too common in the world of jazz.

Christopher Collier, History Scholar and Writer

Christopher Collier was born on 29 January 1930 in New York City, the younger son of Edmund and Katharine Brown Collier. He married Virginia Wright on 21 August 1954; they since divorced. They had two children, Edmund Quincy and Sally McQueen. Collier married Bonnie Bromberger on 6 December 1969. They have one son, Christopher Zwissler, and reside in Orange, Connecticut. Christopher Collier graduated with a B.A. degree from Clark University in 1951, followed by an M.A. degree from Columbia University in 1955 and a Ph.D., also from Columbia, in 1964. He served in the army from 1952 to 1954. He taught American history to junior and senior high school students in Greenwich and New Canaan,

Connecticut, from 1955 to 1961. Since 1961, he has taught history at the University of Bridgeport in Connecticut, where he was promoted through the university's academic ranks rather quickly: from instructor (1961–1964), to assistant professor (1964–1967), to associate professor (1967–1971), to professor of American history (since 1971), and chairperson of the history department (since 1977).

When Christopher Collier writes, he is particularly interested in presenting to his audience some of the complicated, perplexing issues and some of the unvarnished reality about history. In his numerous articles, nonfiction books, and historical fiction novels—whether they are written for history scholars, classroom teachers, or young adults—he has identified many such issues and realities pertaining to the American Revolutionary War. He has studied this historical event extensively. In an article for *Horn Book* titled "Johnny and Sam: Old and New Approaches to the American Revolution," he emphasizes that one cannot teach anything worth learning if one studies and analyzes history in simple, one-sided terms. Such an approach to viewing history, he says, falsifies the past and thereby provides no help in understanding the present or in meeting the future.

In an autobiographical sketch in the *Fifth Book of Junior Authors and Illustrators,* he says he is convinced that when we study history in terms of its complex matters, instead of from a simple or single perspective, we benefit from the memories held by a vast number of people. It is from the knowledge acquired from memories of the past that we can plan and choose which course of action best fits what we want to do. We can make our own plans on the basis of what other people have done—what they have tried to do and failed, or tried to do and succeeded. Without a knowledge of history acquired from the memories of a vast diversity of people, he says, we will never have anything to go on but our own very limited experience (p. 79).

Most of Christopher Collier's writing is addressed to adults, particularly history scholars and classroom teachers interested in history. He has published articles in history journals and served as editor of monographs (highly detailed studies) in *British History and Culture* (1967–1972). He also was editor of publications for the Association for the Study of Connecticut History from 1967 to 1973. Some of his books for adults include: *Roger Sherman's Connecticut: Yankee Pol-*

> *He emphasizes that one cannot teach anything worth learning if one studies and analyzes history in simple, one-sided terms.*

itics and the American Revolution (1971), which is a standard work on its subject, and *Connecticut in the Continental Congress* (1973).

Some of the nine historical fiction novels he wrote with his brother, James Lincoln Collier, have been named as award books by literary critics and literary organizations. Their historical fiction novels *My Brother Sam Is Dead* (1974) and *Jump Ship to Freedom* (1981) both were named for prestigious literary awards.

Notable Writing Collaborators

The books Christopher and James Lincoln Collier have written together take place in parts of the United States where they grew up and with which they are thoroughly familiar: New England, particularly Connecticut, and New York. As members of a collaborative team, the Collier brothers build on one another's talents. Christopher Collier, a professor of history, researches all the historical material and gives a true story with all its details to his brother, James Lincoln, who knows how to write exciting stories. Together they make up some fictional characters. In this way they are able to write books depicting the historical past authentically, while at the same time they create engaging stories full of memorable characters and intriguing action. The books they have collaborated on are published in at least seven languages and have been named for a number of literary awards and citations.

The first book they wrote as a team was *My Brother Sam Is Dead,* and like a number of their other collaborative literary efforts, this book presents to readers some complex issues and some raw realities about war, and it especially gives readers a credible view of the Revolutionary War. A major theme of this historical novel is the divided allegiances that the colonists struggled with during the years 1775–1778. The authors graphically portray the futility of aggression and the agony of a country divided against itself. This fast-paced story was named a Newbery Honor Book and a Notable Children's Book by separate committees of the Children's Services Division of the American Library Association. It was also nominated for the National Book Award in 1975.

The Colliers also emphasize the themes of conflicting loyalties and assaults between groups of colonists during the

collaborators people who work together, especially in the creation of an intellectual work

futility uselessness

subterfuges deceptions

protagonist the main character of a literary work

Revolution in *The Bloody Country* (1976). Set in what is now Wilkes-Barre, Pennsylvania, this story is based on an actual episode during the mid-1700s. It tells what happened when the Pennamites, the older residents of this Pennsylvania valley, claimed that the land was rightfully theirs. With the help of the British and a local Indian tribe, the Pennamites persecuted and tried to drive away the newcomers who emigrated to their area from Connecticut. The authors convincingly depict the harshness of frontier life and the quibbles, subterfuges, and unexpected shifts of people under stress. We see war, extremely bad weather in winter and spring, and the devastating destruction to almost everyone's homes, barns, livestock, and mills when flooding occurs. This flood is caused by the careless chopping down of trees that lined the banks of the Susquehanna River.

Another theme developed in this novel pertains to the real meaning of freedom, especially as it relates to Joe Mountain, a half-black and half-Mohegan boy who is the protagonist's family's slave.

Jump Ship to Freedom, War Comes to Willie Freeman (1983), and *Who Is Carrie?* (1984) make up a series that spans the years just before, during, and just after the American Revolution. A number of the same characters appear in all these novels, but in each book a different African American youth must deal with seemingly insurmountable problems and dangers.

Jump Ship to Freedom, the first in this exciting adventure series, was selected as a Notable Trade Book in the Field of Social Studies in 1981. The story is told by fourteen-year-old Dan Arbus. His father, a slave during the mid-1700s, has earned freedom for himself, his wife, and his son by fighting in the Revolutionary War. Unfortunately, Dan's father drowns at sea and the family's master refuses to turn over the currency called soldier's notes. These rightfully belong to Dan and his mother, who need them to buy their freedom.

The focus of this novel is Dan's effort to find a statesman in the city of New York (at that time the capital of the United States) or someone who would be participating in the Continental Congress in Philadelphia in 1787. Dan must find the right person to help him cash his father's soldier's notes and buy the freedom he and his mother rightfully deserve.

The second book in this series, *War Comes to Willy Freeman,* deals with events prior to those depicted in *Jump Ship to Freedom*. Willy's story begins during the last years of the Revolutionary War, when she is a thirteen-year-old free black girl in Connecticut. Willy is in danger of being returned to slavery because she cannot find the papers to prove she is free. Her father, a patriot, was killed by the British, and her mother has been kidnapped by British soldiers who intend to take her to the West Indies and sell her as a slave. Willy's uncle Jack Arbus (Dan's father) suggests that Sam Fraunce, the owner of the famous Fraunce's Tavern in New York City, might be able to help her find her mother; his tavern is a favorite meeting place for British officers.

Disguised as a boy, Willy makes her danger-filled way to the tavern, where she works until the end of the war. She returns home after the war, goes to the Arbus home, and finds her mother dying. Willy then testifies at the trial in which her uncle Jack sues his master for freedom and wins. (The actual trial depicted in this novel tested the law stipulating that a black man had to be set free if he served in the military. It proved to be a landmark case that ultimately freed three hundred slaves.)

On a number of occasions and under a variety of circumstances, Willy demonstrates that she is a feisty, courageous, and intelligent person. Some readers and critics claim that she is one of the Colliers' most memorable characters.

The third book in the series, *Who Is Carrie?*, tells the story of Carrie, a young black orphan who is determined to learn of her origins. She works in Fraunce's Tavern as a "kitchen slave" and frequently eavesdrops on some of the major figures in the American Revolution. Her eavesdropping enables Carrie to find out some surprising news about her own heritage.

Besides finding this book exciting reading, we can appreciate its authentic historical information about the nation's early leaders, which is presented in a manner that gives us many clear and detailed images, including the city of New York when it was capital of the United States, the inauguration of George Washington as the first president, and the president's mansions—first on Cherry Street and then on Broad Street. We also gain significant insights about the personality of Alexander Hamilton, the first secretary of the treasury, and Thomas Jefferson, who was first secretary of state.

You might be interested in knowing that a reproduction of Fraunce's Tavern—where Dan, Willy, and Carrie worked

patriot one who loves his or her country and supports its authority

and where so much of the action in each of these three stories takes place—exists on the site of the old tavern on Pearl Street in New York City. The original building burned down many years ago, and nobody is exactly sure what it looked like, but the present building is an attempt to reproduce the tavern. A museum upstairs contains numerous pictures, maps, furniture, tableware, and other mementos from the eighteenth century.

Some of the characters in this series use poor grammar, and their language might be described as insensitive, uncouth, racist, and certainly unacceptable by current standards. The authors address this issue head-on in the afterword of each of these books. They explain that they tried to depict the "feel" of the speech of an illiterate slave of the time in a way that would be understandable to modern readers; yet they caution that the language used by these characters should not be taken as historically accurate. As for the language that thoughtful readers might object to, especially the use of the word "nigger," the authors state that this word and others like it were commonly used in America throughout the eighteenth century, and that if they did not use it in these stories, it would amount to a distortion of history.

There are five other books by the accomplished writing team of Collier brothers that might be of interest to avid readers of biography and to history buffs. They are *Roger Sherman: Puritan Politician* (1976), *The Winter Hero* (1978), *Decision in Philadelphia: The Constitutional Convention of 1787* (1987). *The Clock* (1992), and *With Every Drop of Blood: A Novel of the Civil War* (1994). Like their other books, whether written by the brothers as individual writers or in collaboration, these are well worth a reader's attention.

Selected Bibliography

WORKS BY JAMES LINCOLN COLLIER

Cheers (1961)

Somebody Up There Hates Me (1962)

Battle Ground: The United States Army in World War II (1965)

The Teddy Bear Habit or How I Became a Winner, illustrated by Lee Lorenz (1967)

A Visit to the Firehouse (1967)

If you like the works of James Lincoln Collier and Christopher Collier, you might also like the works of Nat Hentoff (jazz), Ann Rinaldi (historical fiction), and William Sleator (science fiction).

Sex Education USA: A Community Approach (1968)

Which Musical Instrument Shall I Play? (1969)

Danny Goes to the Hospital (1970)

Practical Music Theory: How Music Is Put Together from Bach to Rock (1970)

The Rock Star (1970)

Why Does Everybody Think I'm Nutty? (1971)

The Hard Life of a Teenager (1972)

It's Murder at St. Basket's (1972)

Inside Jazz (1973)

Jug Bands and Handmade Music: A Creative Approach to Music Theory and the Instruments (1973)

The Making of Man (1974)

Rich and Famous: The Further Adventures of George Stable (1975)

Give Dad My Best (1976)

Making Music for Money (1976)

The Great Jazz Artists, illustrated with monoprints by Robert Andrew Parker (1977)

The Making of Jazz: A Comprehensive History (1978)

Planet Out of the Past (1983)

Louis Armstrong: An American Success Story (1985; 1991)

Duke Ellington (1985)

When the Stars Begin to Fall (1986)

Outside Looking In (1987)

The Reception of Jazz in America (1988)

The Winchesters (1988)

Benny Goodman and the Swing Era (1989)

The Rise of Selfishness in the United States (1991)

Jazz, The American Theme Song (1993)

The Jazz Kid (1994)

My Crooked Family (1994)

Promises to Keep (1994)

WORKS BY JAMES LINCOLN COLLIER UNDER THE NAME CHARLES WILLIAMS

Fires of Youth (1963)

The Hypocritical American (1964)

WORKS ABOUT JAMES LINCOLN COLLIER

Commire, Anne, ed. *Something About the Author.* Detroit: Gale Research, 1976, vol. 8, pp. 33–34.

Gallo, Donald R. *Speaking for Ourselves: Autobiographical Sketches by Notable Authors of Books for Young Adults.* Urbana, Ill.: National Council of Teachers of English, 1990, pp. 46–48.

Holtze, Sally Holmes, ed. *Fifth Book of Junior Authors and Illustrators.* New York: H. W. Wilson, 1983, pp. 80–81.

Lesniak, James G., ed. *Contemporary Authors.* Detroit: Gale Research, 1991, pp. 92–93.

Moir, Hughes. "Profile: James and Christopher Collier—More Than Just a Good Read." *Language Arts,* March 1978.

Olendorf, Donna, and Diane Telgen, eds. *Something About the Author.* Detroit: Gale Research, 1991, vol. 70, pp. 39–43.

Raymond, Allen. "Jamie and Kit Collier: The Writer and the Historian." *Teaching, K–8,* January 1988, p. 35.

Stine, Jean C., and Daniel G. Marowski, eds. *Contemporary Literary Criticism.* Detroit: Gale Research, 1984, pp. 70–75.

Senick, Gerald J., ed. *Children's Literature Review.* Detroit: Gale Research, 1978, pp. 44–49.

WORKS BY CHRISTOPHER COLLIER

Public Records for the State of Connecticut: 1965–1967

Roger Sherman's Connecticut: Yankee Politics and the American Revolution (1971)

Connecticut in the Continental Congress (1973)

The Pride of Bridgeport: Men and Machines in the Nineteenth Century (1979)

Literature of Connecticut, with Bonnie Collier (1983)

WORKS BY JAMES LINCOLN COLLIER AND CHRISTOPHER COLLIER

My Brother Sam Is Dead (1974)

The Bloody Country (1976)

Roger Sherman: Puritan Politician (1976)

The Winter Hero (1978)

Jump Ship to Freedom (1981)
War Comes to Willy Freeman (1983)
Who Is Carrie? (1984)
Decision in Philadelphia: The Constitutional Convention of 1787 (1987)
The Clock (1992)
With Every Drop of Blood: A Novel of the Civil War (1994)

WORKS ABOUT CHRISTOPHER COLLIER

Alpen, Joyce. "Not a Bad Tory." *Washington Post Book World,* 12 January 1975, p. 4.

Commire, Anne, ed. *Something About the Author.* Detroit: Gale Research, 1979, vol. 16, pp. 66–67.

Gallo, Donald R. *Speaking for Ourselves: Autobiographical Sketches by Notable Authors of Books for Young Adults.* National Council of Teachers of English, 1990, pp. 44–45.

Holtze, Sally Holmes, ed. *Fifth Book of Junior Authors and Illustrators.* New York: H. W. Wilson, 1983, pp. 78–80.

Lesniak, James G., ed. *Contemporary Authors.* Detroit: Gale Research, 1991, pp. 91–92.

Moir, Hughes. "Profile: James and Christopher Collier—More Than Just a Good Read." *Language Arts,* March 1978.

Olendorf, Donna, and Diane Telgen, eds. *Something About the Author.* Detroit: Gale Research, 1991, vol. 70, pp. 36–39.

Raymond, Allen. "Jamie and Kit Collier: The Writer and the Historian." *Teaching, K-8,* January 1988, p. 35.

Stine, Jean C., and Daniel G. Marowski, eds. *Contemporary Literary Criticism.* Detroit: Gale Research, 1984, pp. 70–75.

How to Write to the Authors
Christopher Collier and James Lincoln Collier
c/o Bantam Doubleday Dell Publishing Group, Inc.
1540 Broadway
New York, NY 10036

Hila Colman

by Patricia L. Daniel

In the mid-1990s Hila Colman lived in Bridgewater, Connecticut, with a dear friend in "a very happy relationship." She had lived alone for eight years after the death of her second husband, Louis "Limey" Colman, to whom she was married for thirty years. Colman's two sons, Jonathan and James, have borne her seven grandchildren and two great-granddaughters.

Early Years

Hila Colman was born Hila Teresa Crayder in New York City. Her father, Harris Crayder, was a manufacturer, and her mother, Sarah, was a designer. Sarah Crayder, a Russian Jewish immigrant, worked in the sweatshops of the garment district and died of tuberculosis when Colman was fifteen years old. Colman was closer to her father, but she later realized that her mother's unaffectionate behavior may have stemmed from her concern about transmitting her highly contagious

sweatshops shops or factories in which workers worked for long hours at low wages under unhealthy conditions

Many of the facts about Hila Colman in this article are from a personal interview conducted by the author of this article on 26 April 1995 and are published here by the permission of Hila Colman.

271

disease to her loved ones. In *Something About the Author,* Colman relates that she and her older sister attended a private, all-girl school in Manhattan (Commire, ed., 1988, p. 24).

Colman did not consider her family to be wealthy because she saw how hard her mother worked. "Work, not privilege, was the dominant theme in our house," she says (Commire, ed., p. 24). After her mother's death, her father and a cousin mismanaged the family business and made unwise real estate investments. The family became bankrupt, which meant that Colman had to leave Radcliffe College after two years.

Colman began writing one night in 1947 out of a need to vent her anger. She and her husband had planned to attend a political meeting, but they could not find a baby-sitter for their sons. Her husband assumed that she would stay home and he would attend the political meeting. That night she furiously wrote "Can a Man Have a Family and a Career?" as a spoof on the question usually asked about women. A writer friend read it and gave it to his agent, who in turn sold the article to the *Saturday Evening Post.* Colman began her writing career asking questions that were unpopular and that few had even considered asking.

> *Colman began writing one night in 1947 out of a need to vent her anger.*

protagonist the main character of a literary work

Stories for Young Adults

Ten years later, in 1957, Colman published her first book, *The Big Step,* and as of the 1990s had written at least one book per year. She writes of real people and their struggles. Her stories for young adults involve coming of age; the protagonist, almost always a female, finds her own voice and defines her own values. Family relationships are explored throughout Colman's stories, and there is almost always a social and/or a political issue that is highlighted. Most of her settings are in New York City and Connecticut, both places in which she has lived.

The richness of Colman's stories comes from the realness of her characters. Each of the protagonists is fully developed and grows from her experiences. She allows her characters to question, explore, and discover for themselves. She expects her readers to do the same.

> *Each of Colman's protagonists is fully developed and grows from her experiences. She allows her characters to question, explore, and discover for themselves. She expects her readers to do the same.*

Family Relationships

Colman explores family relationships from the perspectives of parents, children, siblings, and newlyweds. In *The Girl from Puerto Rico* (1961), Felicidad yearns to be a New Yorker. After her father's sudden death, the family leaves Puerto Rico and goes to find a new life as "Americanos." The strength of the family is highlighted by their belief in each other and by their desire for the best for each other.

Felicidad faces each obstacle—the prejudice of being stereotyped, the limited job selection because she is Puerto Rican, and her younger brother's fights—with courage, stubbornness, and thoughtfulness. When she decides to leave New York and return to Puerto Rico, it is her thoughtful choice. Felicidad dreams a dream and makes it come true. In reality the dream is not what she wants for herself or her family. Having experienced New York, she is able to recognize the value of what they had left in Puerto Rico and to choose the best setting for her family.

stereotype to create a character that is not original or individual because it conforms to a preconceived category

Being the younger of two sisters, Colman was very dependent upon her older sister until she went to Radcliffe College, and she was jealous of the closeness her sister had with her mother. These feelings are explored in *Christmas Cruise* (1965). In this story Liz has the opportunity to go on a cruise with her extravagant Aunt Beatrice and cousin Lauren. Liz is excited to be able to do something that her older sister has never done. The real drama takes place within Liz. She discovers that she is the one who has always sold herself short, making herself feel as if she were being left out rather than acknowledging that she is a very different person from her boisterous sister. Throughout this book, individual characters' intentions are not always perceived correctly by the other characters, resulting in hurt feelings. Liz begins to take responsibility for communicating her feelings, rather than keeping silent and holding others responsible.

boisterous rowdy or high-spirited

In *Claudia, Where Are You?* (1969), Claudia runs away from home. Her father is an attorney and her mother is the executive editor of a magazine for younger women. Colman explores family relationships by portraying the mother's and daughter's individual thoughts and feelings about what is important. Claudia could have anything she wants materially, but she has very different values from those of her parents. Claudia sees her parents as fake and superficial; she does not want to be like them. Throughout most of the book, Claudia is trying to make it on her own in New York City. At the same time, her parents are trying to find their daughter and understand why she would want to run away from such a lovely home. Each character grows, but not to the complete understanding of the other. This realistic account of a family's struggles illustrates the huge chasm that exists between many adolescents and their parents, even when everything appears to be perfect. It is not enough for parents to provide material goods; adolescents need to be heard by them. Communication is a two-way street that is traveled by too few.

chasm a marked separation or division

Colman describes her mother as an early feminist who raised her daughters to be able to take care of themselves financially. In *After the Wedding* (1975), Katherine and Peter move out of New York City and rent a partially built house in the country. Katherine is an artist. She loves the setting and its rustic details. Peter works in radio and television; he wants to make a difference in the kind of programs he produces. He decides to go back to New York City and find a job, but Katherine does not want to leave their country home.

They struggle with a long-distance marriage, seeing each other only on the weekends for a while. Throughout most of the book, Katherine and Peter argue with each other, asserting their views of life. Their young marriage is rocky but spiced with romance. Colman presents each lifestyle fairly. The issue is not that one is right and the other wrong, but rather that each is different and a compromise must be reached if their marriage is to work.

In *The Family Trap* (1982), Becky's father dies in an accident at the factory and her mother is sent to a mental institution after attempting suicide. The grim details present an opportunity to explore sibling relationships and growing up. Becky's older sister, Nancy, age eighteen, is bossy and negative. Becky's younger sister, Stacey, age nine, is open to her older sisters' taking care of her, and she receives the best they have to offer. Nancy has had much more responsibility in taking care of their mother than Becky has realized; however, even when Becky becomes aware of this fact, she still resists Nancy's authority.

initiative introductory step

Becky gets a job after school to supplement their meager income. She is very proud of herself for taking this initiative, but Nancy belittles her effort. Becky works after school and on Saturday, and then throughout the summer. Her employer, Mr. Kowalski, is an older widower who prides himself on being a good friend to Becky. He becomes the adult audience and confidant she needs. Becky petitions the court to become an emancipated minor when she turns sixteen years old. She wants the privileges and responsibilities that go with adulthood. She resents answering to her older sister. Becky's boyfriend, Tim, admires her for her strength and determination, but he also tests her resolve to be responsible by repeatedly urging her to have sex with him.

In *Suddenly* (1987), Emily must deal with her guilt and grief after she and Russ accidently run over and kill Joey, the little boy with whom Emily often baby-sat. Russ and his parents recognize that it was a terrible accident, but life goes on. Emily breaks up with Russ because they handle their guilt and grief so differently. Emily's mother admonishes Emily to think of others from their perspective rather than from her own.

Joey's mother has a very difficult time going on with life and chooses to spend her time in little Joey's room. Joey's dad and older brother, Chet, must deal with their anger and grief in losing Joey, but they must also manage their concern and impatience with Joey's mother's handling of her grief. This book is full of emotions, and each is presented as a natural and normal response to death. In addition to Joey's death, Emily's mother considers leaving her husband and confides this thought to Emily. The feelings associated with losing someone are explored from several angles.

Political Issues

Colman is active in politics. She worked with the National War Relief Agency during World War II. She has served on the Bridgewater Board of Education, she has been the chairperson of the Zoning Board of Appeals, and she has been a member of the Democratic Town Committee. She also writes regular letters to her newspaper editor about current issues.

Colman introduces her readers to the democratic process in *Classmates by Request* (1964). The town has recently built a new school for the Negro students (the term used in the book), but the African American leaders have planned a demonstration. Ellen, the daughter of a respected African

American leader, refuses to demonstrate. Her stand is unpopular with her family and friends. She understands that African Americans need to stick together and fight for equality. She knows that the new African American school will be inferior to the white school because of the differences in the curriculum and honor programs available to the white students. She also understands that she is unwilling to sacrifice her senior year and graduation and her dream of going to teachers' college because of segregation. It is the timing that is wrong for Ellen, not the cause.

Carla, the white protagonist, and a few of her friends integrate the African American school, and Carla and Ellen become friends. Carla's father is appointed to head a commission to end segregation. Although he is supportive of the African American demonstration, the African American students' boycott of the new school, and the white students' integrating the new school, he does not appoint Ellen's father to the commission. When the African American leaders decide to expand the demonstration to Carla's father's office, Carla does not understand how he can welcome the demonstration as a necessary part of the democratic process.

In *Bride at Eighteen* (1966), Mike challenges Kate to go beyond her limited experience. Mike is politically active and Kate feels overwhelmed by politics. When Mike says Kate's mother is like sweet people who live good lives but do not get involved with their larger world, Kate does not understand what he means. After Mike and Kate get married, he expects her to make her own decisions and to find her own place in life. She struggles to discover what is important to her and to give voice to her values.

Social Issues

Colman addresses current social issues such as divorce, alcoholic parents, prejudice, and mixed marriages in her stories. In *Mixed-Marriage Daughter* (1968), Sophie learns how discrimination feels when she begins to identify with her Jewish heritage after her family moves to Sophie's mother's hometown. Sophie was not brought up Jewish and does not understand the accepted social barriers between the Jews and the Gentiles in this small community. Her questioning helps

segregation the separation of a race, class, or ethnic group by discriminatory means

boycott a refusal to deal or associate with someone or something

Gentiles people of non-Jewish nations or non-Jewish faiths (sometimes "Gentiles" can mean Christians as distinguished from Jews)

the adults see how their unwillingness to force the issue had perpetuated discrimination.

In *Car-Crazy Girl* (1967), Dina fears she will grow up to be like her parents, drinking sherry and highballs in the morning and throughout the day, and talking around feelings and issues rather than confronting them. Dina loves attention and excitement and wants to experience everything—bad as well as good, pain as well as pleasure. When the school announces a stricter dress code, Dina is ready to rebel. Even though Dina never wore jeans to school, she wears them the day the new code goes into effect. Her boyfriend, Stan, is the long-haired leader of a rock band. Dina and the band members are expelled from school until they agree to abide by the dress code. Stan methodically decides that having long hair is not worth throwing away his future college plans and has his hair cut. Dina is furious with him because he appears to have no will to fight, and she breaks up with him.

Dina has a car wreck and kills her friend. Her parents and their attorney (Stan's stepfather) pressure her to lie about how the accident happened. Dina's decision is critical to the life she will live from then on. If she tells the truth, she will likely go to jail and hurt her parents terribly; but if she lies, she will have decided to live the life her parents have chosen, rather than the one she wanted for herself. Her struggle is tough, and she is the only one who can decide.

Colman's Explorations

Colman's stories involve adolescents who question the current status quo. Because she writes on the cutting edge of controversy, Colman does not offer solutions, but she does make her readers care about the characters and feel what they are feeling. Because her characters question various issues, her readers continue the questioning process long after they close the book. Readers live through the decision-making process of the characters; they experience how to make choices, what to examine, and the natural consequences of choices. Writing is just one avenue that Colman travels as she seeks to make this world a better place. She is politically involved in her local community and politically aware of her international community. Colman draws upon

status quo the existing state of affairs

many of her own experiences in her writings. She explores current issues that have not been resolved; her writings are genuine explorations of complex but everyday situations.

Besides novels for young adults, Colman has written nonfiction books about careers, stories under the pen name of Teresa Crayder, and many magazine articles.

If you like Hila Colman's books, you might also like works by Judy Blume, Will Hobbs, S. E. Hinton, Chris Crutcher, and Rosa Guy.

Selected Bibliography

WORKS BY HILA COLMAN

Novels for Young Adults

The Big Step (1957)

A Crown for Gina (1958)

Julie Builds Her Castle (1959)

Best Wedding Dress (1960)

The Girl from Puerto Rico (1961)

Mrs. Darling's Daughter (1962)

Peter's Brownstone House (1963)

Phoebe's First Campaign (1963)

Classmates by Request (1964)

The Boy Who Couldn't Make Up His Mind (1965)

Christmas Cruise (1965)

Bride at Eighteen (1966)

Thoroughly Modern Millie (1966)

Car-Crazy Girl (1967)

Dangerous Summer (1968)

Mixed-Marriage Daughter (1968)

Something out of Nothing (1968)

Andy's Landmark House (1969)

Claudia, Where Are You? (1969)

The Happenings at North End School (1970)

Daughter of Discontent (1971)

End of the Game (1971)

The Family and the Fugitive (1972)

Benny the Misfit (1973)

Chicano Girl (1973)

The Diary of a Frantic Kid Sister (1973)

Friends and Strangers on Location (1974)
After the Wedding (1975)
Ethan's Favorite Teacher (1975)
That's the Way It Is, Amigo (1975)
The Amazing Miss Laura (1976)
Nobody Has to Be a Kid Forever (1976)
The Case of the Stolen Bagels (1977)
Sometimes I Don't Love My Mother (1977)
Rachel's Legacy (1978)
The Secret Life of Harold the Bird Watcher (1978)
Ellie's Inheritance (1979)
Accident (1980)
What's the Matter with the Dobsons? (1980)
Confessions of a Storyteller (1981)
The Family Trap (1982)
Girl Meets Boy (1982)
My Friend, My Love (1983)
Not for Love (1983)
Just the Two of Us (1984)
A Fragile Love (1985)
Triangle of Love (1985)
Weekend Sisters (1985)
Happily Ever After (1986)
Remind Me Not to Fall in Love (1987)
Suddenly (1987)
Double Life of Angela Jones (1988)
Rich and Famous Like My Mom (1988)

Written Under the Name Teresa Crayder

Kathy and Lisette (1966)
Sudden Fame (1966)
Cleopatra (1969)

Nonfiction

Beauty, Brains, and Glamour: A Career in Magazine Publishing (1968)
Making Movies: Student Films to Features (1969)
City Planning: What It's All About—In the Planners' Own Words (1971)

✍

How to Write to the Author
Hila Colman
c/o William Morrow & Co., Inc.
1350 Avenue of the Americas
New York, NY 10019

Books for Adult Readers

The Country Weekend Cookbook, with Louis Colman (1961)

Hanging On (1977)

Short Stories and Articles

Colman is a contributor to *McCalls, Saturday Evening Post, Ingenue, Ladies' Home Journal, Seventeen, Redbook,* and *Today's Woman.*

WORKS ABOUT HILA COLMAN

Commire, Anne, ed. "Hila Colman." In *Something About the Author.* Detroit: Gale Research, 1988, vol. 53, pp. 22–31.

Caroline B. Cooney

(1947-)

by Donald R. Gallo

Picture an attractive forty-something mother of three grown children playing the organ at the local church or playing the piano for the school music programs in her town. Now try to visualize a person who writes horror novels for teenagers. Caroline Cooney is both of those people . . . and more. She is the author of more than fifty novels—not just of terrifying horror, but also novels about romance, time travel, and serious teenage problems. With more than five million copies of her books in print, she is one of the most successful authors writing for young people today, even though much of her work has not received the kind of attention from critics and scholars that it deserves.

One reason is that many of Cooney's books have been published only in paperback editions, a form that usually is ignored by reviewers in most education and library journals. But teenage readers do not pay attention to whether a book is hardcover or paperback—they only want to know if it is a good story. And because Cooney tells good stories,

All quotations not attributed to a specific publication were made by Caroline B. Cooney during an interview at her home in June 1995 and are published here by the permission of Caroline B. Cooney.

teenagers buy thousands of copies of every book that she writes.

Her success did not come quickly. After graduating from high school in Greenwich, Connecticut, Cooney tried two years of college, as well as a year at Massachusetts General Hospital School of Nursing. She also considered a career in music, having experience playing the piano, the organ, the violin, and the French horn. But she found all these activities too stifling, too limiting. And she knew her musical ability was not good enough to make her a world-class performer. "I'm a really good small-town musician," she decided.

Wanting what she calls "a broader life," and feeling that she "could tell one heck of a story," she began writing while trying to raise three young children. Like any sensible person, she started with what she knew and liked best: historical fiction. Partly because of the influence of an excellent sixth-grade history teacher, she "had a crush on ancient Rome." But none of the eight books she produced was good enough to be published. Nevertheless, growing up with the encouragement of very supportive parents and determined to support herself and her three children after her divorce, Cooney continued to write. She sold several short stories to children's magazines such as *Jack and Jill* and *Humpty Dumpty,* as well as one to *Seventeen,* and in 1979 she finally published a mystery novel for younger readers called *Safe as the Grave.* Next she wrote an adult novel of adventure and suspense about a woman kidnapped by two killers. Called *Rear View Mirror* (1980), it was made into a television movie in 1984, starring Lee Remick.

Boy Meets Girl

Still looking for a comfortable genre that would sell, Cooney next tried a romance novel for young adults. *An April Love Story* (1981) became the first of her many successful romances. Some, like *Nancy & Nick* (1982), stand alone; others became parts of series that include "Cheerleaders" and "Saturday Night." Most of these romances, Cooney says, contain very similar and straightforward themes; they are all basically boy-meets-girl stories. "You can't beat boy meets girl," she claims. Cooney is quoted in *Something About the Author* as saying: "I believe that to love and to be loved are the most fierce desires any of us will ever have, and young girls can never read enough about it" (p. 56). In fact, even in her hor-

"I believe that to love and to be loved are the most fierce desires any of us will ever have, and young girls can never read enough about it."

ror stories and her novels about serious teenage problems, romance always plays a significant role.

Because these romance novels are written for girls, Cooney says they must have a high emotional quality, including "both joy and tears." She also likes all her books to have a "sense of place," so that the location of the town and especially the local high school are important, and all her stories must have a moral. Because there are always descriptions of clothing, makeup, and hair styles in these books, no boy would ever want to read them.

Most of the boys in these books, in fact, usually come off as being clueless about girls' feelings. The boys may be good-looking and even heroic, athletic sometimes and often academically talented, but they are still not very perceptive about emotions. Seventeen-year-old Susan, in *Don't Blame the Music* (1986), even though she is strongly attracted to two different boys in her school, says: "Sometimes I don't think boys can read anything but words. And maybe not even those" (p. 56). Male readers certainly would not take kindly to those sentiments.

In 1983, Cooney had some fun combining romance with a choose-your-own-adventure format, eventually producing four novels in which the reader ("you") is the main character, who is asked to make choices from two alternatives at various places throughout the story. For example, at the end of the first five pages in *Sun, Sea, and Boys* (1984), you have a choice between spending the summer at a wilderness camp in Maine or traveling to New York City with your school's jazz band to play a series of outdoor concerts. In New York, you have to make such decisions as whether to go shopping with a group of girls or see if Alex will accompany you to Bloomingdales. The book has twenty-two different endings, and if you do not like one, you can go back and make different choices so that you end up with the boy you prefer. Pretty simplistic plotting and awfully simple characterizations, but lots of fun for recreational reading.

plot the deliberate sequence of events in a literary work

characterization method by which a writer creates and develops the appearance and personality of a character

Scary Stuff

In 1985, her romance novels for teenagers earned Cooney the Romantic Book Award, but romance was only one of the niches she found for herself. Another was writing horror novels, the first of which was *The Fog,* published in 1989 and

niche place or position best suited to a person

genre type of literature, such as science fiction or romance

trilogy a series of three literary works that are closely related and share a single theme

menacing threatening

followed quickly by *The Snow* and *The Fire,* both published in 1990. Not only was this a new genre for Cooney, but she says it is a type of story she never enjoys reading herself. "They're too scary!" she squeals. Perhaps that is why, although the spooky-looking covers of her horror novels fill the bookstore shelves alongside those written by Christopher Pike and R. L. Stine, hers do not contain the blood and gore typical of most other writers in that field. Nor do dead and dismembered bodies pile up throughout her books (though some characters do die). Of course, there are lots of scary things in her horror novels, not the least of which is an enticing vampire in a trilogy of books, but the atmosphere is the most important ingredient. For example, in *The Perfume* (1992), even the name of the new perfume—*Venom*—creates the menacing feeling in Dove; it quickly brings out a side of her she would rather not have been aware of. And because most of Cooney's stories are told from the perspective of girls, she believes that textural elements—touch and smells and feelings—are essential. In *The Stranger* (1993), for example, Nicoletta feels a creature near her while she is searching for her mysterious classmate Jethro in a cave:

> Its skin rasped against hers like saw grass. His stink was unbreathable. Its hair was dead leaves, crisping against each other and breaking off in her face. Warts of sand covered it, and the sand actually came off on her, as if the creature were half made of the cave itself. (P. 49)

Or in *The Cheerleader* (1991), when Althea encounters the vampire:

> The dark drapery that seemed to be the vampire's clothing shifted and swirled as if it were leaving. But the vampire stood still. The hem of his black cloth blew toward Althea. She stepped back, and the black cloth reached farther, trembling eagerly. The vampire collected it back and wrapped it around himself like a container. (P. 23)

In addition, Cooney believes her books must take a moral stance. These are stories about the battle between good and evil, and good must always triumph. The message in *Twins* (1994), for instance, is stated clearly for the main character: "Mary Lee knew the real horror then. The worst, absolutely worst thing, is to see something wrong, and then just stand there and let it happen" (p. 172).

To those who criticize horror novels, Cooney suggests that these stories have shown male readers that "books are no longer for the squeamish." Given the choice between horror novels and more serious, more substantive books that kids are not interested in reading, "my vote is with books that kids are eager to read," she says in an unpublished speech she gave in Orlando, Florida.

> *To those who criticize horror novels, Cooney suggests that these stories have shown male readers that "books are no longer for the squeamish."*

Critical Acclaim

Cooney, of course, has not limited herself to romances and horror stories. She has also gained critical approval for several books that deal realistically with significant teenage problems. Combining her talent for creating both suspenseful and romantic situations with contemporary teenage issues, Cooney wrote *The Face on the Milk Carton* in 1990. It describes the feelings and events that follow when a high school student notices a picture on a milk carton announcing a young child's kidnapping years earlier. This picture is of her! A review in the 12 January 1990 *Publishers Weekly* praised the book's "strong characterizations" as well as its "suspenseful, impeccably paced action" (p. 62). This novel has become her best-selling book, along with its much-requested sequel *What Happened to Janie?* (1993), and is sure to continue its role at the top because of the 1995 CBS television movie starring Kellie Martin as Janie, with Jill Clayburgh and Sharon Lawrence in the mother roles. *The Face on the Milk Carton* received the International Reading Association-Children's Book Council Children's Choice Award and was also named an American Library Association YASD Recommended Book for Reluctant Readers, and its sequel was an IRA Young Adults Choice.

impeccable flawless

Among Cooney's other award-winning books are *Among Friends* (1987), the story of six students told through their personal journals, which was one of the New York Public Library's Books for the Teenage, and *Twenty Pageants Later* (1991), an ALA/YASD Recommended Book for Reluctant YA Readers as well as a New York Public Library Book for the

coerce to force to make a certain choice

Teenage. *Twenty Pageants Later* resulted from the research that Cooney compiled with the assistance of her daughter Sayre, whom she coerced into entering beauty contests. The novel provides thought-provoking insights into motivations as well as performances in those contests, with such comments as: "[Beauty pageants] don't build character. They diminish it" (p. 105). In the end after watching her older sister struggle through joyous triumphs and heart-breaking defeats, the narrator, Scottie-Anne, learns that she needs to build her own achievements in life.

Another award-winning book that was influenced by the experiences of one of Cooney's daughters is the exciting *Flight #116 Is Down* (1992). This ALA Best Book for Young Adults focuses on the lives and actions of two teenagers, a boy and a girl, who help rescue survivors of the crash of a jumbo jet near their homes. Patrick's actions as a young Emergency Medical Technician reflect the EMS training that Cooney's daughter Louisa received when she was sixteen. In her Fall 1992 *School Library Journal* review, Cindy Darling Codell criticizes the "rapidly shifting viewpoints" and the lack of "finely brushed characterizations" that are evident in such other Cooney novels as *Don't Blame the Music* (another ALA Best Book for Young Adults), but she also noted that this fast-moving, action-packed format is perfect for attracting reluctant readers (p. 107). That, of course, is exactly what Cooney hopes to do with *all* her novels. In fact, having raised a son, Harold, who has always been a reluctant reader and an unenthusiastic student, gave her "a lot more sympathy and understanding for kids who don't want to read. When I write a book, I think about them," she says in *Speaking for Ourselves, Too* (p. 42). *Don't Blame the Music* is also one of the few books in which Cooney provides a male point of view.

reluctant unwilling

Male readers will also appreciate *Emergency Room* and *Driver's Ed,* two of Cooney's books published in 1994. *Emergency Room* focuses on a series of events that various teenagers experience one evening in one city at a city hospital, all of them (but one) based on real, "very scary" things Caroline Cooney saw and experienced at Yale–New Haven Hospital, where she had volunteered every Tuesday evening for five years.

Although not based on any true events, *Driver's Ed* resulted from a combination of imagination and talking with teenagers in various schools she has visited throughout the country and at school and church activities in her town, where she does volunteer work. Focusing on several students in a driver's education class, Cooney shows what happens after two of them steal a stop sign at an intersection where a young mother is later killed because of the missing sign. A 1994 flyer from Bantam Doubleday Dell says that in this "gripping and provocative" story "two high school juniors must learn the hard way that having a driver's license means more than free-dom—it means taking responsibility." The lessons are driven home clearly and effectively without being preachy in the ALA Reluctant YA Reader award-winning novel that every teenager ought to read and think about.

Cooney has also tackled other issues in other novels: divorce in *Family Reunion* (1989), a novel in which, Hazel Rochman, in her review in the 1 November 1989 *Booklist,* says, Cooney "captures relationships with subtlety and candor" (p. 539); the separation of friends caused by graduation from high school in *The Party's Over* (1991), which earned praise, again from Hazel Rochman, in the 15 February 1991 *Booklist,* for Cooney's "frank treatment of the whole high school nostalgia trip and of class and culture differences" (p. 1188); the effects of war on families back home and the role of women in war in *Operation Homefront* (1992), in which the mother of three children is sent off with her National Guard unit in Saudi Arabia during the Gulf War.

candor honesty

nostalgia a sentimental yearning to return to a past time

Where Next?

Although Cooney has had great success in writing horror stories, she is not likely to write any more of them, she says. And even though she began her career by writing historical novels, she is not likely to go back to those either. Instead, in the mid-1990s she enjoyed writing time-travel stories, the first of which is called *Both Sides of Time* (1995) and will be followed by *Out of Time.* "They are such fun to write!" she says. Look also for more adventure stories, like her 1995 *Flash Fire,* a fire rescue story based on the 1993 fires in southern California, along with a novel that could have been taken right out of daily newspapers: *The Terrorist* (1996). In 1996, Cooney was thinking about a third book dealing with Janie.

If you enjoyed *The Face on the Milk Carton*, you might also want to read *Twice Taken* by Susan Beth Pfeffer. And if you like spooky, scary stories, you might like the works of Edgar Allan Poe.

Selected Bibliography

WORKS BY CAROLINE B. COONEY

Novels for Young Adults

An April Love Story (1981)

Nancy & Nick (1982)

He Loves Me Not (1982)

The Personal Touch (1982)

Holly in Love (1983)

I'm Not Your Other Half (1984)

Nice Girls Don't (1984)

Don't Blame the Music (1986)

The Rah Rah Girl (1987)

Among Friends (1987)

Camp Girl-Meets-Boy (1988)

The Girl Who Invented Romance (1988)

Camp Reunion (1988)

Family Reunion (1989)

The Fog (1989)

The Snow (1990)

The Fire (1990)

The Face on the Milk Carton (1990)

The Party's Over (1991)

The Cheerleader (1991)

Twenty Pageants Later (1991)

The Perfume (1992)

Operation Homefront (1992)

Freeze Tag (1992)

The Return of the Vampire (1992)

Flight #116 Is Down (1992)

The Vampire's Promise (1993)

Whatever Happened to Janie? (1993)

Forbidden (1993)

The Stranger (1993)

Twins (1994)

Emergency Room (1994)

Driver's Ed (1994)

Night School (1995)

Both Sides of Time (1995)

Flash Fire (1995)

The Terrorist (1996)

Books for Younger Readers

Safe as the Grave (1979)

The Paper Caper (1981)

SERIES

Follow Your Heart

A Stage Set for Love (1983)

Sun, Sea, and Boys (1984)

Suntanned Days (1985)

Racing to Love (1985)

Crystal Falls

The Bad and the Beautiful (1985)

The Morning After (1985)

Cheerleaders

Rumors (1985)

Trying Out (1985)

All the Way (1985)

Saying Yes (1987)

Saturday Night

Saturday Night (1986)

Last Dance (1987)

New Year's Eve (1988)

Summer Night (1988)

Books for Adults

Rear View Mirror (1980)

Sand Trap (1983)

Books and Parts of Books

Cooney, Caroline B. In *Speaking for Ourselves, Too: More Autobiographical Sketches by Notable Authors of Books for Young Adults.* Edited by Donald R. Gallo. Urbana. Ill.: National Council of Teachers of English, 1993, pp. 42–44.

Unpublished Speech

ALAN Workshop, National Council of Teachers of English annual convention. Orlando, Fla., November 1994.

How to Write to the Author

Caroline B. Cooney
c/o Dell Publishing
1540 Broadway
New York, NY 10036

Works About Caroline B. Cooney

Codel, Cindy Darling. Review of *Flight #116 Is Down. School Library Journal,* Vol. 38, February 1992, p. 107.

Cooney, Caroline B. Bantam Doubleday Dell publicity flyer, 1994

Hile, Kevin S., ed. "Caroline B. Cooney." In *Something About the Author,* vol. 80. New York: Gale Research Inc., 1995, pp. 54–57.

Review of *The Face on the Milk Carton. Publishers Weekly,* 12 January 1990, p. 62.

Rochman, Hazel. Review of *Family Reunion. Booklist,* 1 November 1989, p. 539.

———. Review of *The Party's Over. Booklist,* 15 February 1991, p. 1188.

Robert Cormier

(1925-   )

by Patricia J. Campbell

I t is night. A young boy is beaten almost to death in a fistfight on a stage while the whole school watches and cheers from the grandstand. Two invisible opponents face off in a knife battle to the death. A crippled madwoman seduces a young boy on the phone and then tries to kill him with a poisoned hypodermic. Four nice boys from good families trash a house by ripping and tearing, urinating and defecating. A terrorist stands on a bridge holding aloft the body of the child he has just killed.

Scenes from grisly horror paperbacks? No, these are episodes from the books of Robert Cormier, a writer who has been called the finest young adult novelist at work today. Cormier's stories look unflinchingly at tyranny and the abuse of power, at treachery and betrayal, at guilt and remorse, love and hate, and the corruption of innocence. They do this in brilliant and complex structures full of intricate wordplay and subtle thought. But most of all the books of Robert Cormier are smashingly good stories, full of suspense and

Quotations from Robert Cormier that are not attributed to a published source are from personal interviews conducted by the author of this article between January 1984 and September 1988 and a telephone conversation on 26 March 1995 and are published here by permission of Robert Cormier.

291

> *What kind of writer could be the creator of these brave and tormented people? What kind of person can look so deeply into the heart of darkness?*

Thomas Wolfe
(1900–1938) was an
American novelist.
He wrote *Look
Homeward, Angel*,
which was a realistic
portrayal of Southern
family life.
William Saroyan
(1908–1981) was an
American writer of
short stories, plays
and novels. There is
an article about
Ernest Hemingway
in volume 2.

surprises and dramatic action as his characters struggle—sometimes unsuccessfully—to find an appropriate response to the existence of evil.

The Making of a Writer

What kind of writer could be the creator of these brave and tormented people? What kind of person can look so deeply into the heart of darkness? Some sort of spooky, brooding recluse? Far from it. Cormier (pronounced Cor-MEER) is a slight man with wispy gray hair and a crooked smile like sunshine. He and his wife Connie have lived all their lives in the small New England mill town of Leominster, about thirty miles northeast of Boston. As Monument, Massachusetts, Leominster and the nearby town of Fitchburg are the setting for most of his novels. "I love it here," he once told me. "I like being able to go downtown and run into some guy I was in the first grade with." Their gray clapboard house in a pine-shaded suburb is often noisy with visits from their four grown children and ten grandchildren. Cormier is kind and thoughtful, a devout Catholic, and a man who is happy in his work and secure in a place where his family has roots.

Early in the century Cormier's French Canadian grandfather brought his young family to the United States to seek his fortune in the comb factories of Leominster. There the whole family lived in one of the balconied three-story "tenements" that are typical of the French Hill district. Born on 17 January 1925 to Lucien Joseph and Irma Cormier, he was the second child of eight. With grandparents upstairs and aunts and uncles as neighbors, he was surrounded with love and attention as he grew up. Things were not so easy, however, at St. Cecelia's Parochial Grammar School, where the strict nuns and playground bullies taught him the meaning of tyranny. Young Bob Cormier was not good at sports and was shy with girls, but home was always a secure retreat. Then one day he sat under the playground stairs and wrote a poem for his favorite nun, Sister Catherine. "Why, Bob," she said, after reading it carefully, "You're a writer!" And he knew who he was.

In high school he discovered the books of Thomas Wolfe, William Saroyan, and Ernest Hemingway. He adored the movies, too, and went faithfully to the Saturday afternoon matinees at the Plymouth Theater. He was especially fond of cowboy serials and gangster films. Afterward, because his mother had given up movies as part of a religious vow, he would hurry home and tell her the story, scene by scene—an exercise that taught him how to put together a plot. In spite of these consolations, he remembers adolescence as "a lacerating experience."

At Fitchburg Teachers College, one of his instructors helped him sell his first short story, and Cormier had his start as a professional writer. Soon he was working as a newspaperman for the *Worcester Telegram and Gazette*. At a community dance he met Connie, and in 1948, they were married. In 1955, he transferred to the *Fitchburg Sentinel,* where he was to work for the next twenty-three years. On weekends he wrote short stories, many of which were published in the leading magazines of the day. These pieces were gentle and warm, very different from his novels, and a sampling of them was published many years later under the title *Eight Plus One* (1980). As part of his work at the newspaper he also wrote a column of wistful and ironic musings under the pen name of "John Fitch IV." Long after he had made his reputation as a young adult author, Connie collected some of the best of these writings in *I Have Words to Spend* (1991).

And then his father, the strong refuge of his childhood and the closest friend of his adult years, was diagnosed with lung cancer and died in six months. To come to terms with his grief, Cormier belted out a novel, *Now and at the Hour* (1960). It was immediately accepted for publication, and critics praised it lavishly for its power and honesty. Two more adult novels followed: *A Little Raw on Monday Mornings* (1963), a touching story about a middle-aged woman who gets pregnant by the wrong man, and *Take Me Where the Good Times Are* (1965), a comical tale of a feisty old geezer who runs away from the old people's home.

wistful yearning or longing, sometimes in a sad state of mind

ironic marked by a contrast between what is said and what is actually meant; sarcastic

Cormier's Biggest Novels

One afternoon, when Cormier's four children were in their teen years, Peter, the eldest, came home from his jock high school loaded down with boxes of chocolates to sell. But he did not want to. His father was sympathetic and let him make the choice to refuse. The next day Cormier worried, "What if . . . ?" Nothing happened to Peter, but a story had begun in his father's mind. The result was *The Chocolate War* (1974), a novel that rocked the world of young adult literature.

From the first this story of Jerry Renault, who dares to disturb the universe, was controversial. Critics were shocked by the world of Trinity High School, where the Vigils, a secret society led by the diabolical Archie Costello, vie for power with the vicious Brother Leon. Between them they crush Jerry as he stubbornly persists in his refusal to be part of the school chocolate sale. In the end, when he lies beaten nearly to death, he tells his friend Goober that it is better to give up and sell the chocolates.

It was, and still is, this ending that causes trouble. Readers are used to the lone hero who stands up to the bad guys—but in other stories he always wins out. *The Chocolate War* turns their expectations upside down. "No," they cry, "this is all wrong!" And that, of course, is exactly how Cormier wants us to react. By showing us a situation in which evil wins, he is pointing out that this has happened because the good people have not had the courage to get together and take a stand against it.

But many critics and would-be censors have not understood this. They often call the book "depressing," and seem to feel that by picturing such a dark world Cormier is somehow condoning it or trying to show that all of life is hopeless. Articles and letters in *Newsweek* and librarians' and teachers' magazines have faced off on this issue. Other critics have not been so polite. There have been a number of censorship attacks in which parents, disturbed by the book but at a loss to know why, have tried to get it taken out of the schools by unfounded accusations of sex, dirty words, and disrespect for authority.

The most spectacular censorship attack on Cormier's work began initially not with *The Chocolate War* but with *I Am the Cheese* (1977). In Bay County, Florida, a parent objected to four words in that novel, and before the affair was over, there had been death threats, firebombings, and 200 books banned from the school system. This trouble is surprising, because *I Am the Cheese,* with its theme of menacing and hidden political intrigue, is superficially the least censorable of all of Cormier's young adult novels. In it a boy takes a mysterious winter bicycle journey pursued by unseen forces. At the same time, he is guided by a sinister interviewer to remember that

> *By showing us a situation in which evil wins, Cormier is pointing out that this has happened because the good people have not had the courage to get together and take a stand against it.*

his family was in hiding under the Witness Relocation Program. Not until the end do we find with a shock how the three levels of the plot structure are related.

Taking apart the complex structure is one of the pleasures of reading a Cormier novel in depth. The first time through, the stories read smoothly and easily like good adventure yarns. But a second reading shows multiple levels, shifts in voices and tense, and intricate echoes and interrelated actions that reveal hidden meanings. For example, in *After the First Death* (1979) terrorists capture a school bus and its young girl driver, drug the children and force the girl to drive onto a remote bridge. There they deliver their demands to the army. The General sends his son to them as a hostage, giving him wrong information about the time of the planned attack. When the boy breaks under torture, he must face the fact that his father expected him to do so. But only on a second perusal is it revealed to the careful reader that the boy has killed himself, and it is not his voice but that of the General, driven mad by remorse, that we hear in the first part of the book. Perhaps.

Fade (1988) has an even more complex structure. This tale of a boy who is possessed by the inherited ability to fade into invisibility uses three distinct parts, each with its own characters and style, and all connected seamlessly by the narrative. The novel begins with a gentle Frenchtown coming-of-age story set in the 1930s, shifts into a brittle Manhattan-based examination of the nature of fiction and reality, and ends with a horror fantasy. The first section is autobiographical in setting and in many of the events, and so convincing is its blend of truth and fiction that for months after the book's publication friends took Cormier aside to ask hesitantly, "Bob, can you fade?"

A preoccupation with hidden identity is a thread that runs through all of Cormier's writing. The invisibility in *Fade* is an example, of course, as are the new names of the Farmer family in political hiding in *I Am the Cheese,* the ski masks that hide the faces and humanity of the terrorists in *After the First Death,* and the secret identity of the Avenger, who stalks Jane Jerome in *We All Fall Down* (1991). Barney Snow in *The Bumblebee Flies Anyway* (1983) has lost his identity entirely. Medical experiments in a voluntary hospital for the terminally ill have wiped away his memory, and when he finds out why, a terrible secret is revealed to him. To strike out against the in-

The **Witness Relocation Program** is a federal program designed to protect witnesses whose testimony may endanger their lives.

A preoccupation with hidden identity is a thread that runs through all of Cormier's writing.

evitability of death, he and another young patient reassemble in the attic a wooden model of a little car that they have found in a junkyard, and in a futile but glorious gesture, they send it flying off the roof with another young patient, who has been impatient for the end, as a passenger.

Parallels and doubling are also ways that this passion for secrets and hidden things shows itself. Events often repeat themselves in other forms, and there are a number of paired characters, twins, and too-close brothers and sisters who share hidden links or private knowledge. Names of characters and places, too, are often secrets to be decoded in his work. Secrets abound in *Beyond the Chocolate War,* the sequel that Cormier wrote ten years later in response to pleas from young readers who wanted to know what had happened to the players in *The Chocolate War.* This is his trickiest novel, full of misdirection and surprises, trapdoors and illusions. In it newcomer Ray Bannister uses his hobby of magic to unmask the continuing intrigue at Trinity. Brother Leon gets his comeuppance, but Archie, predictably, slips out of every trap unscathed.

comeuppance a well-deserved punishment or misfortune

The Villains

Cormier's gallery of villains show the many faces of darkness. Because his vision is of the ultimate opposing forces of good and evil, he never humanizes his bad guys by explaining their reasons for cruelty. They are devoted to evil for its own sake. In *The Chocolate War,* for example, Archie Costello, with his cool grace, is the closest to the traditional idea of the gentlemanly Devil. Brother Leon is physically repellent, like some squirming insect. Emile Janza is an animal who reveals the essential pointlessness of evil. Brint, Adam's interrogator in *I Am the Cheese,* is chilling in his systematic and steely coldness. Artkin the terrorist and General Marchand have both sold their souls to the false god of patriotism in *After the First Death.* Lulu, Cormier's only female villain in *In the Middle of the Night* (1995), is grotesque in her obsession with revenge. Harry Flowers, who leads the horrendous house-trashing that opens *We All Fall Down,* seems like a coarser version of Archie. Crudest of all is the racist grocer Mr. Hairston in *Tunes for Bears to Dance To* (1992), who coerces his young assistant into smashing an old man's lovingly carved toy village and

> *Cormier never humanizes his bad guys by explaining their reasons for cruelty. They are devoted to evil for its own sake.*

then reveals his enslavement to evil when he panics at the boy's refusal to complete the act by taking the promised rewards.

By contrast, Cormier's young male protagonists tend to be fearful, shy copies of himself at that age. The girls, who are the objects of their hopeless adoration, have more personality: tough, cocky Amy in *I Am the Cheese,* lovely, brave Kate who drives the school bus in *After the First Death,* Paul's laughing and sensual Aunt Rosanna in *Fade,* and charismatic Cassie, who worries about her mystic link with her dying brother in *The Bumblebee Flies Anyway.* Cormier's only female protagonist is eleven-year-old Darcy in *Other Bells for Us to Ring* (1990), who is both attracted and terrified by the Catholicism of her friend Kathleen Mary O'Hara, and who is desperate for a miracle to bring her father back from war.

Facing Hard Truths

Cormier for years aspired to write a sweet love story, and when Kate appeared in the school bus, so appealing to the young terrorist Miro, he thought it would happen. But that match turned out badly. At last he found his young couple in love in *We All Fall Down,* but in true Cormier style the doomed love affair between Jane Jerome and Buddy Walker is shattered when she finds out that he was one of the vandals who destroyed her house. In his 1995 book, *In the Middle of the Night,* friends and editors tried to prevail on him to allow a happy ending in the romance that would have lightened Denny's obsession with his father's guilt for the long-ago collapse of a crowded movie theater. But Cormier was adamant. "Life just isn't like that," he said.

Cormier has often told interviewers that he goes to the typewriter in the morning to see what his characters are going to do that day. He never outlines his novels ahead of time but lets his subconscious take the lead, working always from an emotion he tries to capture. Sometimes this method leads him astray into pages and pages that later must be discarded. He writes in the morning on his ancient Royal typewriter (he is superstitious about switching to a word processor) and then spends the afternoons walking about or visiting old friends. Revision is what he likes best, the fine-tuning and polishing. He gets hundreds of letters a year

While writing In the Middle of the Night, *friends and editors tried to prevail on Cormier to allow a happy ending. But Cormier was adamant (inflexible). "Life just isn't like that," he said.*

Cormier has often told interviewers that he goes to the typewriter in the morning to see what his characters are going to do that day.

Graham Greene
was an English writer
(1904–1991) who
wrote novels about
guilt, remorse, and
Roman Catholic
ideals.

If you like Robert
Cormier, you might also like
Edgar Allan Poe and J. D.
Salinger.

from young-adult readers and answers each one thoughtfully. An insomniac, he reads at night—Graham Greene is his favorite—or indulges his passion for movies on the VCR.

In recent years the Cormiers have become world travelers, because Bob is highly in demand as a speaker even in faraway Australia. Awards and honors have been heaped on him: an honorary doctorate from his alma mater; the ALAN Award from the National Council of Teachers of English (NCTE) in 1982; the Margaret A. Edwards Award from the American Library Association (ALA) in 1991. His books appear regularly on honor lists. But the award that pleases him most is the California Young Readers Medal, which he won in 1995, because it is voted on by teens themselves and because it means young people have recognized the honesty and integrity with which he speaks to them of the hard truths of being human.

Selected Bibliography

WORKS BY ROBERT CORMIER

Novels for Young Adults
The Chocolate War (1974)
I Am the Cheese (1977)
After the First Death (1979)
The Bumblebee Flies Anyway (1983)
Beyond the Chocolate War (1985)
Fade (1988)
Other Bells for Us to Ring (1990)
We All Fall Down (1991)
Tunes for Bears to Dance To (1992)
In the Middle of the Night (1995)

Novels for Adults
Now and at the Hour (1960)
A Little Raw on Monday Mornings (1963)
Take Me Where the Good Times Are (1965)

Short Stories
Eight Plus One: Stories (1980)
"In the Heat." In *Sixteen: Short Stories by Outstanding Writers for Young Adults*. Edited by Donald R. Gallo, 1984.

Essays

John Fitch IV, pseud. *Fitchburg Sentinel-Enterprise* column, 1966–1978.

"Forever Pedaling on the Road to Realism." In *Celebrating Children's Books: Essays on Children's Literature in Honor of Zena Sutherland*. Edited by Betsy Hearne and Marilyn Kaye, 1981.

"Creating *Fade*." *Horn Book,* March/April 1989, pp. 166–173.

I Have Words to Spend: Reflections of a Small Town Editor. Edited by Constance Cormier, 1991.

"The Gradual Education of a YA Novelist." In *Twentieth-Century Young Adult Writers*. Edited by Laura Standley Berger, 1994.

Media Adaptations

I Am the Cheese. Film. Almi, 1983.

"In the Heat." Audiocassette. Listening Library, 1987.

The Chocolate War. Audiocassette. Listening Library, 1988

The Chocolate War. Film. Management Company Entertainment Group, 1989.

Interviews with Robert Cormier

De Luca, Geraldine, and Roni Natov. "An Interview with Robert Cormier." *Lion and the Unicorn,* fall 1978, pp. 109–135.

Janeczco, Paul. "An Interview with Robert Cormier." *English Journal,* September, 1977, pp. 10–11.

McLaughlin, Frank. *Cheese, Chocolates, and Kids: A Day with Robert Cormier.* Videotape prepared for PBS, no date. Robert E. Cormier Collection, Fitchburg State College, Fitchburg, Mass.

————. "Robert Cormier: A Profile." *Media and Methods,* May/June 1978, p. 28.

Silvey, Anita. "An Interview with Robert Cormier." *Horn Book,* part 1, March/April 1985, pp. 145–155; part 2, May/June 1985, pp. 289–296.

Sutton, Roger. "Kind of a Funny Dichotomy." *School Library Journal,* June 1991, pp. 28–33.

WORKS ABOUT ROBERT CORMIER

Critical Studies—Books

Campbell, Patricia J. *Presenting Robert Cormier.* Updated edition. Boston: Twayne, 1989.

Critical Studies—Articles

Bagnall, Norma. "Realism: How Realistic Is It: A Look at *The Chocolate War.*" *Top of the News,* winter 1980, pp. 214–217.

Carter, Betty and Karen Harris. "Realism in Adolescent Fiction: In Defense of *The Chocolate War.*" *Top of the News,* spring 1980, pp. 283–285.

Clements, Bruce. "A Second Look: *The Chocolate War.*" *Horn Book,* April 1979, pp. 217–218.

Daly, Jay. "The New Repression." *Top of the News,* fall 1980, p. 79.

Gallo, Donald R. "Reality and Responsibility: The Continuing Controversy over Robert Cormier's Books for Young Adults." *Voice of Youth Advocates,* December 1984, p. 245.

Headley, Kathy Neal. "Duel at High Noon: A Replay of Cormier's Works." *ALAN Review,* winter 1994, p. 34.

Knudsen, Elizabeth G. "Is There Hope for Young Adult Readers?" *Wilson Library Bulletin,* September 1981, p. 47.

Lenz, Millicent. "A Romantic Ironist's Vision of Evil: Robert Cormier's *After the First Death.*" *Proceedings of the Eighth Annual Conference of the Children's Literature Association,* March 1981, pp. 50–56.

Lukens, Rebecca. "From Salinger to Cormier: Disillusionment to Despair in Thirty Years." *ALAN Review,* fall 1981, pp. 38–40, 42.

Monseau, Virginia. "Cormier's Heroines." *ALAN Review,* fall 1991, p. 40.

————."Studying Cormier's Protagonists." *ALAN Review,* fall 1994, p. 31.

Nilsen, Alleen Pace. "The Poetry of Naming in Young Adult Books." *ALAN Review,* spring 1980, p. 3.

Nodelman, Perry. "Robert Cormier Does a Number." *Children's Literature in Education,* summer 1983, pp. 94–103.

Schwartz, Tony. "Teen Agers' Laureate." *Newsweek,* 16 July 1979, pp. 87–88, 92.

Stringer, Sharon. "The Psychological Changes of Adolescence." *ALAN Review,* fall 1994, p. 27.

Sutton, Roger. "The Critical Myth: Realistic YA Novels." *School Library Journal,* November 1982, pp. 33–35.

How to Write to the Author
Robert Cormier
c/o Delacorte Press
1540 Broadway
New York, NY 10036

Stephen Crane

(1871–1900)

by Pam B. Cole

When asked to write a brief biography of himself in 1896, Stephen Crane penned the following words: "I . . . do not say that I am honest. I merely say that I am as nearly honest as a weak mental machinery will allow." These words represent Crane's fundamental belief that human beings are imperfect, a theme that he weaves through many of his writings and that helps identify him as one of the first American naturalistic writers.

Many scholars credit Stephen Crane's writings as marking the beginning of naturalism in American literature. His work, as well as that of other naturalistic writers, opposes idealistic portrayals of life and characterizes human beings as shaped by heredity and controlled by the realistic world in which they live. Crane wrote numerous poems, short stories, and novels in which he proved himself a master of irony, imagery, and symbolism, but he is best remembered for *The Red Badge of Courage,* a virtually plotless novel depicting the

> *Crane's fundamental belief was that human beings are imperfect, a theme that he weaves through many of his writings and that helps identify him as one of the first American naturalistic writers.*

psychological complexities of fear, anxiety, and courage in a young male soldier during the American Civil War.

Early Life

Crane was born on 1 November 1871, in Newark, New Jersey, into an aristocratic family, the fourteenth and last child of the Reverend Dr. Jonathan Townley Crane and Mary Helen Peck Crane. Crane's father, an itinerant Methodist preacher, and his mother, a devout Christian woman, reared their children by the strictest moral values, principles from which Crane strayed in later years. Crane's interest in writing was influenced by his family. Both his parents wrote articles dealing with religious and social issues, and two of his brothers were journalists.

itinerant characterized by travelling from place to place

As a child, Crane was afflicted by frequent colds and other illnesses; thus, he did not begin formal schooling until the age of eight, but he did receive his early education from Agnes, his older sister. She remained his closest friend until her death. When Crane was nine, his father died, leaving Crane's mother to rear him and the rest of the children. Crane spent most of his childhood in Asbury Park, New Jersey, where his mother supported the family with her journalism and her adept handling of coal mining stock. Crane loved to play soldier, and despite being delicate, he frequently played baseball, a sport in which he later excelled as a college student.

By the time Crane was sixteen, both he and his mother were writing unsigned articles on shore life for the *New York Tribune*. During his adolescence, he spent a great deal of time among the well-to-do families of New Jersey; however, he developed a dislike for what he viewed as frivolous lifestyles and found himself drawn to lower-class society. Although Crane respected his parents' adherence to their strict religious convictions, he believed that their moral standards shielded them from the unpleasantness and realities of life. He was drawn to all that defied his parents' moral principles and openly rebelled against their beliefs by incessantly drinking, swearing, patronizing brothels, and gambling.

College Years

At age seventeen, Crane attended Claverack College, a military institute that cultivated his interest in the American Civil War and that gave him the military knowledge he would later use in writing *The Red Badge of Courage.* After attending Claverack, Crane made two futile attempts at college. He first spent a semester at Lafayette College, where he flunked, and then he enrolled at Syracuse University. There he was no more successful academically, finding more pleasure in baseball and football than in his studies. Despite his lack of interest in academics, Crane continued to write during his college years.

While at Syracuse University, Crane wrote fiction and worked part-time with his brother as a local news correspondent. After quitting Syracuse in 1891, he worked full-time as a reporter for the *New York Tribune,* spending a great deal of time in the Putnam police court, where he had frequent opportunities to observe the lives of the Railroad Street prostitutes. During this time he lived in poverty among the local artists and lower class along the Bowery—a street in New York City characterized by cheap hotels and saloons. There he experienced firsthand the slum life of New York, absorbing all the realities of poverty, vice, and crime that he depicted so well in his first novel, *Maggie: A Girl of the Streets* (1893).

Maggie: A Girl of the Streets

This book, which was controversial at the turn of the twentieth century, depicts tenement life in the slums of New York in the 1890s. Although readers normally conceive of a hero as a superstar, a champion who performs magnificent deeds, Crane broke from this tradition, choosing for the protagonist of his story a deprived young woman living in poverty. Using the ordinary, real-life events that he observed and experienced while living in the Bowery, Crane elevated Maggie, his main character, to heroic status.

The story is set in the late 1800s, yet the themes in the work ring true even today. The novel is the tragedy of Maggie and her two brothers, Tommie and Jimmie, who are victims of poverty and an abusive home environment. Both their parents drink incessantly, have violent fights, and frequently turn their anger on their children. Tommie dies; so does their father, leaving Jimmie to follow in his father's footsteps. Maggie becomes infatuated with Pete, Jimmie's charismatic friend, who begins escorting her around town. Maggie, innocent and naive, sees Pete as her escape from a world "composed of

Although readers normally conceive of a hero as a superstar, a champion who performs magnificent deeds, Crane broke from this tradition, choosing for the protagonist (main character) of his story a deprived young woman living in poverty.

hardships and insults" (p. 20) and leaves home to live with him. Although the neighbors in the tenement and Maggie's mother view Maggie as wicked, she does not consider herself to be a ruined woman; rather, she views herself as one rescued from a life of misery. For instance, in one scene she displays this image of herself while in a saloon with Pete: walking through the saloon she passes two women with painted faces, and "with a shrinking movement, [she draws] back her skirts" (p. 41).

Pete appears as a gallant knight to Maggie, but eventually he proves himself to be a womanizer. He sends Maggie away when he and Maggie encounter Nell, a woman of questionable character for whom Pete has had a lasting attraction. Maggie, with no place to go, returns home only to be ridiculed by both her mother and Jimmie. Humiliated, she leaves home again and spends the next few weeks of her life as a prostitute on the streets before she is found dead.

Maggie's story—claimed by editors in the 1890s to contain language and content too shocking for publication—explores many themes, including poverty, deceit, and victimization. Pete is in reality arrogant and deceptive; he is a man who views women as mere possessions. In all his actions toward Maggie, Pete reveals himself to be a manipulator: he responds "in tones of philanthropy. He press[es] her arm with an air of reassuring proprietorship" (p. 40). He is proud that Maggie is dependent upon him, and her beauty wins him the admiration of other men. Furthermore, Maggie, a young and romantic dreamer, believes "her life was Pete's and she considered him worthy of the charge" (p. 40). Having escaped her destitute life, she initially believes she has improved herself. Nonetheless, she is a victim: a victim of poverty, of circumstance, of her own naiveté, and of a male-dominated world in which women are merely commodities.

As with many of Crane's works, *Maggie* ends with a twist of irony. Pete has lived his life deceiving women, treating them as possessions, but he, in the end, is also a victim. While in a saloon he buys drinks for Nell and her female friends; he becomes drunk, swears he is a good fellow, and tells Nell that he is attracted to her. Nell and her female friends, who have been using Pete to buy them drinks, show disgust when he passes out. Nell leaves with his money, calling him a fool.

A powerful tale about male and female roles and relationships, *Maggie* was a novel written before its time. Because editors regarded Crane's language as too offensive and the content, though realistic, as too shocking for readers, Crane could find no editor who was willing to publish it. Nonetheless, he borrowed money and had the work published himself under the pseudonym Johnston Smith. The investment, however, was a financial failure. Despite this financial failure, copies of the work found their way into the hands of such prominent writers as Hamlin Garland and William Dean Howells, who were impressed by Crane's style. This literary connection provided a number of opportunities for Crane, among them the syndication of a condensed version of *The Red Badge of Courage* in hundreds of newspapers in 1894 (*Colliers,* pp. 418–419).

Hamlin Garland (1860–1940) was an American writer who wrote Middle Western novels. In 1922, he won the Pulitzer Prize for *A Daughter of the Middle Border*, a sequel to *A Son of the Middle Border*. ***William Dean Howells*** (1837–1920) was an American realist writer.

The Red Badge of Courage

Despite the failure of *Maggie,* Crane did not renounce his love of writing. Having maintained a fascination with warfare, he threw himself into researching the American Civil War. He intensely studied Mathew Brady's Civil War photographs, talked with war veterans, and read various accounts of war, including ex-soldiers' memoirs about their experiences in the line of battle. His research, combined with his personal experience in military school and his close observations of men's struggles on the football field, aided him in writing his most talked about work: *The Red Badge of Courage,* acclaimed by many to be the best war novel ever written.

Published in serial fashion in 1894 by a Philadelphia newspaper and published in its entirety the following year, the novel brought Crane instant recognition. Many critics marveled that an individual who had never experienced war could write such a realistic account of combat. Of all Crane's works, it has received the most attention from critics. Some assert that the story is one of self-discovery and coming to terms with an imperfect world. Others maintain that it is a story of Christian redemption. Still others argue that it is a story illustrating the bestial nature of man.

The Red Badge of Courage recounts a young boy's war experiences. Envisioning himself as a war hero, young Henry Fleming enlists as a Union private in the Civil War. When Henry finds himself on the battlefield, however, he begins questioning his own courage and fears he may "run from the battle." We generally expect a plot when we read; we expect a problem to unfold, to reach a climax, and then resolve it-self in some way. But we do not find such a well-developed structure in *The Red Badge of Courage*. Spanning two days of war in the life of the young hero, the novel appears to be a series of disjointed battle scenes. To many readers the chapters may seem pointless and unrelated; nonetheless, if we read the novel as a psychological study of a soldier's reactions to war, that is, as a novel illustrating the various conflicting emotions that an inexperienced soldier feels in combat and the manner in which a soldier comes to terms with these emotions, then the novel takes on meaning.

Central to the work and to some of Crane's other works as well (for example, the short story "A Mystery of Heroism") are the motivational forces behind courage. Young Henry Fleming's bravery is spurred by a number of complex and often overlapping emotions: pride, anger, doubt, and even fear itself. Henry is proud to be among those fighting in the war; to be a soldier is to be a man. Yet, he sometimes doubts his ability to remain courageous, fearing that he will run when fighting breaks out. And run he initially does. While fleeing, however, Henry accidentally receives a blow to the head. Other soldiers aid him in bandaging his wound, and in the **vainglorious** boast-ful process, Henry feels a vainglorious sense of pride. The blow, mistaken by his fellow soldiers to be a war wound, becomes Henry's red badge, his symbol of courage.

Mingled with the conflicting emotions of fear and courage is anger. Henry is horrified by the ruthless nature of death in war, and at times he feels outrage: he comes to see war as a senseless manner of reconciling differences. As Henry experiences all these conflicting emotions, he becomes a symbol of all humans confronting conflict.

Although in one way the novel may be a psychological study of a soldier's emotional reactions to war, interpreted in yet another way it may represent an individual's spiritual growth. Because his father was a minister and his mother a dedicated Christian, Crane was indoctrinated from birth with religion, but seeing the imperfect world around him, he somehow could not reconcile himself with religious faith. Amy Lowell writes in *Twentieth-Century Literary Criticism*, "He [Crane] disbelieved it [religion] and he hated it, but he could not free himself from it" (vol. 2, p. 130). Biblical phrasings in the novel give it a religious tone, suggesting Crane's preoccupation with religion. For example, feeling guilt and shame for running away from battle, Henry bows his head, and the surrounding insects make a "devotional pause" while the trees comfort him with a hymn. The narrator states, "So it came to pass. . . his [Henry's] soul changed," suggesting the hero's struggle with spiritual growth (p. 192).

Critics have likewise made much of Crane's animalistic descriptions of men and war in the novel. The soldiers "howl," "grunt," "crouch," and have "animal-like eyes." Neither does Crane deny Henry Fleming brutish behaviors:

> [Henry] developed the acute exasperation of a pestered animal, a well-meaning cow worried by dogs. He had a mad feeling against his rifle, which could only be used against one life at a time. He wished to rush forward and strangle with his fingers. He craved a power that would enable him to make a world-sweeping gesture and brush all back. His impotency appeared to him, and made his rage into that of a driven beast. (Pp. 47-48)

Such descriptions, critics argue, suggest Crane's interest in the animalistic nature of human beings.

Whether we read the novel as a psychological study of war, as a story of spiritual growth, or as an examination of the animalistic nature of humans, all readers can identify with Crane's magnificent use of color imagery in *The Red Badge of Courage*. Battle scenes blaze with color: "A sketch in gray and red dissolved into a moblike body of men who galloped like wild horses" (p. 42), and "He [Henry] was aware that these battalions with their commotions were woven red and startling into the gentle fabric of softened greens and browns" (p. 31).

Other Works

In addition to *Maggie* and *The Red Badge of Courage*, Crane completed three other novels: *George's Mother* (1896), *Third Violet* (1897), and *Active Service* (1899). He also published two popular volumes of poetry, many of whose poems concern war: *The Black Riders and Other Lines* (1895) and *War Is Kind* (1896).

irony a situation in which the actual outcome is opposite or contrary to what was expected

Although Crane is best known for *The Red Badge of Courage,* he is considered by many to be a master of the short story. In 1895 he traveled extensively in the western part of the United States and in Mexico for a news syndicate. From these experiences evolved some of his best short stories, such as "The Bride Comes to Yellow Sky" and "The Blue Hotel," two stories that illustrate his superb use of irony. These tales deal with themes such as fear, fate, survival, delusions, deceptions, and the plight of human beings living in an imperfect world—themes also present in his novels.

In 1897, Crane met Cora Taylor (also called Cora Stewart), owner of a hotel of prostitution, and moved with her to England. In the same year he traveled to Cuba, where he spent months in the Cuban jungles reporting on the Spanish-American War. While on this assignment for the *New York World,* Crane's ship sank. He and three other men were the sole survivors of the disaster. The experience provided the seed from which grew the much acclaimed short story "The Open Boat," a survival tale in which a small group of men must battle the natural elements.

Crane uses vivid imagery and symbolism in this story to emphasize both the beauty and the power of natural forces. The disaster, however, combined with his time in the jungle and his general disregard for his health, left lasting marks on Crane. He spent time in Greece covering the Greco-Turkish War and returned to England to write, but his rapidly deteriorating health forced him to travel to a spa in Germany, where he hoped to recuperate. He died there of tuberculosis at age twenty-eight.

If you like Stephen Crane, you might also like war stories by James Lincoln Collier and Christopher Collier and by Walter Dean Myers. Other writers who have written works with survival themes and in a naturalistic style are Jack London and Gary Paulsen.

Selected Bibliography

WORKS BY STEPHEN CRANE

Collected Works

The Works of Stephen Crane, 10 vols. (1969–1976)

The Portable Stephen Crane (1977)

Individual Works

Maggie: A Girl of the Streets (A Story of New York), printed under the pseudonym Johnston Smith (1893)

The Red Badge of Courage: An Episode of the American Civil War, first published serially in 1894 (1895)

George's Mother (1896)

The Little Regiment and Other Episodes of the American Civil War (1896)

Maggie: A Girl of the Streets, revised (1896)

The Third Violet (1897)

The Open Boat, and Other Tales of Adventure (1898)

Active Service (1899)

The Monster and Other Stories (1899; 1901)

War Is Kind (1899)

Whilomville Stories (1900)

Wounds in the Rain (1900)

Last Words (1902)

The O'Ruddy completed by Robert Barr (1903)

The Red Badge of Courage, Mahwah, New Jersey: Watermill Press (1981)

The Black Riders and Other Lines (1985)

Maggie: A Girl of the Streets and Other Short Fiction (1986)

WORKS ABOUT STEPHEN CRANE

Cady, Edwin H. *Stephen Crane.* Boston: Twayne, 1980.

Commire, Anna, ed. *Yesterday's Authors of Books for Children.* Detroit: Gale Research, 1977–1978, vol. 2.

Draper, James P., ed. *World Literature Criticism.* Detroit: Gale Research, 1992, vol. 2, pp. 811–828.

Gibson, Donald B. *The Red Badge of Courage: Redefining the Hero.* Boston: Twayne, 1988.

Johnston, Bernard, ed. *Collier's Encyclopedia.* New York: Collier's, 1995, vol. 7, pp. 418–419.

Kepos, Paula, and Poupard, Dennis, eds. *Twentieth-Century Literary Criticism.* Detroit: Gale Research, 1989, vol. 32, pp. 132–190.

Kimbel, Bobby Ellen, ed. *Dictionary of Literary Biography: American Short-Story Writers Before 1880.* Detroit: Gale Research, 1989, vol. 78, pp. 117–135.

Magill, Frank, ed. *Critical Survey of Poetry.* Englewood Cliffs, N.J.: Salem Press, 1982, vol. 2, pp. 659–665.

May, Hal, ed. *Contemporary Authors.* Detroit: Gale Research, 1983, vol. 109, p. 94.

Olendorf, Donna, ed. *Contemporary Authors.* Detroit: Gale Research, 1993, vol. 140, pp. 96–100.

Pizer, Donald, and Earl N. Harbert, eds. *Dictionary of Literary Biography: American Realists and Naturalists.* Detroit: Gale Research, 1982, vol. 12, pp. 100–124.

Poupard, Dennis, ed. *Twentieth-Century Literary Criticism.* Detroit: Gale Research, 1983, vol. 11, pp. 119–169.

Poupard, Dennis, and James E. Peerson, eds. *Twentieth-Century Literary Criticism.* Detroit: Gale Research, 1985, vol. 17, pp. 63–83.

Quartermain, Peter, ed. *Dictionary of Literary Biography: American Poets 1880–1945.* Detroit: Gale Research, 1987, vol. 54, pp. 48–57.

Stallman, R.W. *Stephen Crane: A Biography.* New York: Brazillier, 1968.

Stallman, R.W., and Lillian Gilkes, eds. *Stephen Crane: Letters.* New York: New York University Press, 1960.

Sufrin, Mark. *Stephen Crane.* New York: Macmillan Child Group, 1992.

Votteler, Thomas, ed. *Short Story Criticism.* Detroit: Gale Research, 1991, vol. 7, pp. 97–158.

Wertheim, Stanley, and Paul Sorrentino. *The Crane Log: A Documentary Life of Stephen Crane.* New York: Macmillan, 1993.

Chris Crutcher

(1946-   )

by Terry Davis

Chris Crutcher is serious in his novel *Chinese Handcuffs* (1989) when he presents information he calls "the secret of life." He makes such an audacious claim because he believes that stories have the power to heal, and because he knows what a great need there is for healing.

Crutcher's Experience

For more than twenty-five years, which is at least twice as long as he's been a writer, Crutcher has worked with young people. In his student years he coached youth swimming, after graduating from college he taught high school, then he became a school director, and then a child-and-family therapist focusing on families involved in child abuse. Over the years he has gained a knowledge of young people, particularly of their pain. "I've just seen so much damage done," he says.

313

As a storyteller, Crutcher tries to prevent some of the damage he's seen as a therapist.

Crutcher believes he has gained "a sense of the connections between all human beings—the ghastly as well as the glorious, an awareness of the damage we do as a society creating unreal expectations for ourselves."

As a storyteller, Crutcher tries to prevent some of the damage he's seen as a therapist. He believes that stories can heal by helping teenagers look at their feelings, or come to emotional resolution, from a safe distance. "If, as an author, I can make an emotional connection with my reader, I have already started to help him or her heal," Crutcher says. "I have never met a depressed person, or an anxious person, or a fearful person who was not encouraged by the knowledge that others feel the same way they do" (*Healing Through Literature,* 1992).

In 1994 the Assembly on Literature for Adolescents of the National Council of Teachers of English (ALAN) cited Crutcher for "significant contribution to young adult literature." Each of Crutcher's six novels for young adults and his story collection have been judged a "Best Book" by the American Library Association, and the ALAN award affirmed Crutcher's rank among the best of the new generation of writers for young adults coming to prominence after Robert Cormier and S. E. Hinton. Three of his novels and one story were in film production in 1995.

In 1995 Crutcher gave up his therapy practice, but he remained coordinator of Spokane's Child Protection Team and a member of the Fatality Review Committee. He believes he has gained, and he hopes his writing reflects from working for twenty years with people in difficult situations, "a sense of the connections between all human beings—the ghastly as well as the glorious, an awareness of the damage we do as a society creating unreal expectations for ourselves, and a different perspective on the true nature of courage."

Cascade and Beyond

Born on 17 July 1946, Christopher C. Crutcher grew up in Cascade, Idaho, a lumber town of 950 residents. It sits in a bend of the Payette River in a mountain valley of the west-central part of the state. Chris liked growing up there. He did not feel isolated or deprived. He lived within walking distance of his grandparents; he worked in his dad's service station and delivered bulk gas and fuel oil to the old mining towns in the mountains, just as Louie Banks does in *Running Loose* (1983); and he kept busy with school activities. He played clarinet in the school band, played football and basketball, ran track, wrote a column for the school paper, and swam for the city team.

Crutcher attributes making those varsity teams to the lack of competition in the small school, but that is partly modesty speaking. He may not have been a gifted athlete in his youth—although he was a good enough swimmer to earn a small-college scholarship, captain the team, and qualify for nationals his junior and senior years—but in his thirties he became a superior distance runner and in his forties a triathlete.

Chris was the middle child. His brother, John, was an excellent student, but Chris and his younger sister, Candy, made average marks. Chris says he observed the amount of study that John put in and decided that scholarship was not his calling. He was not an exemplary student, but neither was he a troublemaker. His father was chairman of the school board, so making trouble would have caused Chris more pain than it would have taken to become a better student. His major misbehavior was failing to live up to people's expectations. "Rebellion felt good," he admits. "I didn't like people telling me what to think."

Chris practiced a modest rebellion with his writing. When he was in eighth grade, the journalism teacher read one of his themes and invited him to write for the school paper. From then through his senior year, he poked fun at people in a column called "Chris's Crumbs." He liked to write, and he particularly liked letting his imagination run. Chris was not in love with reading, however, and one day in that eighth-grade year he responded to a book-report assignment by making up the book. He also raided his brother's storage closet for book reports. When he found something appropriate, he rewrote it with misspellings, reduced the overall quality, and turned it in.

Chris does not admit this instance of plagiarism in order to thumb his nose at the values of diligence and honesty, to gloat about his triumph over authority and tradition, or to suggest that there is no correlation between the effort we put into school and the success we achieve later. He tells the truth about those days because he will not lie to young people about his life. He also believes that adults and young people themselves often create too much pressure to perform, and that an example of someone who did not perform so well in school but did just fine as an adult might have a healthy effect.

exemplary deserving imitation or serving as an example

Crutcher's major misbehavior was failing to live up to people's expectations. "Rebellion felt good," he admits. "I didn't like people telling me what to think."

When he graduated from Cascade High in 1964, Crutcher enrolled at Eastern Washington State College (now University) in Cheney, Washington, a few miles west of Spokane, where he graduated in 1968 with a degree in sociology and psychology. He traveled and worked as a laborer for a year, then returned to Eastern and earned his teaching credentials. He began his career in education as the sole teacher and administrator of a "dropout" school in Kenniwick, Washington. When funding ran out, Crutcher found a position in high school social studies. In 1972 he moved to Berkeley, California, where he worked as a teacher's aide in a kindergarten-through-twelfth-grade private school in Oakland. Soon he was teaching; then he became the school's director. He describes Lakeside School as "the toughest place I have ever been." Lakeside is the model for One More Last Chance High School in *The Crazy Horse Electric Game* (1987).

In 1981 the emotional demands at Lakeside became too heavy, and Crutcher moved to Spokane, resolved to put the helping profession behind him. But six months later he was leading Spokane's Child Protection Team, and in another six months he was working as a therapist in Spokane's Community Mental Health Center.

In the last year of her life, Jewell Crutcher remembered with pride the letters that her son received from mothers of Lakeside students. "They really thought he was wonderful," she said. "I think before maybe their kids had teachers who just put up with them every day. But Chris seemed to care. And that's the core of him right there—the caring."

Revealing the Secrets of Life

Crutcher began writing when he was thirty-five. He always liked stories and playing with words, and his parents were voracious readers. From his mother he learned his love of language, and from his father he learned to observe the life around him to discover the causes of things and their effects. The Dr. Seuss books were among his favorites in childhood, and as he got farther along in school he discovered the narrative poems of Robert Service; he committed several to memory and would recite them whether or not anyone wanted to listen.

Crutcher does not think of himself as a well-read writer, but what he reads, he reads with acute perceptiveness. Among his favorite novels are Harper Lee's *To Kill A Mockingbird,* which he admires for its accuracy about life and its sense of justice and injustice; Joseph Heller's *Catch-22,* for its narrative skill and humor; and *Lonesome Dove* by Larry McMurtry and *Prince of Tides* by Pat Conroy for the power of their stories and their lyric language.

There is an article about Harper Lee in volume 2.

The Prince of Tides was made into a movie that was released in 1991.

Crutcher's greatest skill as a writer is his ability to observe accurately the life around him; and his two greatest assets are his endurance, both physical and emotional, and his experience with people in pain. Because he has observed the causes of so much pain, he has vital—and healing—information to reveal in his stories.

One of the measures of Crutcher's skill is that while his books are highly rhetorical—in the sense that they attempt to persuade the reader to accept certain ideas—they are also among the most popular of the serious novels for young adults. The rhetorical quality in his work is not subtle, but it never overshadows plot or character, because he presents those two elements very powerfully. All Crutcher's books and stories possess heavy measures of magnitude, which is to say that he creates situations filled with conflict, in which a great deal is at stake for his characters.

plot the deliberate sequence of events in a literary work

In his first novel, *Running Loose* (1983), among the many things at stake is mortality. When Becky Sanders crashes her car trying to avoid a motorcycle, and dies, Louie Banks must find a way to live in peace without her. Crutcher always gives his main characters help when the pain comes; to help Louie live with Becky's death, Crutcher created Dakota, the owner of the Buckhorn Tavern, where Louie does clean-up work. Dakota is Louie's friend and a classic mentor, which a Crutcher book is never without. The help that Dakota gives is to tell Louie how the world works—how it really works, as opposed to how people pretend it works. Louie is grieving for Becky and asking "what kind of worthless God" would let her be killed in so senseless a way. And Dakota responds:

"Louie, . . . one thing I'm pretty sure of is that if there's a God, that ain't His job. He ain't up there to load the dice one way or the other . . . . There's one thing that separates a man from a boy, the way I see it, and it ain't age. It's seeing how life works, so you don't get surprised all the time and kicked in the butt. It's knowin' the rules . . . . You go on blamin' God, you get no place. You got to pay attention to how things work. Ya got to understand that the reason some things happen is just because they happen. That ain't a good reason, but that's it. You put enough cars and trucks and motorcycles on the road, and some of 'em gonna run into each other. Not certain ones neither. Just whichever ones that do. This life ain't partial, boy." (Pp. 139–140)

Louie's philosophical conflict is one of many conflicts woven through the novel. The others, such as Louie's battle with an unethical football coach, are the story elements that sustain most readers' interest. Louie's voice, as he narrates the story, is another engaging narrative element.

first person the position or perspective from someone inside the story

Stotan! (1986), Crutcher's second novel, is also narrated in the first person, and mortality is at stake here too, as are athletic competition and romance. In this story, swimming is the sport, and it is a fellow swimmer who is lost to the world and to his friends; disease is the agent of chance. Again, Crutcher presents the theme that "this life ain't partial." Here he speaks through one of the swimmers: "Life doesn't care, guys. It's just there. The only way we have of getting a leg up on the world is to stick together, no matter what." Again, the narrator, Walker Dupree, has a mentor to help him see the world clearly. The speaker is Walker's swimming coach, Max Il Song, and the subject is romance: "I have only one piece of advice about relationships, and I learned it from bitter experience. Be straight. Anything that's unsaid is a lie."

third person the position or perspective from someone outside the story

omniscient having complete knowledge

In his third novel, *The Crazy Horse Electric Game*, Crutcher's writing becomes more sophisticated, which is to say more complex. He presents his material in the third-person omniscient point of view, for example, a manner of presentation that demands greater skill than first-person narration, and the life he reveals to his readers is more harsh. In this book the characters suffer more. *Crazy Horse* is just as funny as Crutcher's two previous books, but the tone is heavier. Even more so than in *Stotan!* there is the sense of how deeply life can hurt us. Dying is one thing, but at least dying is a release from our burdens. Dying does not require anything from us; it requires no strength of character, for example. But living a life full of pain is something else again. Will we inflict our pain on others, or will we learn compassion from our pain?

It is possible that by the time he was writing *Crazy Horse,* all the pain Crutcher was seeing in his work as a therapist was beginning to integrate its way more deeply into his view of the world. He did present a vivid picture of child abuse in *Stotan!,* but the view of life he presents from *Crazy Horse* through *Staying Fat for Sarah Byrnes* (1993) becomes more and more horrific. Still, there is help with the pain. Sometimes the help continues in the form of advice from a mentor figure, and sometimes adults actually intercede on behalf of young people.

The main character in *Crazy Horse,* a great young athlete named Willie Weaver, has been hurt in a waterskiing accident and has lost some of his motor skills. Along with his physical loss comes the loss of an entire privileged way of life. Willie asks the same question that Louie Banks asks: Why? And a woman named Lisa tells him: "God didn't cripple you, Willie. *You* did. You stretched the rules till they broke; had to go a little faster than you could, push out there at the edge because you thought nothing could hurt you."

Chinese Handcuffs is a story packed full of pain. Dillon Hemingway loses his brother to suicide, then discovers that his best friend, Jennifer Lawless, is being abused by her stepfather. It is Crutcher's most complex story, and the center of that complexity is human nature itself. Here, a character states what is probably the major theme in all Crutcher's work:

> A crack appears in the structure we've built to keep ourselves decent, and our own personal evil seeps out. It's one of the hard ways . . . that we learn human beings are connected by the ghastly as well as the glorious, and we need always to walk around inside ourselves looking for those leaks. And plugging them up.

A measure of Crutcher's reputation, and of the book's power, is the column that appeared in *Booklist* in August 1989. It is the policy of *Booklist* to discuss only those books that they recommend, but in the case of *Chinese Handcuffs* they felt the need to explain why they did not recommend "one of the season's most talked about books." The column notes some of the book's weaknesses—unjustified scenes of brutality, authorial intrusion, a breakdown in characterization, and that "the overloaded plot strains the novel's structure and diminishes the vital message Crutcher is trying to convey."

Chinese Handcuffs is not Crutcher's most popular book, but it is the book in which he confronts most directly the subject closest to his heart: the nature of life and the nature of our humanity, and what we must do to find the peace that opens the way to joy. This is the "secret of life" he reveals.

Certainly among Crutcher's most popular books—and among the most praised—is his story collection *Athletic Shorts* (1991). "A Brief Moment in the Life of Angus Bethune" and "In the Time I Get" have sparked the greatest response. All the stories, five of which present characters from the novels, illustrate the theme of "growing—grappling with something tough and finding the courage to carry on" (*Kirkus Reviews,* 1991).

The Deep End (1992), Crutcher's adult novel, is the place for readers to turn to find out the most about Crutcher himself. The main character, Wilson Corder, is not Crutcher, but he's a child-and-family therapist with much of Crutcher's background and personality. In this novel Crutcher exercises his skill with mystery and the suspense elements he began exploring in *Chinese Handcuffs.* Corder is treating a four-year-old boy traumatized by the abduction and murder of his sister, and the murderer turns on Corder and his family. The story relies on plot to a greater degree than Crutcher's previous novels, but theme is never far behind action. One of the prominent themes of *The Deep End* is that of "the tribal father," Crutcher's belief that "every adult has to protect every kid."

All the aspects of Crutcher's storytelling and prose skills come together in *Staying Fat for Sarah Byrnes,* published in 1993. *School Library Journal* called the book "a masterpiece" and recognized its sophisticated characters and plot; and *Publishers Weekly* recognized the "superb plotting, extraordinary characters and crackling narrative." Probably more so than in any of Crutcher's other works, the characters in this story are offered a relief from pain, and nowhere else is

> In *Chinese Handcuffs,* Crutcher confronts most directly the subject closest to his heart: the nature of life and the nature of our humanity, and what we must do to find the peace that opens the way to joy. This is the "secret of life" he reveals.

Crutcher's theme that human beings are both "ghastly and glorious" illustrated in such depth. A comparison of *Sarah Byrnes* with *Chinese Handcuffs* illustrates to the devoted Crutcher reader the extent to which his skill with the narrative craft has evolved.

In *Ironman* (1995), Crutcher creates an engaging wrinkle in the technique of first-person narration by having his protagonist, Bo Brewster, tell the story in letters to the real-life talk show host Larry King. Bo opens the book by telling Larry that he will grant him "exclusive rights . . . the soon-to-be-highly-sought-after memoirs of our country's future premier Ironman, Beauregard Brewster, in the year of his quest to conquer the field in Yukon Jack's Eastern Washington Invitational Scab-land Triathlon." The story's opening words summarize the plot, and along with Bo's physical quest—as always in a Crutcher book—goes an emotional quest. In this case it is Bo's struggle to free himself from his anger and come to some peace in his relationship with his father. Bo's anger-management class is a forum for much humorous and touching discussion. As a reviewer wrote to Crutcher readers about another of his stories, and as is true with so much of his work, "You may not be able to control your laughter or tears" (*Wilson Library Bulletin,* 1990).

Selected Bibliography

WORKS BY CHRIS CRUTCHER

Running Loose (1983)

Stotan! (1986)

The Crazy Horse Electric Game (1987)

Chinese Handcuffs (1989)

Athletic Shorts, story collection (1991)

The Deep End, adult novel (1992)

Staying Fat for Sarah Byrnes (1993)

Ironman (1995)

WORKS ABOUT CHRIS CRUTCHER

Bushman, John H., and Kay Parks Bushman. "Coping with Harsh Realities: The Novels of Chris Crutcher." In *English Journal,* March 1992, p. 82.

Readers who enjoy Chris Crutcher's works might also enjoy the works of Terry Davis and Will Hobbs.

"Chris Crutcher: What's Known Can't Be Unknown." Interview in *Publishers Weekly,* 20 February 1995, p. 183.

Davis, Terry. "A Healing Vision." *English Journal,* March 1996, pp. 36–41.

"Heroes & Villains: Writer Gets Real-Life Inspiration for Stories." *The Free Press,* Mankato, Minn.: 13 April 1994, p. 5.

Jenkinson, Dave. "Portraits/Chris Crutcher: YA Author Bats 4 for 4 on ALA's 'Best Books for Young Adults' Lists." In *Emergency Librarian,* January/February 1991, p. 67.

McDonnell, Christine. "New Voices, New Visions: Chris Crutcher." In *Horn Book,* May/June 1988, p. 23.

Montgomery, Lori. "Idaho Novelist: First Book Wins Raves." In *The Idaho Statesman,* 28 July 1986, p. 80.

Raymond, Allen. "Chris Crutcher Helps Teachers Know Kids." In *Teaching K–8,* February 1990, p. 42.

Smith, Louisa. "Limitations on Young Adult Fiction: An Interview with Chris Crutcher." In *The Lion and the Unicorn,* June 1992, p. 66.

Webster, Dan. "Growing Up: Author Chris Crutcher." In *The Spokesman Review,* 1 March 1992, p. 14.

Webster, Dan. "He's Got the Magic Touch." In *The Spokesman Review,* 12 January 1986, p. E1.

How to Write to the Author
Chris Crutcher
c/o Dell Publishing
1540 Broadway
New York, NY 10036

Maureen Daly

(1921-   )

by Nancy Vogel

Joseph Daly bought his daughter Maureen a typewriter for five dollars after her junior year at St. Mary's Springs Academy in Fond du Lac, Wisconsin. He carried it down to a coal bin that Margaret Mellon-Kelly Daly had hosed out as an office for her daughter, who wanted to write a book. The book became *Seventeenth Summer* (1942), and the typewriter bankrolled a writing career that spans fiction, nonfiction, print and nonprint media. Writing has been Maureen Daly's life, a life filled with love of nature, travel, and family. In fact, it is almost impossible to separate Daly's family and fiction.

The matriarch of modern young adult literature says, "I was born in Ireland, and that is a big factor in my life" ("Re-Making Connections," 1987). Modestly, she maintains, "I'm not capable of writing about ethnic backgrounds other than my own. I don't have any real authority to do that. I could pretend, but I mean I don't feel very sure about it" (Star City Connection speech, 1992). The fictional family in *Seventeenth Summer* reflects her own Irish past.

Quotations from Maureen Daly that are not attributed to a published source are from a telephone interview conducted by the author of this article on 30 January 1993 and are published here by permission of Maureen Daly.

The Green of an Irish Past

The **Great Depression** was a severe recession that began when the stock market crashed in 1929 and that lasted almost ten years. By the winter of 1932–1933, 14 to 16 million American were unemployed. Many died from a lack of food and inadequate living conditions.

> *"We were poor in a temporary way that we knew would not last more than a decade or two."*

Seventeenth Summer, Daly's most famous book, tells the story of Angeline (Angie) Morrow and the events of June, July, and August before Angie goes away to college. Over that summer, she has her first kiss, her first love, and her first parting. Angie, like Daly, is the third-born daughter in her family. In fact, Daly's three sisters—Marguerite, Kathleen, and Sheila—can be seen as parallels for Angie Morrow's sisters: Margaret, Lorraine, and Kitty.

Glancing back at her youth, Daly can say that, all in all, "it was a very unsophisticated time but rather a lovely time too" (Fall English Workshop, 1989). For Daly, born two days before St. Patrick's Day in 1921, adolescence came in the 1930s when *depression* and *recovery* referred more to economics than to psychology. Some years earlier, when the British had threatened to burn out Joseph Daly if he was not gone by the next St. Patrick's Day, the mayor of the tiny town of Castlecaufield, County Tyrone, Ireland, fled to America. A political refugee, he journeyed west to Fond du Lac, Wisconsin, and settled there: "He said it was the only place he saw that was as green as Ireland" ("Re-Making Connections"). His wife and three daughters followed later, and a fourth daughter was born in America. Daly remembers, "Every Sunday we'd have a beautiful Sunday dinner. My mother managed to take the silver and teapots with her" (Fall English Workshop). Daly states, "We had money in Ireland. We didn't when we got here. . . . We took our chances, and loved the country, but we came into a worldwide depression when we came here. . . . We were poor in a temporary way that we knew would not last more than a decade or two" ("Re-making Connections").

Recalling life with her sisters, Daly remembers, "We always wore a lot of flowers in our hair. We just picked them from the garden" ("Let's Talk About It," 1989). In *Seventeenth Summer,* just before she dons her dress of dimity, Angeline Morrow goes "out to the garden to pick bachelor's buttons for my hair in my long white slip, holding it high to keep the hem above the cool dew on the grass" (*Seventeenth Summer,* 1952 ed., p. 54). Among the blooms, Angie, savoring the sensuous moment, pauses to think about the glorious feeling she has because Jack Duluth will call for her soon and take her to the first important dance of her life. Even today, Maureen Daly finds a bouquet intoxicating: I love the things of the earth. My home is filled with flowers" (personal interview). One book has influenced Daly more than any other. As a teenager, she read *Kristin Lavransdatter* by Sigrid Undset, winner of the Nobel Prize for Literature in 1928. This trilogy, Daly has said, remains in her heart (Star City Connection).

Her Most Famous Book

Published in 1942, *Seventeenth Summer* now belongs to the ages. Like *Little Women* by Louisa May Alcott and *Anne of Green Gables* by Lucy Maud Montgomery, Daly's novel is a classic historical text about the growing up of girls. Indeed, it also shares an intimate quality with Anne Frank's *Diary:* both volumes are interior accounts of what it is like to grow up female. All four of these books are classics, and generations of readers have kept *Seventeenth Summer* in print. In fact, the book "seems to have a little, inside, pulsing life that keeps it vibrant. I just got a royalty check yesterday from Putnam and Grosset Group, current hard cover publishers. That means I have received royalty checks twice a year for 50 years—enough to build homes, put children through college, travel around the world. Dear little book" (Letter to Nancy Vogel). Marveling at her classic, Daly can say, "It has no shame about it; it just goes on and on" (Star City Connection).

Why is *Seventeenth Summer* a classic? On one of their early dates, Jack Duluth takes Angie to church, and the sanctuary provides an awesome moment; sitting in the pew, Angie glances at Jack's hands, and for the first time she notices his class ring. By the end of the book, he will give her that ring. Generations of teenagers have seen their own romantic yearnings mirrored in the novel. In a letter, Daly writes, "She (Angie) and Jack kissed and embraced constantly throughout the book and many readers believe that they had their first sexual intercourse experience when they went off together into the woods during a nighttime picnic." For the record, Daly says, "though it wasn't my intent, there is a distinct feeling there that Jack and Angie's romance had become ultimately sexual. I guess it was suggested strongly" (Richardson, p. 425).

In spite of the ambiguity of the picnic scene, the fact remains that Angeline Morrow stays true to her dream. She does not wear Jack's ring, and she spends her last night at home

Kristin Lavransdatter is a trilogy (set of three novels) about the troubled and eventful life of a strong-willed woman who lives in the 1300s in Norway. The three novels are *The Bridal Wreath*, *The Mistress of Husaby*, and *The Cross*.

There are articles about Louisa May Alcott and Anne Frank earlier in this volume. There is an article about L. M. Montgomery in volume 2.

with her family (not with Jack). Serious about a career, Angie goes away to college; Jack Duluth, on the other hand, has dreams of becoming a pilot, but he lacks purpose and motivation. Valuing human relationships and marketplace skills, Angie Morrow desires both. She is a young woman with very contemporary tendencies, tendencies that would have shocked many a mother of the 1950s, the Eisenhower years, when *Father Knows Best* played on television. Daly believes *Seventeenth Summer* presents "the eternal human yearning (at some time in life): 'love me, remember me, I love you.'" Why does the author think the book survives? Daly gives two reasons: "because of a certain evocative poetry in the language and because—innocent as it may seem to some—it portrays first love as an inevitable and tormenting mystery, something better endured if understood" (Letter).

In *Seventeenth Summer,* there are more girls unlike Angie than like Angie. The oldest sister, Margaret, is the fair one; she seems certain to replicate her mother's life, that of a housewife at home. Lorraine, the second oldest, is depicted as the risqué dark woman. Margie, a friend who dates Fitz and double-dates with Angie and Jack, epitomizes the young woman dependent on a man. All these minor characters are foils for Angeline Morrow, Daly's creation of the young woman neither dependent on nor alienated from men. Readers read the book because of Angie, not because of the other characters.

foil a character who, by contrast, highlights the qualities of another character

Daly's special theme is the joy and exuberance of growing up and flowering into an adult. Angeline (Angie) Morrow embodies archetypal themes of love and strength; quite simply, she is a hero for young girls becoming women. According to Daly, "for years and years the Chamber of Commerce in Fond du Lac put out maps for tourist fans to follow while looking for Pete's, picnic grounds, etc." (Letter).

archetypal basic or original (after which other forms are patterned)

Family and Faith

Maureen Daly remembers that her mother "was a great dressmaker, and she was the first person in our little town of Fond du Lac to make evening formals without any straps at all. This is the woman who told us that the Blessed Virgin would blush if we smoked, but she believed in scanty clothing" ("Re-Making Connections"). Having grown up in a family of sisters, Daly's thoughts have been turning to sisters of the cloth, the nuns. Long at home in the Catholic tradition, Daly used to say a little prayer, "Jesus help me," before tests in school. Then, in "The Gift," she writes, "I am a wandering soul, thoughtful, emotional, critical and, in view of what has happened in recent years, strangely—even pathetically—hopeful." Only one sister is still living. Daly's husband, William P. McGivern, also a writer, died of cancer in 1982. Their daughter, Megan McGivern Shaw, mother of two small boys, also died of cancer. Those deaths hit Daly hard. Nevertheless, Daly states, "I have not always gotten what I asked for from God and I certainly never asked for much of what I get. We have had an on-going relationship with periods of doubt, ambivalence, euphoria and sometimes unquestioning trust." She concludes, "I do not seem to live for God, but I do not live without him" (p. 190). Today, Daly's family includes a son, a son-in-law, and two grandsons, as well as her youngest sister.

> *In "The Gift," Daly writes, "I am a wandering soul, thoughtful, emotional, critical and, in view of what has happened in recent years, strangely—even pathetically—hopeful."*

Daly's Signature and Other Work

If Daly's writing has a signature, similes are her trademark. They embellish her pages like grace notes on a sheet of music. About to be kissed, Angie notes, "Behind him [Jack] I could see the high stars and the golf course stretched out silver-green in the moonlight and the fireflies flickering in the grass like bits of neon lighting" (*Seventeenth Summer,* 1952 ed., p. 61). After the kiss, Angie notices a small breeze "as soft and silent as a pussy willow." Another simile can be found in the scene toward the end of the book when Jack and Angie leave the bonfire: "Once I tripped over a vine and it coiled around my ankle like a wet rope" (p. 267). That one echoes the Garden of Eden.

Travel is one of the loves of Daly's life. She speaks Spanish and a Spanish theme can be found in some of her fiction and nonfiction. The McGiverns lived in Málaga for a time, and *Spanish Roundabout* (1960) highlights the cultural and physical geography of Spain. Daly's nonfiction profiles reflect many other backgrounds than Irish. "City Girl," her story about Myrdice Thornton, an African American, won a Freedoms Foundation award; this story appears in *Profile of Youth* (1950).

simile a figure of speech that uses "like", "as", or "as if" to make a direct comparison of two different objects

The **Battle of the Bulge** was fought in World War II, on 16 December 1944. The Germans launched a surprise attack on an American front and advanced into Belgium. This penetration into the front involved many casualties for both sides. However, the American line was reestablished.

As a teenager, Daly began *Seventeenth Summer,* and the whole modern period of young adult literature dates from this book. In 1942, the year of Daly's graduation from Rosary College, *Seventeenth Summer* appeared in print. That summer, she met William P. McGivern at a book-signing party. In fact, she autographed two books for him because he lost one in a taxi. Being Irish, Daly once declared that a house has enough air for only one writer (Fall English Workshop). In her mind, Bill was that writer. This veteran of the Battle of the Bulge wrote more than two dozen novels, and he did screenplays, television programs, and motion pictures. Daly gravitated toward reporting and editing. For years they lived in Europe. Only after her husband's death—and their daughter's—did Maureen Daly McGivern return to young-adult writing. It was a way to keep Bill and Megan close. Megan died on New Year's Eve in 1983, and grief moved in with Daly and stayed and stayed. But when Daly had a flash of insight to write about a *happy* time in Megan's life, the author's resurrection began. As a widow and grandmother, Daly began her own second period of young adult fiction by writing *Acts of Love* (1986), a book depicting Megan's seventeenth summer. *First a Dream* (1990) continues the story. In those two books, Dallas Dobson dates Henrietta (Retta) Caldwell, the teenager modeled on Megan. When their Pennsylvania farm is condemned for a highway, the Caldwells move west, much as the four McGiverns once did.

First a Dream follows the characters to California where Dallas Dobson works at Ranch Arabian and Retta joins the staff of the *Gazette.* Before the summer ends, the young people have taken on adult responsibilities, especially with the birth of Estrellita. Carter Caldwell has much of William McGivern in his character, and Patrick McGivern, Daly's son who teaches Hispanic youth in the Los Angeles area, has a counterpart in Caldwell's son, Carter Caldwell II.

Dealing with Criticism

During an appearance in Nebraska, Daly recalled being challenged by a young man who said he had read one of her books and found it "tame," a word which Daly remembered as "slow" ("I don't know which word is worse really"). She replied, "in any case I said to him, I know the book's slow. It's supposed to be slow, but if it had been written at a greater pace and so on, it would have been off the shelf in six weeks. So, yes, a lot of my stuff is slow" (Star City Connection).

Another time, a high school student in a writing class asked Daly why she did not let her young lovers, Henrietta Caldwell and Dallas Dobson, go to bed in *Acts of Love:* "I said in a flash of adult irritation, 'because then I'd have a short story'" (Program).

Always resolute, Maureen Daly writes her visions: "I didn't care what critics said. . . . I really wrote this book [*Acts of Love*] for myself, just as I wrote *Seventeenth Summer* for myself" ("Main Address"). Along with other young adult authors, M. E. Kerr in particular, Daly sometimes finds her own covers "just distressing." When publishers were preparing to market *First a Dream,* "they asked me in New York if I had any preference for a cover, and I said I'd like some kind of reproduction of Marc Chagall. . . . They said 'that wouldn't sell'" (Star City Connection).

In the mid-1990s Daly was still in print and on the air: she was the restaurant critic for the *Desert Sun,* and she reported monthly to Elmer Dill's Restaurant Review on KABC in Los Angeles as the reviewer from the Coachella Valley. She was writing another book about a young woman, Mariette, who decides to become a nun. Of a trip to Hays, Kansas, in 1989, Daly says, "I developed such a love and such an understanding for this group of women [Sisters of St. Agnes]. I've been with nuns all my life, but I saw what a struggle it was to stay in an order if you wish to do it at this point in time" (Star City Connection). Through the plot of this latest book, Daly says, "I'm trying to equate the feeling that good human beings are godlike no matter whether they're in the convent or out of the convent" (Star City Connection).

At St. Mary's Springs Academy, Sister Rosita told her students, "Do try to write about something you know" ("Let's Talk About It"). Following her teacher's advice, Maureen wrote "Sixteen," a story that won first place in a *Scholastic* contest. Then *Seventeenth Summer* won first prize in the first Dodd, Mead Intercollegiate Writing Fellowship contest. From Fond du Lac to Mombasa, Paris, and Palm Desert, Sister Rosita's precept has been the eleventh commandment for Maureen Daly.

off the shelf no longer displayed in bookstores.

resolute characterized by firmness and determination

Classic novels that may remind you of Maureen Daly's books include *Emma* and *Persuasion* by Jane Austen and *My Ántonia* by Willa Cather. If you like Daly's works, you might also like *Jacob Have I Loved* by Katherine Paterson and *Sweet Whispers, Brother Rush* by Virginia Hamilton. Parallel fiction about young men includes *The Outsiders* by S. E. Hinton, *A Day No Pigs Would Die* by Robert Newton Peck, and *Stotan!* by Chris Crutcher.

Selected Bibliography

WORKS BY MAUREEN DALY

Novels for Young Adults

Seventeenth Summer (1942; 1952; 1968)

Sixteen and Other Stories (1961)

Acts of Love (1986)

First a Dream (1990)

Fiction Collections for Young Adults

My Favorite Stories, edited by Maureen Daly (1948)

My Favorite Mystery Stories, edited by Maureen Daly (1966)

My Favorite Suspense Stories, edited by Maureen Daly (1968)

Children's Books

Patrick Visits the Farm, pictures by Ellie Simmons (1960)

Patrick Takes a Trip, pictures by Ellie Simmons (1960)

The Ginger Horse, illustrated by Wesley Dennis (1961; 1964)

Patrick Visits the Library, pictures by Paul Lantz (1961)

Patrick Visits the Zoo, pictures by Sam Savitt (1963)

The Small War of Sergeant Donkey, illustrated by Wesley Dennis (1966)

Rosie, the Dancing Elephant, illustrated by Lorence Bjorkland (1967)

Nonfiction

Smarter and Smoother: A Handbook on How to Be That Way, illustrated by Marguerite Bryan (1944)

The Perfect Hostess: Complete Etiquette and Entertainment for the Home (1950)

Profile of Youth (1950)

What's Your P. Q. (Personality Quotient)?, illustrated by Eleanor Simmons (1952; 1966)

Twelve Around the World, illustrated by Frank Kramer (1957)

Mention My Name in Mombasa: The Unscheduled Adventures of an American Family Abroad, with William P. McGivern; illustrated by Frank Kramer (1958)

Spanish Roundabout (1960)

Moroccan Roundabout (1961)

Spain: Wonderland of Contrasts (1965)

The Seeing, with William P. McGivern (1980)

A Matter of Honor, with William P. McGivern (1984)

"The Gift." In *God and Me.* Edited by Candida Lund (1988).

Play

You Can't Kiss Caroline (1953)

Autobiography

"Maureen Daly." *Something About the Author Autobiography Series.* Detroit: Gale Research, vol. 1, pp. 69–87.

Interviews with Maureen Daly

Daly, Maureen. "Maureen Daly: One on One." *ALAN Review,* spring 1988, pp. 1–2, 4, 6, 17.

Letter to Nancy Vogel, 3 December 1992.

Personal interview with Nancy Vogel, Palm Springs, 3 August 1989.

Richardson, Lisa Ann. "Books for Adolescents: A Retrospective with Maureen Daly." *Journal of Reading,* February 1993, pp. 424–426.

Speeches

Fall English Workshop, Fort Hays State University, 22 September 1989.

"Let's Talk About It: 'Family: A Reading and Discussion Series.'" Hays Public Library, 22 September 1989.

"Re-Making Connections: Writing the Hard Way." ALAN Breakfast, National Council of Teachers of English Convention. Los Angeles, 21 November 1987.

Star City Connection and the Lincoln [Nebraska] Public Schools, 10 April 1992.

WORKS ABOUT MAUREEN DALY

Books and Parts of Books

Arbuthnot, May Hill. *Children's Reading in the Home.* Glenview, Ill.: Scott, Foresman, 1969.

Bushman, John H., and Kay Parks Bushman. *Using Young Adult Literature in the English Classroom.* New York: Merrill, 1993.

Carlsen, G. Robert. *Books and the Teenage Reader.* New York: Harper & Row, 1980.

Commire, Anne, ed. *Something About the Author.* Detroit: Gale Research, 1971, vol. 2, pp. 87–88.

Fakih, Kimberly Olson. "The Long Wait for Maureen Daly." In *Writers on Writing for Young Adults.* Edited by Patricia E. Feehan and Pamela Patrick Barron. Detroit: Omnigraphics, 1991, pp. 116–122.

Gunton, Sharon R., ed. *Contemporary Literary Criticism.* Detroit: Gale Research, 1981, vol. 17, pp. 87–91.

Nilsen, Alleen Pace and Kenneth L. Donelson. *Literature for Today's Young Adults.* New York: HarperCollins, 1993.

Reed, Arthea J. S. *Reaching Adolescents: The Young Adult Book and the School.* New York: Merrill, 1994.

Vogel, Nancy. "Seventeenth Summer." In *Masterplots II: Juvenile and Young Adult Fiction Series.* Edited by Frank N. Magill. Pasadena, Calif.: Salem, 1991, vol. 4, pp. 1311–1314.

Articles

Alm, Richard. "The Glitter and the Gold." *The English Journal,* September 1955, pp. 315–322, 350.

Burner, Joyce Adams. Review of *First a Dream. School Library Journal,* April 1990, p. 139.

Burton, Dwight L. "The Novel for the Adolescent." *The English Journal,* September 1951, pp. 363–369.

Edwards, Margaret A. "The Rise of Teen-Age Reading." *Saturday Review,* November 13, 1954, pp. 88–89, 95.

Fakih, Kimberly Olson. "The Long Wait for Maureen Daly." *Publishers Weekly,* June 27, 1986, pp. 36, 38–39.

Hendrickson, Linnea. "Quenchable Flames: Expression and Suppression of Sexuality in Three American Novels for Young Adults." *Bookbird,* summer 1994, pp. 20–24.

Monseau, Virginia. "*Seventeenth Summer:* A Modern Old-Fashioned Romance." *ALAN Review,* spring 1988, pp. 5–6.

Review of *First a Dream. Publishers Weekly,* 30 March 1990, p. 64.

Review of *First a Dream.* Books for the Teenage Reader. "Yearnings: 'Give me One Wish. . . . '" Edited by Elizabeth A. Belden, Judy M. Beckman, and Sue Ellen Savereide. *English Journal,* September 1990, p. 92.

"Short Story Awards." *Scholastic: The American High School Weekly,* 1 May 1937, p. 5.

Vogel, Nancy. "The Semicentennial of *Seventeenth Summer:* Maureen Daly's Acts of Love." *Nebraska English Journal,* spring 1992, pp. 7–21.

———. "The Semicentennial of *Seventeenth Summer:* Some Questions and Answers." *ALAN Review,* spring 1994, p. 41.

How to Write to the Author
Maureen Daly
P.O. Box 3875
Palm Desert, CA 92261

Paula Danziger

(1944-)

by Kathleen Krull

Paula Danziger is no ordinary shopper. Known as a flashy dresser, she buys wild jewelry, elaborate capes, and shoes—eight to ten pairs of them at a time—fanciful, sequined and beaded, in every color of the rainbow. Extravagance goes with the territory of being a "brand-name" author—with translations of her books into more than a dozen languages, tours that log up to fifty thousand miles a year and feature her as a flamboyantly funny speaker, young reader medals from Hawaii to Maine, her own television show in England, and a glamorous lifestyle that includes an apartment on the Upper West Side of New York City, a house in rural Woodstock, New York, and spending a good part of the year in London.

The Glamorous Life of an Author

But Paula Danziger's writer-brain never rests, even when she is shopping. In restaurants and stores she constantly eavesdrops for gems she can use in a book (she has been known to ride buses around New York just to study how kids talk), makes up jokes in her head, and weighs whether a piece of material is good or truly great. Danziger's presence—vital, funny, compassionate—pervades her written work in a way that is unique among writers for young adults. To understand her books, it is especially necessary to know about this writer's life.

Danziger was born on 18 August 1944 in Washington, D.C., to Samuel and Carolyn Danziger. She claims that she has known since second grade that she wanted to be a writer: "While other kids had imaginary playmates, I had a follow-the-dot kingdom," she confided in one of several personal interviews conducted over the past few years. "I had the magic pencil, *with* the magic eraser, and this whole town was dependent on me. I'd make their houses for them, extra playmates. If I got angry and didn't like them, I'd erase them." It was a "real control thing," she admits now, "and it's also what I do today—it's what writers do." Somehow she knew that writing would bring success within her lifetime. By third grade she had started practicing her autograph.

Early Influences

"My earliest memory is of going to the library," says Danziger. "Sometimes my mother would shop and leave me there, and I'd have a book finished by the time she got back. The librarian was wonderful. When I read all the children's books she moved me into the adult section." The first book she recalls loving was *The Little Engine That Could*: "I still use that line, 'I think I can, I think I can, I know I can' before anything that makes me nervous—a speech or a big date or doing a TV show."

As a young reader, Danziger was soon polishing off at least six books a week: "I loved books. They were a way to get out of my life. If it had print on it I read it." That meant comics (about Little Lulu, Archie and Jughead and Veronica, superheroes), her mother's nursing books, and her father's law books. The Landmark books helped her with history lessons and were among the few nonfiction books she con-

> She has been known to ride buses around New York just to study how kids talk.

> "I loved books. They were a way to get out of my life. If it had print on it I read it."

The **Landmark books** are two volumes of American history written in 1968 and 1970 by the American historian Daniel J. Boorstin.

tinued to read. Her preference was fiction, including science fiction books by Isaac Asimov and Ray Bradbury. She read all the Nancy Drew and Hardy Boys books as well as the Cherry Ames and Sue Barton nurse stories. She sees no problems with teenagers reading series books and "just laughs" when people get upset about it.

Betty Smith's *A Tree Grows in Brooklyn* was probably the first "YA" (young adult) book that Danziger ever read, or perhaps it was Louisa May Alcott's *Little Women* or Herman Wouk's *Marjorie Morningstar.* "But I think the first YA ever *written* was Jane Austen's *Pride and Prejudice,*" she says. It was in high school that she discovered J. D. Salinger's *The Catcher in the Rye.* "And that was my book. I read it every day for three years. I just felt I wasn't alone, there was hope for me. It's when I knew I could be a writer." Already, Danziger saw writing as salvation: "I remember growing up and having my father yell at me and thinking *while* he was yelling, 'That's okay, sometime you can use this in a book.'" Even as a child, she was able to make that amazing leap— the sign of a born writer—of realizing that misery in the present could make good material in the future.

Danziger has always felt things deeply, particularly when she was young. "You can never be as hurt as you are when you're a child and you don't know you have defenses," she says. By the time she hit adolescence, she was in pain with anger that came from her family life: "There was always tension in my house." She perceived the source of the tension as her father: "He had a very bad temper. He never hit, just yelled. His word was law, and if you disagreed you got screamed at and demeaned. My mother was weak and couldn't stand up to him."

Danziger now feels that her father was scarred from his own younger years. "I don't think he was ever happy," she says. To his daughter he seemed arbitrary and volatile, and the overall feeling remained with her that "nothing I did was ever good enough."

Survival Through Humor

Her strength, weapon, and trademark became a sterling sense of humor. "Humor," declares Danziger, "is emotional chaos remembered in tranquility." Humorists from Mark Twain ("The secret source of Humor itself is not joy but

In addition to *A Tree Grows in Brooklyn*, **Betty Smith** (1896–1972) wrote other novels about girls growing up in poor, urban areas.

There is an article about Louisa May Alcott earlier in this volume and an article about J. D. Salinger in volume 3.

Jane Austen (1775–1817) was an English novelist. *Pride and Prejudice* was made into films in 1940 and 1985.

demean put down or belittle

There is an article about Mark Twain in volume 3.

Lenny Bruce
(1925–1966) was an
American comedian
whose performances
were well known
and controversial for
their daring, slang,
obscenity, and im-
provisation. He was
arrested many times
and died of a drug
overdose.

Elvis Presley
(1935–1977), a
singer, guitarist, and
movie star, was
known as "the King"
of rock and roll.
Ricky Nelson
(1940–1985) was a
star of the very pop-
ular television show
Ozzie and Harriet.
His second career, as
a pop and country
singer, ended when
he died in a plane
crash.

sorrow.") to Lenny Bruce ("All my humor is based on destruction and despair.") might agree. Survival through humor
is Danziger's recurring theme in her books as well as her life:
"It's a way to deal with sadness in life."

While other kids her age had crushes on Elvis Presley
and Ricky Nelson, Danziger had crushes on comedians. She
knew she could make herself laugh a lot—and others, too.
"Apparently I was funny as long as anyone could remember,"
she says frankly. She didn't see the power of her humor at
the time, but now she realizes it was a way to cope: "When
you're funny, you can get very important and angry things
out in a smart way that makes others laugh. People either get
it or they don't, but you've said it and that matters."

School was not a great source of stimulation for Danziger. She claims she stopped liking it in sixth grade. She remembers getting a lot of detention "for talking," and she
used to get A's over F's on papers. "I would turn in something really good," she recalls. "It just wasn't what the assignment was." She admits, however, that she did attend
good suburban New Jersey schools, and in high school, sem-
inars brought in drama critics from New York, and other
speakers, who expanded her horizons.

Later Influences

Danziger was able to get a scholarship to Montclair State
Teachers College. With this and some parental help she
worked her way through and earned a bachelor's degree in
English. (She later earned a master's degree in reading as
well.) She was editor of *Galumph,* the campus humor magazine, and a college librarian introduced her to the first and
most important of her mentors, the American poet John
Ciardi. Ciardi and his wife, Judith, hired Danziger as a
"monster-minder" (babysitter) for their three children, and
she accompanied them to places like the Bread Loaf Conference for writers, where she met notables such as Shirley
Jackson and Archibald MacLeish.

After college, Danziger went on to the career her parents
expected of her: teaching. She taught English in several
New Jersey schools. Her special talents blossomed while she
was teaching eighth and ninth grades; apparently she was a
teacher straight out of a Paula Danziger book. "Another

teacher said that he always recognized my students the year after I taught them," she recalls, "because they didn't raise their hands and they didn't always accept what the teacher said." Kids who were not enthusiastic readers before were usually avid ones by the end of a year with Danziger.

She would probably have endured a long and semi-notorious career as a junior high English teacher but for two serious car accidents in 1970. Being hit from behind by a police car and then, six days later, head-on by a drunk driver changed the course of her life. Forced to quit teaching, she began writing *The Cat Ate My Gymsuit* (1974). If she was ever going to be a writer, she decided, the time was now.

seminotorious somewhat unfavorably known

It All Started with Marcy Lewis

On the first page of *The Cat Ate My Gymsuit,* we find Marcy Lewis full of bile: "I hate my father. I hate school. I hate being fat. I hate the principal because he wanted to fire Ms. Finney, my English teacher." To deal with her rage, Marcy lives within a shell that keeps her safe and protected but also passive, overweight, and bitterly unhappy. Gym class, with its spotlight on bodies, is excruciating for her. The book's title comes from one of the numerous witty excuses she invents to avoid partaking in gym altogether. (It was one of the better excuses Danziger heard during her teaching career.)

It is easy to locate the major source of Marcy's anger. Her father, Martin, is insulting, cruel, and selfish. At age thirteen, Marcy is hardly in a position to move out, and so for the time being she is trapped, powerless—and furious about it. In the course of her relationship with Barbara Finney, the new English teacher, Marcy gradually learns how communication is the one path out of her miserable existence. By the time a crisis strikes and Ms. Finney is fired (for standing up to the school administration), Marcy is a new human being. She is still overweight, still saddled with a destructive father and a weak mother, but active for the first time in her life.

Cat is a work of fiction, but it is the most autobiographical of Danziger's works. She has even been known to have herself listed as "Marcy Lewis" in the telephone directory. (The last name, following Danziger's pattern with all her major characters, comes from a favorite Jewish comedian, in this case Jerry Lewis.) Of this first novel she says, "I wrote about

autobiographical related to the one's own life

what I knew best. I was a fat little teenager from New Jersey who hated school. I'd been a teacher who had taken stands." She drew on her own feelings of raw rage—at social conditions, at parents, and mostly at fathers.

Not all critical reactions to *Cat* were positive, but popular opinion made its author into that rare phenomenon, an overnight success. Probably her best-selling book, it has sold steadily for more than twenty years and is frequently taught in classrooms. One reason for the book's longevity is its biting humor. The jokes are never gratuitous, however, or allowed to interfere with the truly heartrending passages. And Marcy never wallows. She stays light on her feet, and at the end we know her humor makes her a survivor.

gratuitous unnecessary

More Survival Through Humor

After writing two more funny, touching, and hugely successful books—*The Pistachio Prescription* (1978) and *Can You Sue Your Parents for Malpractice?* (1979)—Danziger returned to the Marcy Lewis saga with *There's a Bat in Bunk Five* (1980). She continued her famously winning way with titles in her next two books, which are about Phoebe Brooks and Rosie Wilson. These two "children of divorce" star in *The Divorce Express* (1982) and *It's an Aardvark-Eat-Turtle World* (1985). Subsequent books have taken characters all the way from outer space (*This Place Has No Atmosphere,* 1986) to New York City (*Remember Me to Harold Square,* 1987) and London (*Thames Doesn't Rhyme with James,* 1994). Danziger has also endeared herself to younger readers with the popular Matthew Martin series of four short novels and the best-selling, critically well-received Amber Brown chapter books.

subsequent following

Danziger's books usually appear to bypass the adult critical establishment, reaching readers directly through enormous paperback sales. Critical reception (which has sometimes been glowing, at other times not so kind) has not necessarily been Danziger's main concern. Instead, she says, "What I strive for is that rush of recognition you get from friends—the kind of connection you get when you say something funny and you know that *they* get it." By the time Danziger was writing her fifth novel, the first four had sold more than two million copies in hardcover and paperback.

At one point she was selling 150,000 copies of her books per month.

The Key to Success

Perhaps the biggest reason for her worldwide success is her gift for looking at events through the eyes of a teenager. She says she is appalled "when people say to me it's wonderful how I come down to kids' level. I respond on a level I feel comfortable on." A teenage perspective just happens to be the same as hers. "I'm not like most grown-ups," she admits. She loves pinball and video games, plays jacks on the floor, and has an enormous collection of stickers. She has occasional regrets about not having children or marrying but has proven to be a world-class aunt (in the mode of one of her favorite writers, Jane Austen) and is close to her three nephews and one niece.

The one writer, other than J. D. Salinger, to whom Danziger can point with certainty as an influence was Louise Fitzhugh, an author she very much admires. Fitzhugh's *Harriet the Spy* (1964) is a classic portrait of an outsider (an eleven-year-old budding writer), acute in its depiction of the anger and angst of the psychologically abused child. Like many of Danziger's books, *Harriet the Spy* combines anger and humor to make a witty work of art that appeals to generation after generation. Judy Blume, the writer with whom Danziger is most frequently compared, was not a particular influence, although Danziger admires her work. She also likes the Ramona stories of Beverly Cleary and the Anastasia books of Lois Lowry. "I love a book if it's funny and bright and caring and honest," Danziger says. She loves writers who make her laugh, including Russell Baker, Dave Barry, and Mark Twain.

People are always surprised, says Danziger, by how much labor goes into her books: "They think because I'm funny that it was easy, but I know why words were chosen. I know where I'm going and there's a straight line. It may change but I go back and rework it. I write and rewrite a lot. A book may sound like me talking, but it took hard work to get it that way." One amazing fact about Danziger is that she can write anywhere—on planes, in restaurants, even in the

> *She loves pinball and video games, plays jacks on the floor, and has an enormous collection of stickers.*

angst anxiety or anguish

There is an article about Judy Blume earlier in this volume and an article about Lois Lowry in volume 2.

There is an article about Mark Twain in volume 3.

The **Holocaust** was the mass murder of at least 11 million people, especially Jews, by the Nazis during World War II. The word "holocaust" means "thorough destruction by fire."

Holden Caulfield is the narrator and main character of J. D. Salinger's *The Catcher in the Rye.*

There are articles about Margaret Mahy, Katherine Paterson, and Harper Lee in volume 2 and an article about Robert Westall in volume 3.

defy challenge or resist

dentist's chair. Before computers she wrote in longhand lying in bed on her stomach, with her legs up like a kid, and then transferred the drafts to a typewriter. Now she uses a laptop computer and often writes in her living room on a TV tray. She has never written about her car accidents or other subjects she regards as too painful, such as AIDS (she has had friends who died from AIDS and says, "I just can't detach myself that much") or the Holocaust (except briefly in *Remember Me to Harold Square*).

Danziger appears regularly on television in London to talk about books. She organizes her selections by themes with typical Danziger titles, such as "Characters That I Wish Were Friends" (after Holden Caulfield's desire to call up his favorite authors on the phone); "Books That You Thought Would Make You Puke but You End Up Loving" (classics such as *Pride and Prejudice*); "Because They Make You Do School Reports on Us" (autobiographical books by people like Roald Dahl and Jean Little); "Science Fiction" (Margaret Mahy, Robert Westall); and "The Ten Weepiest Books Ever" (including Katherine Paterson's *A Bridge to Terabithia,* Lois Lowry's *A Summer to Die,* and Harper Lee's *To Kill a Mockingbird*).

May the Shopping Continue

With a funny bone that never sleeps and characters who defy authority while retaining their integrity, Danziger springs from a long tradition that includes Salinger's *Catcher in the Rye,* Fitzhugh's *Harriet the Spy,* Cleary's Ramona books, among others, and going all the way back to Twain's *Huckleberry Finn.* With care and compassion, she hones each element of her novels so that they hit home with their intended audience. She said in 1995 that she plans to continue creating characters who wage war on issues with which one never really stops wrestling. This concern puts her squarely within the tradition of the best of children's literature: the books that last.

Meanwhile, she confesses, "I do like immediate gratification, whether it's food, spending, or whatever." And the shopping is likely to continue. "I live for malls," she says with a smile.

Selected Bibliography

WORKS BY PAULA DANZIGER

Novels

The Cat Ate My Gymsuit (1974)
The Pistachio Prescription (1978)
Can You Sue Your Parents for Malpractice? (1979)
There's a Bat in Bunk Five (1980)
The Divorce Express (1982)
It's an Aardvark-Eat-Turtle World (1985)
This Place Has No Atmosphere (1986)
Remember Me to Harold Square (1987)
Everyone Else's Parents Said Yes (1989)
Make Like a Tree and Leave (1990)
Earth to Matthew (1991)
Not for a Billion Gazillion Dollars (1992)
Thames Doesn't Rhyme with James (1994)
Amber Brown Is Not a Crayon (1994)
You Can't Eat Your Chicken Pox, Amber Brown (1995)

Articles

"The Danziger Prescription." In *ALAN Review*, Fall 1979, p. 7.

"Facets: Successful Authors Talk About Connections Between Teaching and Writing" (co-written with several others). In *English Journal*, November 1984, pp. 24–27.

"I Followed the Sweet Potato." In *Voice of Youth Advocates*, June 1979, p. 8.

"Why I Will Never Win the Newbery Medal." In *Top of the News*, Fall 1979, pp. 57–60.

Other

Introduction to John Ciardi's *Someone Could Win a Polar Bear*. Honesdale, Pa.: Boyds Mill, 1993.

WORKS ABOUT PAULA DANZIGER

Books and Parts of Books

Becker, Margot R. *Ann M. Martin*. New York: Scholastic, 1993.

If you like Paula Danziger, you may also like Judy Blume, J. D. Salinger, and Mark Twain.

Donelson, Kenneth L., and Alleen Pace Nilsen. In *Literature for Today's Young Adults*. Glenview, Ill.: Scott Foresman, 1980.

Krull, Kathleen. *Presenting Paula Danziger*. New York: Twayne, 1995.

Articles

Abso, Jenny. "Older and Wiser?" In *Newsday*, 6 November 1988.

Beeby, Rossyln. "Bad Jokes Fuel for Best-Sellers." In *Sunday Observer* (Australia), 19 June 1988.

Commire, Anne, ed. "Paula Danziger." In *Something About the Author*. Detroit: Gale Research, 1984, vol. 36, pp. 49–56.

Freeland, Dennis. "A Conversation with Paula Danziger." In *Writing!*, November 1988, p. 20.

———. "Paula Danziger's Young Adult World." In *Writer's Digest*, January 1990, p. 40.

Goldberg, Jane. "A Classroom Full of Character." In *Star Ledger* (Edison, N.J.), 24 May 1990.

Haffke, Carol. "A Writer's Childhood Helps Tell the Tale." In *Gold Coast Bulletin*, 16 June 1988.

Hand, Lise. "Author Paula's Whirlwind Visit." In *Sunday Independent* (Ireland), 15 October 1989.

Martin, Sandra. "Kids Love Danziger and Her Funny, Feeling Books." In the *Toronto Globe and Mail*, 2 February 1982.

Reed, J. D. "Packaging the Facts of Life." In *Time*, 23 August 1982, p. 65.

Richardson, Jean. "The Danziger Blitz." In *Publishers Weekly*, 19 July 1991, p. 37.

Sima, Judy. "Paula Danziger." In *Educational Oasis*, January/February 1992.

Tatle, Suzan. "Author Writes for Real Kids." In *Courier-News* (Bridgewater, N.J.), 21 January 1991.

White, Pam. "Teacher's Teen Memories Turn into Popular Books." In *Richmond News Leader*, 29 October 1979.

Youngstone, Wayne. "Students Exercise Creativity: Writer Guides Imagination." In *New Tribune* (Edison, N.J.) 18 May 1990.

How to Write to the Author
Paula Danziger
c/o The Putnam Berkley Group, Inc.
Children's Book Publicity Department
200 Madison Avenue
New York, NY 10016

Terry Davis

(1946-   )

by Jean E. Brown

Whether it is pulling pranks during practice in the gym, getting caught up in a police sweep in Rio, or riding a Harley for the first time, Terry Davis transports us, his readers, so that we share the experience. He said, in a letter to me in May 1995, that as an author, he seeks to "engage the reader while he or she is reading, to make a world of the book take over from the actual world. I want every moment of the book to feel (Yes, *feel,* like in the stomach) real, to make the reader feel the lives of the character, hear their voices." He achieves this kind of connection between the reader and his books by developing characters who are real and likable, and who face challenges, conflicts, and triumphs that readers can imagine and relate to, thus making a strong connection between the reader and the book. In each of his published novels—*Vision Quest* (1979), *Mysterious Ways* (1984), and *If Rock and Roll Were a Machine* (1992)—the main character is a young male who is smart, funny, active in sports, rides motorcycles, and has more than a passing interest in sex.

Quotations from Terry Davis that are not attributed to a published source are from personal correspondence with the author of this essay in May 1995 and appear here by permission of Terry Davis.

A Writer and His Characters

The role of the writer is a special one to Terry Davis. He believes that artists, but especially writers, answer the question, What is it like to be human? In the article titled "Literature Tells Our Family Secrets" (1994), Davis writes: "The answer to this question is: the people who create literature. Writers, movie makers—storytellers. They are the people who tell what it's like to be human. . . ." (p. 27). Certainly, the main characters in each of his books—Louden Swain in *Vision Quest,* Bert Bowden in *If Rock and Roll Were a Machine,* and Karl Russell in *Mysterious Ways* demonstrate what it is to be human as they deal with the circumstances of their lives.

In *Vision Quest,* Louden is riding a high; life is good for him. He is doing well in school; he is determined to bring his very successful high school wrestling career to a challenging conclusion by dropping two weight classes so that he can face Gary Shute, his greatest rival; and he has a good relationship with his live-in girlfriend, Carla, and with his father. He is reflective, thoughtful, open, and funny. But above all else, he has a sense of direction. He is graduating from high school a semester early to work and save money for college, where he wants to study medicine.

While Louden is self-confident, Bert, in *If Rock and Roll Were a Machine,* is insecure. An elementary school teacher has shattered Bert's sense of self-worth, and he is struggling to feel good about himself. Like Louden, Bert takes charge of his life. He seeks ways to establish a sense of identity and new self-worth. He buys a classic Harley-Davidson motorcycle against his parents' wishes. The acquisition of the Harley begins his love affair with classic bikes, and it also begins a significant relationship with Scotty Shepard, owner of the motorcycle shop, who offers Bert a job. Scotty introduces Bert to racquetball and coaches him to work his way up to the top of the B class in local competition, but most of all he teaches Bert about self-worth. At the same time, Bert's talent as a writer is encouraged by his English teacher; he even joins the staff of the student newspaper. As Bert explores his new interests, he gains confidence from his successes and begins to feel better about himself.

Karl, the hero of *Mysterious Ways,* is a young man who must address a series of losses in his life. First, Karl has to deal with the loss of his parents and younger brother, who were killed when their car was hit by a drunk driver. Then a severe arm injury curtails his promising career as a potential major-league pitcher. He loses his sense of well-being as his worst nightmare becomes prophetic. Eventually, he even loses his health.

All three of these characters look inward for solutions to their problems and concerns, but they never lose sight of others. While each of these characters can be considered introspective, they never become obsessively self-absorbed. One of the main reasons for that is that they all have great senses of humor and can make fun of themselves. For example, Louden tells his grandfather that he won't wrestle with him: "You'd just hurt me, and this is my year to be a hero" (*Vision Quest,* p. 75).

Experience and Imagination

Aspiring writers are often told to write about what they know. Terry Davis' works seem to reflect that he has taken that advice, because many of his experiences and interests are reflected in his books. Readers get a flavor of his interests and experiences in the outdoors, sports—especially racquetball and wrestling—and his special love for motorcycles, particularly classic bikes. Davis has owned more than 100 motorcycles in his life, and now, as he said in his May 1995 letter, "I guess we have about fifteen bikes here in Minnesota and back in Spokane where we spend the summer. I buy them cheap, fix them, ride them—my kids ride them too—then I sell them." All these interests appear in his work and in the lives of his characters. Their presence also helps to define the audience who will really enjoy his books. His strong, positive male characters make his books easy for young men to relate to, but his humor and well-developed stories also appeal to young women.

But Davis goes beyond his own experiences in his books. He believes that the imagination plays as significant a role in successful writing as does experience. "A good writer makes everything authentic," he wrote in the same letter. "All good writing rings with authority. I think authority in narrative is created mostly by technique—that is to say imagining accurately, then reporting accurately what you imagined." For example, an experience from his childhood, when a

> *"A good writer makes everything authentic"*

introspective marked by an examination of one's own thoughts and feelings

Spokane is a city in Washington

teacher humiliated Davis and destroyed his self-confidence, becomes a significant event in Bert Bowden's life. Once he presents the situation in *If Rock and Roll Were a Machine,* Davis then imagines how Bert would have handled the situation. He provides two supportive adults—Bert's English teacher, Gene Tannerman, and Scotty Shepard, the owner of a motorcycle shop—to help Bert gain confidence and find a way to confront the teacher. While Bert seeks revenge against the teacher, he learns about both himself and revenge. Thus, Davis began with an actual experience from his own life, made it Bert's experience, then exercised his imagination to determine how Bert would have addressed it.

The major complaint of Davis' readers is that they want more books, but for Terry Davis, it is important to have pride in his work and to feel that he has written as good a book as he can. That kind of self-satisfaction comes from carefully crafting a work, a time-consuming process. In a personal interview in November 1994, Davis said, "I suspect that I may not write more than ten books in my life, but I want them to be good books." He added, "I don't want to give up the things that make my life rich." His family, his dogs, his hobbies, and his work provide the richness in his life and help to fuel his creative imagination.

Qualities of His Writing

There are numerous similarities among his books. Davis creates very strong, positive main characters, who are likable and believable. Both Louden and Bert are high school students, whereas Karl is an older college student who turns twenty-one toward the end of *Mysterious Ways.* All three characters are articulate speakers who reflect on their lives.

Davis uses humor in his books both to capture the reader's attention and to provide the characters with an easy way to reveal their reactions and feelings. All three main characters have a self-deprecating humor that keeps them from taking themselves too seriously. For example, Karl's skin disease is raging out of control while he is in Rio. He receives a letter from a friend who tells Karl of his plan to demonstrate against the Vietnam War during the 1968 Democratic Party convention with some people from Students for a Democratic Society (SDS). Karl's reaction is: "I ought to form

self-deprecating playing down or discrediting oneself; belittling oneself

my own SDS Organization. The initials would stand for Students for Dermatological Subversion. I could turn all the Young Republicans in the whole country into wartcreatures. Singlehandedly I could stop the war" (*Mysterious Ways,* pp. 220–221). Davis also uses humor to capture a sense of comradeship among the characters. Louden and his teammates play tricks on one another during practice, but when match time rolls around they are solidly supportive of each other.

Davis' characters also share intellectual curiosity and a love of learning. "I'm fascinated by learning, like Bert Bowden and Karl Russell and Louden Swain," Davis says. Louden, Bert, and Karl are all readers who recognize the power of a story and its message. Karl takes pride in getting straight A's. Writing provides Bert with the vehicle to sort out his feelings and also to regain confidence about his academic competence. His English teacher, Gene Tannerman, responds to one of Bert's papers by saying, "You're a funny guy, Bert. Smart and funny. These qualities come through in your prose. In class, however, you're one of the living dead, and I want you to come alive" (*If Rock and Roll,* pp. 122–123). Tannerman is helping Bert to recognize that he has the talent and intelligence to succeed. In *Vision Quest,* Louden knows that he wants to continue to think and grow: "Whatever kind of doctor I become, I hope I always make time to read and see movies and talk about them with my friends. I hope I meet people in college who like to do this" (p. 31). All these characters come to realize that it is okay to be both smart and athletic. They realize that books can play a special role in their lives.

> *I'm fascinated by learning, like Bert Bowden and Karl Russell and Louden Swain."*

Life and Career

Terry Davis was born and reared in Spokane, Washington. His books are filled with the people and places of his youth. Spokane and its environs provide the setting for two of his novels and part of the third. Additionally, many of his characters bear the influence of people who have had a significant impact in Davis' life. He describes his youth as being very much like that of Louden Swain in *Vision Quest.* His mother's illness as he was growing up inspired the character of Louden's mother. In fact, as Davis told me in a personal interview in March 1995, "The mother in *Vision Quest* is my mom." He said further: "And the scene where Louden finds her crying in pain is right out of my young life—I was ten or so. The parents are in many ways my parents; one of the ways they're not is that my parents never divorced, although they probably should have." Two of Louden's friends, Otto and Damon Thuringer, the Sausage Man, are also modeled after friends from high school.

In his May 1995 letter to me, Davis describes Karl's girlfriend, Jennifer, as "one of my favorite characters. She's based to a degree on a girl I was fascinated with in college; I guess Jennifer's a girlfriend I wished I'd had." Davis created the relationship between Bert Bowden and his grandparents as a tribute to his own similar relationship. Bert's grandmother is his Grandmother Thompson. The grandfather in *Vision Quest* was like his own grandfather. Like Bert, Davis was also close to his grandfather: "I would like to have my grandfather's kindness," he told me in a personal interview in November 1994. Perhaps *If Rock and Roll Were a Machine* reflects two sides of Davis' personality better than his other books. By his own admission, he is like both Bert and Gene Tannerman, the English teacher, who appears in two novels. Camille Shepard is loosely modeled after Davis' son Pascal, who lives in Paris with his mother.

After graduating from high school in Spokane, Davis, like the main character of *Mysterious Ways,* went to Eastern Washington State University, where he earned a degree in English. His fraternity became a model for the one depicted in the novel. While at Eastern, he became friends with another student named Chris Crutcher. Crutcher credits his reading of the manuscript of *Vision Quest* with encouraging him to begin his own career as a writer of books for young adults. Crutcher is now a successful author of young adult literature, and he continues to work as a family therapist in Spokane. Davis alludes to his old friend in *If Rock and Roll Were a Machine,* when Bert speaks of seeing a therapist, a "Dr. Crutcher."

fraternity a men's student organization formed mainly for social purposes

Vision Quest was both a critical and popular hit. Its success in print led Hollywood to purchase the rights and turn the book into a highly successful film in 1985. Davis feels that the film adaptation was quite faithful to the book.

With degree in hand, Davis went to Rio de Janeiro, Brazil, where he taught English and coached wrestling at the American school from 1970 to 1972. His experiences there inspired parts of his second novel, *Mysterious Ways*. Also a critical success, this novel, like his other two books, was marketed for a young adult audience, although it should have been targeted for adults. The book went out of print, but the Dell Publishing Company plans to re-release it concurrently with the publication of Davis' next novel. "I believe that *Mysterious Ways* is my best book," Davis told me in November 1994. "I don't really have a favorite," he explained further in a May 1995 letter. "I love the experience of writing them all, including *Mysterious Ways,* which was painful to write. The way a writer loves that experience—whether painful or not—is that you are so alive when you are doing it. As I said, you get to be out there, to live that life in a way that's astonishingly close to 'real' living."

After teaching in South America, Davis returned to the United States and attended the University of Iowa Writers' Workshop, where he earned an MFA in fiction writing. During that time, he wrote the beginning and the end of *Vision Quest.* Following his work at Iowa, Davis went to Stanford University (1975–1976) as the recipient of a Wallace Stegner Literary Fellowship. He is currently a member of the English department at Mankato State University in Minnesota, where he teaches courses in creative writing, fiction, and screen writing. Davis married his second wife, Becky, in the mid-1990s. They both brought two children to the marriage. Her two children live with them full-time, while his two visit during the summer. Becky Davis has just had her first young adult novel accepted for publication.

Terry Davis is committed to writing at least three more young adult novels. He told me in March 1995 that he is working on his next book, tentatively titled *The Silk Ball*. It is the story of how the Hmong kid, Cheng Moua, the school newspaper photographer in *If Rock and Roll Were a Machine,* applies to film school at the University of Southern California.

Perhaps Terry Davis best describes himself in the words of Gene Tannerman: "What do I mean by *writer?* What I mean is a professional story writer—someone who sees so deeply and clearly into human life and then writes with such precision, insight, compassion, and imagination about it that the world gives him or her a reward. The reward might not be money; it might be respect. But because there is value, there is also reward" (*If Rock and Roll,* p. 123).

If you like the works of Terry Davis, you might also enjoy the works of Chris Crutcher and Chris Lynch.

Selected Bibliography

WORKS BY TERRY DAVIS

Vision Quest (1979)

Mysterious Ways (1984)

If Rock and Roll Were a Machine (1992)

Article

"Literature Tells Our Family Secrets." *English Journal,* December 1994, vol. 83, no. 8, pp. 27–32.

WORKS ABOUT TERRY DAVIS

Interviews

Brown, Jean E. Personal interviews with Terry Davis at the National Council of teachers of English. Orlando, Fla., November 1994.

———. Personal interview with Terry Davis at the National Council of teachers of English. Minneapolis, Minn., March 1995.

Greenlee, Edwin D., and Arthea J. S. Reed. "Recommended Adolescent Literature." *English Journal,* April 1992, pp. 23, 30.

Roback, Diane, and Richard Donahue. Review of *If Rock and Roll Were a Machine. Publishers Weekly,* 30 November 1992, p. 56.

How to write to the Author
Terry Davis
c/o Dell Publishing
1540 Broadway
New York, NY 10036

Charles Dickens

(1812–1870)

by Laura A. Pritchard

When you hear the name Charles Dickens, what comes to mind? If you think of an old Englishman who wrote long novels and who was probably boring, you are only half correct. Charles Dickens was a prolific writer, considered the greatest English author next to William Shakespeare. He was hardly boring, though. He loved the theater and frequently acted in amateur productions. He dressed flamboyantly. Social reformers, writers, and actors were members of his social circle. Dickens achieved great literary success and public acclaim during his lifetime, yet he could not always enjoy it. He was haunted by his traumatic childhood, and he was insecure in his personal relationships.

Dickens' Early Years

Charles John Huffam Dickens was born to Elizabeth Barrow Dickens and John Dickens on 7 February 1812 in Portsmouth, a city in southern England. In 1814 the family moved to Chatham, a city in Kent, where Dickens spent possibly the five happiest years of his life. While living in Chatham, Dickens did attend school, but he spent more time roaming the woods and exploring the nearby city of Rochester. He was also an avid reader.

In June 1822 John Dickens was transferred back to London, and his salary was insufficient to support his family. Instead of attending school, Charles turned for his education to the streets of London, where he wandered for hours.

Child labor was one way for the family to earn additional income, so at age twelve Dickens began working at Warren's Blacking Warehouse. Despite young Dickens' job, which was to glue labels on pots of black shoe polish, the family's finances became worse. In February 1824 John Dickens was arrested and imprisoned at Marshalsea, a debtor's prison. Most of the family possessions were sold or pawned, and Charles Dickens continued working at the blacking warehouse. In May, his father was released from Marshalsea.

John Dickens rescued his unhappy son from working at the warehouse, but his mother wanted Charles to return to work. She believed that they needed the money he could earn. Charles Dickens never forgave his mother for this harshness.

From 1824 to 1827 Dickens attended school. In 1827, he began his first career, as a junior clerk at a lawyer's office. Then he went to work as a freelance law reporter, which led to his becoming a parliamentary reporter. He worked for two journals from 1830 to 1835. These journalistic enterprises helped him develop as an author.

Everything was not well, however. In May 1830 Dickens fell in love with Maria Beadnell, a pretty and flirtatious young woman. But because she was from a higher social class, she never seriously considered Dickens as a suitor. Nevertheless, Maria teased and encouraged him, and he grew quite obsessive in his love for her. Although by May 1833 the relationship was finished, Dickens failed to recover from the rejection, and his subsequent marriage and his chil-

avid very eager

At the age of twelve, Dickens began working at Warren's Blacking Warehouse, glueing labels on pots of black shoe polish.

debtor's prison a prison where people who could not pay their bills ("debts") were sent. Today this way of disciplining such people is considered backward and impractical.

suitor potential spouse

dren all suffered from it. His writings also suffered; many critics think that he never accurately portrayed adult love affairs.

The Budding Writer

Dickens's first story was published anonymously in 1833 in an obscure magazine. The editor wanted more of Dickens' work, and Dickens happily provided more sketches about life in London. By 1835 he had been invited to be a regular contributor to a newspaper, and a year later *Sketches by Boz* was published to public and critical acclaim. Dickens continued writing, and his reputation continued rising.

anonymously without the author's name

Marriage and Prosperity

Catherine Hogarth was not particularly attractive. She was warm and eager to please, but not lively or imaginative. Dickens proposed marriage and she accepted; they married on 2 April 1836.

By 1837 Dickens was writing *The Posthumous Papers of the Pickwick Club* (*Pickwick Papers*, 1836–1837), *The Adventures of Oliver Twist* (1837–1838), and *The Life and Adventures of Nicholas Nickleby* (1838–1839). Although he worked at a frantic pace, he still found time for social engagements, but Catherine seldom joined him. By 1842 Dickens had also published *The Old Curiosity Shop* (1840–1841) and *Barnaby Rudge: A Tale of the Riots of 'Eighty* (1841), and he was embarking on a his first reading tour of the United States. He had unreasonable expectations of that country, and so he was very disappointed. He attacked Americans in speeches and satirized them in *The Life and Adventures of Martin Chuzzlewit* (1843–1844).

Dickens continued writing, and his popularity grew with the introduction of his Christmas stories. These began with *A Christmas Carol* (1843), and they have shaped our image of a Victorian Christmas. Along with these he published *Dealings with the Firm of Dombey and Son, Wholesale, Retail, and for Exportation* in 1846–1848 and *The Personal History of David Copperfield* in 1849–1850. *David Copperfield*, a thinly veiled autobiographical work, was an immediate success.

satire a method of writing that uses humor and parody to mock or criticize

Victorian relating to the time of the reign of Queen Victoria of England (1837–1901). The ideal Victorian Christmas would include a Christmas tree and decorations, a homemade feast, and a party during which a loving family sings carols together.

autobiographical related to the author's own life

In the 1850s Dickens spent some time in France while continuing to write. He edited two magazines, *Household Words* and *All the Year Round.* He also published *Bleak House* in 1852–1853, *Hard Times for These Times* in 1854, and *Little Dorrit* in 1855–1857.

The Later Years

Although his later years should have been a happy time for Dickens and his family, ironically they were not. The difficulties between Charles and Catherine had escalated dramatically, although they had seven sons and two daughters. In 1857, Dickens fell in love with an actress named Ellen Ternan. The Dickenses bitterly separated in 1858. Dickens tried to keep up appearances, but eventually the separation came to light and created a great scandal. Dickens' reputation, however, was not permanently damaged. Ellen Ternan became a fixture in his life, although their relationship was not publicly known until the twentieth century.

Divorce was against the law in England in Dickens' time.

In 1858 Dickens began a series of dramatic readings of his works and continued them until right before his death. These readings were extremely popular. They reinforced his reputation as the literary genius of his age, and they brought in vast sums of money.

Dickens continued writing. He published *Great Expectations* in 1860–1861 and *Our Mutual Friend* in 1864–1865. Although Dickens' mind was troubled and his health was deteriorating, he embarked on a long reading tour of the United States in 1867. This tour was amazingly successful financially. After his triumphant return home, he prepared readings for his farewell tour of Great Britain. As usual, these readings were extremely popular.

deteriorating becoming worse

While he was on this reading tour in 1869, Dickens' health worsened. By the end of that summer he felt much better, however, and he began working on a new novel, *The Mystery of Edwin Drood* (1870). He was not able to finish it.

In the beginning of 1870 Dickens began a series of twelve public readings, culminating in a private audience with Queen Victoria. Feeling unwell again, he returned to his home, Gad's Hill. He continued writing *The Mystery of Edwin Drood* until the afternoon of his death. That day, 9 June

1870, he felt ill, slipped into a coma, and died, probably of a brain hemorrhage.

hemorrhage release of blood from a burst blood vessel

Dickens' Endurance

Even though Dickens died more than a century ago, he and his works still remain popular. Patrick Stewart, the star of television's *Star Trek: The Next Generation,* successfully performed a one-man show of *A Christmas Carol* for several Christmas seasons. A revival of *Oliver!,* the musical based on *Oliver Twist,* ran to full houses. What is it about these and other of Dickens' works that has made them so enduring?

Oliver Twist

The Adventures of Oliver Twist, or the Parish Boy's Progress was published serially each month from February 1837 to March 1839. Dickens had two purposes when writing the novel: to expose the workings of the Poor Law Act and to offer an accurate portrait of criminal life in London. Many readers and critics disliked the author's depiction of the misery that lurked beneath London's surface. Dickens played the role of ardent social reformer his entire life, and *Oliver Twist* shows his concern for London's poor and their horrible living conditions. Although Dickens wrote the novel in response to Victorian issues that concerned him, *Oliver Twist* is also a modern novel. It can still upset and touch readers.

Britain's **Poor Law Act** of 1834 implied that healthy workers who remained in poverty had failed in a moral responsibility. The poor were put to work in workhouses where conditions were intentionally harsh.

Oliver Twist depicts two worlds: the good, light-filled world of Mr. Brownlow and Rose Maylie, and the dark world of the evil Fagin and Bill Sikes. Yet these two worlds coexist. Oliver wants to cross over from the dark to the light, and through his goodness he is able to do it. Dickens, however, makes Oliver immune to this evil, criminal environment, which many critics feel weakens the novel. Dickens seems to adopt the Conservative (Tory) belief that noble birth and breeding will shine through and triumph. Dickens' way of involving the reader does seem to make Oliver's innocence, and Nancy's love for Bill Sikes, not only plausible but possible.

Critics and general readers alike are frustrated by the many coincidences in Dickens' works. Yet Dickens loved them. He believed that they showed how common coinci-

The **Tories** were a major political party in eighteenth- and nineteenth-century Britain that favored tradition and the monarchy and opposed most social and political reform.

convention accepted literary method or technique

melodrama sentimentality or inflated emotion

dence is in life. *Oliver Twist* uses coincidences, conventions, and melodrama, but Dickens combines these elements skillfully. The reader cannot help being drawn into his story and sympathizing with his characters.

A Christmas Carol

Published in 1843, *A Christmas Carol* was the first of numerous Christmas stories that Dickens wrote. It was always included in his public readings, and it was an immensely popular tale.

A Christmas Carol is less realistic than his other fiction, but then a realistic story could not have elements of the supernatural in it, and *A Christmas Carol* is certainly a ghost story. Freed of realistic bonds, Dickens could include ghosts of Marley and Christmases, and even return to his own childhood in Scrooge's past.

Similar to the light-versus-dark imagery in *Oliver Twist* is the nephew-versus-Scrooge opposition in *A Christmas Carol*. The nephew's Christmas Eve invitation to Scrooge seems like a ritual, with both parties having their set pieces to say. The nephew, however, does see Scrooge's wealth as a reason to be merry, and Scrooge must possess some seed of goodness for his nephew to continue his Christmas Eve invitations and for Scrooge to have such a complete turnaround at the story's end.

David Copperfield

The Personal History of David Copperfield quickly became one of Dickens' most popular works. It was his favorite as well. Before *David Copperfield,* which was published in monthly serial form from May 1849 to November 1850, Dickens had established himself as a great and popular writer. He felt comfortable looking back on his childhood and earlier years.

exorcise remove or expel, especially something harmful or evil

Beginning with the use of his own initials in reverse, Dickens gives clues throughout the novel that *David Copperfield* is autobiographical. This form allowed Dickens to exorcise past demons, yet also to falsify or rework them while writing about his happy, then miserable, childhood. Embarrassed by his father's imprisonment and by his family's financial difficulties, Dickens depicts David's father as dead, but Dickens' father can also be seen in the character of Mr. Micawber. Dora Spenlow, a character based on the real-life heartbreaker Maria Beadnell, is killed by the author.

Throughout the novel something lucky always turns up, while dangers and difficulties disappear. *David Copperfield* is not a realistic novel, but it succeeds in its vision of life from the innocence of childhood to the experience of adulthood.

Another feature of *David Copperfield* is its resemblance to a fairy tale. Good and evil things happen without cause or consequence, inconvenient characters die, and good fortune and coincidences pop up at the right moment. David is the (disinherited) prince, and Agnes is his princess. Betsy Trotwood is the perfect fairy godmother, Peggotty is the faithful servant, and Uriah Heep is the troll. Australia is the never-never land where failures can succeed. The novel, of course, is much more than a simple fairy tale. Although both Copperfield and Dickens seem immature at times, the sadistic schoolmaster and Dickens' self-pity and vengeance make the work much more than a child's story.

sadistic delighting in being cruel to others

A Tale of Two Cities

"It was the best of times, it was the worst of times. . . . " is probably the best-known line from any Dickens work, and it comes from *A Tale of Two Cities*. Yet this novel generally has not been favored by critics. *A Tale of Two Cities* was published in serial form weekly from April to November 1859. Like Dickens' other works, the public loved it. The English had long been fascinated by and somewhat anxious about the French Revolution, and Dickens combined historical drama, social awareness, compassion, forgiveness, and sacrifice to create a serious and very intense novel.

Dickens drew on personal experience for *A Tale of Two Cities,* particularly on the time he had spent in Paris. Some critics see the novel's dramatization of turmoil as representing the turmoil in Dickens' own life, for at this point he was separated from his wife and seeing Ellen Ternan. Sydney Carton and Charles Darnay, two main characters, portray different sides of Dickens. Charles Darnay, who like David Copperfield shares Dickens' initials, tries to shed his family's past but cannot hide from its reach. Sydney Carton redeems

The **French Revolution** (1789–1799) was a bloody and unstable period of popular revolts that resulted in the overthrow of the French monarchy and the creation of the First French Republic.

himself through his love for Lucie Manette. These two versions of Dickens are unified in the novel, and they show the destructive power of the past and the healing power of love and sacrifice.

We also can view *A Tale of Two Cities* as a fable about resurrection. Sydney Carton sacrifices his life, almost in a Christlike manner, to save Charles Darnay and his family. Dickens believed that the hope expressed in the novel is a necessary and vital part of life.

Great Expectations

Like *David Copperfield, Great Expectations,* which was published as a weekly serial from December 1860 to August 1861, has a strong connection to fairy tales and fantasy. In this story, Pip is the prince, and Estella is the beautiful princess. Miss Havisham is the weird fairy godmother, and Magwitch is an ogre. Pip undergoes a magical transformation, but as in *David Copperfield, Great Expectations* is much more than a simple fairy tale.

penal code group of laws dealing with crimes and punishments

In this novel Dickens developed even more as a writer. As in *Oliver Twist,* he attacks a Victorian social issue, this time the penal code and its effects. The novel, while it has a fantasy aspect, also features a strong moral setting. Actions have consequences; privileges have responsibilities. In the plot, Pip's "great expectations," being financed by the criminal Magwitch, symbolize how good and evil—what we desire and fear most—are intertwined. Pip's rise in the world is not the result of magic but rather of an act of theft, which is shameful to him. Estella, the beauty who has tortured Pip but whom he loves anyway, is in fact the illegitimate daughter of Magwitch and the former criminal who is Mr. Jaggers' servant.

betrothed person to whom one is engaged to be married

Another theme in the novel is alienation, or exclusion from society. Miss Havisham, rejected by her betrothed, rejects society and enters a voluntary imprisonment. Her prison is psychological: by isolating herself she has put up barriers to others. Magwitch, on the other hand, is excluded from society because he committed a crime. He is first imprisoned, then escapes to Australia. He cannot reenter society because a death sentence hangs over his head. Both characters are equally bound to their prisons, but Pip is oblivious to it all.

Great Expectations shows Dickens at his most inventive. He uses tragedy and comedy, powerful irony, and social ideas combined with a sweeping vision of human life.

irony a situation in which the actual outcome is opposite or contrary to what was expected

Conclusion

Dickens' genius makes him the central literary figure of his age. He was the first writer to tackle modern problems and the discontent of urban life. He exploited the literary market by appealing to all readers, from the intellectual to the illiterate. People who could not afford to buy the monthly or weekly magazines would rent them from a library, and there were illustrations to help those who could not read well. Installments of the novels were awaited with intensity, and Dickens had an extremely faithful audience.

Dickens' novels are still popular today for several reasons. They capture a complex and exciting time as none of his contemporaries did. He successfully weaves fantasy and fairy tales within a realistic social context. He has a special insight into how children think and feel, and he treats them delicately in his novels, which often show how children should be treated. The works of Charles Dickens appeal to all ages, for all ages delight in his characters and stories.

Selected Bibliography

WORKS BY CHARLES DICKENS

If you like Charles Dickens, you might also enjoy the works of Arthur Conan Doyle, Louisa May Alcott, Robert Louis Stevenson, Edgar Allan Poe, and Lucy Maud Montgomery.

(The dates given here are of a work's first known publication as a book.)

Sketches by Boz, illustrated by George Cruikshank (1836)

The Posthumous Papers of the Pickwick Club, illustrated by Robert Seymour and Phiz (Halbot Knight Browne) (1837)

The Adventures of Oliver Twist; or, the Parish Boy's Progress, illustrated by George Cruikshank (1838)

Sketches of a Young Gentleman, illustrated by Phiz (Halbot Knight Browne) (1838)

The Life and Adventures of Nicholas Nickleby, illustrated by Phiz (Halbot Knight Browne) (1839)

Sketches of Young Couples, illustrated by Phiz (Halbot Knight Browne) (1840)

The Old Curiosity Shop, illustrated by George Cattermole and Phiz (Halbot Knight Browne) (1841)

Barnaby Rudge: A Tale of the Riots of 'Eighty, illustrated by George Cattermole and Phiz (Halbot Knight Browne) (1841)

A Christmas Carol, illustrated by John Leech (1843)

The Life and Adventures of Martin Chuzzlewit, illustrated by Phiz (Halbot Knight Browne) (1844)

Dealings with the Firm of Dombey and Son, Wholesale, Retail, and for Exportation, illustrated by Phiz (Halbot Knight Browne) (1848)

The Personal History of David Copperfield, illustrated by Phiz (Halbot Knight Browne) (1850)

Bleak House, illustrated by Phiz (Halbot Knight Browne) (1853)

Hard Times for These Times (1854)

Little Dorrit, illustrated by Phiz (Halbot Knight Browne) (1857)

A Tale of Two Cities, illustrated by Phiz (Halbot Knight Browne) (1859)

Great Expectations, illustrated from original designs by John McLenan (1861)

Our Mutual Friend, illustrated by Marcus Stone (1865)

The Mystery of Edwin Drood (unfinished), illustrated by Sin L. Fildes (1870)

WORKS ABOUT CHARLES DICKENS

Allen, Michael. *Charles Dickens' Childhood.* New York: St. Martin's Press, 1988.

Andrews, Malcolm. *Dickens and the Grown-Up Child.* Iowa City: University of Iowa Press, 1994.

Butt, John, and Kathleen Tilloston. *Dickens at Work.* London and New York: Methuen, 1982.

Chesterton, G. K., and F. G. Kitton. *Charles Dickens.* London: Hodder and Stoughton, 1906.

Chitlick, Kathryn. *The Critical Reception of Charles Dickens 1833–1841.* New York: Garland, 1989.

Collins, David R. *Tales for Hard Times: A Story About*

Charles Dickens. Illustrated by David Mataya. Minneapolis: Carolrhoda Books, 1990.

Collins, Philip. *Dickens: The Critical Heritage*. New York: Barnes and Noble, 1971.

Davis, Paul B. *The Lives and Times of Ebenezer Scrooge*. New Haven: Yale University Press, 1990.

Fielding, K. J. *Studying Charles Dickens*. Burnt Mill, Harlow, Essex, England: Longman, 1986.

Flint, Kate. *Dickens*. Atlantic Highlands, N.J.: Humanities Press International, 1986.

Forster, John. *The Life of Charles Dickens*. 3 vols. London: Chapman and Hall, 1872–1874.

Greaves, John. *Who's Who in Dickens*. New York: Taplinger Publishing, 1972.

Haines, Charles. *Charles Dickens*. New York: F. Watts, 1969.

House, Humphrey. *The Dickens World*. Oxford: Oxford University Press, 1941.

Hunter, Nigel. *Charles Dickens*. Illustrated by Edward Mortelmans. New York: Bookwright Press, 1989.

Johnson, Edgar. *Charles Dickens: His Tragedy and Triumph*. 2 vols. New York: Simon & Schuster, 1952.

Kaplan, Fred. *Dickens: A Biography*. New York: Morrow, 1988.

Lynch, Tony. *Dickens' England*. New York: Facts On File, 1986.

Martin, Christopher. *Charles Dickens*. Vero Beach, Fla.: Rourke Corp., 1990.

Miller, J. Hillis. *Charles Dickens: The World of His Novels*. Cambridge: Harvard University Press, 1958.

Nelson, Harland S. *Charles Dickens*. Boston: Twayne, 1981.

Page, Norman. *A Dickens Companion*. New York: Schocken Books, 1984.

Stanley, Diane. *Charles Dickens: The Man Who Had Great Expectations*. Illustrated by Diane Stanley. New York: Morrow Junior Books, 1993.

Thomas, Deborah A. *Dickens and the Short Story*. Philadelphia: University of Pennsylvania Press, 1982.

Wilson, Angus. *The World of Charles Dickens*. New York: Viking Press, 1970.

Wilson, Edmund. *The Wound and the Bow: Seven Studies in Literature*. Boston: Houghton Mifflin, 1941.

Scholarly Journals Devoted to Charles Dickens

Dickens Quarterly

Dickens Studies

Dickens Studies Annual

Dickens Studies Newsletter

The Dickensian

Emily Dickinson

(1830-1886)

by William H. Shurr

When Emily Dickinson was a young woman she wanted to write poetry. Her father, the stern head of their New England family, gave her permission to write late at night in her upstairs bedroom when the rest of the household was quiet and asleep. During these late night and early morning hours she produced 1,775 known poems as well as the hundreds of letters that fill three volumes. Her friend Helen Hunt Jackson, who tried to get her to publish her poems, wrote to her, "You are a great poet." So successful was her work that she is now considered to be one of America's finest poets.

She wrote with great care, but also with joy. "I find ecstasy in living," she wrote. In a letter to a friend she set the tone that characterizes much of her writing:

> Oh Matchless Earth—We underrate
> the chance to dwell in Thee.

In one poem she celebrates the beauties of the earth by describing the sun coming up in the morning after she has been working at her desk all night. She could look out her window and see the following scene:

> I'll tell you how the Sun rose—
> A Ribbon at a time—
> The Steeples swam in Amethyst+—
> The news, like Squirrels, ran—
> The Hills untied their Bonnets—
> The Bobolinks—begun—
> Then I said softly to myself—
> "That must have been the Sun"!
> But how he set—I know not—
> There seemed a purple stile+
> That little Yellow boys and girls
> Were climbing all the while—
> Till when they reached the other side,
> A Dominie+ in Gray—
> Put gently up the evening Bars—
> And led the flock away—

+purple

+gate

+Minister

It is important for the reader to catch the tone of energy and intense happiness communicated by this poem, as well as such bright images as the "ribbon," the "squirrels," and the "bonnets." Her vivid use of colors is also remarkable. Some of her lines are harder to figure out; you may wonder who the "little Yellow boys and girls" are. Do you see where the poem switches from a description of sunrise to one of sunset? Some of the music in her poetry comes from her use of rhyming words.

Her Younger Years

homestead house and land owned by a family, often for a long time

Emily Elizabeth Dickinson was born on 10 December 1830 in Amherst, Massachusetts, in the large brick homestead built by her grandfather. Her family had been in this part of New England for eight generations. Her father and brother were lawyers, energetic members of the community who ran a successful law practice and who both served as treasurers for nearby Amherst College. Unlike them, Emily Dickinson rarely left her father's house and grounds during her whole life and rarely saw other people besides members of her immediate family.

Dickinson attended school at Amherst Academy and, for one year, Mount Holyoke Female Seminary in the nearby village of South Hadley. She would have finished this excellent education had poor health not weakened her. Once she went to Washington, D.C., for a short visit when her father served in the House of Representatives. Twice she spent some summer months in Boston for treatment of an eye ailment. Otherwise, she preferred the small world of her bedroom, the kitchen, and her favorite garden where she grew flowers. She must have needed this intense privacy for her reading and writing.

seminary private school

The only existing photograph of her was taken when she was in her early teens and shows a slender girl with large and interesting eyes; she seems to have felt that she was plain looking and described herself as having reddish hair. As an adult she always wore a white dress, but she never explained why she adopted this unusual costume.

She did not publish her poems, though about seven of them were sent by friends to periodicals where they were printed. Instead she wrote her poems for personal friends—several women whom she liked; a noted literary man named Thomas Wentworth Higginson, whose advice she sought; and a clergyman whom she called "my dearest earthly friend," whose name was Charles Wadsworth.

Religion

Her father's New England Puritanism was too grim and stern for her. As an adult, Emily Dickinson did not go to church, but her religion was intense and very personal. Readers can tell from her poems and letters that she knew the stories of the Bible well and many of her writings deal with religious and spiritual matters, as this first stanza of one of her poems attests:

> "Hope" is the thing with feathers—
> That perches in the soul—
> And sings the tune without the words—
> And never stops—at all—

As an adult, Emily Dickinson did not go to church, but her religion was intense and very personal.

She imagines "Hope" as a small bird in her soul—free to fly away if it wishes!

In another poem she calls the beautiful days of autumn (New England's "Indian summer") the "Sacrament of Summer Days"—for her, God is just as present in nature as in the observances and ceremonies of the church. In her letters to friends who suffered from deaths in the family or from serious illnesses, she frequently consoled them with thought of immortality and the life of the spirit after death. The verse form she used in her poems is exactly the same as such famous hymns as "Amazing Grace" and "A Mighty Fortress."

Nature

The second major subject of Dickinson's poetry is her great appreciation for nature. She writes about birds, flowers (many of which she grew in her own garden), bees, cats, and snakes. The following has been a favorite poem of many readers:

+inchworm

> A Bird came down the Walk—
> He did not know I saw—
> He bit an Angleworm+ in halves
> And ate the fellow, raw,
>
> And then he drank a Dew
> From a convenient Grass—
> And then hopped sidewise to the Wall
> To let a Beetle pass—
>
> He glanced with rapid eyes
> That hurried all around—
> They looked like frightened Beads, I thought
> He stirred his Velvet Head
>
> Like one in Danger, Cautious,
> I offered him a Crumb,
> And he unrolled his feathers
> And rowed him softer home—
>
> Than Oars divide the Ocean,
> Too silver for a seam—
> Or Butterflies, off Banks of Noon
> Leap, plashless as they swim.

A good way to understand her poetry is to look at some of the odd use of language in a poem like this one. She writes about drinking "a Dew," for example, and a "convenient Grass," and she uses the word "plashless" to describe swimming butterflies. She seems to invite the reader to try to see how she is inventing her own poetic language, a language unlike that of anyone else.

Love and Friendship

Her third theme was the great poetic subject of love. She begins one poem with the following words:

> **Of all the Souls that stand create—**
> **I have elected+—One—**

+*chosen*

Many people have tried to guess who that lucky person was.

Dickinson occasionally writes about brides and weddings, but with the sense of painful separation from the one she loves totally. Half of her poems were written during the years 1858–1863, the same years in which she was corresponding with her clergyman friend, Wadsworth. After this period she widened the circle of correspondents to whom she sent letters and poems. One of her greatest friends and confidants was her sister-in-law, Susan Gilbert Dickinson, who lived next door.

Dickinson's favorite writers were Charlotte Brontë and George Eliot (the pen name of Mary Ann Evans), both of whom were woman novelists whose stories were about people who marry unhappily. She also liked the romantic love poetry of Elizabeth Barrett Browning.

The poetry of Walt Whitman, who lived at about the same time, is very masculine and public and political, and tends to sprawl into long lines. Dickinson's poetry, in contrast, is very private and nonpolitical; she uses few words and short stanzas. Some of the great events of her day—the Civil War, for example, or the important actions of presidents—are seldom mentioned in her writings, even though her father was a member of Congress and once was encouraged to run for the governorship of Massachusetts.

With words such as "plashless" to describe swimming butterflies, Dickinson invented her own poetic language, a language unlike that of anyone else.

She herself hated the idea of being "public" as she wrote in the following poem:

> I'm Nobody! Who are you?
> Are you—Nobody—Too?
> Then there's a pair of us?
> Don't tell! they'd advertise—you know!
>
> How dreary—to be—Somebody!
> How public—like a Frog—
> To tell one's name—the livelong June—
> To an admiring Bog!

What, in the poem, does she find most unpleasant about having to be an important, public figure? What word would you ordinarily expect to find after "livelong"?

Such an intensely private lifestyle left her frequently feeling lonely. Even her conversations with friends took place, as far as we can tell, mostly in her letters. In one of her poems she describes her writings this way:

> This is my letter to the World
> That never wrote to Me—
> The simple News that Nature told—
> With tender Majesty
>
> Her Message is committed
> To Hands I cannot see—
> For love of Her—Sweet—countrymen—
> Judge tenderly—of Me

Emily Dickinson had great confidence in her own genius, in her own unique way of saying things and writing poetry. She dropped the formal methods of earlier poets like William Wordsworth and Henry Wadsworth Longfellow. She capitalized words when she thought they should be emphasized; she used dashes to tell the reader to pause in reading her poems.

She could be serious about a very serious topic, and yet take a fresh, almost whimsical look at it and see things that no one had ever seen before. For example, in what is probably her most famous poem, she tackles the grim subject of death, but imagines that he is a suitor come to woo her and

whimsical oddly humorous or fanciful

take her on a carriage ride to his serene heavenly home forever. It is hard to imagine a poem more serious, and yet more witty at the same time.

serene   calm and peaceful

> Because I could not stop for Death—
> He kindly stopped for me—
> The Carriage held but just Ourselves—
> And Immortality.
>
> We slowly drove—He knew no haste
> And I had put away
> My labor and my leisure too,
> For His Civility+—

+politeness

> We passed the School, where Children strove
> At Recess—in the Ring—
> We passed the Fields of Gazing Grain—
> We passed the Setting Sun—
>
> Or rather—He passed Us—
> The Dews drew quivering and chill—
> For only Gossamer+, my Gown—
> My Tippet+—only Tulle+—

+a light fabric
+short cloak
+light cloth

> We paused bef FGore a House that seemed
> A Swelling of the Ground—
> The Roof was scarcely visible—
> The Cornice+—in the Ground—

+top of building

> Since then—'tis Centuries—and yet
> Feels shorter than the Day
> I first surmised+ the Horses' Heads
> Were toward Eternity—

+guessed

Her own death on 15 May 1886 was caused by Bright's disease, an illness that affects the functioning of the kidneys. After she died her sister Lavinia found more than 800 of her poems, written between 1858 and 1863, the years when some scholars believe she was in love with the clergyman. They had been sewn into small booklets and

Dickinson's early editors, especially Higginson, changed much of her unusual use of language to make her poetry conform to "normal" literature in English. Her complete poems in their original forms appeared only in the mid-twentieth century.

If you like the Poetry of Emily Dickinson, you might want to read other American poets, such as Maya Angelou, Robert Frost, and Carl Sandburg, Stephen Crane and Edgar Allan Poe were also known for their poetry.

preserved in one of her drawers. Lavinia then found an editor, Mabel Loomis Todd, who arranged for the publication of many of Dickinson's poems and letters in the 1890s. She has had many enthusiastic readers ever since and has earned justified recognition as one of the masters of American poetry.

Selected Bibliography

WORKS BY EMILY DICKINSON

Poetry

Poems of Emily Dickinson (1890)

Poems by Emily Dickinson, Second Series (1891)

Poems by Emily Dickinson, Third Series (1896)

The Single Hound: Poems of a Lifetime (1914)

The Complete Poems of Emily Dickinson (1924)

Further Poems of Emily Dickinson (1929)

Unpublished Poems of Emily Dickinson (1935)

Bolts of Melody: New Poems of Emily Dickinson (1945)

New Poems of Emily Dickinson (1993)

Letters

Emily Dickinson Face to Face: Unpublished Letters with Notes and Reminiscences. Edited by Martha Dickinson Bianchi. 1932.

Letters of Emily Dickinson. Edited by Thomas H. Johnson. 2 vols. 1958.

Collected Works

The Poems of Emily Dickinson, 3 vols. (1955)

The Letters of Emily Dickinson, 3 vols. (1958)

The Complete Poems of Emily Dickinson, (1960)

The Manuscript Books, 2 vols. (1981)

WORKS ABOUT EMILY DICKINSON

Barth, Edna. *I'm Nobody! Who Are You? The Story of Emily Dickinson.* Boston: Houghton Mifflin, 1971.

Bedard, Michael. *Emily.* New York: Doubleday, 1992.

Blake, Caesar R., and Carlton F. Wells, eds. *The Recognition of Emily Dickinson: Selected Criticism Since 1890.* Ann Arbor: University of Michigan Press, 1964.

Greene, Carol. *Emily Dickinson: American Poet.* Chicago: Children's Press, 1994.

Harris, Julie. *The Belle of Amherst (Great Theatre on Video).* Videocassette. Baker & Taylor Video, 1994.

Johnson, Thomas H. *Emily Dickinson: An Interpretive Biography.* Cambridge, Mass.: Belknap Press of Harvard University Press, 1955.

Olsen, Victoria. *Emily Dickinson: Poet.* New York: Chelsea House, 1990.

Porter, David T. *The Art of Emily Dickinson's Early Poetry.* Cambridge, Mass.: Harvard University Press, 1966.

Sewall, Richard Benson, ed. *Emily Dickinson: A Collection of Critical Essays.* Englewood Cliffs, N.J.: Prentice-Hall, 1963.

Shurr, William. *The Marriage of Emily Dickinson.* Lexington: University Press of Kentucky, 1983.

Peter Dickinson

(1927-   )

by Betty Carter

Peter Dickinson was born on 16 December 1927 in Zambia, Africa. His father, Richard Sebastian Willoughby Dickinson, was a civil servant; his mother, Nancy Lovemore Dickinson, was a sculptor. The Dickinsons moved back to England when Peter was seven years old. Shortly thereafter his father died, leaving the family financially strapped though still able to send Peter away to boarding school. After completing his studies there, he won a scholarship to Eton; served in the British Army; and attended Cambridge, graduating in 1951 with a degree in English literature (*Something About the Author,* pp. 23–24).

Early Career

Dickinson joined the staff of *Punch,* a British magazine, where he reviewed detective and crime novels. This work led to his desire to write his own stories rather than continue

civil servant member of the administrative service of a government

Eton College a private secondary school for boys in Eton, Berkshire, England; it is highly prestigious, and many illustrious men have been educated there.

The **Dark Ages** (ca. A.D. 476–1000) was the beginning of the Middle Ages in Europe. The word *dark* referred to a supposed lack of learning, as opposed to the Renaissance, a later period that signified a rebirth of artistry, invention, and scholarly study.

haphazard random

to write about the fiction of others, and he published his first book, the adult novel *Skin Deep,* in 1968. Surprisingly well received for a first novel, *Skin Deep* won the most prestigious prize for British mystery, the Golden Dagger Award. Dickinson's second adult novel, *A Pride of Heroes,* received the same award just a year later, but the writing of this book did not immediately follow that of the first, nor did it lead him to concentrate solely on mysteries. Between these two books, Dickinson wrote *The Weathermonger* (1969), his first work intended for a younger audience. Far removed from the constraints of contemporary detective fiction, *The Weathermonger* takes place in England during an alternative time when, through "the Changes," the island has been thrust back into the Dark Ages, adopting all its characteristic fears of the unknown, especially a belief that machines are the Devil's work and consequently evil.

Although this mixing of genres (from mystery to imaginative fiction), these audiences (from adult to young adult), and these settings (from modern society to an imaginary world) may appear to be haphazard, they define the broad and various directions that characterize Dickinson's later writings. His hallmark is his versatility. Sometimes he allows characters and situations to recur. *The Weathermonger,* for example, concludes the Changes Trilogy (also including, in order of literary progression rather than publication dates, *The Devil's Children* [1970]) and *Heartsease* [1969]), while James Willoughby Pibble, a detective introduced in *Skin Deep,* appears in six other adult mysteries. Some of Dickinson's books, such as *AK* (1992) and *Shadow of a Hero* (1994), deal with political upheaval, while others, such as *Eva* (1989) and the three volumes of the Changes Trilogy, question society's culpability in a modern world that neglects the environment in the former or worships technology in the latter. *The Seventh Raven* (1981) is a taut story confined in a single church, while the main character in *Tulku* (1979) travels halfway across the world. *Healer* (1983) takes place comfortably in contemporary society, *Merlin Dreams* (1988) comes from a legend, and *A Bone from a Dry Sea* (1992) offers a dual story alternating between a modern heroine and a prehistoric one. Despite these differences, several themes and stylistic elements link Dickinson's novels to one another.

The Main Characters

While Dickinson's characters have many of the same hopes and fears as their readers, these characters are nonetheless unconventional. In describing Letta and her grandfather from *Shadow of a Hero,* Dickinson writes: "They shared a sort of outsidishness, accidentalness, not-quite-fittingness as members of the family" (p. 9). The same qualities appear in Barry and Pinkie (*The Healer*), Doll (*The Seventh Raven*), Davy (*The Gift* [1973]), Vinny (*A Bone from a Dry Sea*), Theodore (*Tulku*), and Eva (*Eva*).

Most often this distancing from family occurs long before the novels begin. For example, sixteen-year-old Doll Jacobs, a late-in-life child, acknowledges the circumstances of her birth, feeling that her presence denied her mother a career as a cellist and thus led to a matriarchal favoritism toward her older brothers. In *A Bone from a Dry Sea,* Vinny accompanies her father to an African archaeological dig, partly because their encounters following her parents' divorce eight years previously have been sporadic and unfulfilling. Both Doll and Vinny embrace their respective parents' passions, the former by retaining her affiliation with an annual church opera performance and the latter by seriously studying paleontology. While both experiences allow the girls to see their families more objectively, neither leads the heroine to a more compatible relationship with her detached parents.

Thirteen-year-old Theodore Tewker's distancing from his father comes in the initial sequences of *Tulku.* Set in China during the Boxer Rebellion, this novel begins with an attack on the Reverend Tewker's mission; Theodore flees while all the others in the congregation perish. Although Theodore initially mirrors his dead father's beliefs, a successful escape mandates that he attach himself to a strange group, a surrogate family he neither understands nor is able to feel a part of.

A dramatic incident also divorces Eva from her parents. Critically injured in an automobile wreck, she is saved when her father transplants her neuron memory into the body of a chimpanzee. As Eva increasingly adopts chimp attributes and abandons human ones, she realizes that her survival will come through her mother's loss of a daughter: "Eva still had

The **Boxer Rebellion** (1900) was a bloody uprising in China in which the government and a secret society nicknamed the Boxers attempted to destroy everything foreign. A rescue force from eight nations crushed the rebellion.

mandate   to order

the same Mom she'd always known, but Mom had this new thing, this stranger, this changeling. . . . However much she taught herself to think of this new Eva as that daughter, it wasn't the same as feeling she was" (*Eva,* p. 44).

Eva presents many faces to the adult world: daughter, experiment, celebrity. Dickinson writes, "Her parents and doctors impose an outer shape on her, not realizing that her inner shape will learn to conform to it" (*Horn Book,* p. 162). This conflict between a person's public facade and his inner self marks many of Dickinson's characters. Sixteen-year-old Barry Evans in *The Healer,* for example, "often thought of himself not as Barry but as Bear. Indeed, sometimes he felt as though there were two personalities inhabiting his body" (p. 3). Bear represents a rage that frightens as well as supports the apparently affable Barry, and he, like Eva, must reconcile the dual parts of himself in order to mature.

affable friendly and easy to speak to

reconcile to restore to harmony

The Observing Characters

While young adults populate many of Dickinson's novels, they frequently observe, rather than initiate, the action. Consequently, other characters become the focal point of the story. Nonetheless, these observing characters embody the same elements as do the teenage protagonists. In *Shadow of a Hero* (1994), Letta and her grandfather, a direct descendant from the hero, Restaur Vax of Varina, discuss the burden of an individual being trapped by celebrity status. Grandfather begins,

"A name, you see, has no ideas, and for most of my life I have been not myself but my name. Suppose your name were not Letta Ozolins but, say, Florence Nightingale or Margaret Thatcher or. . ."

"Kylie Minoghe?"

"A singer?"

"Sort of."

"Then people would think of you differently, wouldn't they? They'd expect you to sing, or to order people about, or to want to be a nurse. In my case they expected me to be a hero. . . . People expected great things of me. I would have none of it, and chose to become a schoolmaster. I thought I had found a way to be myself." (P. 21)

Clearly, Grandfather believes that the public persona is far removed from the private self.

Through Daisy Jones, in *Tulku,* Dickinson raises similar issues. Shortly after the attack on the mission, Theodore meets up with her and realizes that, in order to survive, he must join her small troupe traveling through China. Mrs. Jones is an enigma, a person unlike any the sheltered Theodore has ever met. She has a painted face, a salty tongue, a daring and pragmatic nature, an intellectual curiosity, and a manipulative streak, all of which camouflage her loving side to unsophisticated Theodore. Her blasphemy appalls the frightened boy while her openness attracts him. Daisy Jones does not have to reconcile the many facets of herself, but her dominating presence forces Theodore to do so. In the process, Theodore, like Barry and Eva, becomes whole.

The conflicts Dickinson's characters face are frequently moral and philosophical ones such as reckoning with political upheaval or coping with medical ethics. These issues transcend such immediate and personal concerns as dealing with divorce or belonging to a clique. Consequently, a character's physical descriptions and individual nuances often pale before the panorama of broader issues. Partly for this reason, several of Dickinson's characters have been criticized as lacking an emotional core. For example, Paul (from *AK*) lives in the fictional African country of Nagala. Orphaned, he becomes a child warrior who joins a guerrilla band of nationalist freedom fighters. Believing that peace will come to Nagala, Paul buries his gun, an AK-47, only to dig it up later to oppose yet another military coup. Within this political drama, the individual is lost. The reviewer Hazel Rochman comments, "Paul's perspective is like that of a television reporter, a knowledgeable sympathetic witness rather than participant" (*Booklist,* p. 1520). Since Dickinson writes his novels in the third person, this stylistic device may also serve to distance his characters from the reader.

enigma puzzle

Salty means earthy or racy. Someone with a **salty tongue** tends to say improper or indecent things.

third person the position or perspective of someone outside the story

Rich Backgrounds

Whether they are fantasies, historical accounts, or realistic stories, novels need to be believable to their readers. Dickinson piles point upon point to anchor his accounts in reality. Describing his process to Joanna Hutchison, he states, "You're like somebody who is trying to lay a carpet where there's a terrifically strong draught coming up between the floor-boards; the carpet keeps billowing up and so you've to tack it down with detail all the time" (*Children's Literature in Education,* p. 91). Such detail marks Paul's burial of his beloved AK-47.

> Paul slipped away and found a patch of shade by a butcher thorn, where he carefully dismantled his AK, oiling each part, the magazine, the receiver cover, the bolt and bolt carrier, the return spring, the barrel and body, with all the oil he had left. He plugged both ends of the barrel with a wad of oily rag, then wrapped each part in a piece of plastic maize bag, tying them around with trip cord. He made a separate parcel of his eighteen rounds and fitted the whole lot into another bag, which he lashed tight. (P. 20)

This explicit account of the ceremony, typical of Dickinson's detailed renderings, not only underscores the gun's importance as the constant companion of Paul's youth but also anchors the scene with authenticity.

Similarly, *The Seventh Raven* relies on meticulous detail to carry the story. The annual Christmas opera accommodates a hundred children as actors, extras, and members of the chorus. This year, though, there are a hundred and one because the son of a South American diplomat requests a slot at the last minute. He becomes the seventh raven in this elaborate performance, a production far removed from the usual amateur pageants, put on by a corps of devoted professionals who write the script, score the music, paint the scenery, rehearse the cast, coordinate the lighting, and design the costumes. Understanding the amount of behind-the-scenes work, Doll volunteers an afternoon to help Mrs. Dunnitt with the wardrobe. For eight pages the two stitch and talk, with Mrs. Dunnitt offering her opinions on national responsibility and Doll commenting on the power of the costumes to transform the wearer into an intended character. When the church is stormed by a band of revolutionaries intent on kidnapping the diplomat's son, Mrs. Dunnitt disguises the boy in one of her intricate garments and then hides him from the would-be tormentors. The detailed chatter between Doll and Mrs. Dunnitt defines both character and situation, thus allowing the subsequent action to flow naturally from this established base.

Invented documentation, or the fabrication of an everyday world, adds yet another layer of detail. Nagala, Paul's native homeland, is a fictional African nation. Yet Dickinson provides readers of *AK* with a map of the nonexistent country, adding to the credibility of Paul's situation. Similarly, he tacks *Shadow of a Hero* onto a time line detailing the imaginary history of Varina and alternates that modern story with fabricated legend to lend further authenticity to his tale. When Dickinson introduces two native languages, Field and Formal, to Varina, he again builds on seemingly authentic detail to bring that nation to life.

The Gift introduces readers to Davy Price, a sixteen-year-old boy with a hidden talent: he can read the thoughts of others. According to the story, this gift runs in Davy's family, and Dickinson invents a legendary Welsh poem to confirm its existence. Like the map of Nagala and the time line, invented folklore, and imaginary languages of Varina, the rich background develops a strong premise that serves as the novel's foundation.

Religious Themes

Religion enters many of Dickinson's stories, but as an examination of the secular organizations that control it rather than an exploration of particular doctrines. In *The Healer,* for example, he introduces Pinkie Proudfoot, an ethereal child who appears to cure some illnesses by the touch of her hand. Her stepfather isolates Pinkie from her family and friends and sets her up as the center of an elaborate cult, the Foundation of Harmony. There, for a hefty fee, pilgrims without hope seek a remedy for their incurable illnesses. Can

secular not specifically religious

cult a religious group that follows a living leader who promotes unusual teachings or practices

charlatan a fraud or
faker

Dalai Lama the spir-
itual head of
Lamaism, a form of
Buddhism practiced
in Tibet and Mongo-
lia

Pinkie heal the sick? Is her stepfather a slick promoter kidnapping and drugging Pinkie for his own ends, or is he an
idealist who merely wants to help others?

Visionary or charlatan? The question reoccurs in *Tulku*
when Theodore and Mrs. Jones are ushered into Tibet by the
Lama Amchi, who is certain that the future Dalai Lama is a
part of their small group. First he identifies Theodore as the
religious leader, but later he decides that Daisy Jones's un-
born child, a child conceived with Lung, their Chinese guide,
is destined to be the next Lama. Does Ms. Jones indeed carry
a sacred infant, or does she remain in Tibet simply to enjoy
her elevated status?

Peter Dickinson continues the pattern he established
early in his career by writing books that speak to young
adults and children while at the same time authoring a different body of works aimed at adults. His numerous literary
awards highlight the respect others have for his works. In
Britain, Dickinson received the Carnegie Medal for two
books, *City of Gold and Other Stories from the Old Testament*
(1980) and *Tulku*, as well as the Whitbread Award for *AK*
and *Tulku*. Five of his books (*AK, Eva, The Flight of Dragons*
[1979]—a nonfiction book suggesting that dragons exist—
Tulku, and *Bone from a Dry Sea*) have been designated Best
Books for Young Adults by the American Library Association.

Selected Bibliography

WORKS BY PETER DICKINSON

Skin Deep, published in America as *The Glass-Sided Ants'
Nest* (1968)

The Weathermonger (1969)

A Pride of Heroes, published in America as *The Old English Peep Show* (1969)

Heartsease, illustrated by Nathan Goldstein (1969)

The Devil's Children, illustrated by R. Hales (1970)

The Gift (1973)

The Flight of Dragons, illustrated by Wayne Anderson
(1979)

Tulku (1979)

City of Gold and Other Stories from the Old Testament, illustrated by Michael Foreman (1980)

If you liked *Shadow of a
Hero,* you might also want
to read *After the Rain* by
Norma Fox Mazer.

The Seventh Raven (1981)

Healer (1983)

Merlin Dreams, illustrated by Alan Lee (1988)

Eva (1989)

AK (1992)

A Bone from a Dry Sea (1992)

Shadow of a Hero (1994)

WORKS ABOUT PETER DICKINSON

Commire, Anne, ed. *Something About the Author.* Detroit: Gale Research, 1990, vol. 62, pp. 23–32.

Hutchinson, Joanna. "Peter Dickinson Considered In and Out of the Classroom." In *Children's Literature in Education,* 1975, vol. 17, pp. 88–98.

Rochman, Hazel. Review of *AK.* In *Booklist,* 1992, vol. 88, p. 1520.

How to Write to the Author
Peter Dickinson
c/o Bantam Doubleday Dell
Publishing Group, Inc.
1540 Broadway
New York, NY 10036

Sir Arthur Conan Doyle

(1859–1930)

by Ted Hipple

It would be difficult indeed to identify a more universally known fictional character than Sherlock Holmes. Mickey Mouse, perhaps; Superman, maybe. But they began as comic-book figures. Holmes comes from print literature, where he has resided, with frequent trips to stage and screen, since his first appearance in 1888 in *A Study in Scarlet*. That novel was written by his creator (if not always his best friend), Arthur Conan Doyle.

Holmes became and has remained to this day the very embodiment of the detective as observer and logician, examining cigar ash in "The Boscombe Valley Mystery"; noting in "Silver Blaze" that the dog did *not* bark and that, therefore, the murder was committed by an insider the dog knew; using his knowledge of snakes to wreak vengeance upon the killer in "The Adventure of the Speckled Band," the story, by the way, that was Doyle's own favorite among the Holmes tales. When Holmes says, "Come, Watson, the game is afoot," we readers thrill to the chase and gallop onward with him.

> When Holmes says, "Come, Watson, the game is afoot," we readers thrill to the chase and gallop onward with him.

When he makes light of his own mental acuities by saying, "It's elementary, my dear Watson," we see that, in fact, it *is* elementary, and we should have known it all along.

Sherlock Holmes represents not simply detective fiction at its best and most readable and, for millions, re-readable, but also storytelling as high art. We who have come to love Holmes, who seldom let his adventures get far from our bedside bookstand, know that we owe a debt to this man Doyle, a debt he might dismiss with a quickly stamped "paid in full." For, it must be said, Arthur Conan Doyle would very much have preferred that today we read his dozens of other publishing achievements and let the detective rest a bit. In fact, Doyle himself tried to make Holmes rest—by killing him.

Who is this Arthur Conan Doyle, this author who created a giant among literary figures but who, at the same time, questioned the public's taste in making Sherlock Holmes one of their enduring heroes?

> *Yet Conan Doyle never imagined he would be a writer, of romances or of anything else.*

Doyle's Life

Arthur Conan Doyle—he preferred the first name of Conan—was born in Edinburgh, Scotland, on 22 May 1859. Although his father, Charles Doyle, an artist, was ineffectual as an influence on his son and as a means of financial support, Conan's mother more than made up for any paternal inattention. Able to trace her lineage to medieval England, she recounted to young Conan stories of knights and their adventures. She urged him to read Romantic novels: imaginative tales of danger and intrigue in which heroic male protagonists, by virtue of their strong moral character and dogged persistence, achieve their goals against difficult odds. The young Conan proved receptive to these stories, and they stayed with him into his adult years, when he, too, wrote romances and mysteries.

protagonist the main character of a literary work

Yet Conan Doyle never imagined he would be a writer, of romances or of anything else. His wish was to build a career in medicine, and he studied long and hard at Edinburgh University to become a doctor. He succeeded but then discovered that he could not earn a living as a physician, an occupation less lucrative in Doyle's day than today. He had to find another source of income. Writing proved to be that source.

lucrative profitable

In 1879 Doyle sold his first short story and received as much money for it as he had made in a month as a doctor. For the next several years, he worked at the two careers, struggling in both, but with generally better monetary success and more personal satisfaction in literary work. In 1885 he married a wealthy woman, Louise Hawkins, and he was thus able to pursue the work that most pleased him: writing. (In 1907, Doyle was married a second time, to Jean Leckie, a longtime friend, a little more than a year after the death of his first wife; he had five children.)

Doyle wrote short story after short story during the 1880s, and all were widely read. But he always felt that he had a longer work in him, and in 1888 he published *A Study in Scarlet,* in which he introduced to each other and to the world the now-famous characters Sherlock Holmes and his faithful chronicler, Dr. John Watson. Curiously, Sherlock Holmes was not an instant success in England but was popular in the United States, where a publisher urged Doyle to try another Holmes novel; that one became *The Sign of Four* (1890). It was well received in both countries.

chronicler one who records historical events in the order in which they occur without analysis or interruption

Doyle's Other Writing

Although today few readers know of Doyle's non-Holmes writings and even fewer read them, Arthur Conan Doyle was a prolific author, creating short stories, novels, works of nonfiction, political treatises, general journal articles, letters to the editor. None of these was about Sherlock Holmes, and it puzzled—even annoyed—him that his critical reputation and his financial success both soared because of Holmes. Lest Doyle protest too much, however, it must be said that the income he derived from the adventures of his famous detective permitted him to expand his other literary efforts, most particularly his historical and science fiction novels.

prolific producing a large amount

Doyle was proud of his seven historical novels. These were patterned more than a little after the works of an author whom Doyle's mother had urged him to study, the great Romantic novelist Sir Walter Scott. Just as few of Scott's novels are widely read today, *Ivanhoe* and *Rob Roy* excepted, Doyle's are even less commonly found in bookstores or even libraries. The one that most rewards attention is *The White Company* (1891), Doyle's adventure story about knighthood and chivalry in fourteenth-century England. Like most historical romances, this novel offers excitement aplenty: sword fights, tournament jousting, sea battles, a besieged castle.

Doyle also wrote science fiction novels. These, too, enjoy a meager readership today, less popular than the works of novelists of Doyle's own time, notably Jules Verne and H. G. Wells. But at least one of Doyle's science fiction novels is still read: *The Lost World* (1912). In this novel, a flamboyant character named Professor Challenger leads an expedition to South America to find a long-lost civilization. It was, Doyle felt, high adventure, one he intended for "the boy who's half a man and the man who's half a boy."

Beyond the historical and the science fiction novels and stories and the Holmes mysteries is the "nonfiction" Doyle—an unsuccessful candidate for the British Parliament who wrote numerous letters and treatises on issues of the day; a detective himself in writing about the imprisonment of two falsely convicted murderers (his letters helped secure their release); a historian whose works on the Boer War in South Africa and, later, on World War I considerably shaped British public opinion; an author of spiritual treatises. Yet it was the tales of Sherlock Holmes to which he—and we—usually had to return.

The Great Detective

The first two Holmes novels, *A Study in Scarlet* and *The Sign of Four,* set the stage for two more novels, *The Hound of the Baskervilles* (1902) and *The Valley of Fear* (1915), and fifty-six short stories. The latter usually appeared first in English magazines and were later collected into five anthologies (listed in the bibliography). All the Holmes tales are told by Dr. John Watson, Holmes's faithful companion.

But Watson is more than a friend. A singular literary creation in his own right, he is the perfect storyteller of mystery adventures, as he self-effacingly mirrors puzzled readers who, like Watson himself, do not quite understand what is going on and require Holmes's careful deductions to sort it all out. Suppose that Holmes had told his own stories in a first-person narration: "I had this visitor who had a problem and I solved it for her. Permit me to report how I did it." Already a supreme egoist, Holmes would appear insufferable:

Jules Verne (1828–1905) was a French novelist who wrote early science fiction, including *Twenty Thousand Leagues Under the Sea.* **H. G. Wells** (1866–1946) was an English novelist, historian, and science writer. He also wrote science fiction novels, including *The War of the Worlds.*

All the Holmes tales are told by Dr. John Watson, Holmes's faithful companion.

self-effacing keeping oneself in the background

admittedly a marvelous detective, yet one who so commonly bragged about his achievements that we simply would prefer not to be around him. In Watson we readers have a lens through which we can watch from a little distance the great man at his work and, like Watson, be in awe of his commitment and capability.

Watson and Holmes meet in *A Study in Scarlet*. Watson, home from the British wars in Afghanistan, where he had served in a medical capacity and had been wounded, tells a friend that he needs a companion with whom he can share the cost of lodgings. That friend suggests Holmes, who, he believes, "is well up in anatomy, and he is a first-class chemist; but . . . he is a little queer in his ideas." Watson and Holmes get together, and almost the first thing Holmes says to Watson, offhandedly, is, "You have been in Afghanistan, I perceive." Stupefied, Watson later learns of Holmes's considerable ability to deduce much about someone by observation—of language, of clothing, of physical characteristics, of mannerisms. Holmes explains how he knew of Watson's recent past:

221B Baker Street is not a real London address, although millions of tourists try to find it each year.

> Here is a gentleman of a medical type, but with the air of a military man. Clearly an army doctor, then. He has just come from the tropics, for his face is dark, and that is not the natural tint of his skin, for his wrists are fair. . . . His left arm has been injured. . . . Where in the tropics could an English army doctor have seen much hardship and got his arm wounded? Clearly in Afghanistan. (Doubleday ed., vol. 1, p. 24)

Thus began, first, the shared rooms at 221B Baker Street (this is not a real London address, although millions of tourists try to find it each year) and, later, the shared adventures. Doyle had written twenty-four short stories about Holmes and Watson by 1893 but then could do no more. Today we might say he was "burned out," the result of having to create ingenious plots for each story and of having to take time away from what he felt were more important literary projects—his historical novels—in order to satisfy the public clamor for one more detective yarn. He decided to end the Holmes saga. In "The Final Problem" (1893) Holmes and his archenemy, Professor Moriarty, are at the Reichenbach Falls in Switzerland,

ingenious clever

where, locked in hand-to-hand combat, they tumble over the side of the cliff and die. At the conclusion of that story, Watson says that Holmes was "the best and the wisest man whom I have ever known."

Holmes's death caused an outcry among his millions of faithful readers. People wore black armbands, wrote Doyle that he could not let the detective die, besieged the publisher for more stories. Newspapers printed obituaries. But it was all to no avail. Doyle was persistent; he wanted to be an important writer and felt that Holmes kept him from that goal, being a part of what Doyle himself called a "lower stratum of literary achievement." In truth, the creation had dwarfed the creator. Readers spoke less of Doyle and more of Holmes. Each year thousands of letters addressed to Holmes were sent to Doyle. At Doyle's many public readings, the subject was Holmes, not his historical novels. It was time, Doyle felt, to close the book, to say goodbye.

But, as it happened, not forever. In 1902, eight years after the death of Holmes, the great detective reappeared in what is often regarded as the best of the Holmes novels, *The Hound of the Baskervilles*. (Doyle handled Holmes's return by having Watson date the Baskerville story as having occurred before Holmes fell off the cliff in Switzerland.) Almost all the Holmes adventures depict an English weather that is highly suitable for crime—dreary, foggy, rainy, dark—and nowhere is this setting more evident than on Grimpen Moor, a desolate section of rural England where many of the Baskerville family **patriarchs** have met early and violent deaths, some of them apparently frightened into heart attacks by a gigantic hound. Holmes's task is to protect the current Baskerville occupant, Sir Henry, from a similar death, for on Grimpen Moor has been seen of late a gigantic dog with flaming mouth and **luminous** eyes. Holmes and Watson later encounter the animal themselves, and Watson writes, "A hound it was . . . but not such a hound as mortal eyes have ever seen." The hound, as it turns out, is not otherworldly, but rather the work of a malevolent criminal who has painted the dog's face with a **phosphorescent** substance.

The immediate success of *The Hound of the Baskervilles* doubtless inspired Doyle to resurrect Holmes. He did so with a new series of thirteen stories, the first of which, "The Adventure of the Empty House," explains away his death. Holmes had deliberately deceived everyone—including, re-

patriarch male head of a family

luminous glowing light

phosphorescent glowing in the dark

grettably, his best friend, Watson—in order to go undercover in search of international criminals. He has been successful in that endeavor and can now return to life for another series of adventures, stories that Doyle continued until he wrote the final Holmes tale, "The Adventure of Shoscombe Old Place," in 1927, three years prior to his death in Sussex, England, on 7 July 1930.

General Assessment

What has made these Holmes stories so popular with each succeeding generation? First and foremost, they are good mysteries. Virtue triumphs; evil is vanquished—and all of it within a puzzle. They are almost textbook examples of honor and of logical deduction, appealing to what we all want to believe: decency and reason will prevail. Holmes and Watson are engaging characters, the former reed-slim, hawk-nosed, his brooding countenance marked by piercing black eyes. Watson is perhaps more like us, a bit lumpy and out of shape, and almost always baffled by the crime and its causes until Holmes explains how simple it all really is. Described in many of the stories, the lodgings on Baker Street have become for many readers as familiar as their own living rooms; they can imagine Holmes at his violin or chemistry experiments, Watson by the fireplace reading the police reports in the London *Times*.

Doyle's language, although eminently in the style of late-Victorian England, captures readers. It is as if we met him in a pub and, over a pint of his favorite ale, he said, "Let me tell you about this detective I know and his most recent case." His stories are unembellished. We don't look for arcane symbols or extended metaphors. Rather, we seek—and we find—high adventure.

Despite Doyle's own protestations that his Holmes stories were somehow less worthy than his other literary endeavors, the court of popular opinion has rendered a very different verdict: Sherlock Holmes is here to stay, in virtually every part of the world and every language. Doyle's other writings, including his treatises on the wars in South Africa, for which he received a knighthood in 1902, are today literary artifacts that are largely ignored. But Holmes and Watson persist, seeking criminals, preserving British ideals, making the

Victorian characteristic of the time of Queen Victoria of England (1837–1901)

arcane mysterious or little known

symbol anything that stands for or represents something else, for example, "The dove is a symbol of peace"

Readers who enjoy reading the works of Sir Arthur Conan Doyle will also like those by Robert Louis Stevenson, Charles Dickens, Jack London, and Leon Garfield.

world a safer place. The Sir Arthur Conan Doyle who, as a child, had heard stories at his mother's knee, provided his own legacy of adventures that generations of subsequent readers have encountered at the urging of a parent or teacher or librarian. Given the continued popularity of the books and the even greater fame accorded him in stage, movie, and television adaptations, there is every certainty that Sherlock Holmes will be around as long as readers encounter, "Quick, Watson, we must hurry. The game is afoot!"

Selected Bibliography

WORKS BY SIR ARTHUR CONAN DOYLE

A Study in Scarlet (1888)

The Sign of Four (1890)

The White Company (1891)

The Adventures of Sherlock Holmes, short stories (1892)

The Memoirs of Sherlock Holmes, short stories (1894)

The Hound of the Baskervilles (1902)

The Return of Sherlock Holmes, short stories (1905)

The Lost World (1912)

The Valley of Fear (1915)

His Last Bow, short stories (1917)

Memories and Adventures, autobiography (1924)

The Case Book of Sherlock Holmes, short stories (1927)

The Complete Sherlock Holmes, two-volume collection with an introduction by Christopher Morley (Doubleday, 1930)

WORKS ABOUT SIR ARTHUR CONAN DOYLE

Carr, John Dickson. *The Life of Arthur Conan Doyle.* New York: Harper, 1949.

Hall, Trevor. *Sherlock Holmes and His Creator.* New York: St. Martin's, 1977.

Jaffe, Jacqueline A. *Arthur Conan Doyle.* Boston: Twayne, 1987.

Murch, A. E. *The Development of the Detective Novel.* New York: Philosophical Library, 1958.

Lois Duncan

(1934-   )

by Cosette Kies

An unsolved mystery, the murder of her own daughter Kaitlyn, became a very real part of Lois Duncan's life. Before it happened, Duncan had written a number of popular horror and thriller books for teens, but they were all make-believe. One of them, *Don't Look Behind You* (1989), was a typical product of Duncan's fertile imagination, but later it would seem to be an omen of what really happened.

The Killing of Kaitlyn

Duncan has worked hard to achieve and maintain a successful writing career throughout her life. Her most popular books are thrillers for teens, including *Killing Mr. Griffin* (1978), *I Know What You Did Last Summer* (1973), *Stranger with My Face* (1981), *Summer of Fear* (1976), and *Don't Look Behind You*. In *Don't Look Behind You*, Duncan based the central character, April, on her youngest child, Kaitlyn. She had a

The **Witness Relocation Program** is a federal program designed to protect witnesses whose testimony may endanger their lives.

Duncan's daughter Kaitlyn was eighteen years old when Don't Look Behind You *was published.*

prophetic predictive

good time planning and writing the story, using one of her favorite writing devices, the "what if" technique. She imagined what would happen to a pretty and popular teenager if her whole family were forced to go into a witness-protection program. April cannot bear her secret new life in Florida and contacts her boyfriend back in New Jersey. This action breaks the cover so carefully prepared by the FBI, and April finds herself pursued by a hit man named Mike Vamp.

In the story Duncan wrote, April defeats Mike Vamp and saves her family. In real life, however, a different story developed. Duncan's daughter Kaitlyn was eighteen years old when *Don't Look Behind You* was published. An attractive blonde, she had recently been graduated from high school. In August she was shot twice in the head while driving her red car in her hometown, Albuquerque, New Mexico. She died soon after.

The police were sure that the murder had been a random drive-by shooting. But things did not add up for Duncan. There were too many unanswered questions. She started to work on solving the puzzle herself. Duncan reported on her own investigation in her 1992 book, *Who Killed My Daughter?* It describes a fascinating search for details about her daughter's life prior to her murder. Like many teenagers, Kaitlyn had not told her parents everything. Her Vietnamese boyfriend had been involved in shady scams, some of which included Kaitlyn and may have been connected with drugs. Duncan persisted in turning up as many details as possible. She turned to psychics, who helped with leads and interpretations. Among these were some of the prophetic details in Duncan's own books, particularly *Don't Look Behind You.*

The Albuquerque police arrested a suspect whose nickname was Vamp, but they let him go. After showing some interest in Duncan's information, in the end the police maintained that the murder was a drive-by killing. Kaitlyn's old boyfriend disappeared. Duncan and her husband, Don Arquette (Kaitlyn's father), received death threats and lived in secrecy for a while. They left Albuquerque to reside in North Carolina. Although the murder has never been solved (as of 1996), neither has it been given priority in Albuquerque since the initial investigation. Yet Lois Duncan has not given up and is determined to find out who killed her daughter.

Peer Pressure and Moral Issues

A common theme in Duncan's books for young adults is the refusal to give in to peer pressure. Duncan constantly reminds her readers that individuals must take responsibility for their actions. She tells stories about basically good kids who are swayed by the desire to be popular and to be part of a group. She writes about teenagers who possess a realistic combination of good and bad qualities. In Duncan's books, the central characters usually learn to see on their own what must be done, what is right to do. In some cases they have been led astray by friends, in others by adults.

In *The Twisted Window* (1987), Tracy, an unhappy girl, is enchanted by Brad, a new boyfriend, who seems to be on a quest to find his little sister. Tracy acts impulsively, going along with him rather than heeding her doubts. Eventually, she realizes her error and faces the consequences of her actions. In *Killing Mr. Griffin,* four teens are persuaded by Mark, a psychopath, to kidnap their hated English teacher. When Mr. Griffin dies of a heart attack, Mark convinces the others not to tell. The cover-up becomes more and more dangerous. Sue, one of the group, is nearly killed before she can tell the truth about what happened. In *Daughters of Eve* (1979), girls in a select high school sorority fall under the influence of a female teacher whose feminist views have become extreme and twisted by personal events.

sorority a women's student group formed mainly for social purposes

Most of the teenagers in Duncan's stories are basically good people. Some, however, like Mark in *Killing Mr. Griffin,* have abnormal personalities and use others to achieve their own selfish aims. In *They Never Came Home* (1969), practical Joan discovers that her brother, Larry, is basically a bad character who deals in drugs and willfully uses others to achieve his own desires. In *I Know What You Did Last Summer,* selfish, egotistical Barry makes his friends promise not to tell about an accidental homicide. Another of Duncan's interesting, complex characters is Glenn, in *Ransom* (1966), who is unfeeling, manipulative, and amoral.

Duncan is particularly good in creating teenage characters. They are multidimensional, with many different traits. Duncan based some of these personalities on her own five children, their friends, and her own study and reading. As a result, the characters are different and believable. Sue, for example, in *Killing Mr. Griffin,* is not a particularly strong or as-

plot the deliberate sequence of events in a literary work

sertive girl. She is shy, desperately wanting popular friends and yearning for approval from her strict teacher. Yet in the end, Sue has the courage to confess to the killing of Mr. Griffin. In contrast, April in *Don't Look Behind You,* is confident and strong willed, yet impulsive and reckless. The personalities of the two girls are very different, and the descriptions and plots of their stories show these differences clearly. In the end, however, both young women show personal bravery to do what is morally right.

Another appeal of Duncan's work for young adults is her portrayal of adult characters. Adults are not always perfect in Duncan novels. Certainly, adult villains can be found in a number of the books. Other adults, such as parents, are sometimes shown to be flawed, occasionally even vile, such as Janie's abusive father in *Daughters of Eve.* In some cases the parents admit their wrongdoing, such as April's father in *Don't Look Behind You,* who had become involved in drug enforcement without considering the consequences to his family. Some parents, such as Nore's father in *Locked in Time* (1985), are casually loving and realize almost too late the need to be more involved with their teenagers. The villainous adults and teens are easy to recognize, but it is the subtleties and complexities of portraying all the characters that contribute to making Duncan's books so lifelike.

Planning and Plotting

Duncan makes her plots control her books. She does not let the characters take over and change the story line. She has often said in her interviews:

> Although I've been told that some authors start writing with only a general idea in mind and let their stories evolve on their own, I couldn't work that way. My books are tightly plotted and carefully constructed; every sentence is there for a reason. Personally, I can't imagine writing a book without knowing exactly how it's going to end. It would be like setting out on a cross-country trip without a road map.

In a videotape about Duncan's work produced by her daughter, Robin Arquette, Duncan explains how she went about plotting *Killing Mr. Griffin*. She demonstrates on a chart where the action, and particularly the climax, will come in the story. She explains one of the problems with this book. She knew that Mr. Griffin would not be kidnapped and dead until fairly far into the book. Yet she realized how important it was to start the book with something to grab attention. So this is how the story begins: "It was a wild, windy, southwestern spring when the idea of killing Mr. Griffin occurred to them."

The Occult Novels

Some of Duncan's most popular books for young adults use supernatural and psychic themes. When Duncan first started writing these novels, she thought the supernatural elements in her stories added a spooky, scary touch. She did not believe in psychic phenomena then, even though as a freshman at Duke University years before she had participated in one of a series of famous psychic experiments. After Kait was killed, Duncan began to think differently about these paranormal elements. She worked with psychics to get more information about the murder. One of the psychics was remarkably similar to one Duncan had imagined and written about in *The Third Eye* (1984). Events and people Duncan had thought were solely part of her fiction writing became eerie coincidence, possibly precognition (seeing the future). According to Duncan, "The things I've written about as fiction in suspense novels are now part of our everyday lives. We are involved in a police investigation like the one in *Killing Mr. Griffin,* and we are working with a psychic like the one in *The Third Eye.*"

The first book Duncan wrote with supernatural elements was *Down a Dark Hall* (1974). The central character, Kit, finds her exclusive boarding school the scene of personality possession. Famous creative geniuses of the past are invited by the headmistress to take over the bodies of the schoolgirls in order to continue their work. Fortunately, Kit manages to escape. In *Summer of Fear*, Rachel discovers that her recently orphaned cousin, Sarah, is really an evil imposter, a practicing witch. Rachel narrowly thwarts Sarah's scheming. In *Stranger with My Face*, Laurie becomes aware of a mysterious presence in her life who turns out to be an unknown twin sister. Lia teaches Laurie the joys of astral projection,

paranormal not scientifically explainable

> "The things I've written about in suspense novels are now part of our everyday lives. We are involved in a police investigation like the one in Killing Mr. Griffin, *and we are working with a psychic like the one in* The Third Eye."

leaving her body so that her mind and spirit can roam free. Lia, however, really wants Laurie's body for herself. In a fast-paced climax, Laurie triumphs over Lia. The final Duncan occult novel, and probably the best, is *Locked in Time.* Nore discovers that the members of her new stepfamily never age and have been alive for many years. Knowing that she has discovered their secret, Nore's stepmother, Lisette, tries to kill Nore. Nore escapes, and Lisette is killed in an automobile accident with her son. Although Nore has won, she realizes that she will always be responsible for her thirteen-year-old stepsister, who will never get any older.

All the teenage protagonists in Duncan's novels have distinctive personalities, and all possess the courage to do the right thing in the end. In some cases they face fearsome odds in Duncan's carefully planned plots, but by the time the exciting climaxes are over, the young women and men have been able to triumph morally, if not always to their own advantage. The adventures they experience are strengthening and character building.

> **protagonist** the main character of a literary work

Psychic Phenomena

After Duncan's daughter was murdered, Duncan investigated some aspects of psychic phenomena. She became intrigued by the paranormal activities that she had already used in her stories. Although she had formerly believed these misunderstood phenomena to be fantasy, she came to believe that they may be reality. One of the experts she talked with was Dr. William Roll, project director for the Psychical Research Foundation. Together they wrote a nonfiction book, *Psychic Connection: A Journey into the Mysterious World of Psi,* published in 1995. When Duncan was writing her young-adult novels about astral projection, possession, witchcraft, and other parapsychological topics, she did not believe in these phenomena. Later she said, "My experiences with psychic detectives during Kait's murder investigation have forced me to change my mind about what is and isn't possible."

> *"My experiences with psychic detectives during Kait's murder investigation have forced me to change my mind about what is and isn't possible."*

Duncan and Violence

Duncan has always explained the reason for her writing thrillers as "because they're the kind of book I enjoy reading." She writes for teenagers "because I love the sensitivity, vulnerability, and responsiveness of that age reader." Although violence is a feature in many of her suspense stories, Duncan includes only as much as necessary for her plot. She feels strongly that younger children should not be encouraged to read books such as *Killing Mr. Griffin*. She thinks it is important that readers understand the context in which the violence takes place, and that her stories are not suggestions for anyone to imitate.

Duncan wants her readers to enjoy reading. She thinks it is important to write fast-paced stories that are exciting enough to encourage teenagers to read rather than watch television. As she explains, "Today's youth has been raised on a diet of television and has become conditioned to expect instant entertainment. . . . I now find myself forced to use TV techniques to hold my readers' interest."

> *"Today's youth has been raised on a diet of television and has become conditioned to expect instant entertainment. . . . I now find myself forced to use TV techniques to hold my readers' interest."*

Duncan's Life

Duncan always knew she wanted to be a writer. She describes her early life in *Chapters: My Growth As a Writer* (1982). Her descriptions of growing up in Florida seem almost idyllic. During this time she worked hard to become a writer. She published award-winning stories in popular magazines for teenagers such as *Seventeen*. Her first novel, *Debutante Hill* (1958), a romance for teens, won an award when Duncan was still in her early twenties. She decided to use the name Lois Duncan as her pen name because her mother, who also published, had the same name as her daughter, Lois Duncan Steinmetz.

Duncan married at nineteen and had three children. The marriage ended in divorce. Duncan then moved to Albuquerque to start a new life. It was necessary for her writing to support herself and her children, and she wrote many different kinds of stories and articles. She married a second time, to Don Arquette, and they had two children, Don Junior and Kaitlyn. Duncan's books have won many awards, and in 1989 she received the Margaret A. Edwards award for lifetime achievement in young-adult literature.

Duncan's middle years were typical of those of many parents her age: her own children were growing up and having problems during their adolescence. The murder of Kait, her youngest, however, drastically changed Duncan's life in many ways. She believes that she cannot put Kait's death to rest until the murderer is found and convicted. It has been a mystery that Duncan cannot plot and finish herself. She explains, "I was able to give those stories [her thrillers] upbeat endings by cutting them off at points at which everyone was happy. But outside the printed page, we don't have that luxury. There is no way I can rewrite the last chapter of Kait's story."

Until the murder is resolved, Duncan feels unable to write any new young-adult thrillers. In her stories there is always an ending. The ending is not always perfect, but there is a definite resolution of the plot. For Duncan and the real-life mystery of her daughter's death, there has been no resolution as of 1996. The killer, or killers, have not been identified, formally charged, tried, or punished. Proof is needed. Duncan says, "Tips have come in, but we still need concrete evidence. I continue to believe that we will get it."

resolution the solving of a problem

If you enjoy the works of Lois Duncan, you might also want to read books by Joan Lowery Nixon.

Selected Bibliography

WORKS BY LOIS DUNCAN

Novels for Young Adults
Debutante Hill (1958)
The Littlest One in the Family (1960)
The Middle Sister (1961)
Game of Danger (1962)
Silly Mother (1962)
Giving Away Suzanne (1963)
Season of the Two-Heart (1964)
Point of Violence (1966)
Ransom, originally titled *Five Were Missing* (1966)
They Never Came Home (1969)
A Gift of Magic (1971)
Hotel for Dogs (1971)
I Know What You Did Last Summer (1973)
Down a Dark Hall (1974)
Summer of Fear (1976)
Killing Mr. Griffin (1978)
Daughters of Eve (1979)
Stranger with My Face (1981)
The Third Eye (1984)
Locked in Time (1985)

The Twisted Window (1987)
Wonder Kid Meets the Evil Lunch Snatcher (1988)
Don't Look Behind You (1989)
The Circus Came Home (1994)

Nonfiction for Young Adults
Major André: Brave Enemy (1969)
Peggy (1970)

Poetry
From Spring to Spring: Poems and Photographs (1982)
The Terrible Tales of Happy Days Schools (1983)
Horses of Dreamland (1985)
The Birthday Moon (1989)
Songs from Dreamland (1989)

Books for Adult Readers
Point of Violence (1966)
When the Bough Breaks (1974)
How to Write and See Your Personal Experiences (1979)
Who Killed My Daughter? The Story of a Mother's Search for Her Daughter's Murderer (1992)

Autobiography
Chapters: My Growth as a Writer (1982)

Article
"Margaret A. Edwards Award Acceptance Speech." In *Journal of Youth Services,* winter 1993, pp. 108–112.

Interviews
A Visit with Lois Duncan. Videocassette. Albuquerque, N.M.: RDA, 1985.
Sutton, Roger. "A Conversation with Lois Duncan." *School Library Journal,* June 1992, pp. 20–24.

Adaptation
Stranger in Our House. Film for television based on *Summer of Fear,* 1978.

WORKS ABOUT LOIS DUNCAN

Books and Parts of Books
Commire, Anne, ed. *Something About the Author.* Detroit: Gale Research, 1986, vol. 36, pp. 67–72.

Eaglen, Audrey. "Lois Duncan." In *Twentieth Century Young Adult Authors*. Edited by Laura Standley Berger. Detroit: St. James, 1994, pp. 192–195.

Evory, Anne, ed. *Contemporary Authors: New Revision Series*. Detroit: Gale Research, 1989, vol. 23, pp. 129–131.

Kies, Cosette. *Presenting Lois Duncan*. New York: Twayne, 1994.

Articles

Gerlach, Jeanne. "Mother Daughter Relations in Lois Duncan's *Daughters of Eve*." In *ALAN Review*, fall 1991, pp. 36–38.

McElmeel, Sharron. "Interview with Lois Duncan." In *Mystery Scene*, vol. 25, March 1990, pp. 75–76.

————. "Update: Lois Duncan; Was It Really Fiction?" In *Mystery Scene*, vol. 37, (n.d.), pp. 67–69.

Overstreet, Deborah Wilson. "Help! Help! An Analysis of Female Victims in the Novels of Lois Duncan." In *ALAN Review*, spring 1994, pp. 43–45.

How to Write to the Author

Lois Duncan
c/o Delacorte Press
1540 Broadway
New York, NY 10036

Jeannette Eyerly

(1908-   )

by Carol A. Pope

"Why does Father Bobbsey always laugh, 'Ha, ha, ha'?" When Jane Eyerly asked her mother, Jeannette Eyerly, this question about the Bobbsey Twins book she had read most recently, Eyerly knew her query signaled the end of Jane's attraction to the popular children's series. As Jane and her sister Susan, both omnivorous and perceptive readers, moved from reading the Bobbsey Twins books to young adult fiction, they often expressed their disgust over the books they were reading. They complained that the stories, just like those about the Bobbsey twins, were "gum drops." The real world of adolescents they knew was not just filled with going to football games or getting the right boy for the dance. Their friends were confronting problems related to death, sexuality, alcohol, school, and parents, and no one was writing about those complex problems that had no easy answers.

Stimulated by her daughters' desire for real young adult stories, Jeannette Eyerly decided in 1961 that she would try

Quotations from Jeannette Eyerly that are not attributed to a published source are from a personal interview conducted by the author of this article in April 1995 and are published here by permission of Jeannette Eyerly.

403

epistolary novel a novel written in the form of correspondence between characters

writing a book for young adults. She was already an accomplished writer; and, besides being a parent herself, Eyerly had researched and published articles about such child-rearing issues as discipline, children's fears, and children in trouble. She had also coauthored (with Valeria Winkler Griffith) an epistolary novel (*Dearest Kate,* 1961) about a young Catholic girl and the problems she confronted when she went away to college. These writings and personal experiences had not only allowed her to hone her craft as a writer but had also provided her a keen insight into children, young adults, their parents, and their problems.

An Author's Life

Jeannette Hyde Eyerly was born on 7 June 1908 in Topeka, Kansas. Her parents were Robert C. Hyde, a railroad man, and Mabel Young Hyde. She attended Drake University from 1926 to 1929 and graduated from the University of Iowa in 1930 with a bachelor's degree in English and journalism. She married Frank Rinehart Eyerly, who was a newspaper editor, on 6 December 1932. They have two daughters, Jane (Mrs. Lawrence Kozuszek) and Susan (Mrs. Joseph Pichler); six grandchildren (three girls and three boys); and one great-grandchild.

Having moved with her husband from their home of many years to a condominium, Eyerly enjoys writing verse, gardening, cooking, and art. She also gains great pleasure from her daughters, grandchildren, and great-grandchild. The two areas that have been most important to her in her community work are mental health and the Commission for the Blind. Besides being public-spirited and involved in the community, Eyerly has spent many hours talking with students in schools all around Iowa and answering their questions about her books and her writing. She has said that she feels she has led such a blessed life, has been so fortunate in having a career as a writer of fiction, that she "owes" young adults for their support of her work.

Becoming a Novelist for Young Adults

Eyerly's first single-authored book for young adults, *More Than a Summer Love* (1962), was highly successful. Accepted and published without hesitation by Lippincott, it quickly became a favorite of teenage readers. Eyerly has attributed the success of this first book to "knowing her trade" and studying another highly successful novel for young adults, *Seventeenth Summer,* by Maureen Daly. The appealing heroine of *More Than a Summer Love,* seventeen-year-old Casey Cameron, agrees to cancel her exciting visit to New York to spend the summer in uneventful Shady Rock, Iowa. There she helps her grandmother and keeps her company while Aunt Twink nurses Uncle Karl back to health after a bad accident. Shady Rock turns out to be not such a dull place after all, thanks to Casey's investigative journalism, two intriguing boys, a teenage couple that runs away, and a bank crime Casey unwittingly discovers. During the summer in Iowa, Casey makes some difficult but important choices while learning about physical attraction, trust, teenage marriage, and responsibility.

Eyerly's novels are often set in Iowa or New York City, and the teenage characters in them confront such problems as illegal drugs, alcohol, sex, suicide, pregnancy, divorce, and a lack of success in school. Her book *Drop-Out* (1963), which addressed an entirely new topic for its time, tells the story of two teenagers who decide to drop out of school, run away, and get married. Although Donnie, one of the pair, is a good student, she feels isolated from her hot-tempered father, unloved by her preoccupied stepmother, and despised by her younger stepsister. When Mitch, her boyfriend, proposes that they run away during the Christmas holiday, Donnie sees his idea as a perfect escape from her unhappiness. The trials she and Mitch face alone in another city as they look for jobs and stay in separate quarters provide a realistically bleak picture of what life will be like for them. Eyerly remarked that she received lots of letters from teenagers about this book, one of which said, "Until I read *Drop-Out,* I was going to drop out of school. Now I've decided to stick it out until the end of the year." Such letters made her feel that she was making an important contribution to young people and encouraged her to write more real books for real kids.

> *One teenager's letter to Everly: "Until I read* Drop-out, *I was going to drop out of school. Now I've decided to stick it out until the end of the year."*

Listening and Learning

In the next few years Eyerly continued to sharpen her skills as she wrote more problem novels for young adults. She has said that she received good counsel from both her daughters (and later her grandchildren), who critiqued her stories and her writing; from her journalist husband, who read only the finished products; and from her editor at Lippincott, who never had her rewrite but did suggest an important addition to one of her novels, *A Girl Like Me* (1966). The change, which turned out to be a wise suggestion, involved Cass, a supporting character in the novel. The main character, Robin, a well-adjusted teenager with understanding adoptive parents, searches secretly for her birth mother. Her friend Cass, pregnant by Brewster Winfield, son of a wealthy family in town, rejects Brewster's insinuation that she should have an abortion. In the original manuscript Eyerly made no reference to abortion, but her editor's suggestion that she include this possibility led to a scene that contributed to the timelessness of *A Girl Like Me*, which remained popular and in print for over twenty years.

Two novels that Eyerly has said required intense emotional energy were *Bonnie Jo, Go Home* (1972) and *See Dave Run* (1978). In the first novel, Bonnie Jo, lonely and alone, travels from Cedar City, Iowa, to New York City, where she seeks an abortion. Days of wandering the impersonal city, staying in a low-rent boardinghouse, talking with dispassionate doctors, and going to abortion clinics reveal the seamy side of the life of a young girl who makes this choice. In *See Dave Run,* the second novel that Eyerly said really saddened her, Dave Henry is a fifteen-year-old runaway. Vignettes told from a number of his acquaintances' perspectives reveal his intolerable home situation with an abusive stepfather and an alcoholic mother as well as some trouble in school and with the law. Many of the chronicles are told by those who meet Dave along his journey to find his father in Colorado. The last stop on Dave's run, a small-town jail, brings more bad news, even though the sheriff and deputy take an interest in this polite, sad boy. Because she gets so involved with her characters and so invested in their lives, Eyerly said that after writing each of these novels, she had to take a break and write some more uplifting stories to lighten her mood.

After *Bonnie Jo, Go Home,* Eyerly wrote two suspense novels and *He's My Baby, Now* (1977), a story about a teenage boy who tries to find a way to keep the son he has fathered. Surprised that Daisy did not use the money he gave her for an abortion, Charles goes to see his son at the hospital and feels great guilt. After much internal conflict, he refuses to sign the adoption papers and later steals his baby son from the foster family caring for him. This popular book was made into a movie for television, an occurrence for

vignettes short, descriptive literary sketches

internal conflict a character's struggle against himself or herself

which Eyerly says she received more publicity than she would have if she had won a Pulitzer prize.

No teenage problems have been left untouched in the numerous books Eyerly has written for young adults. The temptations of drugs and alcohol and the effects of their abuse show up in a number of her books—sometimes in adult characters, sometimes in teenagers themselves. One particularly well-known novel that exposes the downward spiral of alcohol and drug abuse is *Escape from Nowhere* (1969). Beginning with "Call me Carla," Carla tells her own story of frustration with her mother's alcohol abuse and her father's constant traveling for work so that she can go to finer schools. Alone and vulnerable, Carla succumbs to the escape Dexter offers her through drugs. She finds a new crowd in which she is accepted and follows Dexter until one tragic night when both of them almost lose their way back. Carla learns a valuable lesson: that only she can change her life and herself.

Creating Memorable Characters

One of the qualities that make Eyerly's books so memorable is her ability to create admirable teenage characters. One such courageous teenager is Christina in *The Girl Inside* (1968). Left to live with her unsympathetic Aunt Henriette in a strange town after her mother dies and her father is killed tragically in an automobile accident, Christy has no resources to support her stability. She tries to commit suicide but awakens to find herself in a hospital, where she is given physical as well as psychiatric care. Rescued from her plight by a foster family headed by her understanding lawyer and friend, Dave Keller, Christy begins to emerge from her personal darkness and to enter the outside world again. Unprepared for another personal loss that she must suffer, Christy comes close to slipping back into her painful isolation; however, this time she finds strength and courage through seeking help for herself and reaching out to others. Her inner strength and perseverance rescue her from self-absorption, from "the girl inside," and make her a truly laudable character. She even learns how to befriend and help another girl who is depressed and troubled.

laudable worthy of praise

An active member of the Iowa Commission for the Blind, Eyerly wrote *The Seeing Summer* (1981) about the friendship between Carey and her new next-door neighbor, Jenny, who is blind. Jenny proves to Carey that she can be independent, that there are many activities in which she can participate. The book revolves around Carey's growing acceptance of Jenny as a playmate and friend as well as her respect for Jenny's many abilities. Readers learn, along with Carey, how blind people "see" and about the many strategies they, like Jenny, use to find their way.

In *Someone to Love Me* (1987), Eyerly returned to the topic of teenage sex and pregnancy. Patrice, a quiet sophomore living with her mother because her parents are divorced, is flattered when Lance, a popular senior, notices and pursues her. Anxious to please Lance in any way she can, Patrice allows herself to be swept into a sexual relationship. Even though Lance never takes her anywhere public, Patrice is sure that he loves her and will marry her when she becomes pregnant. Lance, however, has different ideas. Told from a third-person point of view, this story allows the reader to see what Patrice cannot: Lance has used her and now wants no responsibility for his actions. Patrice finds she can depend on her mother, whom she has doubted, and cannot depend on her remarried father, whom she idealized. Though Patrice matures throughout her pregnancy, the real test comes when she must decide whether or not she should keep her baby.

> **third-person point of view** the position or perspective of someone outside the story

Finding the Stories

In a profile in *Speaking for Ourselves, Too* (1993), Eyerly said that, except for her two suspense novels, her books carry a message. "Don't drop out of school. Don't fool around with drugs. Don't make a baby until you are old enough and responsible enough to take care of it. Don't think for a minute that blind kids are any different than you are" (p. 64). Although the messages are there, Eyerly's books do not come off as preachy or didactic. Her themes are those common to all times: coming of age, belonging, making choices, defining the self in a larger world, handling loss, confronting personal limitations. Even though Eyerly began writing her young adult books in the early 1960s, the likable characters, situations, themes, and conflicts are authentic for today's readers. The characters' actions and their internal dialogue strike a realistic chord, and many of the issues are the same as those being faced by young adults today. One notable exception is

> *According to Eyerly, her books carry a message: "Don't drop out of school. Don't fool around with drugs. Don't make a baby until you are old enough and responsible enough to take care of it."*

that Eyerly's books do not specifically focus on minority issues or characters; however, young adults' feelings about being "different" often appear.

Perhaps the reason that Jeannette Eyerly's stories seem so real is that many of them are, indeed, based on actual happenings; the "viable subjects" for books, she has said, "are just out there, if you pay attention." She collects ideas from small newspaper articles, brief stories she hears on the news, or stories she hears from others. She has said that in her "magpie mind" she lets the premise for a story sit for a long time, gathering momentum like a snowball rolling downhill, until she is convinced the idea is a good one. When she hears enough similar vignettes and has given the idea sufficient thought, she may decide that it has universal appeal and warrants a book. *See Dave Run,* for example, evolved from a newspaper story about a teenager who committed suicide in jail. She had the clipping for ten years before it gathered enough momentum in her mind, through the accumulation of similar stories that turned up all around the country, to become a fully developed novel.

Besides collecting ideas about which to write, a writer faces other challenges, one of the most important of which is becoming knowledgeable about the subject and about the audience. Because Eyerly already knew her craft when she began writing fiction for young adults, she knew that she had to be completely informed about her topic and use an accessible, genuine language for young adults. Therefore, before she wrote *Escape from Nowhere,* she did extensive research on different illegal drugs and their effects as well as on alcohol abuse and alcoholism. Similarly, for *Bonnie Jo, Go Home,* she carefully researched abortion policies and procedures in New York City as well as the experiences of girls who had gone there for that purpose. It is her careful attention to these realistic details, as well as her authentic circumstances, characters, and language, that have made Eyerly's books a popular choice for young adult readers.

Other Directions

Having been a successful writer and lover of young adult fiction, Eyerly collaborated with two of her good friends and colleagues Annabelle Irwin and Lee Hadley (who write to-

> *She collects ideas from small newspaper articles, brief stories she hears on the news, or stories she hears from others.*

gether under the pseudonym of Hadley Irwin), on a book entitled *Writing Young Adult Novels* (1988). After parceling out the chapters according to each author's interests, they wrote separately and then circulated the manuscripts to each other. When they had finished the first draft of each planned chapter, they revised and rewrote. The completed text is useful to writers of any novel genre (not just young adult), to college professors of creative writing classes, and to teachers of young adults for their own writing classes. Such catchy chapter titles as "Know the Territory," "Hidden Messages/ Hidden Dangers," and "What A Character!" reveal the pragmatic guidance offered in this readable, reassuring text.

pragmatic practical and realistic, as opposed to idealistic

When asked in 1995 what she was writing, Eyerly mentioned *The Education of Adams Henry,* about teenage children living with an elderly foster parent, and *The Disaster Dog,* a book for children. Both ideas were still building in Eyerly's mind, but she was actually working on an ABC book for adults, using female animals as examples for the letters. Eyerly also writes verse to amuse herself, the latest one to her daughter about six tomato seeds she had sent her mother. Thus, in her career span as a writer, Eyerly has written articles, short stories, young adult novels, and verse.

If you like Jeannette Eyerly, you might also like Lois Duncan, Hadley Irwin, Norma Fox Mazer, and Katherine Paterson.

Selected Bibliography

WORKS BY JEANNETTE EYERLY

More Than a Summer Love (1962)

Drop-Out (1963)

The World of Ellen March (1964)

Gretchen's Hill (1965)

A Girl Like Me (1966)

The Girl Inside (1968)

Escape from Nowhere (1969)

Radigan Cares (1970)

The Phaedra Complex (1971)

Bonnie Jo, Go Home (1972)

Goodbye to Budapest: A Novel of Suspense (1974)

The Leonardo Touch: A Novel of Suspense (1976)

He's My Baby, Now (1977)

See Dave Run (1978)

If I Loved You Wednesday (1980)
The Seeing Summer (1981)
Seth and Me and Rebel Make Three (1983)
Angel Baker, Thief (1984)
Someone to Love Me (1987)

OTHER BOOKS

Dearest Kate, with Valeria Winkler Griffith, under the joint pseudonym Jeannette Griffith (1961)
Writing Young Adult Novels, with Hadley Irwin (1988)

WORKS ABOUT JEANNETTE EYERLY

Gallo, Donald R. *Speaking for Ourselves, Too.* Urbana, Ill.: National Council of Teachers of English, 1993, pp. 63–65.

Paula Fox

(1923-   )

by Connie S. Zitlow

Books make life more interesting, according to Paula Fox. In her works, popular with readers and literary critics, she views life from a young person's perspective yet conveys understanding for adults. She often creates a quiet mood and pace, inviting readers to consider others' encounters with life's surprises and unexplained periods of loneliness. Her original stories stay in readers' minds because her artistry with dialogue, exactness for details, and masterful way with characterization give even her short novels remarkable density. Her writing is imaginative, perceptive, and beautifully crafted because she finds just the right words. "Words, like notes, have tempo and color and innate sequence, and they are as elusive as will-o'-the-wisps" (p. 126), she writes in the March 1995 issue of *School Library Journal*.

Life can be looked at and understood better because stories make recognizable what readers may not have experienced, Fox says. "Great stories give us metaphors that flash

characterization
method by which a writer creates and develops the appearance and personality of a character

metaphor a figure of speech in which one thing is referred to as something else, for example, "My love is a rose"

> *"Great stories give us metaphors that flash upon the mind the way lightning flashes upon the earth, illuminating for an instant an entire landscape that had been hidden."*

upon the mind the way lightning flashes upon the earth, illuminating for an instant an entire landscape that had been hidden" (p. 122). When she and her grandmother saw many episodes of *The Invisible Man,* young Paula realized this story of a person who could disappear and reappear was a literal representation of how she could use memory and imagination to be in two places at once. It is this human capacity to imagine and feel that gives stories meaning. Fox writes to discover connections with herself and others, to explore her characters' feelings, and to find with each book, not answers, but deeper questions about life.

From Place to Place

Fox was born on 22 April 1923. As a child, she seldom saw her father, a traveling playwright and actor, and her mother. Her family moved from place to place, and she attended nine schools by the age of twelve. Maybe because she lived in many places as a child, she has written touching stories about young people in unfamiliar environments who feel alone, even while cared for by a loving adult. In some of her stories, the young person is only temporarily away from family, such as Emma in *The Village by the Sea* (1988) and Elizabeth in *Western Wind* (1993). Sometimes the young person is with one parent in an unfamiliar environment as is the case with Caroline in *The Moonlight Man* (1986) or Tory in *A Place Apart* (1980). Sometimes the child is in a familiar place with both parents, but the isolation is self-imposed, as in *The Stone-Faced Boy* (1968) and *One-Eyed Cat* (1984).

For several years, Fox lived in New York's Hudson Valley with a minister and his invalid mother, an experience she used in *One-Eyed Cat.* The minister was an avid reader and history buff who taught her to appreciate literature and inspired her to become a writer. When he accepted her suggestion for a sermon about a waterfall, she realized what had been implicit in every aspect of her life with him: words contain an energy capable of awakening imagination, thought, and emotion.

At age six, Fox left the minister's home to live in California for two years before going to her grandmother's sugar plantation in Cuba, where she quickly learned Spanish from fellow students in a one-room schoolhouse. Three years later, she and her grandmother, driven out by the revolution of 1933–1934, moved to a small apartment on Long Island.

There is an article about Gary Paulsen in volume 2.

There are interesting parallels between the lives and works of Fox and Gary Paulsen, another popular and critically acclaimed author of novels for young adults. The language in their stories is often poetic and evokes vivid sights and sounds in readers' minds. The places where Fox spent her childhood are different from where Paulsen lived. Both seldom saw their parents, were cared for by various adults, and amid life's confusion, they found freedom and stability in public libraries. For them, reading was everything. As young adults they both worked at numerous jobs. Fox worked for a steel company, a movie company, and a British news service in Paris and Warsaw. She also taught emotionally disturbed children and taught English to Spanish-speaking children. Although not intending to write an autobiography, she has written about the various places she lived as a child and adult. *Lily and the Lost Boy* (1987) is set in contemporary Greece, where she spent several months while her husband was writing there. In this story, surrounded by the places of Greek mythology, twelve-year-old Lily and her older brother Paul meet strange, enchanting, dangerous, and lonely Jack.

Stories and Places Apart

When *Maurice's Room* was published in 1966, Fox was celebrated as one of the finest new writers of children's literature. Her books for young adults have the same characteristics as this charming little book for children. Maurice does not tell the story, but the events are viewed from his perspective. The vivid descriptions of his room, overflowing with street junk or "treasures," such as hanging dried octopus, are funny and imaginative. It is his place, his world apart—a theme of many of her novels. Because of Fox's skill, the frustration of Maurice's parents is understandable but also ironic, as they try to get Maurice "interested in something." Another story, *A Likely Place* (1967), has the same natural, understated perception of how a youth thinks and acts, particularly when adults are demanding and overly protective.

theme central message about life in a literary work

James in *How Many Miles to Babylon* (1967) is loved by the aunts he lives with in Brooklyn, but he is isolated by a

plot the deliberate sequence of events in a literary work

lonely childhood and an impoverished urban existence. A small bewildered victim of an almost overwhelming situation, "Jimmy" leaves school and walks into the hands of thugs. Praising the vivid sensations and atmosphere created by Fox, some reviewers also find the plot heavy; others claimed that its great impact is more important for young people with no knowledge of ghettos than for those who are familiar with the setting (see *Children's Literature Review,* 1976).

Many of Fox's protagonists who are withdrawn take a journey symbolic of their emotional development. *The Stone-Faced Boy,* "spare like the winter landscape of its setting," is a powerful short novel filled with "strong imagery, deep characterization, tension, pain, and also magic," Christine McConnell writes in "A Second Look: *The Stone-Faced Boy*" (p. 219). Shy Gus, the middle child of five, keeps a "stone-face" as a defense against his siblings' battering. Only his sister Serena, the animal lover, does not laugh about his fears. Gus's adventure begins during a snowstorm as strange Great-Aunt Hattie visits and Serena begs him to rescue her stray dog caught in a foxtrap. Later he laughs inside when Hattie recognizes the significance of his quest—the terrifying journey into the dark night. But he will decide when to break the dark, dull little geode stone with its own glow, which Hattie gave him.

geode a stone with an open space inside, which is filled with crystals or minerals; geodes usually look very plain outside and beautifully colorful inside.

Hattie's sense about what is behind Gus's mask is like Fox's insight about her young protagonists. As in many of her novels, the plot of *The Stone-Faced Boy* is believable but of minor interest. It is the characterizations and relationships, the vivid images and poetic language that make her work like "geodes." They might seem simple at first glance, but "nothing is exactly what it looks like," as Fox writes in *Portrait of Ivan* (1969), another quiet sensitive story of a boy's search for himself. A lonely, motherless boy whose father travels, Ivan is cared for by a sympathetic Haitian housekeeper.

Long-haired Ben in *Blowfish Live in the Sea* (1970) is eighteen, the beloved half-brother of twelve-year-old Carrie, who tells his story. She has an eye for detail, a sense of humor, and descriptions fitting her age. Ben, a college dropout, scribbles "blowfish live in the sea" everywhere to represent his disillusionment with his father who sent him a blowfish when Carrie was born, saying it came from the Amazon. In a rundown Boston hotel, Carrie and Ben find his father, an unreliable and pathetic alcoholic. Surprisingly, Ben stays to help with an old motel, his father's latest business venture. *Blowfish Live in the Sea* shows Fox's sensitivity about the relationships between young people and the adults who have failed them.

The Slave Dancer

Fox begins her writing with a person, not an issue—except in *The Slave Dancer* (1973), her historical fiction that won the Newbery Medal. She had thought about and researched the slave trade for more than ten years before writing about it. In this story, as in her contemporary realistic works, she views a harsh and dangerous world with a young person's eyes and feelings. Not abandoned but kidnapped from his home in New Orleans in 1840, thirteen-year-old Jessie is taken aboard the *Moonlight* and forced to play his fife to "dance" the slaves. Jessie is sickened by the smells and sounds of the slaves' suffering in the ship's hold and the hatred and hypocrisy of the crew. At one point, he courageously defies the captain, refuses to play, and finally he and a slave boy escape. This book is Fox's most controversial work. Although some critics saw it as fair and humane, others saw it as racist, excusing the slave drivers as victims of circumstances. Even critics, however, praised her excellent writing. In her Newbery Medal acceptance speech, referring to her own "white childhood" when she never felt free from a dark condition, Fox said enslavers, not the enslaved, are debased by slavery.

A Place Apart and One-Eyed Cat

Like *The Slave Dancer, A Place Apart,* which won the American Book Award, is written in the first person, a variation from most of Fox's works. Thirteen-year-old "Tory" Finch tries to understand life after her father dies suddenly. One day after moving with her mother from Boston, she meets Hugh who is flying a great scarlet kite. He is rich, condescending, exciting, and has also lost his father. With Hugh, Tory travels a little distance from herself, but she has to come to terms with his manipulation and her infatuation. He

slave trade Beginning in the 1500s, Africans were bought and sold throughout Europe and the Americas. Great Britain and the United States abolished the slave trade in the early 1800s, although slavery did not end in the U.S. until the Civil War ended in 1865.

fife a musical instrument similar to a flute but with no keys

> *Fox said enslavers, not the enslaved, were debased by slavery.*

first person the position or perspective from someone inside the story, using the pronoun "I"

pushes her to write a play, then ignores her for the strange and timid Tom Kyle, who looks the way Tory feels: like he does not belong anywhere. Uncle Philip tells Tory she will have to find her place apart. She realizes life's happenings may be chance, but what one makes of life is not.

Ned's internal anguish in *One-Eyed Cat* (1980) is different from Tory's. Responsible for the event that causes him to be alone, he must come to terms with a secret frozen around him. Eleven-year-old Ned is drawn to the attic where his father put his birthday present from Uncle Hilary—a forbidden rifle. Ironically, he thinks if he can shoot it once, he will forget about it. The gun, however, becomes a "splinter in his mind." He is tormented by the memory of a dark shadow and a gaunt, one-eyed cat he sees at Mr. Scully's. Did Ned shoot the cat or was the shadow something else? When asked this question at the 1990 Children's Literature Conference, Fox said, "I don't know, some things cannot be answered." The mood of this psychologically complex but quiet novel is like the large Victorian house on the Hudson River where Ned lives in 1935 with his minister father and mother, who has rheumatoid arthritis. Ned broods over his disobedience and lies. His rich interior monologue contrasts his inability to talk until he opens up to Mr. Scully, who is dying. One moonlit night at the Makepeace Mission, when he and his mother see the one-eyed cat with two kittens, Ned finally takes full responsibility for his act. After telling her, Ned, like the cat, is alive again.

interior monologue
a representation of a character's inner thoughts and feelings

Fox's Techniques

Moon imagery appears in many Fox stories; even Carrie's dog in *Blowfish* is named "Moon." Jessie's coming of age occurs on the ship the *Moonlight;* Ned's self-determination begins in the moonlight; and Catherine Ames calls her elusive father *the moonlight man.* She, like Ben in *Blowfish,* must come to terms with a charming yet weak father who drinks too much and calls his orderly, former wife a daylight person. Catherine finally accepts her parents' twelve-year divorce when she realizes her "moonlight" father is an undependable man who transforms everything he touches. This story about a tenuous father-daughter relationship begins as Catherine waits twenty-one days before her father calls her

tenuous delicate or weak

to join him in Nova Scotia for a summer vacation filled with sunlight and darkness. Harry Ames, who hid from himself as much as from Catherine, finally admits there is nothing funny about the way people betray each other. Betrayal is a theme in many Fox novels.

Although Emma is not betrayed by her parents, she feels alone in *The Village by the Sea*. While her father has heart surgery, she stays on Long Island with kind Uncle Crispin and neurotic Aunt Bea. In spite of her uncle's warmth, it is difficult for Emma to be around her hateful aunt whose voice is "like a razor blade hidden in cotton." Emma's longing for home is lessened when, with her new friend Bertie, she creates a place apart, a miniature village built from beach treasures, to which Emma adds a tiny plastic deer from Bea's forbidden brandy bottle. This place of solace, however, is destroyed by the "sad bad old woman's" hot coal of envy (p. 146).

solace comfort in grief or sorrow

Using her own experience of being nearly homeless as a young woman and the plights of many others, Fox wrote *Monkey Island* (1991). Eleven-year-old Clay is suddenly abandoned by his father, who is desolate after losing his job, and then by his pregnant mother, who is emotionally unable to cope. Clay leaves their welfare hotel in New York and lives in a crate with two homeless men, young Buddy and old Calvin. There are moments of humor, along with desperation, as they run to escape the "stump people," who come with chains and bats yelling "Monkey Island! Where the monkeys live!" (p. 77). Like other Fox characters, Clay is frightened, alone, but extremely brave. Fortunately, he finds his mother, baby sister, and a place he can leave and come back to—a home.

Elizabeth's feeling of abandonment is more like Emma's than Clay's. *Western Wind*, like *The Village by the Sea*, begins as Elizabeth is "sent away" from home and ends as she returns with new understanding. She resents leaving her parents and baby brother to spend a month with her grandmother on a rustic island off the coast of Maine. Elizabeth thinks Gran, a painter, is a strange "encyclopedia of her own interests" (p. 10) but learns from her about intriguing places and poetry, which is "about the hidden and true life inside yourself,' about longing and hope and sorrow," she says (p. 11). Gran's father, like Fox's, was an actor. Her "mother didn't know what a child was" (p. 162). She was left with various people. One rainy night, as they search for

Fox, one of the few Americans to win the Hans Christian Andersen Medal, has written award-winning stories for over twenty years.

motif situation or theme

strange lonely Aaron, Elizabeth finds out that Gran is dying of heart disease—which is the real reason she was sent there to stay with Gran. A great shaft of loss goes through Elizabeth when she thinks about Gran's legacy of family stories and beautiful drawings. "No one would ever see her exactly as Gran had" (p. 201).

Grasping Truth

Fox, one of few Americans to win the Hans Christian Andersen Medal, has written award-winning stories for over twenty years. Her 1995 novel, *The Eagle Kite,* as striking and sensitively told as those that preceded it, shows the suffering and anguish of the whole family when one person is dying of AIDS. Again, with spare yet elegant prose, she conveys universal struggles and feelings. Familiar Fox themes and motifs in this book include a seaside cottage as a place of reconciliation, a mean and angry aunt (as in *The Village by the Sea*), a kite as a metaphor (as in *A Place Apart*), and a sick parent (as in *One-Eyed Cat*).

Fox does not soften realities in *The Eagle Kite,* which is about truth, caring, and coming to terms with loss. Teenage Liam feels anger, fear, betrayal, and loneliness as he tries to cope with his father's illness, which is not the result of a blood transfusion as his mother said, nor is it cancer as Liam told his girlfriend. Buried for several years in Liam's memory is a scene on the beach—his father's embracing a young man. Another burning image in Liam's mind is the scarecrow-looking beggar with AIDS who sits across from their apartment. Healing for Liam begins one Thanksgiving, when he goes to the seaside where his father, with a face like an eagle, has gone to die. As time passes, Liam and his mother learn to love again, not the sick man who wrote, "My two dears. There's hardly anything left of me" (p. 114), but the spirit of the man they once knew. The slow working through of grief is reminiscent of Cynthia Rylant's *Missing May.* The suffering of the AIDS patient and the effect on the family compares to Alice Hoffman's *At Risk.* In *The Eagle Kite,* as in all Fox's stories, there is a wise and compassionate view of the complexities of human nature. Fortunately for her readers, she continues to grasp truth through her remarkable imagination.

Selected Bibliography

WORKS BY PAULA FOX

Novels for Young Adults

Maurice's Room, illustrated by Ingrid Fetz (1966)

A Likely Place, illustrated by Edward Ardizzone (1967)

How Many Miles to Babylon?, illustrated by Donald A. Mackay (1967)

The Stone-Faced Boy, illustrated by Paul Giovanopoulos (1968)

Portrait of Ivan, illustrated by Saul Lambert (1969)

Blowfish Live in the Sea (1970)

The Slave Dancer, illustrated by Eros Keith (1973)

A Place Apart (1980)

One-Eyed Cat (1984)

The Moonlight Man (1986)

Lily and the Lost Boy (1987)

The Village by the Sea (1988)

Monkey Island (1991)

Western Wind (1993)

The Eagle Kite (1995)

Primary Novels for Adults

Poor George (1967)

Desperate Characters (1970), adapted as motion picture by Paramount in 1970

The Western Coast (1972)

The Widow's Children (1976)

A Servant's Tale (1984)

The God of Nightmares (1990)

WORKS ABOUT PAULA FOX

Block, Ann, and Carolyn Riley. eds. In *Children's Literature Review.* Detroit: Gale Research, 1976, vol. 1, pp. 76–81.

Collier, Laurie, and Joyce Nakamura, eds. *Major Authors and Illustrators for Children and Young Adults.* Detroit: Gale Research, 1993, vol. 2, pp. 865–869.

If you like the works of Paula Fox, then you might also like Sue Ellen Bridgers, Brock Cole, Katherine Paterson, Gary Paulsen.

Commire, Anne, ed. *Something About the Author.* Detroit: Gale Research, 1990, vol. 60, pp. 29–38.

Cullinan, Bernice E. *Literature and the Child,* 2d ed. New York: Harcourt Brace Jovanovich, 1989, p. 417.

DeMontreville, Doris, and Elizabeth D. Crawford, eds. *Fourth Book of Junior Authors and Illustrators.* New York: H. W. Wilson, 1978, pp. 135–136.

Fox, Paula. "Other Places." In *Horn Book,* January/February 1987, pp. 21–27.

———. "Hans Christian Andersen Medal Acceptance." In *Horn Book,* April 1979, pp. 222–223.

———. "On Language." In *School Library Journal,* March 1995, pp. 122–126.

Huck, Charlotte, Susan Helper, and Janet Hickman. *Children's Literature in the Elementary School,* 5th ed. New York: Holt, Rinehart, and Winston, 1993.

Lukens, Rebecca J., and Ruth K. J. Cline. *A Critical Handbook of Literature for Young Adults.* New York: Harper Collins College Publishers, 1993.

McConnell, Christine. "A Second Look: *The Stone-Faced Boy.*" In *Horn Book,* April 1984, pp. 219–222.

Nilsen, Alleen Pace, and Kenneth L. Donelson. *Literature for Today's Young Adults,* 4th ed. New York: Harper Collins College Publishers, 1993.

Townsend, John Rowe. *A Sense of Story: Essays on Contemporary Writers for Children.* New York: Lippincott, 1971.

Zeiger, Hanna B. "Paula Fox: *The Moonlight Man.*" In *Horn Book,* May/June 1986, pp. 330–331.

How to Write to the Author
Paula Fox
c/o Orchard Books
95 Madison Avenue
New York, NY 10016

Anne Frank

(1929–1945)

by Elizabeth Wilder Goza

"It's really a wonder that I haven't dropped all my ideals, because they seem so absurd and impossible to carry out. Yet I keep them, because in spite of everything I still believe that people are really good at heart." As Anne Frank recorded these thoughts in her diary during her hiding in 1945, never could she have imagined the fame that they would bring her. Since that time her words have been immortalized as a record of enormous cruelty and shining courage.

Anne Frank's autobiography, originally entitled *Het Achterhuis* and reprinted in English as *The Diary of a Young Girl* (1952), often calls to mind the literature of the Holocaust. The diary touches each reader not only because it is a portrait of a Jewish family in hiding, but because it takes the reader into the private world of a young girl in adolescent transition. Anne experiences the joys and sorrows of youth and reminds each reader of an awkward time full of discovery and disappointment.

The **Holocaust** was the mass murder of at least 11 million people, especially Jews, by the Nazis during World War II. The word "holocaust" means "thorough destruction by fire."

The Diary of a Young Girl has also taken on a life of its own. It has inspired numerous books, a Pulitzer Prize–winning play, a feature film, several documentaries, and a requiem, all of which are based on the life and work of Anne Frank. Since its first publication in Dutch in 1947, Anne Frank's diary has been published in thirty-six countries and has sold an estimated 20 million copies. The universal appeal of this prolific work can be credited to the insight and quality of the author's writing. Anne writes, "I can shake off everything if I write; my sorrows disappear, my courage is reborn. But, and that is the great question, will I ever be able to write anything great?" Anne's triumph is ironic because although the answer to her question is yes, she did not survive to enjoy her success as a writer.

requiem a musical composition honoring the dead

Anne Before the Diary

There are only a few entries in Anne's diary written before her family's decision to go into hiding.

There are only a few entries in Anne's diary written before her family's decision to go into hiding. After the release of *The Diary of a Young Girl,* many historians took up the lengthy task of learning about Anne and her life before the diary. Anne Frank was born in 1929 to Otto and Edith Frank, both of whom were natives of Frankfurt am Main, Germany. Otto Frank served as a lieutenant in the German army during World War I and had always considered himself and his family as German. During the rise of Hitler and the Third Reich, many Jews were sent to "work camps." After Margot, the older Frank sister, was called to leave for such a camp, it became necessary for the Franks to relocate to the Netherlands, and Anne's father secured a home there for the family. This house on the Merwedeplein became Anne's childhood home and a source of many good times and memories.

Work camps are a form of concentration camp, which is a camp for political prisoners. During World War II, many Jews (and members of other ethnic groups) were detained in work camps, where prisoners were deliberately worked to death.

Anne was an active, bright, and extremely intelligent child. She was well liked by her classmates and often the center of attention, and she got into trouble many times with her teachers for talking and entertaining the other students. She refers to several such events in her diary. Anne had many ambitions when she was a young girl, one of which was to become a Hollywood movie star, and as a result she was known for collecting pictures of her favorite actors. Although European, Anne was a typical teenager; she liked visiting with friends, going out after school, and vacationing at the beach on the weekends. The Anne before the diary is a carefree girl whose greatest worries are maintaining her friendships and doing her schoolwork.

Two Dutch writers, Ruud van der Rol and Rian Verhoeven, believed that it was important for readers to know Anne Frank apart from her diary. They felt that Anne's life before hiding has often been overshadowed by the notoriety of her writings and that to truly appreciate her works, readers should know about her life before the diary. In their 1992 book (translated a year later), *Anne Frank: Beyond the Diary,* Van der Rol and Verhoeven include pictures of Anne from birth until the last picture ever taken of her prior to hiding. In her introduction to the book, Anna Quindlen writes:

> There is something so humanizing about these photographs. In them Anne has not yet passed into historical legend. In them the Annex becomes a building again, narrow and unprepossessing. We see the diary with all its teenage blemishes, not transcribed neatly on the page but pocked with pasted pictures, scribbled and haphazard, the work of a girl, not a symbol, not a metaphor. (Pp. xi–xii)

Anne During the Diary

The diary of Anne Frank is a portrait of a girl entering into adolescence and emerging a young woman. When Anne entered the hiding place at 263 Prinsengracht, she was only thirteen years old. Already she had begun to wonder about the questions that many adolescents ask. Anne often queried in her diary: "Am I pretty? Do boys like me? Will I ever be happy? What does my future hold?" Her diary entries reflect the turmoil of adolescence as she is constantly torn between rebellion from and dependence on her parents. While in hiding, Anne writes of the changes in her body, mind, and soul as she is transformed from girl into woman. She also writes of her growing love for Peter, the son of the family that shares the Annex with the Franks. Together, Anne and Peter are able to find comfort in each other's arms as the war wages outside the little window of the Annex.

Anne's descriptions of her changes are sometimes philosophical, and she often reflects on the behavior of humanity in general. She wonders why people behave the way they do as she observes the many relationships in the Annex around her. Anne and her seven companions did not leave the confined space of the Annex for two years. Their proximity and lack of privacy created many uncomfortable moments among the occupants, and Anne was always there to record them in her diary. Her keen insight into the behavior of those around her and of people in general may lead readers to draw their own conclusions about the world around them.

Anne's diary is not only a memoir of a young girl's transition into womanhood; it is also an account of one of the most unforgettable times in world history. This period, as seen through Anne's eyes, is brought to life in each of her journal entries. She makes many references to historical events during the war, including the changes in Amsterdam as the Nazis begin to occupy the city, the onslaught of war as the Allies make their way to the Netherlands, and the sacrifices of gentiles to help those in need.

Allies the countries united against Germany; these included the United States, Great Britain, the former U.S.S.R., France, and China

The diary serves as a firsthand account of the unreasonable demands made on the Jewish residents of Amsterdam during the Nazi occupation. She writes of the laws that required Jews to have curfews, to wear a yellow six-point star sewn on their clothes, and to give up simple pleasures such as bicycling and going to the movies. Anne writes that she and her friends managed to enjoy themselves despite the restrictions, and her ability to focus on the brighter moments during this time is a testament to the strong will of youth in the face of adversity.

During the time covered in the early part of Anne's diary, many Jews were called to leave their homes for work camps. After Margot had been sent such a notice to report for work duty, the Franks decided to go into hiding. With the help of non-Jewish friends, the Franks left their home on the pretext that they had escaped to Switzerland. The Secret Annex, or hiding place, was to be the home of the Franks, the Van Pels (Van Daans in the diary), and Fritz Pfeffer (Albert Dussel in the diary) for almost two years.

While living in the Annex, Anne continues her descriptions and reflections of the war in Europe. She writes of many evenings spent crowded around a radio, each family listening to broadcasts of the Allies' approach. Several times she describes arguments among the adults about the progress of the war and the likelihood of their being freed from hiding. Despite her age, Anne makes many astute political observations and devotes several entries to her own theories about the war and the fate of Jews who were not able to go into hiding. She gives much thought to the senseless rift created by the Nazis between the gentiles and the Jews; however, many of these entries were deleted in early printings of her diary for fear of bringing back old wounds after the war. These entries are included in later editions, and they provide further insight into this period in history.

astute clever; shrewd

Anne also makes many references to the gentiles who played a major role in maintaining the families while they hid. The five people responsible for helping the Franks to hide were all connected with Otto Frank's business and were close friends of the family. Their real names were Miep Santrouschitz (known as Miep Gies after her marriage) and her fiancé Jan Gies, Bep Voskuijl, Victor Kugler, and Johannes Kleiman. As with all names in the diary, Otto Frank had them altered in accordance with Anne's wishes. Anne's contact with her protectors helped her conclude that, despite the horrible atrocities being committed around her, people were still good at heart and willing to help those in need.

The popularity and universal appeal of Anne Frank's diary may be credited to its role as a historical account of World War II. The historical documentation, accompanied by Anne's detailed description and insightful narration, challenges and entertains the reader throughout the diary.

Anne After the Diary

Anne's diary concludes in August 1944, three days prior to the betrayal and arrest of the residents in the Secret Annex. In 1991 Willy Lindwer, a Dutch filmmaker and son of Jewish parents who survived the Nazi Occupation in hiding, undertook the task of recreating Anne's subsequent ordeal. His documentary, *The Last Seven Months of Anne Frank's Life*, was published in 1991 in book form, and it is a firsthand account of those who spent time with Anne in the last months of her life.

After leaving the Annex, Anne and her family spent time in three different camps: Westerbork, Auschwitz, and

Bergen-Belsen. Early on in the camps Anne was separated from her father. She was able to stay close to her mother and sister, however, and several survivors who knew the Franks during this time commented on the strong bond between the Frank women. Despite the jealousies and arguments described in the diary among Anne, her mother, and Margot, those feelings seem to have faded in the camps, as the three turned to each other for strength and hope. Although separated from her parents and other occupants of the Annex after Auschwitz, Anne and Margot managed to stay together until they died.

For his documentary, Lindwer interviewed six women who knew and had contact with Anne and Margot during their time in the camps. His work presents a grim yet strangely uplifting picture of Anne's life after the diary. Many of the women Lindwer interviewed said that Anne kept her optimism until the end and managed to smile and have happy words for all those around her. Although Anne no longer had her diary with her and was unable to record her experiences in the camps, there are several surviving accounts from this period. Perhaps one of the best known is *Night,* written by Nobel Prize–winning author Elie Wiesel. *Night* is a first-person narrative of Wiesel's experience in Auschwitz. He has written several other works, all of which deal with the Holocaust. Etty Hillesum's *Letters From Westerbork* is also a firsthand account of life in a concentration camp. Like Anne, Etty lives in the Netherlands, and her descriptions of Westerbork shed light on the female experience in a concentration camp.

The Diary Takes on a Life of Its Own

After the liberation of the Jews in 1945, Otto Frank returned to Amsterdam, hoping to locate his family. With the help of Miep and Jan Gies, Otto reestablished his business and began to search for Anne and Margot. During his search, Otto discovered that the other occupants of the Annex had all died in camps, and he later received a letter indicating that Anne and Margot had both died in March 1945.

Upon hearing the news, Miep, who had been saving Anne's diaries in case she returned, handed the books and pages over to Otto Frank. Gies had been able to retrieve the diaries after the police had raided the Annex and taken away the people in hiding. She knew there would be little time to remove any items from the Annex but had been immediately drawn to Anne's diary as an important keepsake.

After receiving the diary from Miep, Otto set out to get Anne's work published. He had always known about his daughter's dream of becoming a writer, and he wanted to get the diary published in her memory. The journey to get Anne's diary published was in itself an epic, and only after a long struggle was Otto able to write in his personal journal the single word BOOK, meaning that he had finally carried out his daughter's wish. In 1947, fifteen hundred copies of Anne Frank's *Het Achterhuis* was published through a Dutch publishing company.

Despite the triumph of finally getting his daughter's diary published, Otto Frank faced further struggles. Soon after the diary was released in Europe, critics and scholars began to question the work's authenticity. Many claimed that *Het Achterhuis* was the work of a mature, accomplished writer and could not have been written by a thirteen-year-old girl. Through extensive examination and scientific testing, however, it was proven that the diary is the work of a single author. It has since become well known that the undisputed author of the diary is indeed Anne Frank.

The Diary's Universal Appeal

Anne Frank is perhaps one of the best-known figures of the twentieth century. Her honesty, innocence, and optimism in the face of horror is a tribute to the human spirit. In 1994 another diary was released that serves as a firsthand account of a young girl's experiences during a war. *Zlata's Diary,* written by Zlata Filipovic in Sarajevo during the war in the former Yugoslavia, has also received worldwide acclaim, and many have compared it to *The Diary of a Young Girl.* Readers are attracted to these personal accounts because they have a great deal of truth and insight in them without the political slant of many writers of history. Anne Frank was one of the many young writers who are willing to examine themselves and the world around them in a telling and touching manner.

In the 1990s, in Bosnia and Herzegovina, Serbs expelled Muslims and Croats from Serb-controlled areas in a policy known as "ethnic cleansing." The massacres of civilians in this war led to the creation of a Yugoslav War Crimes Tribunal to punish those responsible.

Conclusion

Very few students leave school without having a chance to read Anne Frank's *Diary of a Young Girl*. Many adults return to her book later in life as a nostalgic reminder of their youth. Perhaps Anna Quindlen, writing in the introduction to *Anne Frank: Beyond the Diary,* said it best:

> Now wife and mother, even-keeled and middle-aged, all those things that Anne never had a chance to be, I cannot read it without feeling the pall, the enormous tragedy that hangs over the entire enterprise, whose essence is contained unadorned in the final sentence of the epilogue: "In March 1945, two months before the liberation of Holland, Anne died in the concentration camp at Bergen-Belsen." (P. ix)

If you like *The Diary of a Young Girl,* you might also like the works of Maya Angelou, Bette Greene, and Lois Lowry.

Selected Bibliography

WORKS BY ANNE FRANK

Frank, Anne. *The Diary of A Young Girl*. New York: The Modern Library, 1952.

Branouw, David, and Gerrold Van Der Stroom, eds. *The Diary of Anne Frank: The Critical Edition.* Translated by Arnold J. Pomerans and B. M. Mooyaart. New York: Doubleday, 1989.

Frank, Otto, and Mirjam Pressler, eds. *The Diary of Anne Frank: The Definitive Edition.* Translated by Susan Massotty. New York: Doubleday, 1995.

WORKS ABOUT ANNE FRANK

Adler, David A. *A Picture Book of Anne Frank.* New York: Holiday House, 1993.

Birstein, Anne, and Alfred Kazin, eds. *The Works of Anne Frank.* Westport: Greenwood, 1959.

Gies, Miep. *Anne Frank Remembered: The Story of the Woman Who Helped to Hide the Frank Family.* New York: Simon & Schuster, 1987.